The Crimes of Wildlife Trafficking

This book examines trade and trafficking in endangered animal species and how the trade increasingly puts large numbers of nonhuman species at risk. Focusing on illegal trafficking, the book also discusses the harmful aspects of the trade and trafficking which is taking place in concordance with laws and regulations. Drawing on the findings of empirical research from Norway and Colombia, the study discusses how this global, transnational trend is addressed, and features of the trade and the ways in which it is controlled in the two case study locations. It also explores the motives driving the trade, and the consequences in terms of animal abuse and environmental harm. The book discusses whether internationally agreed measures, such as international conventions, actually help prevent the trade. Possible ways to address the harms of wildlife trade are considered, including a total ban. The work draws on a green criminology and eco feminist theoretical framework to provide a broad perspective on concepts such as harm, animal rights, species justice and speciesism.

Ragnhild Aslaug Sollund is Professor of Criminology at the Department of Criminology and Sociology of Law, University of Oslo. Her research is in the field of green criminology, specifically wildlife crimes, and she has published widely on this and related areas.

Green Criminology

Series editors: Michael J. Lynch
University of South Florida, USA

Paul B. Stretesky
University of Northumbria, UK

Now two decades old, green criminology – the study of environmental harm, crime, law, regulation, victimization, and justice – has increasing relevance to contemporary problems at local, national, and international levels. This series comes at a time when societies and governments worldwide seek new ways to alleviate and deal with the consequences of various environmental harms as they relate to humans, nonhuman animals, plant species, and the ecosystem and its components. Green criminology offers a unique theoretical perspective on how human behaviour causes and exacerbates environmental conditions that threaten the planet's viability. Volumes in the series consider such topics and controversies as corporate environmental crime, the complicity of international financial institutions, state-sponsored environmental destruction, and the role of non-governmental organizations in addressing environmental harms. Titles also examine the intersections between green criminology and other branches of criminology and other areas of law, such as human rights and national security. The series is international in scope, investigating environmental crime in specific countries as well as comparatively and globally. In sum, by bringing together a diverse body of research on all aspects of this subject, the series makes a significant contribution to our understanding of the dynamics between the natural world and the quite imperfect human world, and sets the stage for the future study in this growing area of concern.

Other titles in this series:

Green Crimes and Dirty Money
Edited by Toine Spapens, Rob White, Daan van Uhm and Wim Huisman

The Crimes of Wildlife Trafficking
Issues of Justice, Legality and Morality
Ragnhild Aslaug Sollund

For more information about this series, please visit: www.routledge.com/Green-Criminology/book-series/GREENCRIM

The Crimes of Wildlife Trafficking

Issues of Justice, Legality and Morality

Ragnhild Aslaug Sollund

Routledge
Taylor & Francis Group
LONDON AND NEW YORK

First published 2019
by Routledge

2 Park Square, Milton Park, Abingdon, Oxfordshire OX14 4RN
52 Vanderbilt Avenue, New York, NY 10017

Routledge is an imprint of the Taylor & Francis Group, an informa business

First issued in paperback 2020

British Library Cataloguing-in-Publication Data
A catalogue record for this book is available from the British Library

Library of Congress Cataloging-in-Publication Data
Names: Sollund, Ragnhild Aslaug, 1959– author.
Title: The crimes of wildlife trafficking : issues of justice, legality and morality / Ragnhild Aslaug Sollund.
Description: Abingdon, Oxon ; New York, NY : Routledge, 2019. | Series: Green criminology | Includes bibliographical references and index.
Identifiers: LCCN 2018040608 | ISBN 9781472417749 (hardback)
Subjects: LCSH: Wildlife crimes. | Wildlife smuggling. | Wild animal trade—Moral and ethical aspects. | Wild animal trade—Law and legislation.
Classification: LCC HV6410 .S65 2019 | DDC 364.16/2859—dc23
LC record available at https://lccn.loc.gov/2018040608

ISBN: 978-1-4724-1774-9 (hbk)
ISBN: 978-0-367-66211-0 (pbk)

Typeset in Galliard
by Apex CoVantage, LLC

The author has received support from The Norwegian Non-Fiction Writers and Translators Association [NFFO].

Contents

Tables

Preface and acknowledgements

Writing this book has been an on and off again project for many years, which has run parallel to my increasingly deeper engagement with the field of green criminology. It is a book that could not have been produced without the help and contributions from many. First, I am very grateful to David Rodríguez Goyes for his help in compiling interviews in Colombia, for the discussions along the road and for the friendship we have developed as time progressed.

All interviewees in Norway and Colombia who have participated in the research and who have helped me accessing data also deserve my sincere thanks: without you, there would have been no book. You have given me a lot of insight into the problem of wildlife trafficking which I hope I have been able to bring forward.

I am further very grateful to Avi Brisman for reading and insightfully commenting on the manuscript in its final stage, and for always being helpful and supportive. I also thank Kerry Fast for her proof editing.

In addition I want to extend my heartfelt thanks to other of my green criminology colleagues who particularly have contributed with discussions and collegial support during the years, to Piers Beirne, Nigel South, Rob White, Jenny Maher, Daan van Uhm, Reece Walters, Tanya Wyatt, Rune Ellefsen and Siv Runhovde.

The research on which the book is based has received funding from the Norwegian Animal Protection Fund, which helped me with costs related to data collection, for which I am also grateful.

The research was further partly conducted for the EFFACE project, European Union Action to Fight Environmental Crime, https://efface.eu/. Jenny Maher and I did the wildlife trade case study of the project, some of which has been explored in further depth herein. I am grateful also to colleagues of EFFACE, particularly Teresa Fajardo de Castillo, Christoph Stefes and Anna Rita Germani, as well as to Christiane Gerstetter for discussions and project management.

I further want to thank the editors of Routledge, Alison Kirk and Alex Buckley, both for their patience and also for their help in getting the manuscript into production. Many thanks also to series editors Michael Lynch and Paul Stretesky for allowing the book to be included in the series.

The Department of Criminology and Sociology of Law at the University of Oslo has offered splendid working conditions and good colleagues, for which I am grateful.

I dedicate the book to my daughter and best friend, Vilde, to whom I am grateful for all support and for our conversations. Last, but not least: This book would not have been produced had it not been for my friendship and love for our parrot companions, Pottifnatt, Kåre, Line and Tinga, who inspired me to do research into the harms of wildlife trafficking. I also dedicate this book to their memory.

Oslo, August 8, 2018

Figure 0.1 Trafficking victims at Centro de recepción y rehabilitación de fauna silvestre, in Bogotá.

Source: © David Rodríguez Goyes with permission from CRRFFS

1 Introduction to the legal and illegal abduction, theriocide and trafficking of endangered animals

The legal and illegal trade in free-born animals is an increasing problem worldwide. It is causing the extinction of many species, destruction of entire ecosystems and unspeakable harm to each individual who is victimized. Usually, the human society is recognized as the victim of the illegal wildlife trade because local communities lose 'resources' when non-human animals are illegally abducted and killed and because of threats against human security when terrorist groups are involved. In this book, however, the main concern is the direct victims. My main motives for this research are the serious dangers the trade poses for species survival and the ecosystems that are home to the trafficked victims, and last but not least, the harms committed against each individual animal as s/he is turned into a commodity – dead or alive. My focus on animals does not imply that I do not find the illegal trade in endangered plant species important. To the contrary, this trade can destroy ecosystems just as effectively as removing an animal species from its ecosystem can. However, the fact that nonhuman animals, like human animals, are sentient beings (Regan 1987) who therefore suffer from being abducted from their habitats, turned into property, and trafficked and sold, just as humans would suffer under such treatment, has determined my focus. In an anthropocentric world, those who are most often applauded are those who side with human interests. Still, my hope is that this book will move readers and policy makers to think of animal trafficking as a parallel to human trafficking and appreciate the harms involved in the trade, whether legal or illegal. Although human slavery has not de facto ended with a declaration of human rights, this declaration has contributed as a support for a general legal ban of this phenomenon, thus strengthening human rights and dignity (Sollund 2013b). A prohibition against animal slavery and trafficking could do the same.

This should indicate that I adhere to the perspectives and values raised in the field of green, or ecoglobal, criminology (see, e.g., Beirne 2014; Beirne and South 2007; Brisman and South 2014; Ellefsen et al. 2012; White 2013), and my concern is both with what is currently criminalized and punishable (although maybe not *punished*) and that which is harmful but not (yet) acknowledged as 'crime' (see Hillyard et al. 2004; Sollund 2015c; South 1998, 2008; Lynch and Stretesky 2014; Walters 2010; White 2013). Green criminology is a fast-developing field of criminology with a particular concern for harms and crimes committed against the natural environment and those who live in it (e.g., White 2011, 2013; Sollund and Brisman 2017; South 1998; Benton 1998; Beirne and South 2008; Brisman and South 2014; Lynch and Stretesky 2014; Lynch et al. 2015; Sollund 2015a). Rather than having an anthropocentric point of departure only, concern for ecosystems and non-human animals is widely recognized, as is a focus on power structures that permit such harms (e.g., White 2013; Beirne 1999, 2009; Brisman 2014; Brisman and South 2014; Lynch and Stretesky 2014; Stretesky et al. 2013; van Uhm 2016b; Sollund 2008b, 2011, 2012a, 2013b, 2015a; Wyatt 2014b; Goyes and Sollund 2016; Maher and Sollund 2016 a,b). Considering myself a green criminologist, I have a particular concern for the ***direct victims*** of wildlife trade and wish to draw attention to them more than to the illegality involved in wildlife trafficking (henceforth WLT) because, as I will discuss, this breach of law is one in which the direct victim is most often overlooked as the crime is treated as a conflict between the state and the offender (Christie 1977). Accordingly, one issue to be discussed in this regard is whether the laws and regulations governing the animal trade harm the animals more than they protect them. Furthermore, laws and regulations change with time, yet the harm involved in animal trafficking remains constant.

This research thus adopts a critical victimology perspective – a non-speciesist approach focused on animals as the first and most important victims of the trade (Fitzgerald 2010; Maher and Sollund 2016a, 2016b; Wyatt 2013). Animal abuse has for nearly two decades been included as a legitimate field of green criminology in its own right (Beirne 1999, 2009; Cazaux 1999; Sollund 2008b, 2012a; White 2013). The research described in this book follows this tradition.

My purpose with the book is consequently neither to provide an overview of WLT, whether legal or illegal, nor to produce an overview of all the different instruments available internationally to control and prevent the trade. This was done extensively by Wyatt (2013), Schneider (2012) and, in the EU context, by Fajardo del Castillo (2016). Rather, my intent is to conduct a close analysis of what motivates the different actors involved in the trade (buyers/consumers of live animals and animal products, abductors/killers/traffickers of free-born animals) and to explore different dimensions of the trade and the ways in which trafficking is controlled and prevented in two countries: Norway and Colombia.

In this first chapter I will define central concepts concerning wildlife trafficking. I will then provide an introduction and brief overview of the phenomenon of the trade and trafficking in endangered animal species. What usually receives attention is the *illegal* trade in endangered species, whatever the species, although special attention is given to iconic species like elephant, rhino and tiger. This was the case at the London conference held in February 2014 (Foreign & Commonwealth Office 2014), with British royalty playing an important part and from which an international declaration against wildlife trafficking was produced, signed by 40 countries in addition to the European Union. In this book, I do not exclude the victims of the *legal* wildlife trade because, from the perspective of the animals, whether they are trafficked legally or illegally is irrelevant. Still, given my background as a criminologist and the data sources on which this book is based (see Chapter 2 on methodology), I have a special interest in discussing the effects of criminalization and regulation of this harm, and also the effects (or lack of effect) of punishment currently applied when a criminalized act of animal trafficking is committed.

The term 'wildlife' is usually applied to both animals and plants, e.g., by TRAFFIC[1] that states on its website, 'TRAFFIC believes in a world where wildlife trade maintains wildlife populations and contributes to sustainable human development.' Both plants and animals are regarded as resources that are there for human benefit. My focus, however, is on individuals of animal species, rather than on the illegal trade in endangered timber, medicinal plants and orchids, because I don't think animals' purpose in life is to provide resources for humans. Like Wyatt (2013: 21), I include in my research animals who are bred as a commodity or provide service to humans, whether for medicinal use or for entertainment, and who are not domesticated in the sense that they are physically and psychically ill-adapted to a life of captivity under human control. Burgener and colleagues (in South and Wyatt 2011: 546) suggest the following definitions for trade and trafficking:

> Trade encompasses collection, harvesting, possession, processing, acquiring or transporting of wildlife for the purpose of purchasing, importing, exporting, selling, bartering or exchanging. Wildlife trafficking or the illegal wildlife trade is the specific name of the green crime that involves the illegal trade, smuggling, poaching, capture or collection of endangered species, protected wildlife . . . derivatives or products thereof.

As this is an anthropocentric definition, I amend it in a way which serves more justice to the victims:

> *Trade* [[2]] encompasses legal and illegal abduction, possession, processing, acquiring or transporting of free-born animals for the purpose of purchasing, importing, exporting, selling, bartering or exchanging them through taking them as captives. *Trafficking* in free-born animals involves the legal and illegal trade, smuggling, abduction, theriocide and collection of animals pertaining to (often endangered) animal species, either alive or by turning them into products.
>
> (Sollund 2013b: 319; emphasis original)

Although I dislike the term 'wildlife,' I will retain it when discussing illegal wildlife trafficking (IWT) and wildlife trafficking (WT) for simplicity's sake, where it refers to the practices of illegally or legally taking/abducting animals from their habitat, and killing, transporting and trading them.[3] But these terms will be used interchangeably with 'trafficking in free-born animals,' even if I find them problematic. While the term 'trafficking' implies that the trade is illegal,[4] my reason for applying the term, irrespective of legality, is that the legal status of the harm is irrelevant for the animal victims involved; their victimization is my main concern.

Furthermore, even though animals are bred in captivity, they are still ill-adapted to humans and human conditions. Consequently, parrots and reptiles who are bred for sale in the pet[5] trade, tigers and bears who are bred and kept captive for traditional Chinese medicine/traditional Asian medicine (TCM/TAM), and animals kept in zoos are included in the definition of 'wildlife trafficking.' The black bears who are captured to be caged so that their bile, a traditional medicine, can regularly be collected through a hole in their stomach and black bears who are bred for this reason in Asia to supply the market with bear bile (Foley et al. 2011) are both wildlife. Tigers are exploited because various body parts are seen as efficacious; for example, their whiskers are a good luck talisman and their bones are believed to hold special curing properties, for which reasons they are also bred in captivity. These animals are also subject to wildlife trafficking, even though by definition many of these are not born free. Lions, bred to be killed by trophy hunters in canned hunts, are also regarded as incorporated into this definition.

CITES[6] – the Convention on International Trade in Endangered Species of Wild Fauna and Flora (henceforth either 'CITES' or 'Convention') – regulates the trade in endangered species. The Convention currently has 184 parties to the convention, including the EU. The purpose of the Convention is not to ban trade in free-born animals, but to prevent trade leading to species extinction. CITES is an anthropocentric instrument which sees 'wildlife,' whether animal or plant species, as resources for human use (Sollund 2011; Goyes and Sollund 2016). Species are listed in three appendices: Appendix I includes species threatened with extinction. Trade in individuals of these species is permitted only in exceptional circumstances. Appendix II includes species not necessarily threatened with extinction, but in which trade must be controlled in order to avoid utilization incompatible with their survival. Appendix III species are those that are protected in at least one country, and for which the country asks CITES for help to control the trade.[7] If listed in one of the CITES appendices, animals are covered by the Convention whether or not they were free born or bred. Whenever possible, I will clarify whether the animals I am discussing were bred to be trafficked or were taken from their habitats. I will further return to a discussion about CITES in Chapter 12.

A green criminologist trying not to write anthropocentrically encounters many problems. For example, the term 'animal' is othering because it implies a sharp contrast between humans and other animal species, as it underlines and creates differences rather than recognizes our shared features and interests. 'Animal' implies all non-human animal species are the same, rather than the multitude of different species with different capacities and interests. The division is illogical because humans have much more in common with some other species, for example, orangutans and chimpanzees, than some non-human species have with each other, for example, a chimpanzee and a crab. Authors arguing for non-speciesist language have resolved the problematic nature of the word and the meaning of 'animal' in different ways: nonhuman animal (Nibert 2002: 23), animals other than human animals (AOTHAs) (Beirne 1999: 118), and other than human animals (Kheel 2008). The human species, however, is still the yardstick, and other species remain a unified category rather than being recognized for the diversity they truly represent. These designations still leave us with the othering of nonhuman species through language and do not free us from a contrasting of humans and 'the rest,' so these solutions remain unsatisfactory. One can also opt for abbreviated terms – 'companion animals' becomes 'compans' (Sollund 2011). This is easier to write, but fails to add significantly in other respects because 'animal' is retained. Perhaps for simplicity, one could also choose 'nhanimal' for nonhuman animal.

One issue in this regard is that the word 'human,' and by extension 'humane,' holds positive connotations for most humans in contrast to 'animal' and 'beast' (Adams 1996). Derridá (2002) convincingly explores the word 'animal' as a construct that reflects no ontological reality. Beirne (2007), from a constructivist perspective, also argues for the consequence of non-anthropocentric language, emphasizing like Derridá the importance language has in shaping our thoughts and attitudes, and consequently also our world as we see it and act in it (see also Searle 1995). Still for Beirne, style wins in the choice between 'nonhuman animal' and 'animal.' Lacking any really good alternatives, I choose, like Beirne, to prioritize style and remain with the term 'animal,' rather than the heavy 'nonhuman animal,' a solution with which I am not entirely happy. To emphasize that they are individuals rather than objects, I use 's/he' rather than 'it' and 'who' rather than 'that' when referring to animals.

In relation to the specific topic of this book, the fact that animal victims are often taken from where they were born as free individuals is an important part of their victimization and the abuse they suffer; they are turned into captives with the trauma this involves, and if not killed, turned into commodities. This dimension involves the contrast between 'domesticated' and 'wild' and should be transparent in the language used to address the problem. This, however, is also tricky. As argued elsewhere (Sollund 2014), 'domesticated' should imply that someone is made part of the household, like some animal species were ten thousand years ago when humans started to keep pigs, cows and sheep (Børresen 1996; Nibert 2013; Noske 1989). The term 'domestication,' or in Norwegian '*temme*,' has implications derived from an anthropocentric mindset. It indicates that animals are adapted to a human household and that the animal, during this process, has been subjugated to the human, and thereby her/his own natural ways of living have been oppressed/eradicated to better meet human requirements. Some of the first animals who were 'domesticated' may have been and still are comfortable in an enclosure or barn if sufficiently spacious; however, in today's factory farms, many animals do not feel at home in the captivity of their concrete craters and many are not used to humans because so much husbandry is automated (Børresen 1996; Risan 2003, 2005). The term may no longer be justified the way it used to be. Nibert (2013), therefore, uses 'domesecration' rather than 'domestication,' which he defines as

> the systemic practice of violence in which social animals are enslaved and biologically manipulated, resulting in their objectification, subordination

> and oppression. Through domesecration, many species of animals that lived on the earth for millions of years, including several species of large, sociable Eurasian mammals, came to be regarded as mere objects, their very existence recognised only in relation to their exploitation as 'food animals' or similarly socially constructed positions reflecting various forms of exploitation. (12)

Nibert sees domesecration as enslavement and exploitation rather than as a process of mutual benefit. Animal species that most frequently are defined as domesticated, thus positioning them as part of the household and even the family, are dogs and cats.

'Domesticated' is often contrasted with 'wild.' This means, according to *The Free Dictionary*, uncivilized, barbarous and savage,[8] and is therefore also an alienating term for the description of animals because of its implication that nonhuman animals are uncivilized, unpredictable, fierce and dangerous in contrast to humans (although indigenous peoples also have been labelled this way).[9] The term 'tame' further implies that an animal from the outset is wild – s/he is uncivilized, unpredictable and dangerous and in opposition to human – and, therefore, through the process of taming is turned into an object under human control. The meaning of 'tame' in *The Free Dictionary* is 'changed by man from a naturally wild state into a tractable, domesticated, or cultivated condition – an animal who is not fearful of human contact' and 'who is lacking in spirit or initiative; meek or submissive: a tame personality.' Thus, taming or domesticating an animal implies a transformation from being who s/he was meant to be to being someone and something else – there *for* someone – a human.

The combination of 'wild' and 'life' to make 'wildlife' creates a single category for animals and plant species that obscures all individuality of those within it. As White (2013) observes, the categories that humans position animals in are 'inherently anthropomorphic categorizations in the sense that the ways in which animals are categorised reflect human interventions over time and human notions of usefulness' (117).

Another frequently used anthropocentric word is 'poaching.' This can easily be replaced with 'abduction' (Sollund 2011) or 'theriocide,' which is analogous to homicide (Beirne 2009, 2014),[10] depending on the act. I reject 'poaching' because it implies that animals are property, whether private property, as in animals in game parks, or the property of the state. In these cases, poaching is perceived in conventional/conservation criminology terms (see Hill 2015; Pires and Moreto 2011) as a crime consisting of killing/taking animals without permission. Here, then, the crime is against the person who or the state that owns the animals, rather than a crime against an animal. The focus should be on the harm that is committed against the animal victim.

Norway is preponderantly a receiving country for trafficked animals, and Colombia is a country that is preponderantly a source country. Using rich qualitative data, I will discuss different arrays and motives of people's involvement in the trade and also the ways in which the problem is addressed in two countries, with the main focus on Norway. As I will argue, much animal trafficking takes place within nation states, rather than across international borders, and these crimes are often more of a national than a transnational problem. First, a brief history of animal trafficking is in order.

The deep roots of animal trafficking

Trafficking in animals has been occurring for centuries. The Vikings traded in furs from Scandinavia and Russia to Constantinople (Logan 2013), and in Norway, the use of and trade in predator birds, such as hawks and falcons, has a history going back hundreds of years; the rules attached to property practices of hawks were regulated in the 12th century in *Frostatingsloven* (the law of Frostating) and *Gulatingsloven* (the law of Gulating) – Norway's oldest laws from the courts (Thorsen 2007). Falcons were caught and given as gifts in order to secure political alliances. Håkon Håkonssøn, king in Norway between 1217 and 1263, sent hawks and falcons to the English king in 1224 (Thorsen 2007: 88). In the 18th and 19th centuries, animals were trafficked from African colonies: dead for museum collections and alive for zoos (Thorsen 2013).

By tracing the histories of exotic animals at Gothenburg's Natural History Museum, Thorsen (2013) demonstrates that both live and dead animals were in great demand in the late 19th and early 20th centuries. The museum received animals from a range of suppliers, such as big game hunters, scientists and sailors. She shows how hunters treated their victims as goods by conserving their pelts/skins and how museum staff detailed their size and weight in order to ready them for display. She also describes how monkeys were kept as companion animals or in menageries. Menageries were also part of the French court, and Gålmark (2016) discusses how Olympe de Gouge, the author of the Declaration of Women's Rights, took many of these exotic animals into her home as companions (see also Beirne 2014).

van Uhm (2016b, 2018) also discusses the history of trafficking and shows how it has century-long – even millennia-long – roots in ancient Egypt, and continues today, whether that is trafficking of monkeys as companion animals, caviar and other animal delicacies, animal parts used for traditional Asian medicine, or ivory for decorative purposes. As will be shown, the trade in free-born animals also has century-long traditions in the other case study location, Colombia.

In sum, humans' exploitation of animals for various purposes, including trading them as commercial commodities, has a long cultural tradition, in which the economy in WLT is central. Lynch and Stretesky (2014: 179) suggest that environmental crimes should only be explored in light of the political economy and from the perspective of production theory. This approach is too limited, however. Intertwined in capitalism and consumerism are cultural features, such as doxic speciesism (Sollund 2012a; Lie and Sollund 2017) and meat normativity[11] (Gålmark 2008) that are among the most important structural features of globalization that drive species extinction. While WLT most certainly has been crucial in sustaining capitalist economies and political alliances, it is necessary to remember that it was taking place *prior* to capitalism as we know it today. While the fundamental reason for why animals are traded as commodities is economic, animals' roles in cultural and religious practices are important too (e.g., Nibert 2013; Noske 1989; Villamar et al. 2015). Thus, the great variety of the trade requires phenomenological, cultural and contextualized analyses.

Wildlife trafficking: a brief overview of its features

The illegal trade in free-born animals and products made from their bodies is one of the fastest growing illegal trades worldwide (e.g., Steiner 2014). It is positioned repeatedly alongside the drug trade, the illegal arms trade and human trafficking in terms of its economic value (South and Wyatt 2011; Warchol 2007; Wyatt 2013; Zimmerman 2003). Tourism, migration and the internet play a crucial role in the global expansion of the markets, with the internet playing an extremely important role in the offer–demand exchange. According to a study by the International Fund for Animal Welfare (IFAW), the US is responsible for two-thirds of the trade, nearly ten times more than the second- and third-ranking countries – the UK and China. Of the eight nations involved in the study (Australia, Canada, China, France, Germany, Russia, the US and the UK), IFAW (2008) found that

> of the 7,122 auctions, advertisements and communiqués reviewed in this study, 5,223 (73.3%) offered elephant products. Elephant products, predominantly ivory, were the most commonly available products in six of the eight countries profiled, with the United States responsible for ten times more ivory listings than the next closest country (the United Kingdom). (10)

Abduction from and theriocide of animals in their habitats entail a significant threat to many animal species. This includes the trafficking of a large number of parrot species destined for the international pet market (Eniang et al. 2008; Gonzales 2003; Herbig 2010; Pires and Clark 2011; Pires and Taylor 2011; Pires and Moreto 2011; Sollund 2011; Wright et al. 2001; Berkunsky et al. 2017), as well as great apes (gorillas, chimpanzees and bonobos) and other primates, who are abducted for use as research subjects, for bushmeat (Boekhout van Solinge 2008a) and for the pet trade (van Uhm 2016b). Big cats are traded dead and alive for traditional medicine and the use of their skins as cultural and souvenir apparel (only 3,890 tigers remain in the wild according to WWF).[12] Reptiles are traded for medicinal purposes (Alves et al. 2008; Lin 2005), as exotic pets (Natusch and Lyon 2012; Wilgen et al. 2010) and for meat (e.g., Gibbon et al. 2000).

Abduction and theriocide are facilitated by deforestation and the construction of forest roads that make the animals more accessible (Boekhout van Solinge 2008a, 2008b; Mowbray 2015). Bushmeat is not only sold in markets in Africa, but exported to Europe and has been found in London markets (Sollund and Maher 2015), and unidentified meat from Africa has been confiscated at the Oslo Airport.[13]

Analysis of seizures from EU Customs authorities shows that 60% of traded ivory was categorized as 'personal effects,'[14] 22% came as mail parcels and 9% came concealed in freight or transport (Interpol/IFAW 2013: 20). This means that Customs confront specific challenges concerning the control of freight transport, a topic that will be treated in relation to the Norwegian data in Chapter 6.

Most often, the value and cost of the legal and the illegal trade are estimated economically. The economic value of the legal wildlife trade is approximately 323 billion USD, while the illegal trade, although highly uncertain, is roughly several hundred billion USD annually (Traffic 2017). Figures for the illegal trade in wildlife range from 6 billion USD a year (Warchol 2007) to 10 billion USD a year (Schmidt 2004) to as high as 20 billion USD (Alacs and Georges 2008; South and Wyatt 2011). The legal trade is estimated to be anywhere from 5 to 50 billion USD a year (Reeve 2002: 10) to 159–160 billion USD (Duffy cited in White 2011: 55; Schneider 2008; Warchol 2007). van Uhm (2016) confirms that 'if there is an assumed legal wildlife trade of €86 billion, the illegal wildlife trade would be roughly estimated at €21.5 billion worldwide from which €9.5 billion relates to the EU' (91). In addition, economic damage to communities and societies occurs when, for example, species drawing visitors become extinct, causing tourism revenue to cease. The market is steadily increasing (Broad et al. 2003; Rosen and Smith 2010; Stoett 2002) and is attracting organized crime (see Milliken and Shaw 2012; van Uhm 2016b; Wyatt 2013). Because of dark figures (such an unregistered crime) and under-enforcement, establishing the number of victims and their economic value and value of the products made from their bodies is impossible.

Conceptualizing the trade in economic terms overlooks the suffering and deaths involved. The illegal trade in endangered species is not only causing unspeakable suffering for the direct victims involved, but it is also increasingly said to cause social unrest when, for example, guerrilla groups, perhaps in league with organized crime groups, traffic large quantities of animals and animal products illegally and fight over elephant tusks and rhino horns (e.g., Wyatt 2013). According to the European Commission (EC [2014a]), the resale value of rhino horn is estimated at €40,000 per kilo (current price per kilo of gold is approximately €31,000), while raw ivory prices reach €620 per kilo on the black market. Tiger bones sell for up to €900 per kilo (EC 2014c). Unsurprisingly, armed conflict between rangers protecting the animals and the groups who try to kill them have unfolded. An estimated 1,000 rangers have been killed during operations aimed at protecting animals in the last ten years around the world (EC 2014a; see also Minnaar 2014). According to EC (2014a),

> The increase in wildlife trafficking is mainly driven by a high and growing demand for wildlife products, notably in parts of Asia, by poverty, weak governance, instability and crisis situations in key source regions, and facilitated by gaps in enforcement and insufficiently deterrent sanctions.[15]

A quick Google search confirms that eBay is an important connecting link between buyers and sellers of ivory. eBay has officially taken a stance against commercializing ivory, as its website states: '*eBay has decided to institute a global ban on the sale of all types of ivory. This global ban will be effective January 1, 2009.*'[16] However, as will be discussed in relation to a Norwegian case, traders in ivory circumvent this ban by labelling ivory as 'faux ivory,'[17] although many items, such as antiques, obviously contain real ivory.

There are exceptions to the ivory ban, depending on when the ivory item was crafted. According to an Interpol and the International Fund for Animal Welfare investigation into the illegal ivory trade on the internet, ivory is considered antique or pre-CITES if the raw ivory was acquired or introduced into the EU before the adoption of the Convention or if the worked ivory (meaning not raw ivory, but it being worked in some way to produce an artefact) was acquired more than 50 years ago. These ivory items are subject to less strict regulations. Commercial trade within the EU in these antique ivory items is allowed with certification. For the commercial trade of worked ivory items which are more than 50 years old, no certificate is needed. If the ivory item is not antique, an import and/or export permit must be obtained to prove its legality. Exemptions to the Convention also exist, provided the items are personal effects. The CITES legislation includes various categories of personal effects ivory that are listed in Appendices A and B. Importing ivory, which is listed in Appendix A as a personal effect, requires an export and import permit which must be presented to Customs before entering the EU. An import permit is not needed for personal effect ivory listed under Appendix B. In both cases, however, an export permit from the country of origin is necessary (Interpol/IFAW 2013: 10). In the case of Norway, the Norwegian Environment Agency has restricted the practice in order to close the loopholes which exist in defining ivory (or other CITES products) as personal effects because of the massive volume of the global internet trade and the pressure it puts on many species (Miljødirektoratet n.d.).

The Interpol/IFAW report (Interpol/IFAW 2013) also establishes that the internet trade of ivory is a major problem in the EU, especially in Western Europe. The time frame studied for the report was only a few hours per day in nine countries over a fortnight. A conservative estimate was that 4,500 kilos of ivory were traded during this brief time (11). According to the report, significant loopholes in the legislation of the internet trade of ivory exist:

> There is no obligation on the side of the seller to prove on the Internet that the ivory item for sale complies with the existing legislation; there is no obligation to inform the buyer of existing regulations; and there is no obligation for the website owner to comply with existing legislation.
>
> (15)

This implies that buyers may be ignorant of the fact that they are committing a crime when they purchase ivory through internet auctions. It does not imply that they are not committing a crime, because being unaware that one is committing a crime does not absolve an offender in other kinds of crimes.

van Uhm (2016b) found in his study (using EU TWIX[18] data) that many of the items sent to the EU are ordered via the internet, and that the probability of detection is small, as Customs officials check as little as 2% of all packages (104). Some 2,500 seizures of wildlife products are made every year in the EU (van Uhm 2016b). Certain rare species of birds, coral, fish and tortoises are also trafficked from EU Member States, within the EU or to third countries (EC 2014a: 4). Europe is also a main arena and receiver for parrot trade. When one of the largest bird traders in Europe was found guilty of large-scale illegal animal trade within a criminal organization in the Netherlands and legal imports of protected birds were banned due to avian influenza, other criminal groups immediately filled the gap. Couriers repeatedly smuggled birds from Suriname through Spain into the Netherlands. Often, imported animals are said to be destined for a zoo that is involved in the process, but in fact, the animals are illegally sold to other customers.

In the last 15–20 years, there has been a considerable boom in keeping exotic animals as pets and extraordinary animal products being sold over the internet, at auctions and in pet shops (e.g., Lavorgna 2014, 2015; van Uhm 2016b: 16). In Norway, the internet is used to connect sellers and buyers on the sale of fish, coral and parrots. The internet has now replaced traditional marketplaces, which has created a global problem because it demands tremendous resources and priority to control, including expertise that most police forces worldwide lack. Whether for medicinal products, meat consumption or other purposes, there is an increase in the worldwide trafficking, use and exploitation of free-born animals. This can be seen in relation to how food habits worldwide have changed with globalization and the ensuing cultural exchange, for example, pizza and sushi, traditional Italian and Japanese foods, can be found and consumed worldwide.

The role of the internet and other media in increasing the demand for wildlife is not limited to actual transactions. For example, YouTube videos of 'cute' animals, like a loris being tickled, make people want to have a slow loris themselves and disregard – or do not know – that tickling a slow loris is abuse (Nekaris et al. 2013, 2015). Likewise, videos of parrots singing and dancing contribute to a representation of parrots as attractive, funny and charming, which also makes people want them. But such videos fail to show how complicated it is to keep a screaming, messy parrot as a companion, resulting in parrots being passed from person to person, lacking liberty, and suffering from inadequate food, shelter and care (Engebretson 2006). Indeed many parrots, especially wild-caught birds, do not allow petting and respond to such attempts with painful bites, which can result in their resale on an internet site (Nekaris et al. 2013). The popularity of J. K. Rowling's *Harry Potter* series, where owls are used to transmit messages, resulted in a dramatic increase in the demand for owls in Java and Bali to such an extent that the owls previously referred to as Burung Hantu (ghost birds) were referred to as Burung Harry Potter, leading Nijman and Nekaris (2017) to suggest that they be listed as protected species. The authors refer to the increase in the trade of owls as a delayed effect, the greatest increase taking place when the citizens there first gained access to the internet, and the growth of internet groups, such as on

Facebook, generated more hype regarding owls as pets. The authors also point out the high 'turn over' as many owls die before they are sold and that it is hard to determine what species the owls are because they are kept in small, dark cages, making identification difficult, indicating also the harms they are subjected to.

In a similar wary, growing Chinese and Vietnamese middle classes have led to an increased demand of rhino horn, bear and tiger products, which, according to cultural beliefs, contain special medicinal properties and are used in traditional medicine (Emslie in Warchol 2007; Lee 1996; Lin 2005; Minnaar 2014; van Uhm 2016b). Arguably, what triggered the demand in rhino horn substantially around 2008 was a politician in Vietnam claiming to have been cured from cancer by rhino horn (Watts 2011). This is an example of how quickly and broadly wildlife consumption spreads. Crushed rhino horn has been seen as a status symbol and is also believed to cure hangover, and is therefore served in drinks. Rhino horn is also used in Yemenite dagger handles (Wasser et al. 2008). The trade in rhino horn has increased so dramatically over the past few years that the species is now critically endangered.

Pangolins are also threatened, with six of eight species classified as near threatened or endangered on the IUCN (International Union for Conservation of Nature) Red List. Trafficking in pangolin species is increasing as they are used in TCM (Zhou et al. 2012), as well as for food.

Primates are abducted to become laboratory animals for Western pharmaceutical companies (Lemieux and Clarke 2009: 451; Goyes and Sollund, in press). According to Zimmerman (2003), between 200,000 and 600,000 primates are trafficked for this purpose yearly, not the least from and also within Colombia to be experimented on for a malaria vaccine by scientist Manuel Elkin Patarroyo (Goyes 2015; Maldonado et al. 2009, see Chapter 9). Ten percent of the 10,000 primates used in test research in EU laboratories per year are abducted from their habitats (ADI 2009).

In many countries, the abduction and killing of free-born animals can be attributed to cultural practice. In Colombia, turtle meat is an Easter specialty, despite turtles' protected status, songbirds are kept in homes, and taking parrots from their nests has become an annual tradition in Peru (Gonzales 2003). I return to these points in Chapters 9 and 10.

In addition to causing the death of innumerable animals and species extinction, eating free-born animals has also caused zoonotic diseases, such as Ebola, HIV and monkeypox. Moreover, the emergence or re-emergence of many zoonotic diseases including yellow fever, Lyme disease, hantavirus pulmonary syndrome, Nipah virus encephalitis, influenza, rabies, malaria and human African trypanosomiasis have been linked to anthropogenic habitat changes (Kurpiers et al. 2016). To glorify aspects of culture and traditions in order to argue for the legitimacy of harmful practices would thus amount to harmful culture and moral relativism.

Endangered species, whether dead or alive, appeal to collectors: rare parrots (Pires and Clark 2011; Pires and Moreto 2011), raptor birds for falconry (Wyatt 2009, 2011), bird eggs (Nurse 2011, 2015), rare aquaria species (Mazurek 2017),[19] amphibians, anteaters and sugar gliders. How animal collecting plays into illegal killing and taking of wildlife will be examined in relation to specific court decisions in Norway in Chapter 4. Pet stores and breeding facilities are used to disguise trafficking, a point that will be discussed in relation to the research findings in both Norway and Colombia.

The offenders: buyers, abductors, killers and middlemen

Just as the offenders on the demand side of the illegal and legal animal trade are varied, so are the actors who abduct, kill and traffic the victims. Wyatt (2013: 82–93) identifies seven categories of offenders.

1 Subsistence abductors/theriociders (my preferred terminology to replace her 'poachers/harvesters') are people living in close contact with the natural environment and who have a long tradition of living on the exploitation of a particular species.
2 Opportunistic abductors/theriociders (again my preferred terminology) are people living in proximity to nature who take advantage of a 'moment in time' and because 'this is what they have always done' (Gonzales 2003; Leberatto 2016); for example, taking a parrot from its nest during nesting season to make additional income or killing animals to sell their pelts.
3 Specialist abductors/theriociders (as above, my chosen terminology) are those who are calculated in their capture of animals. They target particular species to sell to middlemen or in markets. As Wyatt (2013) explains, 'they could be filling an order for a particular "specimen" that has come through the transnational organised crime network from a wealthy buyer' (85). These categories are not clear cut. Categories 1 and 2 and categories 2 and 3 can merge, and what constitutes 'organised' is subject to discussion. For example, in line with my Colombian interview data (see Chapter 10 and Goyes and Sollund 2016), the order for an animal comes from an urban middleman, who sends a person to a particular place, where a person who lives in proximity to nature is willing to fill the order for extra income. The middleman's henchman then brings the animal back to the city where the middleman passes the victim on to his client, the purchaser. Both those who abduct the animals and the middlemen may act opportunistically making extra income from trafficking (Leberatto 2016).
4 Traffickers/smugglers work within or across national borders and are motivated by profit. According to Wyatt (2013: 85), they may be acting on their own or as part of a network.
5 Individuals, whether part of a network or trafficking for themselves or for others. A key group of offenders involved in animal trafficking and trade are the middlemen. They are not necessarily part of organized crime, defined as a hierarchical, long-standing criminal network (Hagan in Wyatt 2013: 87). Wyatt describes the middleman as someone who moves stolen goods within a network, most often as 'disorganised crime,' although there may be some organisation and structure to such actions.

6 The individuals in crime networks who form part of the middle stage of the smuggling of wildlife constitute more or less organized networks – a category I return to when discussing the findings from Colombia. Rather than characterising WLT as *organized* or *unorganized* crime, it seems that the concept of *networks* would be more fruitful (van Uhm 2016b). People profiting from WLT are organized but not necessarily as part of a formally organized crime group, yet definitions in this respect are fluid, and acts which are defined as organized crime in one context, for example Norway, are not considered so in another. One argument for applying the term 'organized crime' rather than 'network crime' is that the former emphasizes the seriousness of the crime and the threat this constitutes for animals and the ecosystems they belong to, such as when keystone species are lost (Mills et al. 1993). 'Organized crime' tends to attract more attention and greater efforts are made to impact it than 'network crime,' if this term is even used. Networks are necessary in many instances of WLT, whether to secure buyers, to organize transport or in the abduction/killing of animals (van Uhm 2016b). When animals/products are trafficked across borders, a higher level of sophistication and organisation is required. van Uhm's (2016b) study of wildlife trafficking of animal products for TCM, sturgeon caviar and live Barbary macaques for the 'pet' trade, led him to conclude that

> dynamic alliances developed in order to transfer the illegal wildlife from the source to the destination countries. The chain of the illegal wildlife trade consists of different stages, actors and networks. The wildlife moves along a hub of contracts from the source areas to the final destination.
> (243)

7 Criminals who can be characterized as members of organized crime groups, for example, those involved in rhino horn and elephant ivory trafficking. Increasingly over the past few years, claims by the EC, the UN (UNODC 2013) and Interpol have been made that organized crime groups are involved in wildlife trafficking, hence this kind of crimes should be regarded as serious, transnational organized crime (CITES Secretariat 2013a,b). As Interpol (n.d.) states on its website:

> A significant proportion of both wildlife and pollution crime is carried out by organised criminal networks, drawn by the low risk and high profit nature of these types of crime. The same routes used to smuggle wildlife across countries and continents are often used to smuggle weapons, drugs and people. Indeed, environmental crime often occurs hand in hand with other offences such as passport fraud, corruption, money laundering and murder.
> (Interpol n.d.)

According to Europol, the role of organized criminal groups in wildlife trafficking within the EU is increasing, based on the expectation of high profitability with low risk of detection and low levels of sanctioning (EC 2014a, 2014b).

Claims about the connections between wildlife trafficking and organized crime[20] have been made elsewhere (e.g., Alacs and Georges 2008; Ellis 2005; Lowther et al. 2002; Renctas 2001; Schneider 2012; South and Wyatt 2011; Warchol et al. 2003; Wilson-Wilde 2010; Wyatt 2011, 2013; Zilli 2011; Zimmerman 2003). A concise – or consistent – explanation of what 'organized crime' is has been lacking. The UN Convention against Transnational Organized Crime (Article 2a) defines 'organized crime' as:

- A group of three or more persons that was not randomly formed;
- Existing for a period of time;
- Acting in concert with the aim of committing at least one crime punishable by at least four years' incarceration;
- In order to obtain, directly or indirectly, a financial or other material benefit.

(UNODC 2015)

To distinguish these groups from the many others containing three or more people and working in concert for an extended period (what Wyatt [2013: 88] refers to as 'disorganised crime'), theUnited Nations Office on Drugs and Crime UNODC (2015) website also states: 'the true defining characteristics of organised crime groups under the Convention are their profit-driven nature and the seriousness of the offences they commit.'

Despite the definition put forth in the UN Convention against Transnational Organized Crime, 'organized crime' is defined in various ways in the academic literature. Schneider's (2012: 52) definition involves more than two people committing crime over time with the capacity to operate outside their countries' boundaries. Wyatt (2013) argues that the IWT market is not necessarily consistent with official understanding of organized crime and groups; instead, she suggests that organized crime in relation to IWT 'is violent, long-lasting, structured, rationale, and adaptive, with networks to legitimate and illegitimate industries' (90).

In paragraph §60 of the Norwegian Penal Law,[21] punishment may be doubled if a crime, punishable by more than three years, is committed as part of 'organized crime,' defined as conspiracy among three persons or more. This has included considering organized crime charges for wildlife trafficking and applying it for wildlife crimes against protected wolves (Sollund 2015b, 2017c).

Schneider (2012) calls for further research to understand the connection between organized crime and IWT, suggesting that the bird trade is linked to Asian, European and Latin American groups, the ivory and rhino horn trade to Asian and African groups, the trade in reptiles and insects to Asian and European groups, the trafficking of tigers and tiger parts to Asian and Chinese triads, and trade in wild game to Asian and Chinese triads, as well as to African groups (5, 7; see also Ellis 2005). In 2011, the last Vietnamese rhino was found dead with its horn removed.

Milliken and Shaw (2012) identify organized syndicates involved in pseudo trophy hunts in South Africa, trafficking rhino horn to Asia. Organized groups involved in IWT are reportedly well-resourced (heavily armed and mobile with the necessary resources to carry out bribery and complicated trafficking operations) and able to fight rangers protecting wildlife (Schneider 2012; Wyatt 2013). According to Wyatt

(2011, 2013), the falcon trade in Russia is not only connected to organized crime groups, who sell a single falcon for up to 100,000 USD, but also to terrorism; revenue from this IWT is used to purchase weapons and support training camps for terrorists. There is growing concern that terrorist groups, such as Al-Shabaab, are using ivory to finance rebellion and war. Crosta and Sutherland (2012), who investigated the involvement of Al-Shabaab in trafficking ivory through Kenya, determined that the trade could be supplying up to 40% of the funds needed to pay its fighters. Ivory has thus taken the role of conflict diamonds (Boekhout van Solinge 2008a, see also Brisman and colleagues 2016). Evidence also suggests that rebel groups in Sudan kill elephants in order to finance weapons (Warchol et al. 2003).

The Asian-Pacific region is responsible for a quarter of the world's IWT (Lin 2005: 201). Elliot suggests that environmental crime here, including IWT, 'generates the kinds of "pernicious effects on regional stability and development," [and] the maintenance of the rule of law and the welfare of the region's people' identified by the ASEAN Declaration on Transnational Crime as matters of serious concern (2007: 499). Organized crime groups in Colombia and Mexico also corrupt law and order, which, indirectly, leads to social insecurity (Lawson and Vines 2014; Schneider 2012; Wyatt 2013).

A connection between drug crimes and wildlife crimes is often made (e.g., South and Wyatt 2011; Wyatt 2013; Zimmerman 2003), and it is, therefore, one of the issues relevant for this project. Such a link, however, can be difficult to establish as the diversity of actors involved in the trade makes it difficult. That traffickers may carry double contraband will be shown in the analysis of the Colombian data.

Before turning to methodological approaches applied in this research and its findings, I will describe the legal framework for wildlife trafficking.

The legal framework, the CITES and EU regulation

The purpose of CITES is not to prevent trade in endangered species, but to secure the survival of endangered species through regulation so that humans can continue to exploit them, since non-human species are regarded as resources. In July 2018, there were 183 member states to the Convention. Article 1 of the CITES, which was adopted in 1973, lays out the rationale of the agreement:

> Recognizing that wild fauna and flora in their many beautiful and varied forms are an irreplaceable part of the natural systems of the earth which must be protected for this and the generations to come; *Conscious* of the ever-growing value of wild fauna and flora from aesthetic, scientific, cultural, recreational and economic points of view; *Recognizing* that peoples and States are and should be the best protectors of their own wild fauna and flora;
>
> *Recognizing*, in addition, that international co-operation is essential for the protection of certain species of wild fauna and flora against *over*-exploitation through international trade.
>
> (Preamble to the CITES; emphasis added)[22]

Thus, fauna (another anthropocentric mass term) is 'part of nature,' which must be protected for human generations to come. Fauna (and flora) hold a number of different values – cultural, economic and recreational. Peoples and states own their flora and fauna: animals are property. Under CITES, these 'resources' must be protected against *over*exploitation, not exploitation per se. As the Convention explains:

> CITES regulates international trade in close to 35,000 species of plants and animals, including their products and derivatives, ensuring their survival in the wild with benefits for the livelihoods of local people and the global environment. The CITES permit system seeks to ensure that international trade in listed species is *sustainable, legal and traceable.*
>
> (emphasis added)[23]

Because CITES is a convention regulating trade, for which continued trade is a goal, it is not designed to tackle illegal trade. As stated by Sina and colleagues (2016), however,

> Article VIII.1 CITES recommends the adoption of domestic criminal sanctions for the violation of CITES norms, so it establishes '1. The Parties shall take appropriate measures to enforce the provisions of the present Convention and to prohibit trade in specimens in violation thereof. These shall include measures: (a) to penalize trade in, or possession of, such specimens, or both; and (b) to provide for the confiscation or return to the State of export of such specimens.'
>
> (6)

CITES CoP11[24] specifies that 'Parties should advocate sanctions for infringements that are appropriate to their nature and gravity,' and the International Consortium on Combating Wildlife Crime adopted a toolkit dedicated to wildlife and forest offences to help the states comply with these provisions (Sina et al. 2016: 15; Sollund and Maher 2015; UNODC 2012).

Whether or not the toolkit is applied and how the different parties to the Convention choose to enforce CITES varies, and as will be shown in the case of Norway, the authorities may aim for only minimum standards, both in terms of the priority of cases and in the level of sanctions applied.

The three appendices of CITES are important insofar as they categorize species according to their degree of endangerment:[25]

1 Appendix I shall include all species threatened with extinction which are or may be affected by trade. Trade in specimens [sic] of these species must be subject to particularly strict regulation in order not to endanger further their survival and must only be authorized in exceptional circumstances.
2 Appendix II shall include:

   (a) all species which although not necessarily now threatened with extinction may become so unless trade in specimens [sic] of such species is subject to strict regulation in order to avoid utilization incompatible with their survival; and

(b) other species which must be subject to regulation in order that trade in specimens [sic] of certain species referred to in sub-paragraph (a) of this paragraph may be brought under effective control.

3 Appendix III shall include all species which any Party identifies as being subject to regulation within its jurisdiction for the purpose of preventing or restricting exploitation, and as needing the co-operation of other Parties in the control of trade.

4 The Parties shall not allow trade in specimens [sic] of species included in Appendices I, II and III except in accordance with the provisions of the present Convention.

This is regulated by the requirement that animals and plants which are listed in the appendices are accompanied with the required export, import and re-export permits issued by the source and receiving countries.

Concern for the animals involved is mentioned in a few instances:

Article III.2 (c): a Management Authority of the State of export is satisfied that any living specimen [sic] will be so prepared and shipped as to minimize the risk of injury, damage to health or cruel treatment.

Article III.3 (b): a Scientific Authority of the State of import is satisfied that the proposed recipient of a living specimen [sic] is suitably equipped to house and care for it.

The intrinsic value of the animal and her/his interest in not being trafficked are not mentioned, however, and what 'the risk of injury, damage to health or cruel treatment' would be is not defined, nor is the requirement for being 'suitably equipped to house and care for' him/her. Animal welfare, their intrinsic value and whether this should entitle them to rights and a different conservation regime are points to which I return in Chapters 12, 13 and 14.

Arguably, the rationale behind CITES is outdated because of the knowledge now available about the capacities and needs of free-born animals. For example, biologist Hessen (2013) argues that humans and other animals do not differ in any significant way in their capacity to feel fear, pain or pleasure. This is rather obvious and an understatement if looking into the work of Bekoff (2006), whose research documents the clear notion of justice that animals apply when engaging in play.

That the EU is a large and expanding market for wildlife trade is confirmed by a WWF/TRAFFIC study (Engler and Parry-Jones 2007), which shows that the EU ranks as the top global importer by value for caviar, reptile skins and live reptiles. In 2005, the legal trade in wildlife products in the EU had an estimated declared import value of €93 billion, and €2.5 billion when excluding timber and fisheries. The EU jointly joined the CITES as a member in 2015. As EU membership has expanded, the magnitude of the EU market for wildlife and wildlife products has also increased (cf. Cowdrey 2002). EU regulations regarding the protection of wild flora and fauna are Council Regulation (EC) No. 338/97.[26] The aim of the EU Trade Regulation is to enforce CITES within the EU and provide additional measures for the conservation of species in trade. Council Regulation (EC) No. 865/2006[27] sets forth the rules concerning the implantation of the first. Although Norway is not an EU member, EU regulation is still worth mentioning in this study because Norway is a European country and strongly connected to and subject to EU legislation through its membership in the European Economic Area. With the EEA agreement, Norwegian legislation is not only subjugated to much EU legislation, but also of 600 Norwegian laws, about 170 contain EU law, and 6,000 EU acts have been implemented in Norway since Norway joined the European Economic Area agreement in 1994 (NOU 2012: 2, 20–22).

Through the EEA agreement, Norway has access to the inner market of the EU (NOU 2012: 2; Store Norske Leksikon 2014), and this has implications for IWT. The EU regulation about WLT includes four appendices, which follow CITES logic:

> Appendix A contains a) Appendix 1 species, for which the Member States have not entered a reservation; b) any species in demand which is either threatened with extinction or so rare that any level of trade would imperil the survival of the species.
>
> Appendix B contains a) the species listed in Appendix II to the Convention, other than those listed in Appendix A, for which the Member States have not entered a reservation; b) the species listed in Appendix I to the Convention for which a reservation has been entered; and c) any other species not listed in Appendices I or II to the Convention, which is subject to levels of international trade that might not be compatible with its survival or with the survival of populations in certain countries, or with the maintenance of the total population at a level consistent with the role of the species in the ecosystems in which it occurs. Furthermore, and as in the case with CITES, similar species to those in danger are protected to ensure the effectiveness of controls on trade in specimens of such species in appendix B. Species that constitute an ecological threat to wild species of fauna and flora indigenous to the Community are also listed in Appendix B.
>
> Appendix C contains Appendix III species of CITES and the species listed in Appendix II to the Convention for which a reservation has been entered.
>
> Appendix D contains a) species not listed in Appendices A, B and C which are imported into the European Community in such numbers as to warrant monitoring; b) the species listed in Appendix III to the Convention for which a reservation has been entered.[28]

In sections 11 and 12 of the EU regulation, there is also some superficial mention of the interests of the animals who are trafficked, indicating that they are individuals, not only 'specimens':

> 11) Whereas measures should be taken to minimize the adverse effects on live specimens [sic] of transport to their destination, from or within the

> Community . . . 12) or where they are exported or re-exported from the Community; whereas there should also be facilities guaranteeing that live specimens [sic] are adequately housed and cared for.

Again, what is adequate housing and care is not specified.

The EU has focused on the illegal wildlife trade in the past few years through the commissioning of research (Sollund and Maher 2015;[29] Sina et al. 2016), the EU action plan against wildlife trafficking (2016), and the recent donation of €30 million to combat IWT in eastern and southern Africa and the Indian Ocean (CITES 2017).

Both Norway and Colombia are parties to the CITES. Laws and regulations which apply in Norway are sketched out under the chapters concerning the country,[30] while the legislation in Colombia is included in an appendix of the book.

The outline of the rest of the book is as follows: In Chapter 2, I describe the methodology employed for this research, including my ethical and philosophical points of departure; in Chapter 3, I describe Norwegian trafficking cases, including seizure data from Customs and analysis of verdicts; in Chapter 4, I dive deeper into cases involving trafficking *to* Norway to show the diversity of motivations and species involved through analysis of case files and verdicts; in Chapter 5, I explore and analyze trafficking cases within and *from* Norway; in Chapter 6, I discuss law enforcement of WLT in the case of Norway, using interview data with representatives of law enforcement agencies, in Chapter 7, I address reptile trade in Norway, which was banned during most of the time for this research but is now partly legalized; while Chapter 8 offers a brief summary of the findings from the Norwegian data. In Chapter 9, I begin the description and analysis of the Colombian data, starting with an overview of wildlife trafficking in Colombia; in Chapter 10, I describe the various categories of victimization of the WLT in Colombia and the various modus operandi of offenders; in Chapter 11 come description and analysis of law enforcement of WLT in Colombia; Chapter 12 includes a discussion about how to respond to WLT, which is proceeded on a more philosophical level in Chapter 13, where I discuss and enhance the analysis and discussion of victimization for the animals involved. In the last chapter, 14, I end the discussion proposing theoretical perspectives through which the harms of WLT can be addressed, such as animal rights and care ethics. I end the book with this discussion since the attribution of rights and the application of care ethics should be the baseline for how we treat each other, whether we differ in terms of gender, species, age or other physical phenotypes. It can therefore provide scripts for how we should act also towards the free-born animals who are so heavily exploited in the WLT.

Notes

1 https://www.traffic.org/about-us/our-mission/

2 In the EU, regulation trade is defined as 'the introduction into the Community . . . and the export and re-export therefrom, as well as the use, movement and transfer of possession within the Community, including within a Member State, of specimens [sic] subject to the provisions of this Regulation; while transit,

refers to the transport of specimens [sic] between two points outside the Community through the territory of the Community which are shipped to a named consignee and during which any interruption in the movement arises only from the arrangements necessitated by this form of traffic.' http://eur-lex.europa.eu/legal-content/EN/ALL/?uri=CELEX:31997R0338

3 Another definition of 'wildlife' (Spanish: *vida silvestre*) is the one applied in Colombia, where an animal, according to law, is *silvestre* when it has not been genetically modified by human breeding (anonymous interviewee, Colombia).

4 For example, the US Fish and Wildlife Service defines wildlife trafficking as 'the poaching or other taking of protected or managed species and the illegal trade in wildlife and their related parts and products.' www.fws.gov/international/wildlife-trafficking/

5 The term 'pet' is anthropocentric and implies a bond of affection between owner and animal, and that the animal exists to be 'petted' and 'coddled' and to provide some kind of social and emotional satisfaction for the human owner. The term 'pet' implies this is the *purpose* of the animal, who exists *for* a human, rather than for him/herself, thus denying the intrinsic value of the animal, while extrinsic factors like sociability, fluffiness, etc. are appreciated – again by the human. Concerning wildlife trade, many animals who are trafficked as part of the so-called 'pet trade' will never be included as social beings in a family, however, but used as part of a collection, to display status, for entertainment, or as decoration.

6 https://cites.org/

7 https://cites.org/eng/disc/how.php

8 *The Free Dictionary* has among other definitions the following for savage: 1. Not domesticated or cultivated; wild: *savage beasts of the jungle.* 2. Not civilized; barbaric: *a people living in a savage state.* 3. Ferocious; fierce: *in a savage temper.* www.thefreedictionary.com/savage. The Oxford English Dictionary defines 'wild' when concerning an animal as 'living in a state of nature; not tame, not domesticated.' www.oed.com/view/Entry/228988?rskey=k90nBc&result=1#eid

9 This implies that animals cannot have culture, which is counter to research (Laland and Hoppit 2003). It would depend on species, is a large discussion and consequently is not one I will enter herein.

10 Beirne (2014: 49) uses 'theriocide' to refer to the act when a human/humans kill a nonhuman animal. The killing may be socially acceptable or unacceptable, legal or illegal. It may be intentional or unintentional and may involve active maltreatment or passive neglect. Theriocide may occur one-on-one, in small groups or in large-scale social institutions. The numerous and sometimes intersecting sites of theriocide include intensive rearing regimes, hunting and fishing, trafficking, vivisection, militarism, pollution and human-induced climate change.

11 'Meat normativity is the institutions, structures, relations and acts upholding the norm of other animals as objects for human use in whatever way they find appropriate, especially as matter in the production of everyday "meat"; "meat" thus being presented as the natural, indispensable and normal protein for humans' (Gålmark 2008: 102).

12 www.worldwildlife.org/species/tiger

13 Interview done with Customs officials as part of my pilot study.

14 Items made of ivory that are carried on the person or in the personal luggage of travellers coming from a third country are regarded as personal effects. This can be, for example, a tourist souvenir or a hunting trophy brought back from a holiday destination (Interpol/IFAW 2013: 21).

15 Communication from the commission to the Council and the European Parliament on the EU Approach against Wildlife Trafficking Brussels, 7.2.2014. https://eur-lex.europa.eu/legal-content/EN/TXT/?uri=COM%3A2016%3A87%3AFIN

16 Brewer-Hay (2008). www.ebayinc.com/stories/news/ebay-to-institute-global-ban-on-ivory-sales/ (emphasis original).
17 www.ebay.com/sch/sis.html?_kw=Beautiful+Antique+Bone+Faux+Ivory+Folding+Fan www.ebay.com/bhp/faux-ivory
18 Trade in Wildlife Information Exchange. A database on seizures and offences reported in 28 member states of the European Union. www.eu-twix.org/
19 The concept 'aquaria' or 'ornamental' fish is a symptom of the use value of the fish, rather than of the fish as a sentient being with intrinsic value; it is speciesist and anthropocentric.
20 Part of this text is previously published as Sollund and Maher (2015).
21 https://lovdata.no/pro/#document/NL/lov/1902-05-22-10/§60?searchResultContext=1109
22 www.cites.org/eng/disc/text.php
23 www.cites.org/eng/news/pr/2014/london-conference-20140214.php
24 The 11th meeting of the Conference of the Parties to the Convention on International Trade in Endangered Species of Wild Fauna and Flora held in Gigiri (Kenya) from 10 to 20 April 2000.
25 www.cites.org/eng/disc/text.php
26 http://rod.eionet.europa.eu/instruments/584
27 http://eur-lex.europa.eu/LexUriServ/LexUriServ.do?uri=CONSLEG:2006R0865:20120927:EN:PDF
28 For further details, see http://eur-lex.europa.eu/legal-content/EN/ALL/?uri=CELEX:31997R0338
29 In the EFFACE project, European Union Action to Fight Environmental crime – 2012–2016 (https://efface.eu/), wildlife trafficking was one of the topics studied.
30 I am grateful to David Rodríguez Goyes for putting the information about legislation together for me.

2 Methodology and ecophilosophical orientation

This project is based on grounded qualitative methods (Glaser and Strauss 1967), focusing on the deeper subjective meaning of experiences for individuals (Thagaard 2011: 38) and of phenomena. While this phenomenological approach is most often used to explore how experiences are understood and to frame the life world of humans, in this book, I extend this approach to include non-human animal victims. The underlying foundation of this is to actively apply intuition and empathy (Donovan and Adams 1996; Kheel 1996; Sollund 2017a), in order to try to *understand* and *feel* the experiences of the animal victims of the trade and the harms done to them. I am, of course, also interested in how my human informants perceive their reality, the WLT and the ways in which this harm is addressed, and in relation to reptile keepers I also use my intuition and empathy to fully comprehend their experiences, yet my compassion with the animal victims is my guide. While I have a green criminology–grounded point of departure, I will allow my findings to direct me theoretically. As a green criminologist, I am theoretically and intellectually open minded in that I employ perspectives that can add value to the analysis of my empirical findings (see Brisman 2014; South 2014; South et al. 2013; White 2008).

The locations and framework of this research

Norway is a northern country at the very edge of Europe, home to roughly 5,000,000 people, of which about 750,000 are immigrants or children of immigrants.[1] Norway has a long coastline and borders Sweden, Finland and Russia. These borders are porous, with many unmonitored crossing points. Being a Schengen member makes Norway responsible for the outer borders of Schengen Area. As mentioned, Norway is an affluent country due to a large oil industry, which began in the 1960s with the discovery of oil in the North Sea. This allows Norwegians to travel a lot, and many have the means to purchase material goods, including products made from animals during travel or on the internet. Norway has traditions involving predator birds, but today birds of prey are usually sought by collectors, both Norwegians and foreigners. Norway is a consumer country more than a supplier country for WLT.

Colombia is a country rich in biodiversity and therefore a source country for WLT. As I will show, much of this trafficking, legal and illegal, takes place within its borders or to/from neighbouring countries. Animals are used as pets (*mascotas*), eaten during festive seasons, used for medicinal products and may be used to display status. (For example, the drug baron Pablo Escobar had a private zoo of large species.)

While Norway is a peaceful, stable democracy, Colombia has been riddled by conflicts and civil war for more than half a century. Control and enforcement of IWT, therefore, may not be high on the country's agenda, but for reasons other than what can be observed in Norway.

Norwegian data

For this project, I conducted 17 interviews in Norway between 2010 and 2015 that lasted from one to two hours. They included individual and group interviews with police officers of different ranks and with different positions in police organizations and with Customs officers at different levels, including some at Oslo Airport and the Customs Directorate. Interviews were based on an interview guide, which ensured that the same topics were covered in all interviews but allowed me to pursue topics which arose unexpectedly and also ensured that interviewees had room to elaborate on their fields of expertise and their experiences. Interviews were recorded and transcribed.

I also interviewed a veterinarian of the Norwegian Food Safety Authority[2] and had several email conversations with a leader there. I further did an interview with an employee of the Norwegian Environment Agency,[3] and yet with another veterinarian to learn about her experiences with 'exotic' animals. I had a conversation and many email exchanges with a forensic expert on wildlife, carried out several informal conversations with police officers and state prosecutors, and observed Customs at Oslo Airport. I interviewed five people who had taken reptiles illegally to Norway and/or kept reptiles illegally in order to explore their motives in engaging in such acts as well as to explore the meaning the animals held for them. Excerpts from the interviews will be used extensively to ensure the interviewees are not misrepresented and to show typical features of the findings, such as narratives that were repeated by several.

Interviews were carried out in the offices of interviewees, such as in the Eco Crime Unit[4] and Customs Directorate where I had several interviews, in my office, or with reptile keepers at cafes. One interview was conducted by phone, and one police officer responded by email. Interviewees are anonymized when possible. When this was not possible, interviewees[5] were asked if they could be cited. The project was approved by Norwegian Social Science Data Services (NSD), and other necessary permissions were provided by the director general of the Higher Prosecution Authorities (*Riksadvokaten*) and the Customs Directorate. These were necessary for me to get access to CITES confiscation reports and police files related to penal cases. The 125 confiscation reports from the Customs Directorate are the reports Customs officers completed when animals (or any illegal goods) were seized at Norwegian borders. They contain information about the animal/object/goods seized, information provided by the person involved about the reason behind the act and a brief explanation of the crime. The reports document seizures from January 2008 to June 2017, but most likely do not cover all existing confiscation reports from this period, because pre-2014 reports were not provided systematically and seizures were under-reported.

I began data collection for this project in late fall of 2010 and concluded it in the fall of 2017. This longitudinal approach gave me the opportunity to follow several confiscation cases through the judicial system to their end, whatever the outcome, and to explore development in the field concerning priorities of control and law enforcement. Penal cases, including interrogation reports, photographs and confiscation reports, were secured and analyzed in line with the policies and confidentiality requirements of NSD,[6] as well as with the ethical guidelines of the Norwegian National Research Ethics Committees (NESH 2014).[7]

By means of critical discourse analysis, I examined several penal cases,[8] including police case files and verdicts, to discuss central topics and exemplify typical offences. Critical discourse analysis aims to reveal the role of discursive practice in the maintenance of the social world, including social relations with unequal relations of power (Jørgensen and Phillips 2002), such as the human–animal relationship. This means that I looked particularly for the ways in which speciesism plays itself out in the discourse in the verdicts and how abuse of the animals involved is overlooked because they are rarely regarded as victims. I also looked at discourse that refutes a hypothesis implying that this is the case. The penal cases that I examined for this research include 87 cases coded[9] as 2510 (illegal importation of alien wildlife species, a breach of Wildlife Law §47) and 723 cases coded as 5901 (illegal importation/dealing with exotic species §30 nr. 76, a breach of the Animal Welfare Act).[10] I focus only on a few of these penal cases, however, so that I can provide an in-depth analysis. Some of these cases include confiscation reports if they involved animals crossing an international border. In addition, I analyzed eight penal cases including verdicts that were connected to CITES cases. These were found at Lovdata.no,[11] a database of Norwegian laws, regulations and important verdicts. Three of my analyses pertain to the same case because it was appealed to the Supreme Court. Finally, I was given access to CITES statistics by Customs and the police. Several cases appeared in the media during the process of this research.

Colombian data

Fourteen interviews were conducted in Colombia. These interviews were conducted in 2013 by David Rodríguez Goyes, with two exceptions. One was an interview that I conducted in 2013 via SKYPE from Norway with staff of Centro de Rehabilitación de Fauna Silvestre – Secretaría Distrital de Ambiente (Centre for Rehabilitation of Wild Fauna – District Secretariat of the Environment, henceforth CRRFFS), in Bogotá. Goyes arranged the interview and was present in Colombia during the interview. The second interview conducted by me took place with Claudia Brieva Rico in connection with a visit to Unidad de Rescate de Animales Silvestres (Unit for the Rescue of Wild Animals) at the Faculty of Veterinary

Medicine at the Universidad Nacional de Colombia (URRAS) at the National University in Bogotá. For the other interviews, I suggested possible stakeholders and IWT experts that Goyes could target for interviews. Goyes made the initial contacts and conducted his interviews using an interview guide based on the one I used in Norway, which was reworked to suit the interview settings. Goyes asked follow-up questions at his own discretion. Interviews were conducted with members/staff of the following entities and organizations (governmental organizations [GOs], non-governmental organizations [NGOs] and foundations): Universidad de Colombia; Secretaría Distrital de Ambiente (District Secretariat of the Environment); Corporación para el Desarrollo Sostenible del Norte y el Oriente Amazónico (Corporation for Sustainable Development of the North and East Amazon); Ministerio de Ambiente y Desarrollo Sostenible (Ministry of the Environment and Sustainable Development); Asociación de Veterinarios de Vida Silvestre (Association of Wildlife Veterinarians); TRAFFIC (Latin America); Fundación ProAves[12] (Foundation ProAves [For Birds]); CRRFFS; and Entropika. The following people in Colombia asked to be credited for their participation in the project: Claudia Brieva Rico, URRAS, Bernardo Ortiz von Halle, TRAFFIC, Javier Cifuentes, CRRFFS, Wilfredo Pachón, Corporación para el Desarrollo Sostenible del Norte y el Oriente Amazónico, Claudia Rodríguez, Ministerio de Ambiente y Desarrollo Sostenible, and Angela Maldonado, Entropika.

While the project ran for over seven years, the data analyzed in this book provide a picture primarily of the situation in the period interviews were done and data collected. Improvements (or lack of improvement) may have been made to address the situation after the data collection, which these data do not represent. Although the data include some statistics, they are not extensive enough to provide a total overview of registered CITES cases in either of the research locations, particularly in Colombia where my statistical data are from Bogotá. In Norway, I found that not all cases[13] have been registered in the statistics provided to me by the Customs Directorate. Still, I regard them as sufficient to reveal a picture of the trade. Nor do the interviews, being qualitative data, necessarily represent all the existing wildlife trade in the two countries or the ways in which it is policed. To assess this more broadly, law enforcement agents in all police districts in Norway and Colombia should have been interviewed. The data are broad and rich enough, however, to provide in-depth information about trends of the trade; the motives of offenders; the priorities, weaknesses and strengths of law enforcement agencies; and the consequences of trafficking for the direct victims – the animals themselves – in Norway and Colombia.

Situating myself in relation to the research: autoethnography and ecofeminist care ethics[14]

My research topic, the legal and illegal trafficking in animals, was not randomly chosen nor do I claim to be neutral, in the sense that I myself have no personal feelings invested in the research. I have a vested interest in animal trafficking victims because of my experiences and because of my empathetic feelings towards non-human species. While I situate my research within the framework of green criminology with an emphasis on harm, I am also inspired by other theoretical directions. My own awakening to the horrors of WLT came about by coincidence and stems from my personal experiences with parrots, whom I suspected were victims of trafficking. They joined my household in different ways; they were abandoned birds, and yes, they could be problematic: Kåre held a distinct antipathy and aggression towards my male friends and family members. Pottifnatt and Jacoline were dedicated to destroying the interior of my house; Jacoline made nests in the kitchen cupboards, tearing out the wood, and Pottifnatt destroyed my books. The screaming of Pottifnatt and Kåre could wake up the devil himself, if they felt abandoned and did not want to fly to me in my apartment. And little Tinga's need to always be with (on) a human was irritating for some, but never for me. Pottifnatt, Kåre and Jacoline (Line for short), two blue-fronted Amazon parrots and one African grey, all showed behaviours which made me suspect they had been trafficked from South America and Africa. They were afraid of sticks and thread and could become hysterical if confronted with any of these. If I as much as lifted my flute, Pottifnatt would fly frantically through the rooms and scream hysterically, before I had even played a note. Tinga, an *Ara nobilis* (Hahn's macaw), was most probably bred in Norway, while the others came to Norway before the ban following Norway's entry as a party to the CITES in 1976 or were illegally trafficked thereafter.

My lengthy experience with parrots has thus provided me with both direct and indirect empirical and theoretical insight which I have further sought to expand and verify in my research, in matters concerning their victimization, their needs and the reason why people engage in the trade as consumers. An important reason why this autoethnographical experience can be applied as a grounding for systematic research is that the social distance which would otherwise have existed between my birds and me was reduced through daily, social interaction and replaced by empathy and love.

These experiences also facilitated rapport with several of my interviewees, including people who also had animal companions and were therefore engaged in animal welfare and wildlife issues, whether as police officers, Customs officials, veterinarians or reptile keepers. Interviews with reptile keepers expanded my insight into why people keep reptiles that countered my pre-understanding (Gadamer 1975).

According to Ellis and Bochner (in Anderson 2006: 387), evocative autoethnography foregrounds the writer's personal stories. Analytical autoethnography connects to 'some broader set of social phenomena than those provided by the data themselves.' Theoretically, my autoethnographical approach cannot be categorized as either evocative or analytical but draws on both approaches. My experiences mostly form a point of departure for my research, yet they are an important foundation for the ways in which I reflect on my findings. These reflections are, at times, painful, but invariably productive, and without these experiences, my research would not have taken the course it did. As Atkinson et al. observe,

> [auto]ethnographers-as-authors frame their accounts with personal reflexive views of the self. Their ethnographic data are situated within their personal experience and sense making. They themselves form part of the representational processes in which they are engaging and are part of the story they are telling.
>
> (Atkinson et al. 2003: 62 as cited in Anderson 2003: 382)

An autoethnographic point of departure and the reflexive process it entails is yet another personal and emotional experience, building on my previous life with parrots through which I question my motives and feelings in order to gain insight into the parrot trade that goes beyond my own subjective experiences. This implies a kind of introspection through which I, during my research and writing, aim to expand knowledge that reduces the harms brought on by the wildlife trade: it is by no means and should not be seen as a value-free position. To the contrary, it is loaded with ethical and moral bias that I hope will move readers to act to diminish the harms of the trade.

In a way, my parrots have also been my informants; they have shown me through their presence and behaviour what trafficking victims experience. Parrots are very often 'secondhand' birds who, in captivity, pass through multiple hands of people who do not always treat them well. While attractive to many buyers who may want a funny, talking bird, parrots are complicated, demanding individuals, whom many find too hard to handle. They are noisy, bite hard, make a lot of mess and destroy a lot of things. Buyers of animals constitute the market for WLT, but they also feed the market with their animals, once they feel incapable of taking care of them, and sell them off at markets again (Leberatto 2016). Parrots, just as other animals abducted from their habitats, may be hard to handle. Leberatto found, in his study from Peru, that parrots may also, with luck, grow to be quite old, and people seldom plan for such longevity. Owners' life situations change as might their commitment to keeping parrots. Parrots are then often sold again – in Norway through the website Finn.no. Kåre was an example of such retrafficking; he had been placed in many different homes and had the voice of many people. He sang like an old woman (did she die?), he cursed like a vulgar man, he yelled 'Papa!' and he told us in the family to shut up in an angry man's voice if we raised our voices, or alternatively, asked us in a shivering voice to please stop the noise. He was possessive and jealous, but towards me, incredibly lovely. Line liked to walk on the floor where she had easy access to my kitchen cupboards to carve the wood out, underlining that parrots nest in holes. She would also suddenly jump out of the kitchen attacking someone's feet with a decisive bark (showing she was used to the company of dogs and that she had learnt to bark from them) and regarded the kitchen as her domain. On other occasions, she meowed softly for some cuddling, indicating that she had also lived with and learnt from cats. Pottifnatt made it plain to me that he cared for my company and started turning me into his flock by flying after me from room to room. Tinga seldom left my shoulder unless forced to or if he had some creative enterprise going on, like picking the strings of a banjo or guitar, demonstrating parrots' affection, creativity and playfulness. My birds showed me that parrots need a flock and are born to be free. I am forever grateful for what they taught me about the great personalities and extraordinary intelligence and charm of parrots, and I miss them daily. Since they died, I feel a vital part of me is missing – as though I were amputated. In all of the parrots and other animals who are forcefully abducted by humans and denied the lives they were entitled to, I see my own birds – this is my motivation. By situating myself in relation to my research, I avoid presenting myself as an invisible, anonymous voice of authority, but rather as a real, historical individual with concrete, specific desires and interests (Harding 1987: 9).

An ecofeminist perspective and neutral research

In this research I further aim to position feminism more solidly in the field of green criminology, as this has been identified as a gap within the field (South 2014: 12), but most of all, because I regard ecofeminism as an important perspective with which to explore the issue at hand. The debate concerning scientific neutrality as a requirement for securing valid data grew out of debates in the 1970s and 80s over positivism. It has grown old, and frontiers between different positions have softened. Despite this, I think the issue of value-free research as an ideal for researchers is still a topic worth addressing as it prevails as a more or less declared ideal for research. The question is whether being value-free or neutral in order to avoid bias is at all possible or even desirable. As Harding and Norberg (2005) note, 'value-free research is an unachievable ideal.' Becker, however, contended that value-free research was impossible and stated in 1967 that the question, therefore, was not *whether* we take sides, but *which* side we are on (239).

Harding (1995) also notes, with reference to Novick and Proctor, that 'asserting objectivity sometimes has been used to advance and sometimes to retard the growth of knowledge, and the same can be said of assertions of relativism' (333). Citing Proctor (1991), she claims that 'neutrality, the central requirement of the conventional notion, has been used as "myth, mask, shield and sword"' (Harding 1995: 333). The then prevailing scientific methods were critiqued by feminist, anti-racist, postcolonial, environmental and other movements, whose proponents were demanding social justice because of the distorted results from research in the natural and social sciences. This led Harding (1995) to state that 'the prevailing standards for good procedures for maximizing objectivity are *too weak* to be able to identify such culture-wide assumptions as androcentric or Eurocentric ones' (333–334; see also Harding and Norberg 2005, 2010; emphasis original). The answer, according to Harding, is to invoke 'standpoint epistemologies to provide a kind of method for maximizing our ability to block "might makes right" in social sciences' (1995: 331). Researchers who find themselves in structurally determined power positions, such as white Western males, may be particularly poorly equipped to identify oppressive features of their own beliefs and practices (Harding and Norberg 2005, 2010). This perspective can be expanded to include, not only the position of diverse groups of women (as different from those of men), but also other oppressed individuals, like animals, and our relationship to them. Just like the feminist methodologies of the 1970s challenged hegemonic ideals of science that, they claimed, were tainted by androcentrism, such feminist methodologies can be employed to demask other doxic (Bourdieu 1995) oppressive structures, such as the human oppression of non-human animals (Sollund 2012a). Levins and Lewontin (in Harding 1995) state that the ideal of neutrality has raised demands on the researcher that her research and the results not be guided by feelings: 'The demand for objectivity, the separation of observation and reporting from the researchers' wishes, which is so essential for the development of science, becomes the demand for separation of thinking from feeling' (334).

Dorothy Smith (1974: 7) points out how (male) research failed in representing women:

> The two bases of knowledge and experience don't stand in an equal relation. The world as it is constituted by men stands in authority over that of women. It is that part of the world from which our kind of society is governed and from which what happens to *us* begins. The domestic world stands in a dependent relation to that other and its whole character is subordinate to it. The two difficulties are related to one another in a special way. The effect of the second interacting with the first is to impose the concepts and terms in which the world of men is thought as the concepts and terms in which women must think their world. Hence in these terms women are alienated from their experience.

We can extend such recognition to include animals; their interests are usually not taken into account and they are understood through an anthro(andro)pocentric lens (Kheel 2008). We are surrounded by animals, whether in the form of products, such as clothing and food, or as compan(ion)s. They constitute the basis for human 'civilisation' (Nibert 2013) and they are also socially important in our lives. Still, they are more misrepresented in sociological inquiry than women have ever been, particularly in studies focusing on trafficking. While we recognize the social value of our companion animals because they are of social value to *us*, when the costs of IWT (and note that legal trafficking is seldom a topic) are discussed, the animals' social value for each other or their intrinsic value are seldom considered.

Androcentric, Eurocentric, class-exploitative and racist ideologies – and I would add speciesism to this list – have been institutionalized and as such are ingrained in the fabric of scientific research, constituted as objective and neutral, according to Harding (1995):

> Objectivism[15] defends and legitimates the institutions and practices through which the distortions and their often exploitative consequences are generated. It certifies as value-neutral, normal, natural and therefore not political at all the policies and practices through which powerful groups can gain the information and explanations that they need to advance their priorities.
>
> (337)

I will turn to a critique of conventional criminology to show why I find my approach not so much a matter of choice, but a *must*, if one is to address adequately the evils of WLT.

Critique of conventional criminology approaches

The reason why I employ the approaches as detailed above is that I find conventional criminology perspectives and methodologies insufficient for the study of legal and illegal wildlife trafficking. A number of scholars and researchers have applied traditional criminological perspectives, such as situational crime prevention, to this field (Hill 2015; Lemieux 2014; Lemieux and Clarke 2009; Pires and Clarke 2011; Pires and Moreto 2011; Warchol et al. 2003). While helpful, such work does not question the underlying foundations of harm connected to wildlife trafficking. For example, in the abstract of their article, 'Solutions That Can Overcome the "Tragedy of the Commons,"' Pires and Moreto (2011) state that 'the "tragedy of the commons" dilemma occurs when individuals working independently of one another, will *overuse* a *common-property resource* for short-term benefits while decimating *the resource* for long-term use' (101; emphasis original). Pires and Moreto continue: 'This [tragedy of the commons] is often found in the field of "wildlife" crimes where species become *overexploited* to increase short-term profits while *endangering and eliminating a natural resource for future users.* Wildlife crimes suffering from the "tragedy" need to be prevented in order for species to avoid extinction while also *conserving a natural resource that monetarily benefits numerous people and their respective communities*' (101; emphasis added).

Pires and Moreto do not take a harm-based perspective, but a legalistic one, defining wildlife crime as (1) poaching for trade or personal possession; (2) illegally killing for bushmeat; and (3) killing animals due to human-animal conflict. The authors in their choice of approach acknowledge that it is the criminalized wildlife crimes that are of interest to them – that animals are a resource (capital) – a 'common good' – and that this resource or common good should be managed to ensure human benefit.

This does not mean that situational crime prevention measures will not be useful in preventing criminalized wildlife trafficking (see Hill 2015; Wellsmith 2010). Such empirical examples clearly prove the importance of providing incentives to local communities that are involved in these crimes, such as encouraging them to protect the targeted species. But Pires and Moreto (2011) are critical of the role of activists. While they acknowledge that their participation has contributed greatly to drawing attention to and providing responses that address wildlife-related crimes, they see the need for direct involvement of criminologists because 'arguably, criminologists may be able to provide a perspective to address "wildlife"-related crimes that is disconnected from the ideological rhetoric which may be present amongst such circles, hindering objective policy implementation and analysis' (118).

According to this line of reasoning, the ideologies of animal welfare groups, such as the International Fund for Animal Welfare, an organization that has been at the forefront in the fight against the illegal wildlife trade, prevent these groups from identifying viable policy solutions. The authors recognize that even criminologists are value-driven, but as they see it, apparently, they are more able to maintain neutral, distant analysis, which is seen as beneficial:

> With the involvement of criminologists in researching wildlife crimes, more viable solutions can be developed and implemented that help facilitate persons to sustainably trade species as well as prevent poaching and the subsequent illegal trade. As described in this paper, SCP is one possibility in which criminologists can be directly involved.
>
> (Pires and Moreto 2011: 118)

The application of crime prevention theory to the field of wildlife crimes, as exemplified above, also demonstrates that their research is criminology in a conservative form being focused on what is criminalized only, applying conventional models. While not discarding their findings as unimportant, I maintain that this body of literature supports the status quo: animals are either desired as objects (Pires and Clarke 2011) or they are exploitable common goods which must be preserved, thus following the anthropocentric values of the CITES.

Pires and Moreto and others working in the realm of conservation criminology (e.g., Gibbs et al. 2010; Lemieux 2014) essentially endorse or otherwise fail to condemn wildlife trade as long as it is sustainable and legal. In my view, potential animal abductors/killers could be sensitized to protect animals, not because they are *capital*, but because they are *sentient beings*, and such awareness can, for example, be created through public campaigns and education beginning in school in kindergarten.

What Pires and Moreto (2011) refer to when they talk about criminology is criminology dependent on a masculine discourse of impartiality. This then would stand in contrast to the feminine as explicated by Gilligan (1982) in her critique of Freud. As Smart (1989) writes of Gilligan, '[she also draws attention to the fact that] it is the masculine mode, deemed to be inexorable, unemotional, impersonal, and objective, which coincides with cultural expectations of justice and sound moral judgment' (73). This critique is in line with the critique raised against Regan and Singer by Adams (1996) for 'reiterating a patriarchal disavowal of emotions as having a legitimate role in theory making' (173).

Far from being objective or neutral (or perhaps even indifferent) concerning the findings of my research, I acknowledge from the outset that I have an agenda.

In line with standpoint theory (Harding 2004), my position is that I wish animals to be acknowledged as victims, I wish harms committed against them to be recognized as crimes and I wish the foundation of speciesism as well as its consequences to be scrutinized and prevented. These views may be regarded as limiting my analysis and conclusions; however, I think it is fair to state that these are my values, because these values are also those in which my research agenda, research questions and interview guides are embedded. That said, I can still treat my data with an analytical distance (Ellefsen 2017), communicating results that counter my conception of justice; criminalizing animal trafficking, for example, although justified in my view, may not be the best solution to help trafficking victims.

Rather than hiding my motives, I explore them epistemologically. In this, I accept that science is a socially and culturally embedded activity (Gould 1996: 21). Consequently, governing epistemologies and beliefs cannot but affect research agendas, and all research is a child of its era (e.g., phrenology). It is my goal, rather than being kept back by doxic beliefs such as speciesism into which I was also socialized, to challenge them and provide suggestions for radical solutions, to avoid modifying or contributing to systems that are profoundly unjust. To succeed in such an endeavour, one needs to explore critically taken-for-granted assumptions and personal experiences in which presuppositions (pre-judices [Gadamer 1975]) are embedded and through which they are defended and legitimized (Presser and Taylor 2011).

Thus, while interested in the individual suffering of animal victims of trafficking, this must also be seen in the context of the overall social structures of our societies and the ways in which norms are fortified and prolonged in legislation. As Harding (2004) says:

> It is not individual, personal, 'subjective' error to which feminist and other social critics of science have drawn attention, but widely held androcentric, Eurocentric and bourgeois assumptions that have been virtually culture-wide across the culture of science.
>
> (339)

Thanks to the challenging of ingrained ideological assumptions of superiority, it has become possible to explore individual wrongdoing and injustice. Through demasking the features of society that facilitate abuse and exploitation, many women have been ascribed victim status of domestic violence and sexual abuse. As a parallel to doxic discrimination of women, which, at least in the Western world is no any longer as acceptable as it used to be, speciesism is doxic and condemnable (Sollund 2012a).

Gilligan (1982) found that as long as the categories by which development is assessed are derived from a male perspective, divergence from the masculine standard can be seen only as a failure of development (390). When arguing for an ecofeminist approach in research concerning human-animal relations and exploitation of animals, I risk being accused of doing neither proper criminology nor complying with the academic epistemologies established in the discipline. But because I acknowledge that the inspiration I have for my research is based in personal experiences and the emotions necessitated by them, I cannot honestly discard them as guides in my research.

Rather than separating thinking from feeling, I argue we think *because* we feel. Feeling is fundamental for thinking and questioning taken-for-granted truths. Intuition and sensitivity for the positions and suffering of others, whether human or non-human, are necessary requirements both for initiating research of oppressed groups and for disseminating their experiences.[16] A feminist care-ethics theory has therefore been suggested by feminist scholars (e.g., Adams 1996; Donovan 1996; Kheel 1993, 1996, 2008; Kemmerer 2011), which I will return to in Chapters 13 and 14.

Patterns of abuse and oppression have their source in androcentric culture and power (Adams 2015; Gålmark 2008, 2016; Kheel 2008; Nibert 2002), and, as will be shown, men are also the most frequent perpetrators in the legal and illegal trafficking of free-born animals. The combination of a lack of empathy and self-ascribed rights to commit abusive acts, for example, those legitimized through legal hunting practices, may be very destructive on a large scale. From my ecofeminist perspective (see Donovan and Adams 1996; Gaard 1993; Kheel 2008; Sollund 2013b), I acknowledge that the ideals that govern our treatment of animals in nature are tinted by patriarchal values through which, for example, a boy's killing of an animal through hunt is regarded as a rite of passage that transforms him into a man, thereby glorifying the act of theriocide (Connell 2005; Fine 2000; Kheel 2008: 49, 125, 129). Indeed, the rationale for nature conservation is to provide sufficient prey for male hunters, as Theodore Roosevelt argued (Kheel 2008: ch. 3). Similarly, Aldo Leopold saw hunting as culturally advanced and contributing to the moral improvement of the human race (read: men). In contrast, sociologist Nibert (2013) argues that humans' domesecration and killing of animals have contributed greatly to moral decay and a society that encourages warfare and slavery. I concur with Kheel (2008) that the dominance and exploitation of the natural world is based in gendered ideas and masculine ideologies, supported by an economy that regards free-born animals as exploitable resources and that such ideas define the relationship between humans and the natural world (16–17). Following from this, and as reflected in CITES, animals are resources that humans can exploit as long as we ensure that such exploitation does not bring about the species' extinction. Animals in nature, therefore, are not accorded individual (non-economic, non-material) value or individual rights; they have value only as part of a species that is important for an ecosystem.

Essentially, CITES takes the perspective that species should be preserved for future generations of humans, while individual animals are of lesser importance (Kheel 2008: 128). I will explore not only the logic behind the way free-born animals are treated and protected in conventions, laws and regulations, but whether the crimes against them are gendered. As a reaction to the kind of nature management that appears in CITES and in Norway's wildlife laws, a movement of compassionate nature management has emerged, which combines perspectives of animal welfare and species survival (Ramp and Bekoff 2015). Here, the individual, intrinsic value of each animal is taken into account, as is the role s/he plays in relation to her/his social unit and population.

Although the ideologies and values pertaining to hunting are predominantly patriarchal (Kheel 2008) or 'manly' (Presser and Taylor 2011), being a woman does not automatically make one identify with animal victims. Many women would be offended by such a presumption, for example, the increasing number of Norwegian women who hunt for pleasure (Sollund 2015b). To identify with the suffering of others, as Cohen (2001) and Christie (1975) claim, one needs to have or feel a certain level of social proximity/affinity. This proximity and ensuing empathy with animals often depends on personal experiences with animals, and even then, people fail to recognize and empathize with animal victims because they are of the 'wrong species': for example, a fox who is hunted is shown no empathy, whereas a hunter's dog is. Perhaps women hunters distance themselves from their animal victims for fear of simultaneously distancing themselves from the comradeship of hunting, and thus the male values and status they achieve through partaking in male activities.

I define my research interests to include the nature, causes, prevention and punishment of crime and harm as they relate to justice. Harm, injustice and oppression are central elements in WLT, and these phenomena and perspectives are decisive for my choice of field.

Empathy is central to the way I perceive the harms of wildlife trafficking. In this sense, my topic of study and the ways in which I approach the topic, including my own motivation and interpretation of my data through this lens of empathy, are part of the process. To provide an example: When I saw a Cuban Amazon parrot in a tiny cage with only dry, light bread to eat and dirty water in a cup hung up on a restaurant wall in Havana, I was less interested in whether the restaurant owner bought the bird legally than in the harm he was causing by treating the bird in this way; my senses established that this was abuse and a crime to the bird. If it is indeed illegal, it can facilitate action and reaction, although in this case, it did not.[17] To expose such crimes – to reveal, analyze and explain the harms involved in them in order to prevent them – is my goal of my research. I therefore take as a beginning point for my research the inherent violence and oppression of the acts in question and let the harms of these acts and the empathy they evoke guide my analysis of the ways humans treat animals. In the following, I will further clarify my philosophical lens and point of departure for the research.

To see and empathize with the other[18]

One can attempt to truly see the other as your *next*, the beings with whom one relates who are entitled to concern – like discussed by Lévinas (Aarnes 1994), Berger (2009) and Derridá (2002). Bergo (2006) argues that according to Lévinas, it is in *seeing* the other's face, through recognizing the other as one worthy of moral consideration, that a moral responsibility towards the other arises:

> It is an interpretive, phenomenological description of the rise and repetition of the face-to-face encounter, or the intersubjective *relation* at its

Figure 2.1 Cuban amazon (*Amazona leucocephala*) abducted from the forest to be of entertainment for guests in a restaurant in Havana; fed only bread, and with dirty water and dirt all over the cage; no wooden sticks s/he needs to sit on and for stimulation

Source: © Ragnhild Aslaug Sollund

> precognitive core; viz., being *called* by another and *responding* to that other. If precognitive experience, that is, *human sensibility*, can be characterized conceptually, then it must be described in what is most characteristic to it: a continuum of *sensibility and affectivity*, in other words, *sentience and emotion in their interconnection.*
>
> (n.p.; emphasis added)

While Lévinas wrote about the human face-to-face encounter and the moral and ethical responsibility arising from it for the human other, Berger and Derridá are concerned about animals as the other, worthy of recognition and empathy. Berger (2009) describes the experience of meeting the eyes of caged animals in the zoo and how keeping animals in enclosures prevents humans from seeing them:

> The zoo cannot but disappoint. The public purpose of zoos is to offer visitors the opportunity of looking at animals. Yet nowhere in a zoo can a stranger encounter the look of an animal. At the most, the animal's gaze flickers and passes on. They look sideways. They look blindly beyond. They scan mechanically. They have been immunized to encounter, because nothing can any more occupy a *central* place in their attention.
>
> (37)

Thus, the animal is *looked upon*, but s/he is not *seen*, and s/he is not perceived as anyone, as someone to whom the person looking can relate. Neither does the animal see under these conditions. Often the glance will be empty, resigned or purely desperate. S/he is deprived of her being her because she is forced into the denigrating position of being caged. Many animal owners, although unfortunately not all, see an animal when they relate personally to the animal under their 'ownership' (Sollund 2009). This is easier when the animal in question is not in a cage. A caged bird, for example, becomes a 'cage bird,' and the bird is identified as a specific kind, through which the cage comes to define the bird and prevents the owner from seeing *who* the bird is. The bird and the cage, in other words, become one entity.

Bekoff (2006) criticizes the doubts some scientists raise about animals sentience, and describes how different persons, when looking into the eyes of animals in distress, feel obliged to help:

> Eyes tell it all and, if we can stand it, we should look into the fear-filled eyes of animals who suffer at our hands, in horrible conditions of captivity, in slaughterhouses and in zoos, rodeos and circuses. Dare to look into the sunken eyes of animals who are afraid or feeling other sorts of pain, and then try to deny to yourself and to others that these individuals aren't feeling *anything*.
>
> (31; emphasis original)

Looking into an animal's eyes, it becomes hard to maintain that animals lack feelings (Berger 2009). To recognize the animal implies to establish an empathetic bond, which is affected when the animal suffers. When people cannot bear to look at pictures of animal suffering and when producing footage of animal suffering is criminalized (Shapiro 1994), is this not precisely because people are prevented from recognizing the fear and pain animals suffer by those who hold an interest in continued animal exploitation, such as when authorities encourage and economically support meat production? And when people refuse to look at such footage, is this not because they in their hearts feel compassion and cannot bear to watch the suffering, just like they will cognitively disassociate themselves from pictures of human catastrophes (Cohen 2001)?

To share personal experiences with animals or humans alike is *not*, I emphasize, a condition for empathy; empathy can and should therefore be guiding one's choice of method as well as the nature of analysis, by which one attempts to imagine what it feels like to be in the skin of the targets of the research.

Denial becomes the negation, the flip side, of empathy. Forcefully obliging people to see photos of animal suffering can make them shut off; it can thus produce the opposite effect because of the pain and discomfort inherent in empathy. And perhaps this is partly the reason why otherwise empathic humans fail to include animals within their circle of moral concern. This does not mean that the compassion and empathy many feel towards animals cannot be used as an active tool and moral guide. By acknowledging the direct connection and relatedness that are produced through empathy, the only consequence if we are to produce a just world for non-human species is to stop regarding wild animals (or other animals) as exploitable resources that can be used and/or killed as long as their species survives.

From this discussion that forms a basis for the concluding chapters of the book, I turn to findings from Norway.

Notes

1 Statistics Norway. (2015). Available at: www.ssb.no/befolkning/nokkeltall/befolkning. Accessed 1 February 2015.
2 The Norwegian Food Safety Authority is responsible for all animal welfare, including all husbandry, in Norway and the veterinarians here thus take care of (or kill) animals when they are seized on borders. The name and area of responsibility of the Authority reflects that animals are preponderantly perceived through their value as food.
3 When I interviewed him (twice), he was chair of the standing committee of CITES.
4 The Eco Crime Unit prosecutes cases of fundamental significance and decides which cases they will prosecute. The Eco Crime Unit was established in 1989 and is a state prosecutor with national authority. Rules for eco crime are established in påtaleinstruksen kapittel 35.
5 Some interviewees were hard to anonymize because they are unique in having their position, or there are few persons working on the topic in a department.
6 www.nsd.uib.no/nsd/english/index.html
7 www.etikkom.no/en/

8 All excerpts from interviews, case files, verdicts and confiscation reports are translated from either Norwegian or Spanish by me.

9 As coded in the police central penal case statistics system, STRASAK. First, statistics were provided to me by the police, then, based on these, I contacted the police districts in Norway which had such cases registered in their district after permission for this was obtained from Riksadvokaten (The Higher Prosecuting Authorities). I was then sent the physical documents from all of the Norwegian police districts that had cases that could involve CITES species.

10 Lovdata. (n.d.d). *Lov om dyrevelferd.* [online]. Available at: http://lovdata.no/dokument/NL/lov/2009-06-19-97. Accessed 19 January 2015.

11 https://lovdata.no/ Lovdata is a foundation privately owned by the Ministry of Justice and the Faculty of Law at the University of Oslo. The database includes the primary court sources that regulate citizens' duties and rights. This includes laws, regulations, verdicts from courts of appeal and the Supreme Court and decisions from the European Court of Human Rights.

12 ProAves website, Fundación ProAves 1998 initiative of a group of Colombian conservationists interested in saving the yellow-eared parrot. ProAves's mission is to protect birds and their habitats in Colombia through research, conservation actions and community outreach. ProAves is a registered non-profit organization with free membership, open to all who share the vision to prevent the extinction of threatened species and protect key sites. ProAves is a UK-registered charity that supports the work of Fundación ProAves in Colombia. www.proaves.org/about-proaves/?lang=en

13 For example, I received seizure reports concerning parrots that did not appear in the statistics I received for the period when the seizures were made.

14 Parts of this section has been published previously in Sollund (2017a).

15 Harding (1995) suggests 'objectivism' rather than 'objectivity,' which she thinks will enable scientific projects to escape the influence of powerful social tendencies: 'Such an analysis leads to one obvious possibility: to separate the goal of maximizing objectivity from the neutrality requirement in order to identify the knowledge-limiting values and interests that constitute the project in the first place' (337–338).

16 Ferrell (1997) similarly argues for empathy during fieldwork to understand and analyze criminalized behaviour, but also the situation for crime victims. See Natali and McClanahan (2017) for a discussion of the use of photographs in interviews with environmental victims.

17 Instead, the restaurant owner called the police. When the police arrived, they had no interest in whether the bird was CITES-listed or in her living conditions.

18 This has partly been published in Sollund (2017d).

3 Animals and animal products trafficked to Norway

In this chapter I will present an overview of cases concerning various forms of trafficking to Norway. Before I present the findings from the Norwegian case study, I will provide an overview of the legal framework in this country.

The legal framework in Norway

Norwegian legislation contains several regulations which prohibit the importation of live animals to Norway from abroad: The CITES regulation of November 2002 nr. 1976[1] was revised in 2013 and is today incorporated into the Wildlife Law[2] (*Lov om jakt og fangst av viltet – viltloven*), the Nature Diversity Act (*Naturmangfoldsloven*),[3] and Law of Import and Export Regulation from June 6, 1997 (*Lov om innførsle og utførsleregulering*),[4] and the Law concerning environmental protection of Svalbard and Jan Mayen.[5] As I will show, however, what laws are applied in CITES cases depends on judges' discretion, or rather their judicial competence concerning CITES legislation.

The Wildlife Law applies to animal trafficking and punishment for trafficking of live or dead animals, eggs and animal products. The regulation is based on Wildlife Law §26[6] and §56, which dictates a maximum penalty of two years imprisonment. If the offence also constitutes a breach of the Nature Diversity Act, §29,[7] however, the maximum sentence is three years prison under particularly aggravating circumstances, for example if the crime is organized (Sollund 2017b). A regulation based on the Animal Welfare Act,[8] the Regulation against the Import, Trade and Keeping of Exotic Species ([FOR-1976-11-20-3),[9] is often applied. The maximum sentence is three years. As will be shown, police and Customs are consistent concerning neither which laws and regulations they apply for CITES crimes nor in their penal case statistics, and often in the case of exotic species it is not clear whether the animal in question is CITES listed, often because to establish this is not a priority for the police or Customs (Sollund 2013a; Sollund and Maher 2015; Runhovde 2015). This makes it hard to get an overview of cases that involve CITES species, which is perceived as problematic by control agents themselves. As the interviewee in the Customs Directorate explained in relation to crimes concerning nature diversity:

> First we must see if it is regulated according to this law, and then that law, and then we really get in trouble. We need a very clear and transparent set of rules to relate to. If not, this task will not be prioritised.

In 1979, Norway adopted the Convention on the Conservation of European Wildlife and Natural Habitats (Bern Convention), which was ratified in 1986. The convention's goal is to protect its free-born species to ensure they do not go extinct; in Norway a particular concern is for the large predator species: wolf, wolverine, brown bear, lynx and golden eagle.

The CITES, the Nature Diversity Act and the Wildlife Law are all concerned with species survival and biodiversity, rather than the individuals of the species, which are subject to abduction and theriocide. A study of verdicts for the illegal killing of Norwegian predators found that a crime is regarded as more severe depending on how vulnerable the species is, and that the Animal Welfare Act is used when the species the animal victim belongs to is very endangered, for example the wolf (Sollund 2015b, 2016b, 2017b). This suggests that we 'value' species based on how vulnerable they are, but some species may have become vulnerable precisely because of our lack of concern, which results in them being listed as endangered.

The Norwegian Environmental Agency is the formal 'owner' of all wildlife in Norway and is responsible for implementing CITES in the country. It is also the agency which is consulted by Customs when animals are seized, to establish whether CITES species are involved. The Norwegian Environmental Agency regulates – extends import and export permits – that are required for Appendix I, II species, upon application.

The Food Safety Authority is the entity responsible for animal welfare in Norway, which takes care of the animals who are seized, whether at Oslo Airport, other Customs points along the Norwegian-Swedish-Finnish-Russian borders, at ferry stations, or when police seize animals in private homes.

Økokrim (the Norwegian National Authority for Investigation and Prosecution of Economic and Environmental Crime [*The Eco Crime unit*]) is the central unit for investigation and prosecution of such crimes and the main source of specialist skills for the police and the prosecuting authorities in their combat against crime of this kind. In addition, there are police specialist investigation groups on environmental crime in each police district. They are also responsible for other environmental crimes, however, and therefore must prioritize their resources.

Seizure data and confiscation reports from Customs

I will begin by looking at Customs statistics and confiscation reports to assess what kind of animals are trafficked to Norway and the circumstances relating to these crimes.[10] Seizure report data are included in a table as an appendix to the book.

Data were first provided to me in the form of Excel sheets consisting of statistics of both plant and animal species which had been seized by Customs at

Norwegian borders. Later, I received access to the confiscation reports, which provided more in-depth information about each seizure. It is clear that the seizures listed are not all seizures made during the period of the research, because there are confiscation reports and verdicts/fines relating to seizures that were not found in the Excel sheets. That Customs statistics are not reliable was also confirmed by the CITES/Norwegian Environment Agency interviewee who said that huge seizures do not appear in their statistics, nor do the statistics reflect seizures made within Norwegian borders. Consequently, these statistics unlikely present the full picture but will still give a good indication of what is confiscated in Norway. The inaccuracy in the statistics may exemplify the lack of priority given to these cases, a point to be further discussed in Chapter 6. I present first Tables 3.1a and b, which provides an overview of both animal and plant seizures between 2002 and 2010. The table indicates an increase in WLT over these years.

The Table 3.2 presents seizures of CITES I- and II-listed animal species made by the Norwegian Customs Directorate between 2008 and 2014.

The Customs Directorate also has statistics for wildlife trafficking in species that are not CITES listed, such as dogs. I find this information useful because it provides a broader picture of animal trafficking to Norway, whether in CITES-listed or non-CITES-listed species. Animals who are trafficked pertain often also to species that at some point may become CITES listed, such as bird and reptile species, as soon as the species have been 'overexploited,' since the logic of CITES is that trade in a species persists until the species reaches a critical state (Sollund 2011).

While a considerable number of seizures of CITES- and non-CITES-listed species are registered, it is still, however, hard to determine what these numbers reflect. Are they the actual numbers of seizures and products/animals made at all Customs stations? Have Customs officers sent in all confiscation reports? Have they reported all seizures and are these reports correct, that is, are species registered correctly as CITES or non-CITES species? And finally, they reflect only what has been registered and reveal nothing about what has transpired under the radar of Norwegian Customs. I will return to this when I discuss the interviews with Customs Directorate and frontline Customs officers. First, I will look at the information provided through the total number of confiscation reports that I received from Customs to see how CITES seizures were carried out, and the modus operandi and motives as stated by offenders, or as these appear due to the category of the seizure (in Appendix 1 of this book). The reports span from January 2008 to July 2017, but are not likely all the confiscation reports that exist, since the Customs Directorate staff member who searched for the relevant reports said he could not detect them in their system. Furthermore, his replacement was reluctant to provide me with these reports later during the project. It is also very possible that not all confiscation reports were properly registered as CITES cases, as suggested by the interviewee from the CITES/Norwegian Environment Agency.

When possible, I have followed cases from the moment when a confiscation of an animal was made by Customs inspectors to the conclusion of the case, to see what happened to the animals when they were trafficked alive and what kind of punishment, if any, was meted out to the offender.

Table 3.1a Overview of CITES confiscations

Number of seizures/number of individuals/items

Animals/product seized	*2002*	*2003*	*2004*	*2005*	*2006*	*2007*	*2008*	*2009*	*2010*
CITES animals other than mammals or birds (usually reptiles)			4/9	2/3	1/1	5/9	5/6	5/7	3/5
Bird eggs									
Live birds							2/51		
Live mammals									
Plants	7/153	6/184	4/133	2/1302	3/185	2/2213	24/3902	49/6750	15/14655
Products/KG									
Products/litres									5/2.5
Products/*N*[11]	39/475	34/726	43/614	25/596	15/404	17/100	14/35	30/5072	22/15031
Total confiscations	**46/628**	**40//910**	**51/756**	**29/1901**	**19/590**	**24/2322**	**45/3994**	**84/11829**	**45/29693**

Table 3.1b Overview of non-CITES confiscations

*Goods seized**	*2002*	*2003*	*2004*	*2005*	*2006*	*2007*	*2008*	*2009*	*2010*
Bird eggs	2/240	1/4							
Other live animals (usually reptiles)	8/14	11/27	12/55	10/62	9/26	13/38	7/23	9/397	14/38
Live birds	7/23	2/10	3/15	1/2	2/2		4/51	5/24	
Live mammals	5/13	4/5	10/37	3/4	18/29	21/58	27/38	25/88	4/14
Animal/bird seizures	22/290	18/46	25/107	14/68	29/57	34/96	38/112	40/541	27/66
Total	**44/580**	**36/92**	**50/2014**	**28/136**	**58/114**	**68/192**	**76/224**	**79/1050**	**45/118**

Table 3.2 CITES I and II confiscations in Norway, personal and mail/courier deliverances, animals and animal products[12]

Year	*Live birds*	*Live reptiles*	*Other*	*Dead/stuffed/ body parts, incl. taxidermy*	*Product*	*Total N*
2008	4	8	27	3	2	44
2009		5		2	226	238
2010	4	2	2	3	11	22
2011	33	1	236	67	6	343
2012		5		10	48	59
2013		1	567	19	157	744
2014	14		242	114	20[s]	390
Total	55	22	1074	218	470	1839

Table 3.3 Categories of cases from Customs confiscation reports 2008–2017

	Live animal	*Parts/products*	*Unknown/non-CITES*
Mammal	1	26	9
Bird	7	23	6
Reptile	13	26	4
Fish	0	10	1
Amphibian	2	0	0
Arthropod	1	1	1
Mollusca	6	1	0
Annelid	1	0	0

In terms of the nature of the trafficking, the largest category (71 instances) consists of people who brought the product/animal with them from abroad, whether by car, plane or ferry, usually to Kristiansand from Denmark. The next largest category (46) consists of trafficking by mail. Shipping by freight, which is how coral is usually sent, is another modus of trafficking, but it is not possible to determine such circumstances from these seizure reports. The issue of freight companies and why goods sent by them may go under the radar of Customs will be discussed separately in Chapter 6.

Customs seizure reports from Norway: species, products and modus operandi

The seizure reports from Norwegian Customs present a diverse picture of animal victims and offenders. Traffickers can be categorized according to their motivation. While live animals, such as the Bengal cat, birds and reptiles, are trafficked by individuals who want them as pets, animals are also trafficked by people who want to profit from the pet wildlife trade. Pet trafficking is also committed by tourists who do it on a whim, for example, buy a tortoise in a market and then traffic the animal in their pocket or in a more planned fashion. Reptile traffickers can be deliberate about crossing a border with the least risk of being detected by Customs, for example, by driving two cars in tandem where the second one bringing the animal crosses only if the first car drives through unhindered (Sollund 2013a).

Another large category is tourists who buy skins and products, often unaware of the illegality of what they are doing. The head of the standing committee of CITES whom I interviewed had this to say about this category of consumer:

> Many tourists will say that the little they buy can hardly matter, but this is what drives the trade. It is the taking of products from nature to cover the market and the tourist market is one of the biggest. So that is a bad excuse.

Animals or animal parts are also trafficked as medicinal products, reflecting the place TAM has in wildlife trafficking (van Uhm 2016b). It is reasonable to assume that many of those trafficking TAM products have a migrant background, demonstrating the effect of globalization on WT when migrants bring their cultural traditions with them to new settings. For example, the persons who were caught for taking pills and plaster made of tiger, leopard and Musk ox had Chinese names and the products were brought/sent from China.

Collectors form another category. They buy animal/animal products (stuffed birds or predator pelts, for example) to add to their collections. A final category is trophy hunters who bring home, or have sent home, the carcasses of their victims. The majority of these offenders are male, as are reptile traffickers.

The (former) head of the standing committee of CITES, working at the Norwegian Environment Agency, further categorized the Norwegian trafficking picture as follows:

> One category is the profiteers, for example internet-based companies that make money by not following the rules, often run by one person only. We have a few of these in Norway. Another group is large commercial actors, for example, one selling medicinal products. And this is perhaps the scariest group because of Norway's adaptation to the EU and the free float of trade in the inner market, so we depend a lot on the freight companies, that they know the rules which they are obliged to, or they will lose their permissions to clear goods through Customs.

Trafficking offences are usually punished by a fine, ranging from 3,000 to 20,000 NOK (about €3,000–20,000). To impose a fine is an administrative sanction which Customs is allowed to do after directions made by the Ministry of Finance in cases that are considered not to be serious, according to §16-9 of the Customs Act.[13] Consequently, it is up to the Customs officer to determine on the spot the seriousness of the offence and respond accordingly. Evidently, trafficking in endangered species is not regarded as a serious offence in Norway, as imposing a fine is the most frequent response. While many CITES offences may go by undetected, the same interviewee believes the Customs Directorate when they state all CITES offences are reported to the police:

> And that is also my impression when talking to Customs control stations. And usually they are taken to the police and the reaction is a fine. And most accept a fine ranging from 3–10,000 NOK, and then the case is concluded. While, if the case goes to court, there are not many cases, and the few I have seen, we usually lose.

If the fine imposed by Customs/police is not accepted by the offender, the offence is reported to the police who decide whether to prosecute. Often, however, the case will not be prosecuted and no reaction will follow due to lack of priority, depending on the gravity of the case. When seized, the illegal 'goods' will be confiscated according to the regulation of Customs determining the application of fines.[14] For example, on March 30, 2014, a man arrived on the ferry to Kristiansand from Denmark with 44 parrots, but he had the necessary CITES permits for only 36. The 'surplus birds,' one *Barnardius xonarios* parrot and seven *Agapronis* parrots, were offered to Kristiansand Zoo, but were rejected. Subsequently, the birds were killed. This offender was fined 20,000 NOK. As a general rule, the trafficked animals are confiscated and then usually killed by the authorities. Similarly, animals are killed as outcomes of cases that go to court. For example, in the Bengal cat case, the cat was confiscated and killed and the reason stated in the verdict was the importance of enforcing CITES, the Bengal cat being an endangered species. The logic behind this is that the animals are regarded as just any other illegal 'goods,' and that in order to enforce the law, the offenders may not keep the illegal goods, since then legislation adhered to CITES would not be enforced.

According to a Customs officer who is a CITES expert and situated at Oslo Airport, live CITES animals arrive only about four times a year, although non-CITES-listed animals arrive frequently according to the border veterinarian located at the airport. When CITES animals are trafficked alive, they are usually destined for the pet trade. Most frequent are tortoise and bird species. But, anecdotally, interviewees were aware of other incidents. According to one Customs officer: 'A few years ago, a slow loris [CITES I] arrived. He was packed in a towel under his [the trafficker's] jacket. But he was stopped because we knew him as a big trafficker of steroids;[15] he arrived then from either Malaysia or Thailand.'

The slow loris was re-homed at Kristiansand Zoo and was fortunate not to be killed, but the paradoxical way of enforcing CITES – euthanizing/killing confiscated animals – is present in other cases which will be treated in more detail below. I will return to a broader discussion of this in Chapter 13.

The gendered nature of trafficking

Nearly 90% of trafficking offenders in Norway are men. This strengthens the assumption raised initially that most offenders of wildlife crimes are men and that

Table 3.4 Gender of traffickers in the three trafficking categories

	2007	*2008*	*2009*	*2010*	*2011*	*2012*	*2013*	*2014*	*2015*	*2016*	*2017*	*TOTAL*	*%*
Category 1													
Male	0	5	1	3	5	3	3	4	0	2	0	26	89.7
Female	0	0	1	0	0	1	0	0	0	1	0	3	10.3
Category 2													
Male	1	3	4	1	8	6	1	11	17	14	3	69	88.5
Female	0	1	0	0	2	1	0	2	2	1	0	9	11.5
Category 3													
Male	0	2	1	2	0	4	0	1	1	0	0	11	91.6
Female	0	0	0	1	0	0	0	0	0	0	0	1	8.3
Total	1	11	7	7	15	15	4	18	20	18	3	119	89.1 male 8.9 female

this is a gendered crime. However, it must be added that men are in the majority as the culprits of *all* crimes, so in that sense wildlife trafficking is no different from other crimes. For example, according to Statistics Norway's[16] overview of all charges for crime in 2016, the total number of persons charged was 169,496, of which 145,031 were against men and 24,465 were against women, only about 14% of the total.[17]

Concerning who is apprehended at borders and consequently registered in relation to wildlife trade, this may be the result of selective control, that is, Customs officials make judgments based on former experiences that men are more likely to be carrying illegal goods than women are, causing a control effect in the sense that more frequent control of a certain category of individuals will produce more seizures within this category. This would be relevant particularly in the 'no goods to declare' zones, because in the 'goods to declare zone' travellers declare their goods. As Runhovde (2015) shows, Customs bases many of its decisions about which people to inspect on a 'gut feeling.' The Customs inspectors' use of discretion based on previous experience strengthens the circle of inspection in which men are initially stopped more often than women, resulting in seizures, thus strengthening the circle of inspection. There is no reason to believe that men travel more than women, so the person search results in the following table may be the result of Customs inspectors' gendered use of discretion. Table 3.5 shows the number of persons and their gender as well as whether the seizure was made of a post package or during a personal search.

While the gender of a person travelling through Customs may play a role in a Customs inspector's decision to conduct a search, this 'inspection effect' is reduced significantly when it comes to posted packages, because the package information that is available may not reveal or reflect the gender of the sender or recipient. This is so particularly with foreign names that a Customs inspector may be unable to distinguish as male or female. A factor of importance for the decision to conduct a search is, for example, the country from which the parcel is sent. Here, too, men are overrepresented, which suggests that whether

Table 3.5 Gendered[18] Customs inspections of persons

Modus	*Male*	*Female*	*Total*
Category 1: Live animals			
Post	2	0	2
Searched	24	3	27
Category 2: Animal parts/Stuffed products			
Post	40	6	46
Searched	29	3	32
Category 3: Non-CITES or unknown species			
Post	1	0	1
Searched	63	7	70
Total	106	13	119

trafficking by post or cross-border travel, male offenders are far more numerous or are more frequently caught.

In what follows, I will detail the crimes committed by one of the offenders, starting with a relatively recent case, which will be discussed in view of a case from the end of the 1990s.

Parrot trafficking conviction 1

The first case concerns one individual who was convicted several times for parrot trafficking and wildlife crimes. There are *four* verdicts pertaining to this person: December 3, 2013 (Halden tingrett [Halden District Court] [13–156198MED-HALD]); May 29, 2015, from Borgarting lagmannsrett [Court of appeal[19]], ([14–094257AST-BORG03]); January 20, 2014, from Dalane tingrett ([TDALA-2013–175645–]), appealed to Gulating lagmannsrett; September 3, 2014 ([14–09847AST–GULA/AVD1]). The verdicts concern three incidents: two parrot trafficking cases and one concerning the illegal taking of a sea eagle egg. According to a note made on one of the Customs confiscations reports, the offender had also been caught for trafficking parrots in 2000 (27 individuals) and in Gothenburg, Sweden, in 2007. Because I do not have these verdicts from Sweden and do not know more about them, I will omit these incidents from my analysis of his crimes. In the verdict from December 3, 2013 (13–156198MED-HALD), he was sentenced for trafficking four African grey parrots on November 21, 2010, and trafficking eight on November 20, 2011.

The offences he was charged with are the following, based on the verdict (13–156198MED-HALD).

1 On Sunday, November 21, 2010, at 14:55 at Holtet in Halden,[20] he imported from Sweden parrots protected under the CITES, 594 litres of beer, 15.84 litres of cider, 15.25 litres of wine, 10 litres of liquor and 1,000 grams of tobacco without presenting these for Customs inspection.
2 On Sunday, November 20, 2011, at 04:00 at Holtet in Halden, he imported from Sweden five litres of wine, 23.76 litres of beer, 27.72 litres of cider, 1.10 litres of alcopops and eight live parrots that are protected under the CITES without presenting these for Customs inspection. The border crossing post is unattended.

For the first offence, he was initially fined 25,000 NOK, which he apparently contested, as this charge was added to the case for the second charge. In the details of the first fine, the birds were not mentioned, only the alcohol he smuggled was. In a Customs document, the birds were listed, but as another species of lesser monetary value – 200 rather than 5,000–7,000 NOK. This means little weight was put on the birds in this case.

Following the November 2010 offence, the four parrots, all African greys, were killed by the authorities on order from the Norwegian Environment Agency,[21] the reason being they were only CITES II species.[22] Although the judge decided in this case that an unsuspended 30-day prison sentence should be applied for preventative reasons, the delay in the judicial proceedings resulted in the judge stating that the 30-day prison sentence should be replaced by a two-year suspended sentence. In addition, the offender was fined 5,000 NOK and the birds and alcohol were confiscated.

What happened to the birds who were seized in 2011 is not revealed in the verdict from the first trial, but according to interview data, some were saved, others killed. That the fate of the victims in the case is not clarified in the verdict is a significant point, in my view, since it underlines that the case concerns the offender and the state, whereas the direct victims are exterminated and made invisible.

In the second verdict, from January 20, 2014 (13–175645MED-DALA + 13–175658MED-DALA), the same offender was convicted for breach of the Wildlife Law (*Viltloven*) and also for a breach of the Nature Diversity Act for taking an eagle egg from a nest and illegally possessing it.

1 On Monday, April 16, 2012, the two offenders travelled together to Eigerøya in Eigersund, where there was a breeding pair of sea eagles. The intention was to observe and photograph the eagles, but also to collect an egg.
2 On April 26, 2012, he had in his possession a sea eagle egg that was unregistered,[23] without the requisite permission.

It was the opinion of the court that these acts were done deliberately and that the offenders attempted to conceal their crime when they were confronted by a police officer who was surveilling the nest and observed their crime. When the police searched the offenders' homes after their arrest, they found and seized several boxes with bird eggs, including a sea eagle egg in the parrot trafficker's house.

In this verdict, it is regarded as aggravating that he had been convicted before for similar crimes, and thus he received a 45-day unsuspended prison sentence. In addition, he had to pay 2,000 NOK for procedural expenses. The offender appealed this case and in the verdict from the Norwegian Court of Appeal, *Gulating lagmannsrett* (201414–09847AST – GULA/AVD1), regarding the sea eagle egg – the third verdict pertaining to this man – his prison sentence was reduced to a 30-day suspended sentence because of judicial delays.[24]

In the first trial, from Halden District Court on December 13, 2013 (13–156198MED-HALD), the defendant was convicted under the Wildlife Law for breach of §26.9, which concerns the importation and exportation of wildlife. At this same trial, he was also convicted under Customs Law[25] §16–1 for illegal importation of goods. He received a 30-day, conditional prison sentence, suspended for two years. The 12 parrots and the considerable amount of roughly 692 litres of alcohol and the kilo of tobacco in his possession were confiscated, and he was ordered to pay a fine of 5,000 NOK. The court found that the defendant intended to sell the 'goods' (including the parrots), rather than keep them for personal use, and treated this as an aggravating factor in issuing its sentence.

The offender appealed the verdict from Halden District Court to the Borgarting Court of Appeal (LB-2014–92357)[26] regarding the parrot and alcohol trafficking based on the application of the law, the punishment and the assessment of evidence. The verdict of this appeal, to a large degree, concerned the application of laws in this case, and consequently, whether it was correct to convict the trafficker under the Wildlife Law in the first trial – a point which was disputed by the state prosecutor. Paragraph 2 of the Wildlife Law states that 'wildlife' is 'understood [as] all wildlife of terrestrial mammal species, birds, amphibians and reptiles' (*Med vilt menes i denne lov alle viltlevende landpattedyr og fugler, amfibier og krypdyr*). Despite this clear language of the law defining 'wildlife,' the judges examine the preparatory work (the legal history) of the law (Ot Prop 54 1992/93: 27), which revealed that 'wildlife' covers individuals of all species and subspecies capable of surviving free and potentially breeding in the Norwegian wild. The judges further found that

> the Wildlife Law was directed at species that could cause harm to Norwegian nature, and that nowhere in the Wildlife Law was it argued nor did it refer to exotic species that cannot survive in the Norwegian wild. The aim of the law implies that such animals are not covered by the law.

The judges stated that there were other laws in the Constitution that regulated the importation of animals, for example, §47 of the Wildlife Law, but that the accused had not been charged under this paragraph, which may have been because, while this paragraph concerns importation, it provides for a generalized permission to import African grey parrots.[27] The judges further stated that at the time this verdict was given, a relevant paragraph in the Nature Diversity Act,[28] §29, had not yet been implemented. (It was implemented on January 1, 2016, while the verdict was issued on January 20, 2015.) They continued by referring to CITES regulation §5 (based in the Wildlife Law §26.9) and Section 1.3 of the Law of Import and Export Regulation (*Lov om innførsle og utførsleregulering*). They explained that the concerns behind regulating the importation of animals that cannot do harm to the Norwegian wild were addressed adequately by this law and by CITES regulations §§1 and 2.

According to the judges, *no* exception was granted for 'ordinary cage birds or exotic pets which have traditionally been kept in Norway, according to §7 of the Wildlife Law (which pertains to Norwegian wildlife).' They also said that if such animals were included under the Wildlife Law, it 'would have been illegal to keep budgerigars, hamsters, rats or guinea pigs in cages. This is obviously not the case.' Therefore, the court concluded that the original intent of the law was to cover Norwegian 'wildlife' and indicated that exotic animals of this nature were not included in the law.

Parrots and other birds are traded extensively and, in large measure, are victims of the wildlife trade. That the judges regarded African grey parrots as 'cage birds,' thereby allowing the cage to define them (see Sollund 2009), is salient proof of this victimhood. In so doing, the judges accepted that parrots are traded as pets, rather than offering them the protection to which they should be entitled precisely *because* they are victims of such trade. The judges failed to acknowledge that the cage was the consequence rather than the point of departure.

This interpretation of the law concerning CITES-listed species is interesting because it is a strong indication that these African grey parrots had been caught in Africa and subsequently trafficked to Europe. When I asked the interviewee from the CITES/Norwegian Environment Agency if there was reason to believe these birds were trafficked from their habitats, he replied,

> It is a very great danger because the trade worldwide is huge. I would say that in the 80s and 90s the vast majority were caught in their habitat. The avian flu reduced the trade, but still it will take place because one would want to sell them as cheap as possible. And that can be achieved by buying them for next to nothing in Africa. Then you can compete in the European market. And one should wonder, when it costs 10,000 [NOK] to buy an African grey in Norway that is hand bred, and then one must cover salaries, electricity, rent, etc., and a profit. But in Netherlands, you can buy these birds for 1,500 and, therefore, we have always thought these were wild caught.

My interviewee's statement resonates with the findings of van Uhm (in Sina et al. 2016), who interviewed staff from the Dutch Crime Squad about the involvement of organized crime groups in wildlife trade. Van Uhm learned that criminal groups immediately filled the gap when imports of protected birds were banned due to avian flu. Couriers repeatedly smuggled birds from Suriname through Spain into the Netherlands. A common method was to hide the animals or products in concealed compartments in luggage or on the smuggler's body. It was therefore possible that not only were birds from Suriname being trafficked to the Netherlands, but that the African grey parrots in the above case may have been trafficking victims because of the global reach and ongoing nature of trafficking by groups specializing in the illegal parrot trade.

The judges in the Norwegian court, however, after the lengthy discussion of whether the African grey parrots consisted of 'wildlife,' decided that they were *not* wildlife but illegal *goods*. Therefore, they concluded that the trafficking of the parrots was *not* a breach of the Wildlife Law due to these parrots' inability to survive were they to be liberated in Norway. They were not 'wildlife' but 'cage birds,' the court reasoned, and thus §5 of the CITES regulation applied. The court also explained that according to §18 of the Law of Import and Export Regulation June 6, 1997, nr. 32 §4, the defendant was eligible for a maximum prison sentence of six months, rather than two years for breach of the Wildlife Law. Because the Law of Import and Export Regulation applied, rather than the Wildlife Law, and because the statute of limitation for the former was two years, the court reversed the offender's conviction of the first offence, the trafficking of the four parrots (and alcohol possession) in 2010.

The court decided that he should receive a combined punishment for the parrot cases in question and the case from Gutating Court of Appeal (the verdict of

September 3, 2014, concerning the sea eagle egg). Since it had been three and four years respectively since the crimes were committed (since the case from 2010 had exceeded the relevant statute of limitations), the defendant was punished with a sentence of (only) 60 days conditional prison of which 45 days were suspended for two years. The unconditional part of the prison sentence had already been served in custody. Because of the delay in the judicial system, the judges did not impose a fine.

Parrot trafficking conviction 2: should lessons be learnt from an earlier sentence?

I now go back in time, to the first sentence I have been able to locate that concerns the trafficking in live CITES animals, from 1998. It is troubling that in the above case, the judges did not bother to look into previous CITES verdicts concerning the parrot trade. This one such case should have been of particular interest. This verdict was issued in Sarpsborgs Magistrate Court on November 17, 1998 (Sarpsborg forhørsrett [1998] 98–00805 F), thus many years prior to the African grey cases treated above. As the case was treated in a Magistrate Court, this means, as it was also underlined by the judge, that the offender had already confessed to the crimes. It involved a man found guilty of smuggling, with an intent to sell, 41 birds listed in CITES I and II – predominantly parrots including African greys and Amazon parrots – as well as eight macaws, an iguana, two boa constrictors, and 50 terrapins. Altogether, he trafficked 147 birds and 122 other animals. In issuing its verdict, the court stated that the offence was regarded as particularly serious because of the large number of animals, because the 'goods' were meant to be commercialized, and because live animals and birds represented a considerable risk of contagious diseases. The court also treated the offender's prior criminal history as an aggravating factor because of his prior criminal history: he had been fined previously for trafficking exotic animals in breach of CITES I and II. The state prosecutor of the case in 1998 stated that this was the biggest case of its kind in Norway. In 1996 and 1997, the offender travelled on 11 occasions to Sweden and the Netherlands to buy animals and then smuggled them to Norway. The offender, however, admitted to 20 trips for the sole purpose of buying and trafficking animals, but he was convicted only for the 11.

The same defendant was convicted for breach of the Customs Law and for breach of the Law of Import and Export Regulation for trafficking CITES-listed animals to Norway. He was also convicted of bringing live animals to Norway in breach of the Animal Husbandry Law,[29] for selling animals without authorization from the district veterinary, and for breach of the Animal Welfare Act.

The court found the offender guilty of a serious breach of the Customs Law. Such a serious breach of the law must, it was stated by the judge, entail a harsh punishment for preventative reasons. Finally, the court further found the offender guilty of a serious breach of CITES regulations, which the judge considered to be a major international problem. The offender's claim that the birds were bred in Sweden and the Netherlands, rather than from the countries that form natural habitats for the birds, was not regarded by the court as ameliorating. It was regarded, however, as aggravating that the offender chose to traffic the animals illegally to avoid the paperwork of acquiring export and import permits. Because he moved in circles of people who specialized in exotic birds and also bred birds, he was well aware of the CITES regulations, the court claimed. Ignorance of the law, anyhow, by no means frees anyone from guilt.

All the animals were seized by the authorities and several of them were diagnosed with psittacosis and salmonella. The accused claimed that while they were in his custody, they had showed no signs of these diseases. Because the diseases may have developed after they were seized, this was not regarded as an aggravating circumstance. The offender was charged, however, with a breach of the Animal Husbandry Law for importing animals without permission from *Statens dyrehelsetilsyn* (the state animal health control agency, no longer active, and replaced by the Food Safety Authority). What happened to the animals after their confiscation is unknown.

The offender was sentenced to 120 days in prison, money he had from his illegal activities worth 38,950 NOK was seized, and he was prohibited from possessing non-Norwegian species for five years.

An appeal was heard in Borgarting Court of Appeal on May 10, 1999. The appellant claimed that the Magistrate Court had erred in convicting him for a particularly serious breach of Customs Law §66 (which concerns the potential punishment if the breach of law is regarded as particularly serious and concerns many goods).[30] The Borgarting Court of Appeal disagreed, emphasizing that the very large number of animals in the offender's possession reflected an intent to sell. The Borgarting Court of Appeal also noted that many of the animals were listed in CITES I and II and that the accused had been fined previously for the illegal import of animals. The court thus ruled that the appellant should still be convicted under §66, but regarded as an extenuating circumstance the fact that the man had recently obtained other (legal) employment and had four children. The court of appeals also found persuasive the appellant's contention that he had been taught a lesson and would desist from all fauna crime. As such, the Bogarting Court of Appeal found the verdict of the Magistrate Court too harsh and reduced the sentence to 120 days in prison, making 60 days conditional and suspended for two years.

So, in view of this and the above cases, it appears it pays for an offender to appeal a sentence. One should think further that in other, later trials attention would be paid to the outcome of previous similar cases, which could have served as a guide for sentencing in the same category. This was not the case here.

What this case also teaches us is that it appears that while there are rules regarding the facilities used for imported animals, no such rules exist for birds bred in Norway (other than the provisions of the Animal Welfare Act).

Supreme Court verdict, trafficking in animal products

Supreme Court case (Høyesterett 2003 HR-291-a-Rt) sheds light on the motives of traffickers of large numbers of animal products. In this case, the defendant was first convicted in the Oslo Magistrate Court for importing 271 artefacts, including bows and arrows decorated with feathers from between 10 and 20 CITES I- and II-listed parrots, as well as two margays and two boas.

At the first trial, the defendant was convicted of breach of the Customs Law and the Law of Import and Export Regulation and sentenced to 90 days in prison, of which 30 days were conditional. In addition, all items that he had attempted to import were confiscated. The court treated as an aggravating factor the finding that the offender had imported the artefacts as part of his business with the intention to sell them.

The verdict was appealed by both the state prosecutor and the offender. Both appeals concerned the sentence. Before the trial, the state prosecutor had altered the charge to include (1) breach of the Customs Law and (2) breach of the Law of Import and Export Regulation and its adhering regulations. The offender's defence lawyer claimed the Customs Law did not apply because the man had not physically carried the items across the border himself. He had also declared the bows and arrows, and thus he was not attempting to smuggle them into the country. The Borgarting Court of Appeal, however, rejected this argument, explaining that declaring goods is mandatory and that by not identifying the artefacts as containing endangered animal products, the offender had misled Customs officials, as well as KLM, who shipped the artefacts.

The following is taken from the verdict from Borgarting Court of Appeal:

> It is regarded as aggravating that the case concerns a considerable number of protected animal species. The convicted has acted with pure profit motives. The feathers are used decoratively on artefacts which were to be commercialised in his business. Furthermore, he was aware of the prohibition against the import of such goods, as he had read about it at Customs. He admitted to the offence in the Magistrates Court and acknowledged his uncertainty about the legality of the import. That he said something else in the Appeal Court was not given weight. Neither did the Court put any weight on the offender's claim that indigenous people do not kill birds to get their feathers, as the feathers were not necessarily sourced from indigenous villages. In any circumstance, the birds must have been caught and the business of the offender, therefore, contributes to the decimation of the specific bird populations. The Court therefore agreed with the state prosecutor that the punishment should be 90 days imprisonment.

A mitigating circumstance was the delay in the judicial system, for which the offender was not to blame. It took three years from when the crime was committed until the trial. Thirty of the 90 days were therefore made conditional, with a two-year suspension. The court concluded that the offender's appeal be rejected.

The offender next appealed the above verdict to the Supreme Court based on the application of the Customs Law, the finding of guilt and the sentence. The Supreme Court accepted part of the appeal on March 7, 2003, rejecting the question of the applicability of the Customs Law. The Supreme Court judge then declared that he agreed with aspects of the offender's appeal.

The Supreme Court held that the wrong paragraph had been applied in the Court of Appeal and that because the offender did indeed present the goods for Customs inspection, he was acquitted on this point. The judge stated, 'In my view the act which is given as the basis for the indictment's part 1, is not the same punishable act as the state prosecutor claims "nn" [name of offender] should be convicted for. Therefore he must be acquitted for this.'

Concerning the issue of sentencing, the judge found that for general deterrence reasons, the appropriate sentence for a breach of the prohibition against import and export of CITES-listed products as part of a business – especially when it involves a considerable number of animals – should be an unconditional prison sentence. An appropriate sentence would therefore be 45 days in prison. The judge, however, reached the conclusion that in this case, the prison sentence *should be* conditional. This was because too much time had elapsed in the case. The case was first sent to the Magistrate Court more than a year after the offence took place, and this was a fact for which the offender could not be blamed. In addition, according to testimony, he admitted to the offence immediately.

The five judges in the Supreme Court acquitted the offender for breach of the Customs Law but convicted him for breach of the Law of Import and Export Regulation and sentenced him to a 45-day conditional prison sentence suspended for two years.

That the offenders in the above cases were given mild sentences because of procedural delay in the judicial system is, as shown, a theme in these penal cases. These delays may be caused by a lack of priority on the part of the police and state prosecutors who are responsible for investigating the offences and bringing them to trial.[31] Whether this is actually the case will be discussed further in Chapter 6. Before doing so, however, I examine, in Chapter 4, variations in the abuse of animals in the wildlife trade.

Notes

1 https://lovdata.no/dokument/SF/forskrift/2002-11-15-1276?q=CITES
2 http://lovdata.no/dokument/NL/lov/1981-05-29-38. This law was revised in 2009.
3 http://lovdata.no/dokument/NL/lov/2009-06-19-100
4 http://lovdata.no/dokument/NL/lov/1997-06-06-32
5 Lov av 15. juni 2001 nr. 79 om miljøvern på Svalbard (svalbardmiljøloven) § 26 annet ledd, lov av 17. juli 1925 nr. 11 om Svalbard § 4, samt lov av 27. februar 1930 nr. 2 om Jan Mayen § 2.
6 Wildlife Law §26 concerns the King's right to give concessions to Point 5: catching wildlife for transferring it alive to another area. Point 8 concerns importation and exportation of dead and alive wildlife and eggs.
7 §29, concerning importation and releasing alien organisms.
8 http://lovdata.no/dokument/NL/lov/2009-06-19-97
9 FOR-1976–11–20–3 Forskrift av 20. November 1976 om forbud mot at fremmedartede (eksotiske dyr) innføres, omsettes eller holdes som husdyr, selskapsdyr eller i fangenskap på annen måte, (§1). http://lovdata.no/dokument/SF/forskrift/1976-11-20-3
10 Some seizure overviews also include plants, to provide some information about the trafficking in endangered plants versus animal trafficking.

11 E.g., pills, plasters and other, such as belts, shoes, ivory items.
12 Species that are confiscated alive or in form of products include alligator, armadillo, brown bear, butterflies, coral, crickets, crocodile, elephant (ivory), hippo, leopard turtle, musk deer, parrots, predator birds, primates, pythons, tiger (including Siberian), seahorses, spiders and wolves.
13 https://lovdata.no/dokument/NL/lov/2007-12-21-119
14 www.toll.no/no/verktoy/regelverk/tollabc/16/16-9/
15 All steroids are illegal in Norway.
16 www.ssb.no/sosiale-forhold-og-kriminalitet/statistikker/lovbrudde/aar
17 Whether this is also caused by undercontrol and thus lack of detection of crimes committed by women due to normative gendered expectations is a discussion I must leave aside here.
18 The gender of the offenders is usually established in the seizure reports.
19 In Norway, there are four court instances: Forhørsrett, Tingrett, Lagmannsrett and Høyesterett (Magistrate Court, District Court, Court of Appeal and the Supreme Court). In the first instance, Forhørsrett, it is a requirement for the case to be treated there that the offender has confessed to the crime. Cases treated in the District Court can be appealed both by the state (prosecutor) and the offender, both in regards to the issue of culpability and the sentencing to the Courts of Appeal (Lagmansretten), of which there are six. Concerning appeals to the Supreme Court, this will accept only appeals concerning the proceedings, the application of law, and the punishment. An appeal to the Supreme Court cannot be founded in errors concerning proofs relating to culpability (Store Norske Leksikon 2017). The Supreme Court also treats cases of relevance beyond the specific case in matter, since it is the court of precedent.
20 Near the Swedish-Norwegian border where there used to be a Customs station.
21 Most likely my interviewee in the Norwegian Environment Agency, the former leader of the standing committee of CITES.
22 Timneh grey and Africa grey parrots were moved from Appendix II to Appendix I of CITES in October 2016 and to Appendix A of the EU in February 2017.
23 He had not previously reported to the Norwegian Environment Agency that he had in his possession an egg of an endangered species, which is a requirement. If the egg had been registered then that could have proved his innocence.
24 If the treatment of a case takes unreasonably long, then the general practice in Norwegian courts is that the punishment is reduced, since this is regarded as an extra burden for the offender.
25 https://lovdata.no/dokument/NL/lov/2007-12-21-119
26 https://lovdata.no/pro/#document/LBSTR/avgjorelse/lb-2014-93257?searchResultContext=1117
27 Because this species is CITES II listed, such birds may be imported only if accompanied by the correct paperwork, which is provided by the Norwegian Environment Agency, the Norwegian CITES authority.
28 https://lovdata.no/dokument/NL/lov/2009-06-19-100
29 LOV 1962–06–08 nr. 04: Lov om dyrehelse (husdyrloven). [Law of animal health]
30 Later suspended and replaced with Law of Customs and Transfer of Goods. https://lovdata.no/dokument/NL/lov/2007-12-21-119?q=Tolloven
31 However, such delays concern many types of cases, not only CITES, and may thus be considered a general problem in the Norwegian judicial system.

4 Court cases exemplifying the variations of wildlife trade and animal abuse[1]

In this chapter I examine cases that I discovered in Customs seizure reports, such as the first case I discuss below, cases about which the police informed me or ones I found in the form of verdicts in Lovdata.no.

Ivory smuggling and eBay shopping

My analysis of this case is based on Customs confiscation reports, Customs reports to the police, correspondence concerning the verification of species, photographs and reports of police interviews (including quotations from transcripts) with the offender, etc.

This case came under investigation during the first seizure on November 1, 2012, and was finally concluded in Dalane District Court on October 28, 2015 (15–156399ENE-DALA), when the offender was sentenced to conditional prison time of two weeks suspended for two years, and ordered to pay a fine of 15,000 NOK. The majority of the animal products, including stuffed animals and animal parts, were bought through eBay.

Police and Customs reports refer to different dates when parcels addressed to the accused were first checked and seized because they contained illegal wildlife products. In one report, the police state that Customs opened ten parcels from different European countries, all addressed to the offender. Six of these contained ivory. Another police report stated that Customs intercepted ten parcels addressed to the offender. Eight of these contained ivory, one a stuffed bird and one a deer's head. This report also said that there were similar unsettled cases against the same man. Yet another seizure of parcels addressed to the offender revealed two containing 12 CITES-listed products: eight made from ivory, three made from hippo teeth and one stuffed falcon. Other Customs confiscation reports pertaining to this man dealt with Nile crocodile heads (CITES I).

In a report of a confiscation made by Customs in the fall of 2012, items were found to have been sent from many different private addresses in several European countries, as well as from companies specializing in internet auctions.

Following the seizure of the parcels, the police went to the offender's home with a search warrant. Here they found a chaotic collection of more than 10,000 animals/items, according to one of the investigating police officers (Istad and

Vigane 2016) and the man's own assessment of the collection. Many of the stuffed animals and birds were of species protected under the Bern and CITES, such as wolverine, lynx, grey wolf, and several hawk, eagle, owl and falcon species. In addition to the ivory items and the predators, he had several reptile skins, a cobra, a stuffed monitor lizard, a very large number of stuffed wading, predator and song birds, bats, fox, otter and hare, and pelts from different animals. Further, he had a skull of a bat (*Pteropus vampyrus*), two stuffed fruit bats (*Cynopterus brachyotis*), one set of paws from a lion and one set of walrus teeth were also found. There were glass showcases containing stuffed animals, preponderantly birds, everywhere in the house.

In the police interview reports, it appears that the offender had feverishly purchased items through internet auctions. He had as many as 200 simultaneous auction bids. According to the interview report, 'it was almost like an obsession for him. . . . Ten to fifteen parcels would arrive daily.' In another interview report, the police stated that 'it became like an obsession to acquire things cheaply; he learnt the tricks of how to succeed with this. At times it was like a gambler's addiction; he therefore won many auctions.' He purchased items from many different auction websites including eBay, Skanfil and Finn.no. He also travelled to Denmark and England to buy items, always directly from people, rather than from shops. In an interview he stated that he panicked when parcels kept arriving; he felt he had lost control and so hid the parcels unopened in the attic. He did not want his family to see them. He further explained that he had been collecting marine items since childhood – especially from the whale-hunting period, such as narwhale ivory[2] – a hobby he was introduced to by a relative in Norway. Because he was unemployed, he had a lot of time to spend on his stuffed animal collection. In fact, he had bought whole collections of stuffed birds from death estates.

The accused revealed he was aware that labelling ivory as 'faux' or naming it 'ox bone' was a well-known strategy among ivory collectors who made internet purchases and from traders (Interpol/IFAW 2013; see also Davenport 2014). Elephant ivory may also be sold as mammoth or hippo ivory, or detection may be evaded through misspelling the word 'ivory,' or by omitting it entirely in the ad (IFAW 2008: 15).

Motivation: the thrill of collecting

Collecting may be fundamental for humans and non-humans and be deeply ingrained in us. According to Rigby and Rigby (in Case 2009: 739), an early collection of seal impressions is dated to the 5th century BCE, indicating that collecting has a long tradition. As gatherers, humans have depended on their capacity to forage food found in nature, and collecting is a very frequent pass-time. Collecting is defined as follows:

> If the predominant value is representative or representational, i.e., if said object or idea is valued chiefly for the relation it bears to some other object

or idea, or objects, or ideas, such as being one of a series, part of a whole, a specimen of a class, then it is the subject of a collection.'

(Durost, in Pearce 2003: 157)

Pearce adds that this understanding holds the valuable distinction between objects held *for use*, broadly conceived and objects held as *part of a sequence*: it is the idea of series or class which creates the notion of the collection (Pearce 2003: 159).

A collection and the activity of collecting holds many sociological and psychological meanings (McIntosh and Schmeichel 2004). Pearce's description above can be applied to the ivory collection of the accused; the photographs in the case documents and the description of the items in the verdict demonstrate that the ivory items collected by the offender were decorative, rather than functional, e.g. a person's bust, thereby emphasizing their value as collectables. Collectors may collect for leisure, aesthetics, competition, risk, fantasy, a sense of community, prestige, domination, sensual gratification, sexual foreplay, a desire to reframe objects, the pleasing rhythm of sameness and difference, ambition to achieve perfection, extending the self, reaffirming the body, producing gender identity and achieving immortality (McIntosh and Schmeichel 2004). McIntosh and Schmeichel point out that all these motives involve self-fulfilment or self-enhancement. Collectors may further be categorized as (1) passionate collectors, obsessive and emotional and willing to pay any price for the right item; (2) collectors for whom collecting is an investment; (3) the hobbyist who collects purely for enjoyment; and (4) expressive collectors who collect as a statement of who they are (87). The accused may fit into several of these categories, except that of inquisitive collector, as he did not resell what he collected. Regarding the stuffed animals, their skins and furs, collecting these seems to have been for the offender an attempt to constitute some kind of series, being spread around the house as decoration rather than having some other use.

A study by Formanek (2003) of why people collect revealed a number of motivations. Collecting may hold meaning (1) to the self, (2) and to others. It may be a means of (3) preservation, restoration, history and a sense of continuity, (4) financial investment. (5) It may be an addiction. The last category may be of particular interest in the present case judging by the hundreds of dead animals and animal products in the man's house. For the accused, collecting began as enjoyment, something he was introduced to as a child, but became more than a hobby. In the end it was also a statement of who he was and where he came from; both the man and family members, having worked as sailors and in similar positions, had collected items related to the sea. As he was unable to work due to an occupational injury, his passion for collecting seems to have gradually increased until it turned into a compulsive disorder. The way in which stuffed animals were piled up around the house indicates he had lost control of these collections.

Ivory is appealing for various reasons: it is rare and therefore valuable, it is beautiful and therefore enjoyable and in a collector's mind, collecting ivory is an activity which the collector can continue to pursue because the collection is never complete. In this way, it gave meaning to the offender as a replacement for waged labour. As poetically stated by Danet and Katriel (2003),

> In our opinion, in its contemporary form, and perhaps in all ages since it first blossomed about 3,000 years ago . . . collecting is an aesthetic activity that gives expression to the universal experience of the ephemerality of human existence.'
>
> (236)

More prosaically, one can state that consumerism drives collectors. The accused in this case did not even stop to admire or systemize his collection; he merely purchased items for it. This may be counter to the ordinary drive people have to collect. Clifford (2003) describes the collection process as 'an excessive, sometimes even rapacious need to *have* [which] is transformed into rule-governed, meaningful desire. Thus the self that must possess but cannot have it all learns to select, order, classify in hierarchies – to make "good" collections' (260). In the present case, the urge to *have* seems to have overruled the urge to *systematize* and thus refine and 'culturalize' the collection. His collection was not something he took pride in; on the contrary, he was ashamed of the way he had purchased items, indicating he could not prevent himself from participating in auctions. Although precious items of ivory may serve to ascribe social status to a collector because of their worth, in the present case, it seems that craving these items, or perhaps even more craving the act of purchasing, was an important motive. There may have been, however, several related motives for the offender's engagement in IWT. I will treat them separately and then proceed to discuss how to prevent people with similar motivation from getting involved in this crime.

Internet auction addiction?

Collecting ivory was a compulsory act of addiction on the part of the offender; the police interviews suggest that the compulsion was reinforced by the mode of purchase, which can be compared to a gambler's addiction. For gamblers, the internet provides ample opportunity for indulging their addiction at any time of day, thus amplifying the situational and structural factors facilitating the activity (Griffiths 2003) and making it harder to resist the temptation. In the same way, internet auction websites provide collectors with similar opportunities. Structural characteristics are viewed by Griffiths as those that are responsible for the reinforcement of the addiction and which may satisfy gamblers' needs and actually facilitate excessive gambling. Technological advances can have a significant impact on the development and maintenance of gambling behaviour. Factors which facilitate the purchase of illegal ivory on the internet are the privacy of one's own home, where the passion can be acted out, the pressure during the process in which one must act swiftly in order not to lose the bid, the reward being close at hand and the attraction of the beautiful item, including its rarity and aesthetic value. In relation to gambling addictions, Griffiths (1999: 268) states that addiction is essentially about rewards and the immediacy of rewards. Therefore, the more potential rewards there are, the more addictive the activity is likely to be. In the present case, rewards came with far more certainty than in gambling, and may, therefore, have had an even greater effect on the offender's motivation to make purchases. The rewards were also highly cherished, at least during the auctions. The offender's description of acting 'like [he was] obsessed' may, however, suggest that the possibility of winning the auction drove him to proceed as much as the desire for the objects. Therapists are beginning to consider online auction addiction as a medical disorder under the rubric of internet addiction (Peters and Bodkin 2007).

An additional element of internet auctions is the competition between the bidders. Other elements than pure luck, which is more prevalent in ordinary gambling, come into play, such as the capacity of bidders to psychologically foresee the actions of their opponents during the auctions. Consequently, the taste of victory and of having deserved to win the auction may be sweeter and function as an enticement to proceed. The statements of the accused in the police interrogations, however, indicate that his internet auction participation was compulsive in nature, suggesting an 'online auction addiction'. Such an addiction is defined as 'the compulsive need to participate in online auctions that over time generate harmful consequences for the consumer' (Peters and Bodkin 2007: 3). The harmful consequences meant are not those for the animal victims, but the direct harmful effects to the accused himself – committing criminal offenses and spending his resources on IWT.

A third important motive for his addiction was his lack of work and the considerable time he had on his hands as a result. Waged labour is what provides meaning to life for many (see Jahoda 1982; Sollund 2004), and when waged labour is absent many will seek other ways to create meaning and self-realization. By turning into an expert on (dead) wildlife[3] and through possessing and building his collections, the accused may have achieved a satisfaction he otherwise would have lacked in life due to his situation.

The verdict in the ivory/collector case and the application of law

In 2013, the Norwegian attorney general stated that combatting environmental crime was a priority for the police and that the work to reveal serious environmental crimes should be enhanced. It was further stated that the police has a central role in reducing such crime through rapid investigations of breaches of environmental legislation.[4] He recommended that since investigations of economic and environmental crimes shared many features, these investigations should be carried out by the Eco Crime Unit to ensure competence building and the necessary specialization. In order to develop these teams, they should be shielded from doing other tasks and there should be collocated teams in each police district (Riksadvokaten 2013: 9).

The police investigator in the above case, who was also a coordinator of environmental cases in the police district where the offender lived, stated at the outset of the investigation that he thought this case would be big, and an important CITES conviction. There were various developments, however, in the course of the investigation that had an important impact on the final verdict, which may suggest that police specialization may be counteracted by a lack of judicial specialization. A similar dynamic unfolded in the parrot case heard in Borgarting Court of Appeal.

The argument of the judges in the parrot case (14–093257AST-BORG/03) was that this case should (could) not be prosecuted under the Wildlife Law because the parrots were not Norwegian wildlife, but 'cage birds.' Their decision not to apply the Wildlife Law but CITES regulation §5 and the Law of Import and Export Regulation §1.3 had consequences for both the parrot sentence and this ivory/collector case.

The Eco Crime Unit of the police prosecuted the case in February 2014, due to its special responsibility for investigating and prosecuting environmental crimes, while the local police district continued the investigation. In January 2015, the offender was indicted and charged with importating 254 items of ivory, nine items of alligator, one skull of the bat species (*Pteropus vampyrus*), two stuffed fruit bats (*Cynopterus brachyotis*), two shipments of crocodile items, three hippo teeth, lynx products (three skulls, one set of claws and a pelt), one wolf skull, one set of lion paws, six snake skins/stuffed snakes, including four cobras, two turtle shells, two narwhale horns, three skins of water monitor (*Varanus salvator*), one set of walrus teeth, one stuffed honey buzzard, one stuffed hen harrier, four stuffed owls, two stuffed peregrines, one Eurasian hobby (*Falco subbuteo*), and one great white shark tooth (Istad and Vigane 2016: 40).

The indictment was based in Wildlife Law §56, part I, (see also §26, nr. 99) and in the CITES regulation, §18, part I. Because the verdict described above from the Borgarting Court of Appeal was not appealed, however, and the court in that case applied the Law of Import and Export Regulation rather than the Wildlife Law (carrying a lesser sentence of six months rather than two years), the same law had to be applied in the Dalane District Court ivory/collector case.[5] The statute of limitations are also different for the two laws: two years for the Law of Import and Export Regulation and five years for the Wildlife Law. The first indictment included far than in the final 2015 indictment. Because many of these crimes had taken place more than two years before, they fell outside the statute of limits (Istad and Vigane 2016: 40). For this reason, the offender was convicted only of importing 28 ivory items, rather than the hundreds of animals/products he had actually imported and which were included in the initial charges.

The offender was convicted in Dalane District Court on October 28, 2015 (Dalane tingrett 2015). The proceedings took only 40 minutes, since he had confessed. The offender was convicted of importing 28 ivory items without the requisite export and import permits required in CITES, according to the Law of Import and Export Regulation §4, part I, cfr §1 and Regulation of November

15, 2002, for the enforcement of CITES, §18,cfr §5, parts I and II.[6] These paragraphs concern the import of wildlife, and of particular interest is §18 concerning punishment:

> Breach of the regulation or decisions based in the regulations is punishable under the following laws: For living or dead wildlife or products thereof, the Wildlife Law of May 29, 1981 nr. 38, §56 about wildlife shall apply.
>
> For other species or products thereof, the Law of Import and Export Regulation, of June 6, 1997, nr. 32, §4 shall apply. [My translation and edits.]

The judge stated that the court was unaware of previous Supreme Court verdicts which could have a bearing in this matter. This clearly shows that the court had not gone to the trouble of doing a simple search in the database https://lovdata.no/, which contains previous verdicts of principal importance that could have served as precedent. There are several CITES verdicts in the database, including a Supreme Court verdict from 2003 (see previous chapter),[7] which included a statement on the importance of enforcing CITES for preventative reasons. This was also included in the verdict from 1998, in which the offender was sentenced to four months of prison for trafficking CITES-listed species. In no other CITES verdicts, however, have I seen a reference made to these two important verdicts.

The judge stated that it was important to react harshly to CITES crimes for reasons of general deterrence. That said, because the offender had confessed, he had saved the judicial system for considerable expenses, which was regarded as a mitigating factor. The court also treated the fact that the case had remained so long in the judicial system, as a mitigating circumstance. The verdict consisted of a 14-day conditional prison sentence, suspended for two years, and a fine of 15,000 NOK (approximately €1500). In addition, the 28 ivory items were confiscated.

Based on the analysis of these cases, it appears that judges have little interest in this type of crime and therefore do not prepare properly for trials, given that they do not identify previous relevant CITES cases. They also lack knowledge about this type of crime and the growing awareness about these crimes internationally, particularly the UN and EU's recent action plan against wildlife trafficking.[8] It is likely that if there had been specialized judges with expertise in environmental crimes in general, and wildlife trafficking crimes in particular these crimes would have had a different outcome. A conclusion of the EFFACE project, based on research of various environmental crimes in the EU and beyond, was that environmental crimes should be treated seriously by criminal law (Faure et al. 2016). It is to little avail having the specialized Eco Crime Unit or dedicated police investigators if their well-prepared cases result in insignificant punishment because of uninformed, generalist judges.

Many of the cases from Norway that I have examined involve offenders who have committed a long list of crimes, of which some of which may be connected to wildlife crimes, but others of which may have very different motivations. A typical scenario is that the police come to the home of an offender for one reason, e.g. drugs, and while they are there they end up finding evidence e.g. of a reptile. It is unknown why the police first came to the home of the offender in the case in the next section, but his crimes included fraud, wildlife crimes, animal abuse and food crimes.

In the next section, I will look into the collector/taxidermy business for which the offender possessed both live parrots for the pet trade and a large number of dead animals and body parts, all part of his business.

Case: taxidermy and the pet trade: trafficking in dead and live endangered birds and predators

Verdict 14–06830MED-TONS details how on January 23, 2013, a man trafficked with him from Denmark to Norway four parrots, one illiger's macaw (*Primolius maracana*, CITES I), one hooded parrot (*Psephotus dissimilis*, CITES I) and two blue-headed parrots (CITES II).[9] For this he was charged for breach of Wildlife Law §56 and CITES regulations. He also trafficked to Norway from Sweden a dove referred to as 'yellow-breasted earth dove' (*Gulbrystet jorddue*) in 2010. The reason he was trafficking these birds is not indicated in the verdict, but he bred and sold parrots, which suggests they could have been laundered into his business as locally bred.

The man, who was a taxidermist, was also charged for breach of Wildlife Law §56 (cfr. §49) from 2009 to 2013 for having received and kept the following dead animals without registering them in the Norwegian Environment Agency database for dead wildlife: nine peregrine falcons, one goshawk, one European green woodpecker, two dead owls (*Strix aluco*) and one sparrow hawk. He was also charged with keeping in his freezer the following dead animals and animal parts: one grey wolf pelt, one musk pelt, one grizzly bear pelt, one grizzly skull, one wolf skull, eight peregrines, two gyrfalcons and one hawfinch. He also had four stuffed owls (*Strix aluco*). He was further charged with having a (dead) sea eagle and a goshawk, without keeping them chipped, which is a requirement to enable the authorities to assess whether he had property rights to the stuffed birds of endangered species, which is a breach of Wildlife Law §56. He was further charged with having a (dead) sea eagle without registering it in the Norwegian Environment Agency database. The man was also charged with breach of the Tax Law for not having reported 122,700 NOK as income from his taxidermy activities, and for breach of the Law on Value Added Tax (VAT Act) (*Lov om merverdiavgift*) for failing to register his business, despite having commercial activity worth 72,000 NOK subject to taxation. Finally, he was further charged with fraud for failing to report income equivalent to 122,700 NOK, while simultaneously benefiting from disability benefits worth 260,715 NOK.He was further charged for breach of the Weapon Law for keeping two shotguns unsecured.

The trial took place December 1–3, 2014, and the offender pleaded guilty to all charges. The state prosecutor wanted him to be sentenced to 120 days in prison, in addition to the confiscation of 46,269 NOK (gains from the illegal activities), one wolf pelt, one grizzly pelt, one grizzly skull, one wolf skull, eight peregrine falcons, three gyrfalcons, one European green woodpecker, one musk ox pelt, four owls, one sea eagle, one golden eagle and one goshawk. There was no mention in the verdict of the fate of the live birds.

His file also contains details of his life up until the charge. He is described as 'always having had a great interest in nature. He had been an eager hunter all his life and in 2003–2004 he started breeding and selling birds.' In 2006–2007, he built an extension on his house where he conducted his taxidermy activities as a hobby. On October 23, 2012, his house was searched by the police in relation to another unrelated case. (No mention was made about why this was done.) The police found both living and dead animals and the Norwegian Environment Agency demanded an investigation. The house was searched again in March 2013 and the police found more than 100 individuals in different freezers on the property. Live and dead animals, computers, mobile phones and GPSes were confiscated. The Eco Crime Unit took over the investigation in July 2013.

The court found that the man had deliberately breached CITES regulations when bringing the parrots to Norway, in car via Sweden from Denmark. It was also found that he had brought a non-native species to Norway – the dove. If this man had not been apprehended at the border, these birds would likely to have become a part of his live bird pet business.

In addition, the court found that the offender had committed the crime of keeping dead wildlife without registering it in the database of the Norwegian Environment Agency, and that he had kept unchipped wildlife – the sea eagle and the goshawk. The court also found the offender guilty concerning the point in the charge of keeping unregistered wildlife older than 2005. He was further found guilty for tax evasion and fraud, in addition to being guilty of keeping shotguns unlocked.

He was convicted on all charges, including breaching a number of laws concerning the protection of endangered wildlife. The offender had been convicted previously for breach of the Customs Law (without the verdict specifying for what) and for bodily assault (*legemsfornærmelse*), but the court gave this no weight. In sentencing, the court determined that the fraud and the failure to register dead wildlife in the database should both result in a prison sentence, while the other breaches of law should result only in fines but, they were, however, still regarded as aggravating. He was sentenced to 90 days in prison and levied a 46,269 NOK fine. In addition, one wolf pelt, one grizzly pelt, one grizzly cranium, one wolf skull, eight peregrine falcons, three gyrfalcons, one hawfinch, one musk ox pelt, four cat owls and one golden eagle were confiscated.

Concerning the database for taxidermy through the regulation for authorization the taxidermists are given room to conduct their business, also in the private market. One hundred and forty persons (45% of the total 255 registered taxidermists) are given access to the database which contains more than 9,600 registrations of dead animals (Norwegian Environment Agency 2016). Of the 255 persons registered as taxidermists by the Norwegian Environment Agency, 15 are women, only 5.8% of the total. This supports again my position, that the stuffing and collecting of free-born animals, whether legally or illegally, are gendered practices: Just like men are most often the killers of the animals, it is also men who like to stuff them.

The authorizations and the Norwegian Environment Agency's publication of the list of authorized taxidermists give these persons an advantage. The system is also based on trust. This, the court found, justified a strict sentence. All the charges, except fraud and failure to register dead wildlife, were regarded as aggravating, while the defendant's confession was regarded as an ameliorating circumstance, saving the court time and money. The court also noted the two-year lapse from when the Norwegian Environment Agency demanded an investigation until the trial and found this to have been difficult for the offender. He was sentenced to 90 days in prison and to have 1 wolf pelt, 1 grizzly pelt, 1 grizzly scull, 1 wolf scull, 8 peregrine falcons, 3 gyrfalcons 1 European woodpecker, 1 musk ox pelt, 4 owls and 1 golden eagle confiscated.

It is interesting in this case that it concerned both live and dead animals. The man had a profitable business that involved taxidermy and breeding and selling live parrots. This dual interest allowed him to disguise his crimes as legal activities; as said, it is not illegal to breed and sell CITES-listed birds in Norway, neither is it illegal to stuff endangered animals if done in compliance with the rules. It is illegal, though, to import endangered animals without proper CITES permits. It would have been interesting to know the basis for the fine he was levied earlier for breach of the Customs Law and whether his crimes related to that case were similar to those he was convicted of in 2014.

It is also interesting that the man stated in court that he had a genuine interest in nature and hunting. Apparently, his interest in nature consisted of killing, stuffing and imprisoning animals, rather than observing them. It is tempting to suggest that his interest and engagement in nature was dependent more on domination and destruction than on respect. His taxidermy activities also suggest that rather than seeing the animals as individuals, he objectified them as merchandise, as collectables or for display.

I also note that his trafficking crimes were punishable by means of fines, whereas his fraud was punishable with a prison sentence. Thus, crimes against living individuals are regarded as much less serious than economic fraud against the state – money is valued more than protecting endangered animal species.

Trophy hunting and wildlife collections: crimes of 'masculinity'?

Collecting seems to motivate men to partake in wildlife trafficking, whether they kill, abduct and/or trade dead animals, whether mammals or birds are stuffed and put on display or kept alive and caged. Collecting takes place within Norwegian borders, but apparently, birds are also trafficked from Norway, as in the Finnish case.

It is uncertain whether the experience of bird and egg collecting is comparable to killing and collecting trophies; it perhaps has similar features when the killing of large birds of prey is involved. The golden eagle is a big animal with a wingspan of up to 2.2 metres, and consequently killing him/her may produce a sensation of conquering an animal, which supposedly increases a man's sense of masculinity through which he regards himself superior to the animal. When big predator birds are killed in Norway, however, it seems to be more related to 'hate crimes' (Hagstedt and Korsell 2012), in which the birds are regarded as enemy, like other large predators.

As discussed in another study concerning the illegal killing of large predators in Norway (Sollund 2016b), it is hardly a coincidence that *all* offenders in the verdicts presented above are male. According to Nurse (2013: 135–136),

> Many wildlife crimes also involve appropriate male [sic] behaviours such as aggression, thrill-seeking, or having an adventurous nature. . . . [W]hile masculinities may not be the cause of all animal harm, it is certainly a factor to be taken into account in some wildlife crimes and some companion animal abuse.

In Norway, of the 482,000 registered hunters in 2015/2016, of a total population of 5,258 million, people, only 13.1% were women.[10] This is a substantial disparity, and the large total number of hunters in Norway demonstrates the normative climate for such acts; hunting is perceived as tradition, sport and leisure, further solidifying its acceptability and desirability (see Nurse 2013, 2015).

The overall majority of offenders of *any* crime, however, are male. In Norway, of all charges for crimes in 2014, 85% (78,995) were against men, while 15% (12,860) were against women.[11] Of the 7,864 charges concerning crimes against life, body and health, 88% (6,968) were charges against men, while 12% (896) were against women.

When more men than women are involved in crimes against animals, this may merely reflect that it is men who are behind *most* crimes, especially violent crimes. When men hunt this likely has to do with ideals and expressions of masculinity as is the case with trophy hunting. Usually those who kill a large predator will have him/her stuffed or the head mounted for display, thereby adding glory to the killer, and a story for him to tell. In fall 2016, Norway decided that 47 of the then total 65 Norwegian wolves should be killed. Eleven thousand hunters registered to partake in the hunt (Sollund 2017b). There are several reasons why killing an endangered animal is so appealing to so many. First, the wolf is for many an object of hatred, especially for farmers and hunters (Hagstedt and Korsell 2012; Sollund 2016b), because they 'take' prey, for example elk, from hunters and also constitute a threat to their hunting dogs. Second, among hunter peers, the display of one's kill of a wolf results in an elevated social status (Hagstedt and Korsell 2012). This, in turn, is connected to ideals of masculinity: conquering nature through killing large predators, demonstrating the ability to 'overpower' others, expressing aggression and thrill-seeking through which killing becomes an entertainment and leisure activity (Nurse 2011, 2013; Sollund 2015b, 2016b, 2017b; White 2016b). Killing may contribute to the additional instrumental value in what surrounds the hunt: the comradery of hunters, an enhanced sense of masculinity (Brandth and Haugen 2006; Bye 2003), and a feeling of power and reward through killing an animal (Bye 2003; Presser and Taylor 2011). As a hunter William Taylor says, what he enjoys most is the 'challenge, being present in the moment, excitement, learning, the beauty of the surroundings and the social bonding' (Presser and Taylor 2011: 488; see also Bye 2003).

Trophy hunting and collecting constitute a large threat to many endangered animal species (Hall et al. 2008). It has a centuries-long tradition, and as shown by van Uhm (2016b), the global trade in wildlife escalated in the early modern period (±1500–1800 CE) with the advent of European imperialism and colonialism in the Age of Exploration (see also Thorsen et al. 2013). Animals were shipped from the colonies to Europe to be exhibited dead or alive in menageries and zoos (van Uhm 2016b: Chapter 1). That such collections were not only historical displays of status for powerful men, but still exist today, is exemplified by the host of a birthday party my daughter attended as a child. When I arrived to fetch her, I saw a collection of stuffed animals that he had killed, including crocodiles, a polar bear, three big cats, a leopard and a large number of birds of prey. The hunter himself had said in media interviews that he frequently goes hunting; his stories include killing a black bear in Alaska and a lion in Africa.

About the lion theriocide, he boasted that in the village near where he shot the lion, the people were so happy he had killed the 'dangerous lion' that they carried him around in triumph. The idol of this man was Ernest Hemingway for the ways in which he "lived out the 'man in himself." By killing animals, especially endangered predator species, he enhanced (a) his collection, (b) his reputation as a hunter, (c) his self-awareness in terms of ideals of masculinity and (d) the thrill of the moment. To hunt demands that the animal be objectified and othered (Sollund 2016b, 2017b; White 2016b: 303). Hunting, whether legal or illegal, does not take place in a social vacuum, and the undergirding of the norms and values of the hunting subculture is important (Nurse 2011, 2015), as is the more general normative climate that favours hunting (Sollund 2015b, 2016b, 2017b).

'Conquering' an animal and later boasting about it by displaying the victim is a way of displaying 'genuine' manhood. As Fine (2000) states in the case of hunters in Michigan, 'There is no question that many men who took (and take) to hunting do so because it is considered one of the few remaining authentically masculine and white, male-only activity left in a feminized and integrated world' (816).

One may speculate, however, whether men's desire to conquer and dominate nature goes far beyond that of women hunters. A number of feminist scholars claim that the exploitation of the earth and nonhuman species is rooted in patriarchal power structures and androcentrism (see Adams 1996; Birkeland 1993; Collard 1989; Donovan 1996; Donovan and Adams 1996; Gaard 1993; Gålmark 2008; Kheel 1993,1996, 2008; Noske 1989). These feminists critique the elevation of masculine values and traits, such as the perception that killing animals in a hunt is noble (see Kheel 2008), rather than an act of violence. While women may turn to hunting because of a desire to be on par with men or to embody male values that are privileged over female ones, many are unlikely to hunt for this reason.

Luke (1998) thus maintains that contemporary hunting by North American white men is structured and experienced as sexual activity. He describes how animal killers describe their relationship to their victims in terms otherwise reserved for the relationship between partners: love, caring, intimacy and marriage (628). Luke interprets such vocabulary, not with the meaning such words would usually evoke, but that '"Love" here simply means the desire to possess those creatures who interest or excite the hunter: Taking possession typically entails killing the animal, eating the flesh, and mounting the head or the entire body' (629). The sexualized experiences many male hunters have in killing do not represent deviations, according to Luke. Rather, 'within certain patriarchal social structures the disposition to take sexual pleasure in the domination and destruction of other living beings is a normal part of a man's fulfilment' (633).

'Love' as it is used here evokes associations with rape and violence. The hunters themselves, however, may see such acts as romantic (Collard and Contrucci 1989). This conflation of concepts and acts, which are diametrically different in character, sheds some light on the passion with which many men dedicate themselves to theriocide and accumulating trophies to prove their manhood.

On the other hand, perhaps there is nothing paradoxical about connecting violence with sexuality and love. That many people incorporate a violent element into their sexual activities is well known. However, it is well documented that rape is about domination and therefore more an act of violence than of sex (Brownmiller 2013; Sollund 1999; Palmer 1988). Acts of rape or homicide – violence that is directed to other human beings and also to non-human animals (Beirne 1997), can be seen as a desire to (re)gain control in a world that is anomic (Sollund 2001). This need for control may motivate hunters in a context where such killing is illegal and rules set by the state are not accepted (von Essen and Allen 2015). However, in relation to trophy hunting of endangered species for the purpose of displaying them as tokens of masculinity, this is less likely the motive.

In the next section, I discuss a case that highlights the vulnerability of animals in an anthropocentric world, and also demonstrate that categorizing them determines what form of abuse, trafficking and theriocide they suffer.

Case: trafficking raccoons, nose bears and raccoon dogs to Norway, abusing farm animals and committing hunting crimes

Because the acts of the offender described in verdict 13–137704MED-KISA/06 from Kristiansand District Court (2013) are multiple and varied, I cannot describe all the crimes involved in the case, but will focus on the crimes committed against animals. It should be mentioned though, that the first charges both directly and indirectly concerned animals, as the offender demanded state compensation for attacks on his sheep by animal predators. In Norway, the state compensates farmers generously if their animals are killed by endangered large predators. There are two regulations prescribing this, one for domesticated animals (cows, sheep, goats, horses, herding dogs, guard dogs and hunting dogs)[12] and one for reindeer.[13] The result is, that every year farmers/reindeer keepers[14] receive compensation for a much larger number of animals than the few predators in Norway could possible take. For example, in 2003, compensation was given for almost 31,800 sheep, or nearly 25% of the total 130,000 sheep that graze in the summer. Only 2,300 were actually proved to have been taken by predators (Grønli 2004). In addition, annual licensed hunts are organized to deal with predators. In 2017, compensation was paid for 1,849 sheep, and in the winter of 2017–2018, authorities authorized the killing of *42 wolves, four bears, 113 wolverines and 38 lynx in licensed hunts*, despite the fact that these species are very or critically endangered (Mathismoen 2018). Wolves who have been killed in these licensed hunts include packs living within designated wolf zones who did not take sheep; rather they were killed for 'public interest of considerable importance'[15](Sollund 2018b). Regional predator boards (*Rovviltnemnder*) decide the level of protection endangered predator species will receive (Sollund 2015b, 2016b, 2017c), but the members of these local boards are sheep owners and hunters. According to Martinsen, the head of the Norwegian animal protection organization NOAH, wolves are responsible for only 2% of the deaths of the 100,000 sheep who die yearly in pasture; 80% of those who die do so from injuries and disease. Sheep thus die yearly for a number of reasons other than predator attacks; diseases carried by ticks spread by deer, who are overpopulated because of a lack of predators, are the most frequent cause of death Lenth et al. (2018).

The charges in the raccoon case

In the racoon case, the offender was charged with misleading the county governor (*fylkesmann*) of Vest-Agder by claiming compensation of 667,772 NOK for the loss of 246 animals (209 sheep and 37 goats), which he claimed had been taken by wolves. He was also charged with breach of the Wildlife Law for releasing alien species: Between July 1 and November 15, 2011, he trafficked two raccoons, three mountain coaties (*nesebjørn*, *nasuas*) and four raccoon dogs from Sweden to Norway without permission from the Norwegian Environment Agency. He also failed to secure them properly so one or two of the raccoons escaped sometime in October 2011. This was regarded as particularly aggravating because of the threat they pose to the Norwegian wild. He was further charged under Wildlife Law §56 for keeping wildlife illegally in captivity; between July 1 and November 15, 2011, he kept seven raccoons, five mountain coaties and four raccoon dogs without permission. He was further charged with breeding raccoons (five kits) and nose bears (two cubs). For the crimes related to these animals, he was also charged with breach of the Animal Welfare Act, concerning the regulation prohibiting the import of exotic animals.

In addition, he was charged with breach of the Animal Welfare Act for purposefully or by severe negligence failing to care adequately for the animals. Between

July 1 and November 15, 2011, he failed to care properly for sheep #8013 and #9528[16] who had inflamed legs. Sheep #8013 had to be euthanized. He was also charged for purposefully or with severe negligence breaching the Animal Welfare Act and regulation concerning care for sheep and goats because he did not bring in 32 goats from the pasture (*utmarksbeite*) when severe weather threatened.

Moreover, he was charged with (1) breach of the Animal Welfare Act for not caring properly for six of his 28 pigs – providing them a comfortable, dry, draft-free, warm, clean shelter – whom he kept outside; (2) not providing adequate care for two horses and four ponies, who were also kept outside; and (3) failing to repair the floor in a sheep pen, so that one sheep broke through and injured her leg. In addition, he was charged with slaughtering pigs on his farm, using a hammer to kill them. The problem for the court was more that the meat was not properly registered than that harm had been committed to the animals, even though killing pigs with a hammer was described as 'hazardous.'

Apart from these crimes against animals, he was charged with breach of the Food Law for (1) selling meat that had not been subject to an inspection; (2) for not properly tagging his sheep and goats; (3) for buying and moving two cows without reporting it and for failing to tag them; and (4) he also kept four llamas and two alpacas who were not tagged. The practice of IDing animals has a long tradition, and much could be said about it being an abusive practice which is done only for the benefit of facilitating their reproduction by which they are transferred into commodities (Cazaux 2007). In Norway, domesticated animals are IDed by tagging, while free-born animals, for example, wolves and reindeer, are collared for surveillance purposes (Tønnessen 2013). Being tagged or carrying heavy neck devices is of course painful, but these harms will not be further explored here (but see Cazaux [2007] for more on the topic).

The offender was also charged with breach of the Wildlife Law for hunting crimes. Between September 25, 2010, and September 29, 2011, he shot several deer and foxes without a hunting permit. It appears from the sentence that he failed to pass the mandatory shooting test required for a hunting permit. On this occasion, he used ammunition that was illegal, because it was not expanding bullets, and thus having only 15% of the effect of permitted ammunition. For this he was charged with breach of the Wildlife Law because he caused unnecessary harm to the animals he killed.

There were also additional charges made against him by the state prosecutors in Agder for breach of the Wildlife Law for caging two American chipmunks and for breach of the Animal Welfare Act for importing exotic species.

Overall, 23 charges were filed against the man for breach of nine different laws and a number of paragraphs of laws and regulations.

The verdict in the raccoon case

For his crimes, the offender was sentenced to one year and three months in prison. He did not lose the right to keep animals; his breaches of the Animal

Welfare Act were not considered severe enough. He was, however, banned from hunting for five years because of his inhumane hunting of deer and fox. He was also required to pay back the compensation of 680,937 NOK given to him by the state within two weeks of the verdict.

The equipment he had for the trafficked animals, such as enclosures and cages were confiscated. He was also required to pay procedural costs of 28,125 NOK. In addition, he was convicted to the confiscation of 9,800 and 204,469 NOK to cover for the compensation he had claimed improperly from the state.

The man failed to comply with a long list of laws and regulations detailing proper husbandry. I am less concerned, however, with these breaches than by the description of this man's actions in the verdict concerning his abusive treatment of animals. He had hundreds of animals under his care for whom he failed to provide precisely that – care. He killed free-born animals with illegal ammunition causing them to suffer, and he also trafficked animals and kept them captive. These crimes also involved, although unintentionally, releasing 'alien species' into the Norwegian wild, thus endangering Norwegian ecosystems and animal species. The raccoon dog, as described in the sentence, is a severe threat to Norwegian birds and amphibians as s/he can adapt easily to the Norwegian climate. Experience has shown that this species has exterminated birds and amphibians in large areas in Finland. Raccoons have parasites which can transfer to humans as well as to wild species. The court thus regarded this contagious potential as an aggravating factor. The charge of keeping chipmunks arose after the police searched the farm and found the other animals, meaning that the man was determined to keep alien wildlife on his farm. The court also considered this as an aggravating circumstance.

His actions harmed many animals but despite this, his relatively harsh sentence was in response to fraud more so than his crimes against animals, although the judges held that the punishment was also due to the trafficking. The court stated though that in isolation, the hunting crimes would also have resulted in a prison sentence. The judges emphasized that it was very easy to commit fraud when demanding compensation from the state for loss of livestock to predators because the system is based on trust and discretion. What is not mentioned is that such claims affect ordinary citizens' attitudes towards predators and their right to be in the Norwegian wild. For example, media articles often include photos of sheep torn to death. When claims are made that predators take far more sheep than they do, this stigmatizes wolves, turning them into enemies, rather than accepting them as a part of Norwegian fauna. It then also becomes easier for predator boards to authorize licensed hunts (Sollund 2016b, 2017b).

Considering the harm inflicted on the animals in his possession, the court's judges did not deprive the offender of the right to keep animals, allowing him to pick two species among pigs, goats, sheep, cows, poultry, horse. He was thus allowed to continue farming. The judges stated that 'the breaches of the Animal Welfare Act he is convicted of are not the most egregious of crimes. To condemn the man to not rightfully be able to keep a fishpond in the garden, dogs or canaries seems inexpedient.'

I do not know why the judges found that keeping animals under the conditions the offender did, resulting in death for some of them, was not serious. It also seems strange that the judges so candidly allowed him to own other animals, canaries, dogs and fish, given his history. The judges display speciesist attitudes insofar that they ruled that some animal species more than others may be placed at risk in the hands of a careless owner. Although there are many regulations concerning the keeping of animals for food production (Ellefsen 2013b), anyone 16 years or older can buy an animal in Norway. That people should possess a 'right' to keep an animal in captivity can of course be disputed from a species justice perspective (White 2013). In the next chapter I will present the problems of the animal trade within and *from* Norway.

Notes

1 Parts of this chapter have been previously published as Sollund (2015).
2 Whale hunting in Norway and Japan is ongoing, despite the 1986 International Whaling Commission moratorium and CITES protection. The peak of whaling in Norway was in the late 1800s and took place in the Antarctic and in Norway as well as in open seas. Many whale species were driven to the brink of extinction until the foundation of the International Whaling Commission and the moratorium. Norway opposes the moratorium and more than 10,000 minke whales have been killed in Norway since (Martinsen 2013: 103–105).
3 The police reports showed, however, that several of the dead animals in his house were categorized incorrectly according to species.
4 http://riksadvokaten.no/filestore/Dokumenter/2013/Rundskrivnr1for2013-Mlogpriforstraffesaksbehandlingen.pdf
5 Interestingly, while in the African grey/eagle egg case the judges did not look into previous verdicts, in the ivory case this was an issue for the prosecutor and determined its outcome.
6 https://lovdata.no/dokument/NL/lov/1997-06-06-32/%C2%A73#§3
7 https://lovdata.no/pro/#document/HRSTR/avgjorelse/hr-2003-291-a?searchResultContext=1121
8 http://ec.europa.eu/environment/cites/trafficking_en.htm
9 Since the Latin name does not appear in the verdict, it is uncertain what species these were. It is most likely blue-headed cacique parrot (*Pionus menstruus*).
10 www.ssb.no/jegerreg/
11 www.ssb.no/sosiale-forhold-og-kriminalitet/statistikker/lovbrudde/aar/2015-10-29?fane=tabell&sort=nummer&tabell=242555
12 Forskrift om erstatning når husdyr blir drept eller skadet av rovvilt (Regulation about compensation when domestic animals are killed or injured by predators) https://lovdata.no/dokument/SF/forskrift/2014-05-30-677
13 Forskrift om erstatning for tap og følgekostnader når tamrein blir drept eller skadet av rovvilt (Regulation about compensation for loss and following costs when domesticated reindeer are killed or injured by predators) https://lovdata.no/dokument/SF/forskrift/2001-05-04-468
14 The Sami people, Norway's indigenous population, keep reindeer.
15 The predator boards confirmed their decision to have 47 of the total population of 67 wolves in Norway (70%) killed in 2016, a decision that was later overruled by the Minister of Climate and Environment in 2017 but proposed again in 2018. Eleven thousand hunters signed up for the ecogenocide (Larsen 2012). These packs were not a threat to sheep, but threatened the interests of hunters

and forest owners who benefited by retaining their hunting rights – an interest defined as being of 'particular public interest', by a judge in Oslo District Court where he rejected a temporary injunction to stop the wolf hunt brought by WWF Norway on January 5, 2018.

16 That animals are numbered rather than named is part of the alienation process inherent in industrialized farming, by which they are objectified, rather than attributed with personhood.

5 Trafficking within Norway and from Norway to other countries

In the previous chapters I have addressed cases that concern trafficking *to* Norway, in this chapter I will discuss cases in which Norway is a source country for WLT. Several decades ago, the smuggling of eggs and chicks from predator birds to abroad was occasionally documented in Norwegian newspapers. Interview data will establish how this problem is addressed. For example, people are stopped at the border with incubators when entering Norway, but people leaving the country are very seldom inspected. This may indicate that bird and egg trafficking from Norway is insufficiently addressed.

However, through my data it appeared other more unexpected species may also be trafficked as part of the international 'pet' trade, an issue I will explore in the following, through a case in which reptiles were trafficked and suffered abuse, while the mice were victimized as feed for the reptiles. I follow the case from the initial police investigation until the verdict was finally given in the Oslo District Court.

Case: reptile trafficking from Norway, as described in the investigation material and interviews

The case differs from those discussed in previous chapters, in that the modus operandi of the offender(s) is different, yet similar to the internet ivory case described previously in that it starts out like a seemingly huge case, but concludes with lenient punishment.

On September 4, 2013, the Environment Division of the Oslo police entered a private residence in Oslo. They had received a tip from Interpol that snakes were being imported into Australia. The concern of the Australian authorities was not only the snakes, but also the cockroaches that accompanied the snakes as food. Nineteen reptiles, including a jaguar carpet python (*Morelia spilota*), had been found accidently when a man who had recently moved discovered a parcel containing the reptiles at his new address. The parcel also contained five thousand Australian dollars. A man had come to the address twice and inquired about the parcel, saying he had intended to rent the house and therefore had directed mail to it (but said he changed plans).

The Australian police revealed that 14 parcels had been shipped from Norway to four different male recipients in Australia. The trafficking took place from August 16, 2011, until the last seizure on April 2, 2013. The peculiarity of trafficking snakes to Australia was commented on by the police in an interview: 'It is a bit like bringing fish to Lofoten.'[1]

The Norwegian offender's name was connected to an internet reptile shop on two occasions; he had previously been convicted for trafficking snakes in Norway. The police were convinced that he sold endangered reptile species that he had bred from his internet shop and from which he profited greatly. The police revealed that he had had many telephone conversations with persons in the Czech Republic, Denmark, Germany, Spain and Sweden, thus they suspected he was part of an organized criminal network. In the offender's house, the police found 240 CITES-listed animals, including geckos, lizards, monitor lizards and mice. Several of the reptiles were dead or dying, as were the mice that were used to feed them. One of the monitor lizards had been injured by a heat lamp placed above his/her cage. In the house of the offender's mother, the police found 119 new-born dead piglets and thousands of dead mice in two freezers. Most of the live reptiles were killed by the authorities, while some were taken to a zoo in Kristiansand.

The police believed the offender had bred the reptiles and shipped them to Australia and other countries. When I interviewed police, they believed they would be able to charge him with organized crime and money laundering, as well as with breach of CITES and the Animal Welfare Act. In the press conference that followed his arrest, the police described this as 'cynical profit-motivated animal abuse.' In the interview, the police said, 'This was to go as far as we could [in the description of the case], to show that here the experienced police officer was shocked.'

During the investigation, the police discovered that the offender had had 165 currency transactions amounting to 550,000 NOK to and from 19 different countries between August 2008 and April 2013, while during the same period, he had registered an income of only 590,000 NOK. The police suspected that these transactions were connected to his illegal enterprise, and that as a result, his income from it must be much more than he declared – for example, one reptile alone was priced on his internet shop at 5,000. Also, the offender's mentally handicapped sister and fiancée were involved in money transactions. The police found the 5,000 Australian dollars in the parcel supported their suspicion that large amounts of cash were involved. Finally, between January 12, 2012, and July 18, 2013, the offender had also deposited an unaccounted for 220,000 NOK to his bank account.

The bank account statements showed that prior to making the deposits, he travelled to Sweden and Germany, making the police suspect that he travelled to these countries to buy reptiles. His account transactions also showed his card was used at a well-known reptile fair in Hamm, Germany (see Sollund 2013a), which Auliya et al. (2016) describe as an important marketplace in Germany for wild-caught reptiles and which is the largest market for reptiles in the European Union.

The Australian police revealed that an additional 25 parcels had been sent to the same address in Australia, and one parcel had been sent from the same address to Italy, containing an Australian blue tongue lizard. The similarity in the way this reptile was packed and the way the reptiles were packed who were sent to Australia, and the fact that the same name appeared in both shipments, convinced that police of a strong organizational relationship between the Norwegian and the Australian arms of the organization, which the police suspected had been in operation since 2011.

Concerning the two Australian suspects, one had been fined for similar crimes before (6,000 and 60,000 AUD), and both were involved in a larger international network profiting from reptile trade.

The modus operandi was the same in all cases. Parcels were sent to addresses where currently no one lived. The offenders then went to these addresses and picked up the parcels. It was only coincidence that police were alerted to the shipment that sparked the investigation.

Initially the police planned to charge the Norwegian offender with organized crime (§60 in the Norwegian Penal Law), and it was this that allowed them to tap the suspect's phone. According to the police, the case was prioritized because the potential it held for correction for money laundering, organized crime, and breach of CITES, as well as potential punishment for serious environmental crime, since §152b could come into play.[2]

As one of the police interviewees said,

> It was the size of it, the international aspects, it was simply a highly unusual case involving rare or exotic animals, so all in all it was a wrap that made the whole section realise that we were doing pioneer legal work, and to associate this, organised crime with exotic animals.

Another police officer interviewee added,

> So these were very complicated investigations, they involved the data crime unit, internet, the case required letters rogatory abroad, only the process with taking DNA samples from the snakes; we had to apply for export [CITES] permits, and those on the other side [in Australia] needed import permits, and it was Australia that initiated this [the investigation].

Cooperation was also complicated because of different time zones and because the police in Norway and Australia are organized differently, thus making it complicated in the initial stages to know who to deal with.

The final charges in the reptile trafficking case

In the initial charges as of July 23, 2013, the Norwegian offender was charged, along with others, with profiting from an illegal act, thus breaching Penal Law

§317. It was regarded as serious because of the nature of the crimes from which the gains were derived, the value and the regularity of the act. He was also charged for having transferred 555,003 NOK, on 165 occasions, to bank accounts abroad. The money was claimed to have been gained from criminal acts.

In the final indictment of March 17, 2016, however, the charges were changed. Now he was charged with breach of the Animal Welfare Act §37 for seriously neglecting to provide care for animals in his custody, including adequate food, clean water, protection from injury and veterinary care when necessary. The crime was regarded as severe because of the number of animals involved (210 exotic animals, including endangered lizards and snakes listed in the CITES appendices) and their condition. The majority of the animals lacked clean water and fresh food, there were remains of dead mice used for food in the cages, three snakes and a gecko were found dead and several animals were very sick. He was found guilty.

Charges for breach of the Animal Welfare Act were also laid under §37, part II, concerning the prohibition against feeding animals live food, having fed live mice to the reptiles.

He was further charged with breach of the CITES for exporting exotic animals including CITES-listed boas and for importing CITES-listed reptiles. In addition to the charges involving animal abuse, he was charged with breach of Penal Law §102 for having kept many illegal doping substances at his home, including testosterone pills. Compared to the initial police investigation and their suspicion that other serious crimes were involved, the final indictment was far more limited, and the charges for being involved in organized crime were omitted. When I questioned the police lawyer in charge of the prosecution about this, he said the reason for this was that these were the only crimes they could prove.

The verdict in the reptile trafficking case

The verdict was given in Oslo District Court on November 30, 2016. Nearly three years and three months had passed since the police first entered the offender's home. The trial lasted three days, and the accused pleaded guilty to some of the charges concerning breach of the Animal Welfare Act for severe negligence of care. He plead guilty to point II of the charges, feeding animals with live mice, and III, breach of the CITES for having exported boas.

The state prosecutor argued the accused could be acquitted on point IV of the charges, for having imported CITES-II listed pythons, but that for the other charges he should be sentenced to eight months in prison, have his terraria confiscated and be ordered to pay procedural costs of 5,000 NOK, as per the indictment. The defence attorney argued that he be acquitted on charges IV and V (the drug charges) and that the remainder of the charges should be treated in the most lenient manner. He was able to persuade the court.

The accused stated in court that he, in 2004, had imported 30 carpet python snakes to Norway from Sweden, all CITES II listed. He added that he had not imported any more reptiles and that the confiscated snakes were offspring of the initial animals he had bought in Norway. The monitor lizards were acquired from Sweden in 2011, but he was unaware of this until he received them.

The court found him guilty of breach of the Law of Import and Export Regulation, §4, part I (and CITES regulation §5, part I), for which the maximum prison sentence is six months or a fine, or both. Likewise the defendant had breached the Wildlife Law, but because of the statute of limitations, he was acquitted for this part of the charges, just like the offenders in the parrot and ivory cases.

The court found that he had sent one parcel to Australia containing one adult carpet python and 19 juvenile carpet pythons. Concerning 13 more parcels that had been sent to Australia, the court found it likely that he did, indeed, send these parcels, but the court lacked information concerning who the recipients in Australia were and the content of the parcels. Therefore, they found that they lacked the necessary proof to convict him on these charges.

Concerning the breaches of the Animal Welfare Act, §37, severe negligence in care, the court found that the prosecutor had it proved beyond reasonable doubt that the lack of care for the animals was more serious than stated by the accused, and that this was a breach of §24 of the Animal Welfare Act concerning adequate care, food, etc. The veterinary report stated,

> The majority of the snakes lacked water, and the water bowls in the cages were either empty or the water was very dirty, and foul smelling. The majority of the snake cages were dirty, with excrement and old food (moldy or dried mice cadavers). Live mice were found with two of the juvenile snakes. Two of the snakes had eye inflammations and the infected eyes were probably blind. This was probably the result of incomplete molting and attempts to remove the skin, causing the normal skin over the eyes to be injured. Several of the snakes were dehydrated and had not molted completely. Several of the snakes had mites. Three snakes were found dead in their cages. Two monitor lizards had scars on their backs, probably from burns caused by heat lamps. A gecko was found dead in its cage. Several of the animals were in bad shape, several of the snakes' skins appeared loose. Several of the animals were aggressive and angry. The air in the room was dense and foul smelling.
> (Oslo Tingrett 2016)

Likewise, the court did not doubt this description of the situation; however, it did not find it proven that the scars on the monitor lizards were caused by lamps, as they could have been caused by fights. At the same time, they did not consider what might have caused such fights, and that such fights could have been the consequence of abuse – being cramped in narrow boxes, lacking food and water. Otherwise, the court accepted the description and found a lack of appropriate care.

The court did not find trust in the testimony of the accused that the lack of care had been of short duration and that the reason the animals did not have water was that he was treating them for mites. The court agreed with the veterinarian report that suggested that the reptiles were aggressive because they were hungry.

The court also found that despite the fact that the animals had suffered from neglect for some time, the evidence was not a sufficient basis on which to establish whether the neglect had resulted in animal harm, which was necessary to establish whether it was serious neglect. From the testimonies of the veterinarians, the court assumed that snakes could tolerate lack of food and water better than mammals and birds, as well as a relative lack of space, hygiene and ventilation because reptiles are cold-blooded. The judge further stated that the veterinarian's assessment of the condition of the reptiles was based only on inspection; no autopsies had been performed to establish cause of death and harm caused by the accused's actions. Furthermore, 210 animals were alive, and only three to five were dead, implying that the harm and suffering were limited at the time of the seizure. The court found beyond reasonable doubt that the accused understood that he failed to provide good care and that this caused the conditions described above.

The accused was convicted with of §37, part I, and §24, part I, a and b, concerning adequate food and water, protection from parasites and the need to euthanize sick animals as soon as possible. The court did not, however, find that the accused engaged in *serious* neglect. Even though the inadequate care encompassed more than 200 animals and was deliberate, the court did not find that the animals had suffered abuse or harm.

Concerning the charges for feeding the reptiles with live mice, which is criminalised in Norway, this was proved beyond reasonable doubt. The court distrusted the accused's explanation that he had only fed the reptiles with live mice 2–3 times, since there were cages with very many mice, and also very many mice of different sizes were found in the freezer, a fact counting against the explanation given by the accused that he kept the mice alive to have feed of different sizes available.

However, the court did not find that these acts were so extensive they could constitute gross violations. The court made reference to two other verdicts that had been given in the Supreme Court in 2016, where the central points regarding the punishment were whether the abuses were gross negligence. One case concerned a man who neglected to provide his 92 cows with food and water, after which they died. For this, he was convicted to one year and eight months in prison (HR-2016–2285-A). The other case concerned a man who drowned his dog by tying him to a concrete metal tube and tossing him over a bridge, for which he was sentenced to 120 days in prison (HR-2016–295-A).

The court, in the present case, found that they could not be proved to have caused the reptiles great harm, and that the correct punishment for the lack of care for the reptiles in isolation should be a 120-day suspended prison sentence.

Instead the court determined that the correct punishment for feeding the reptiles live mice, isolated, should be 30 days suspended imprisonment, importing snakes, in isolation, merited 30 days suspended imprisonment.

The remainder of the sentence concerned the drug offences, for which the offender was convicted of breach of Penal Law §162, part I, concerning illegally producing, importing, keeping, acquiring or sending drugs. For this offence, the court reasoned a five-month suspended prison sentence would be appropriate.

The court decided the offender should be sentenced to a total of four months suspended prison time and levied a fine of 15,000 NOK, as well as procedural costs of 3,000 NOK, and the confiscation of the equipment used for the animals. While the punishment for the offender was lenient, the other individuals involved in the case – the animals – were seriously victimized.

When are acts of animal abuse seriously abusive, and who count as victims?

The judges stated the crimes – animal abuse and trafficking – were serious. When it came to sentencing, however, these findings were ignored. In employing the Animal Welfare Act, §3 did not come into play, although it contains the clause, 'Animals have intrinsic value independent of their use value for humans.' While this may seem as a revolutionary statement, this is undercut by the following statement from the Act: 'Animals shall be treated well and be protected against *unnecessary* strain and harm' (emphasis added). This implies that animals can be subject to strain and harm as long as this is regarded as necessary, with necessary being defined from an anthropocentric perspective rather than from the perspective of the animals. From an animal welfare position, animals do not have rights, meaning rather that animal welfare legislation sanctions ongoing animal abuse (Ellefsen 2013b; Francione 2009, 2014; Svärd 2008). The use of the animals in the reptile case could by no means be regarded as necessary. Keeping reptiles in private homes, whether Norwegian or foreign, was illegal (see Chapter 7 for elaboration on the legality/illegality of keeping exotic reptiles in Norway); that is, keeping domestic reptiles would be encompassed by the Wildlife Law, in that it is illegal to take free-born animals into private homes, so that keeping foreign free-born reptiles would be criminalized[3] by the legislation described in Chapter 2, including the CITES regulation. Feeding live mice to reptiles could never be deemed a necessary harm, like killing animals for human consumption is defined as necessary. Therefore rather than the court applying this paragraph, the paragraphs referred to in the sentence concerned proper care, which of course the animals did not get. But the overarching question would then also be, would not this keeping of reptiles and the treatment of the mice have entailed strain and harm whether or not they had been subject to obvious neglect, as in this case?

The necessity of inflicting harm on animals may therefore be flexible and discussed in view of the continued exploitation of minks and foxes in small cages for fur production (Ellefsen 2013a; Sollund 2008a). This is a harm that is outlawed in many countries and, which will be phased out in Norway in 2025, precisely because of its abusive character. Locking undomesticated, active predators that naturally roam long distances into small cages where they can hardly move should be a breach of the Animal Welfare Act (Sollund 2008a), yet this industry has been maintained and the fur farmers subsidized, despite growing protest for many years.[4] In view of such treatment – and as long as this is permitted – just like other abuse against animals people use, such as cows, chickens and pigs ,is permitted; the minks and foxes are not accorded intrinsic value precisely because of their use value; this abuse was regarded as necessary, despite the harm and strain inflicted on them (e.g., Beirne 1999, 2009; Francione 2009; Larsen 2013; Sollund 2008a, 2012a; White 2016a; Wyatt 2014b).

Undoubtedly, concerning the reptiles, having lived under the conditions that are described in the sentence must have implied both strain and harm, being subject to thirst, starvation and infections to such a degree that several even died as a consequence. For the mice, being fed to the snakes while still alive must have produced the greatest of fear and for the mice that were still alive in the cage with their predators, it is almost impossible how they must have felt – almost, but not entirely.

While reptiles well may eat live rodents in the wild, the mice in the cage have no escape. Mice, as other mammals, are animals with well-developed cognitive abilities (Pearson 2003). They have also developed to escape their predators, although naturally they will not always succeed, and must therefore have been constantly in a flight mood, yet perhaps starvation and thirst in their case slowed down their natural awareness and flight reactions.

That the court was so imprecise concerning the number of dead animals also indicates the lack of intrinsic value the court ascribed to each of them. The court did not say exactly how many animals were found dead among the 210 reptiles; there were, however, 'many dead mice'. To explore the issue of the usual significance of the *quantity* of deaths, it is worthwhile looking to other court cases, as the Supreme Court reference cases used by the present court. In the case of the 92 cows, the farmer suffered from depression because his father, diagnosed with Alzheimer's, could no longer help him on the farm, and therefore he did not go to the barn to see to the cows. For starving 92 cows to death, he was convicted to one year and eight months imprisonment. In the present reptile case, the exact number of animals who died is not even given. The animals who died were already dead when the crime was discovered, this could also have been the fate of all the reptiles and mice who were still alive. Most of them were killed anyway after confiscation, a point I return to, and we don't know how many of the reptiles were taken by the zoo.

There seems to be another element of speciesism involved in the court's determination that this was not gross negligence, because '210 animals were alive, and only 3–5 animals were dead, indicating the harm and suffering were limited at the time of the seizure' (Oslo Tingrett 2016: 8). It appears big domesticated mammals such as cows enjoy more protection under the Animal Welfare Act than do reptiles and mice. The mice may have seemed insignificant to the court, little as they are and of no use, except as 'lab mice,' and consequently nothing was said about their suffering.

When taking a more empathetic non-speciesist approach, however, it is obvious that the mice suffered given that they were sentient, intelligent mammals. Pearson (2003), in an article in *Nature*, describes how scientists have long used a factor called general intelligence, or 'g,' to rate people's brainpower, a measure that uses verbal, logical and mathematical tasks. A person with a large 'g' tends to score high in IQ tests and perform well in school and work. Experiments assessed this feature of the mouse brain and found that mice also have a version of 'g,' indicating they are intelligent too. Concerning the pigs found in the freezer of the offender's mother, we know nothing about how they came to be there, or why the offender had them, so I will leave these out of the discussion, except to say that it would probably have been in the interest of the pigs to live (depending on what kind of life they would have had in the Norwegian pig meat industry (Sollund 2008a, 2014; Wyatt 2014b)).

As shown, the abuse of the reptiles is detailed in the sentence, however, the court doubts the *degree* of suffering. It seems thus that the court was unable to empathize with the suffering of this kind of animals, and like in the case of the mice this is also interesting from a non-speciesist perspective. *Her er du!*

Like the mice, the reptiles were victims of speciesism. With their prehistoric appearance, reptiles often elicit little empathy and are often alienated and the subject of phobias. As observed by Öhman and Mineka (2003), 'fear and respect for reptiles is a likely core mammalian heritage. From this perspective, snakes and other reptiles may continue to have a special psychological significance even for humans, and considerable evidence suggests this is indeed true' (5). The court even said that despite all their injuries, and the fact that they had been subject to excessive heat, lack of fresh air, lack of fresh water and lack of food, the prosecutor had not proved that they had suffered. Then there is the matter of their intelligence. An animal cognition study (Manrod et al. 2008) confirms high cognitive learning capacities in monitor lizards. Also, anole lizards have shown high behavioural flexibility and the capacity to solve problems (Leal and Powell 2012).[5] Given reptilian intelligence, the reptiles in this case also likely suffered from lack of stimulus and captivity.

When the court sentenced the offender to only a suspended prison sentence for abusing and causing the death of so many animals, the one-year, eight-month prison sentence for the offender in the cow case and the three-month prison sentence for killing one animal in the dog case, seem comparatively much harsher. The dog, for instance, was hit on his way to the water and then suffered three to four minutes before drowning, while the reptiles and mice suffered for a long time before three to five of them finally died. After the seizure, they were, with a few exceptions, all euthanized.

It is likely that these different court approaches to animal abuse are linked to what kind of species were involved, rather than the actual extent of suffering inflicted upon them and how many animals were involved. Familiarity and size are likely factors, as well as the ways in which these species are viewed: snakes are demonized, white mice (which the mice in this case were) are experiment material (see, e.g., Regan 2004), while dogs are humans' companions with a high cuteness factor, and cows have been valued by humans as an agricultural resource for more than 18,000 years (e.g., Nibert 2013; Noske 1989). The point here is that detailed laws govern how cows are to be treated because of their utility for humans, which is not the case for reptiles and mice. Furthermore, cows and dogs are positioned within the moral circle in Western culture, thereby deserving some level of compassion (Hallsworth 2008).

Most of the animals involved in this case were ultimately killed, if they did not die because of their maltreatment. That most of the survivors were killed by the Food Safety Authority is a fatal consequence of the authorities' ways of dealing with victims of crime when they are animals. The Norwegian authorities do not employ a critical victimology perspective (Fitzgerald 2010; Moore 2005; Sollund 2015b, 2017b; Maher and Sollund 2016a, 2016b) that includes animals. While the offender was convicted of animal abuse, the animals were doubly victimized by being euthanized (Maher and Sollund 2016a, 2016b). That being euthanized is considered as attending to the welfare of the animal implies that animals, unlike human animals, have no interest in life itself. But when reptiles and birds are killed by veterinarians, I doubt they *see* the animals and appreciate the fear in their eyes. The abyss created by the animals' 'animalism' (Derridá 2002) prevents them from being seen by the humans who are in charge of their fate.

In the next section, I explore the trafficking of Norwegian birds, first through a case involving a Finnish abductor/collector who also operated in Norway, then through Norwegian Supreme Court verdicts.

Bird crime and trade

A Finnish citizen was sentenced in the Finnish Österbotten District Court in 2015 to one year's conditional prison stay and a fine of €250,000[6] for illegally collecting approximately 8,700 eggs, mainly from Närpes, Finland. The eggs were also collected from Finnmark in northern Norway in 2008 and 2011, and according to the report from the Norwegian Environment Agency, eggs were also taken from Norwegian national parks. They included endangered species. The eggs were assessed at a value of €700,000. Finnish authorities have established fixed fines to be paid for different species according to their economic value, e.g., a gyrfalcon is worth €6,391, an eagle €7,400 and a golden eagle €4,877 (Enger 2013). At the offender's house, authorities also found about 3,000 stuffed and frozen birds. As part of the verdict, the eggs were confiscated, and the court emphasized the economic aspects of the crimes. The Norwegian Environment Agency reported him to the police for breach of the Nature Diversity Act and the Wildlife Law.

Since the case concerned a Finn travelling to Norway to collect eggs, the Norwegian and Finnish police had to cooperate. A name of a Norwegian man appeared in records found in the house search of the Finnish offender, but this person, when called as a witness, denied any knowledge of the Finnish offender.[7]

The Finn could have been sentenced to an unconditional two-year prison term, yet the Finnish Court levied a considerable fine instead. The application of fines, rather than a suspended prison sentence, can be viewed as having a greater deterrent effect than a conditional or even unconditional prison sentence when the size of the fine is big enough to impact the offender's life, which one must assume was the case here. There is a contrast between the amount of the fine in the Finnish case and the amount of a fine imposed for trafficking in Norway, especially when it is imposed by Customs, although as said there is a tendency that they may be on the increase in Norway due to more prioritization of environmental crimes over the last years. The Finnish sum of the fine also signals the huge economic gains possible in wildlife trafficking.

In an article (Enger 2013) featuring an interview with Eco Crime, and *Statens naturoppsyn*,[8] retired police officer Terje Axelsen makes it clear that fauna crime is a big problem in Norway, particularly concerning falcons, other raptor birds and eggs. Axelsen, who is also a hobby ornithologist and specializes in this kind of crime, explained that before *Statens naturoppsyn* and the Eco Crime Unit were established, taking Norwegian birds was easy, and all kinds of birds were trafficked to Europe. According to him, there were groups with networks in Denmark, England and Germany who traded Norwegian birds. In the previous decade, it appears that people from Belgium, China, Denmark, England, Netherlands, Sweden and Vietnam had been apprehended throughout Norway in the possession of birds and eggs. According to Axelsen, a common modus operandi is to pay two visits to Norway, the first in the spring to map nests and take photographs, the second to abduct the birds. Alternatively, information about nesting locations is purchased from knowledgeable Norwegians (Enger 2013: 26). Again, according to Axelsen, it is men who are involved in this type of wildlife trafficking:

> It is like this kind of hunt of endangered predators attracts a certain type of men, of all ages. To plunder nests, collect live golden eagles, to catch cat owls in traps [*stolpefeller*], only men do that. I will characterise them as sick collectors.

This statement is consistent with my findings throughout the book that men are the offenders behind most of these crimes.

It appears that the Norwegian enforcement authorities may have to do a considerable job to detect crimes of nest plundering and bird trafficking in and from Norway. One of the environmental coordinators in the police, with whom I conducted an email interview, confirmed the problem:

> The authorities have quite a good overview of the localities and will soon register if anything happens. This was the reason why in Agder, we could presume that the golden eagles were 'disappearing'. By looking at the composition of the population in the area, nature scientists assumed golden eagles were illegally shot/captured. It appears they were right. We have received the rings of the birds delivered anonymously.

Trafficking in birds from Norway, particularly birds of prey, was also identified as a problem by the CITES/Norwegian Environment Agency interviewee who said a gyro falcon could be sold for half a million NOK in some Arab countries, where they are 'desperate for these birds.' The demand for falcons is confirmed by Wyatt's (2011, 2014a) study of the Russian wildlife trade, where birds trafficked for falconeering is a significant problem with complex features involving many actors (see also Dixon et al. 2011). Customs interviewees also confirmed a case of falcon trafficking from Norway to Germany in the 1990s (see examples of Supreme Court cases below), but except for the Finnish case, there are no recent verdicts concerning trafficking in falcons or other birds of prey from Norway.

Confronted with this, an interviewee in Customs said trafficking birds from Russia might be easier than from Norway, but that the problem in Norway is also that of illegal capturing:

> Bird skins for stuffing, there is a gigantic market for this in Europe. People want complete collections with summer feathers, winter feathers, etc. And there are people in Norway who stuff animals all the time, so yes, we have the problem here as well. . . . I see there is a market for this in Norway, particular as it is. And, for example, in Copenhagen Zoo, they have snow owls and polar owls and golden eagles, etc., and peregrines and they get children every year, and then they kill them and skin them and sell them. And then Norwegian taxidermists buy those skins with CITES permits, we must assume they have things in order then. I see these coming in regularly. And then they stuff, let's say a snow owl, you pay 500 for the skin and stuff it, and sell it for 5,000, so it is business. I am surprised that there actually is a market like that in Norway, year after year.

The Finnish and the reptile trafficking cases are clear examples of the transnational character of wildlife trafficking, which also underlines the need for cooperation at the international level in order to solve and prosecute cases. In interviews, advisors in the Customs Directorate maintained that Norwegian Customs cooperates on Scandinavian, European and international levels, strategically and in relation to intelligence, but also when needed in relation to specific cases, as in the reptile case. Norwegian Customs and police do not work in isolation; at least formally they cooperate with Europol, Interpol and the Worlds Customs Organization (WCO). There is both a Norwegian police officer and a Norwegian Customs officer stationed at Europol. However, none of the interviewees could recall having ever received any concrete intelligence information relating to CITES. What information they do seem to receive concerns what is seized in various airports, and in this way Norwegian Customs may acquire information about source countries. This is information they then transmit to Oslo airport Customs. So, Customs may learn more generally about the modus operandi of wildlife traffickers but do not receive specific intelligence information from either of their partners in Norway or abroad, whether among police or Customs agencies.

Supreme Court decisions concerning bird (and other animal) crimes

One of the ways of collecting endangered species is to kill them and stuff them. I will briefly present three Supreme Court verdicts concerning the illegal killing of endangered birds, all from 1990.[9] One also concerns crimes against other animals.

It appears from a Supreme Court decision (Høyesterett–Rt-1990–203) that one offender in the years 1982–1987 had killed a large number of protected birds from which he had profited economically. The birds were frozen, and his intention was to sell them so they could be stuffed, as he had previously made a profit doing so. He was convicted to 120 days in prison, of which 60 days were suspended for two years, and he was deprived of the right to hunt and capture animals for five years.

In another case (Rt-1990–156 [40–90])[10] in which the offender profited from his crimes, he was sentenced to prison for one year and two months, of which ten months were suspended for two years. He was deprived of hunting rights for five years and the dead animals were confiscated. Economic gains of 50,000 NOK made from the crimes were confiscated. The Supreme Court verdict (Rt-1990–156 [40–90]) states that the offender had engaged in extensive activities of illegal hunting and capture of animals for more than four years, including a range of endangered bird species that had complete, legal protection. The offender had acted zealously and with considerable knowledge and for economic profit. He had previously been fined for breach of protection rules under the Wildlife Law. In this case, it also appears that the state (*Viltfondet*), the owner of all wildlife in Norway, did not confiscate the animals who, according to the offender, had been trafficked to Norway from abroad in large numbers. These were species not found in the Norwegian wild. The reason they were not confiscated was that they were foreign and consequently not property of *Viltfondet.* He had also trafficked a number of animals from other Nordic countries. This trafficking was not listed as one of the crimes for which the offender was found guilty. It was only mentioned in relation to the right the state had, or did not have, to confiscate the dead animals. This, despite the fact that Norway is a signatory to the CITES with ensuing obligations of law enforcement for breaches of the convention. Consequently, it should have been established whether these animals pertained to species that were endangered outside Norway. Much of the dispute in this case concerned whether the state had the right to confiscate the killed animals, since this was the basis of the appeal. The impression created by the verdict is that the man profited greatly from selling these endangered animals turning them into products, most likely as stuffed animals.

The third case from the Supreme Court from 1992 (Høyesterett–HR-1992-60-B – Rt-1992-559)[11] concerns breach of Wildlife Law §3 for capture of more than 160 protected birds between 1983 and 1990. Five of these were seasonally protected (geese and ducks); the rest were protected year round. These species included four that at the time were vulnerable: golden eagle, gyrfalcon, Eurasian eagle owl and black woodpecker (*Dryocopus martius*). The offender had caught 79 goshawks, who together with the majority of the other birds of prey were released at some point. The number of birds who died during capture, in captivity or when seized was therefore smaller than the total number of birds captured. The defendant was also convicted for breach of the Animal Welfare Act because he caught them in traps and for using live animals as bait. The police also found 83 protected birds in a freezer that were kept for a friend who was supposed to stuff them. It was unknown whether he sold live or dead birds; he must have bartered some birds for other services. The judges pointed out that it was mitigating circumstance that the majority of the birds were released. It was, however, regarded as a considerable harm to nature to have kept them captured because it interfered with reproduction and the feeding of offspring. In addition, considerable weight was placed on the fact that the offender also illegally killed six elk and a roebuck. Previously, he had killed 13 animals, but the statute of limitations had expired for some of those cases so they could not be tried in court. The offender was sentenced to six months in prison and he lost the right to capture and hunt animals for five years. Five traps, five rifles, ammunition and all the dead birds were confiscated by the state.

The number of individuals in the above cases, as well as in the Finnish case where birds and eggs were trafficked from Norway, indicates these acts are more characterised by professionalism, with several people involved, than just one offender committing wildlife crimes. Even though the offenders may have been passionate collectors, one must assume that they recognized the importance of limits (although the ivory case, discussed in Chapter 4, may contradict this). However, it is unlikely they as collectors wanted many birds of the same species for personal use, and consequently, they must be commercializing the others. This is confirmed by the Customs Directorate:

> We know that it is well organised and probably also *very* well organised, but we are not good enough at catching them as they cross the border. We suspect quite a few, and then we warn all the border controls about cars or vessels if necessary and about persons, and try to stop them. We also warn neighbouring countries, and Germany, for example. Germany is often mentioned [as an offenders' country]. And provided we have a liaison officer in Germany we also warn German authorities. But unfortunately, little of what we warn about is caught by inspection.

I asked whether they were particularly vigilant during breeding season, and the Customs officers confirmed this to be the case in northern Norway. The problem is there are large stretches of empty land:

> If you try to catch people like this by driving around, it is rather transparent, and they are clever. We assume they camouflage their actions in elaborate ways because they usually manage both to enter and leave. It was easier in the 90s when we would stop people in the bay with incubators. And those were not illegal to bring in, and made it easier to keep an eye on them right? But then they would leave by other means, probably driving through Sweden or Finland. So it is not easy and we have many crossing points, limited resources and often the control points are unmanned.

It is confirmed both by the Finnish case and from interview data that foreigners travel to Finnmark (Norway's most northeastern county) where they have established contacts who point out nests. They arrive with a GPS and are able to leave quickly, making them very difficult to catch. The Customs officers emphasized the need for intelligence work in cases, such as Germans leaving nesting boxes in Finnmark, to which they return the following year to empty them of eggs. One of the Customs Directorate interviewees confirmed that inspections of people leaving the country are lower than of people entering.

I now turn to a deeper exploration of the enforcement of the law in relation to endangered species from the perspective of control agencies themselves.

Notes

1 Lofoten, in northern Norway, has substantial fish stocks.
2 Referred to as *generaklausulen mot faunakriminalitet* (the general clause against fauna crime) (Istad 2008).
3 These crimes took place before the partly decriminalization of alien reptiles in Norway on August 15, 2017.
4 The animal rights organization NOAH annually organizes protests against fur farming in several Norwegian towns. In 2017, 9,000 persons protested outside the Parliament in Oslo.
5 A problem with both studies (Manrod et al. 2008; Leal and Powell 2012) is their lack of animal/research ethics. In the monitor lizard study, the researchers put live mice into tubes for the monitor lizards to catch, through a hinged door. The lizards would access the mice through rotating the tube and opening the door with their foreclaws or snout or by using gravity. The lizards then would insert their head, grab the mice and retire from the tube before swallowing the mice alive. While the authors state that being fed 'live prey' contributes to psychological well-being for the reptiles, little regard is paid to the mice who 'did not appear highly reactive to the presence of the monitors before capture, and any stress they experienced seemed far less than in most current mouse behavioural testing and phenotyping protocols' (Manrod et al. 2008: 269). It seems thus as if some stress must be accepted for 'lab mice' and that these experiments did not cause them more suffering than 'normal.' Little is said, however, about the highly unusual circumstances in which the mice were prey, compared to how they are prey in nature, and how this may have impacted their behaviour. In the other experiment with anole lizards (Leal and Powell 2012), the anoles used in the experiments were abducted from their habitats, meaning that the researchers had participated in wildlife trafficking. I am hesitant to credit these researchers for their work, as citing them may encourage this kind of research. However, because the animals are dead and the results clear concerning the establishment of the cognitive capacities of reptiles who suffer tremendously from the pet trade, I hope a greater good will come of my use of these studies, although I hope such experiments will be banned in the future.
6 Information from the Eco Crime Unit, Norway.
7 He said something else of interest which indicates that the abduction and killing of Norwegian free-born animals has been going on for a long time. The man was a taxidermist, and said that 30 years ago he received a visit from a man who was very interested in Norwegian polar foxes and birds. He carried a big box with maps, and the witness showed him on these maps where he could find the animals.
8 The fieldworkers of the Norwegian Environment Agency.
9 Høyesterett–Rt-1990–203 and Høyesterett–Rt-1990–156 (40–90). https://lovdata.no/pro/#document/HRSTR/avgjorelse/rt-1990-203-25a?searchResultContext=1004
10 https://lovdata.no/pro/#document/HRSTR/avgjorelse/rt-1990-156-27b?searchResultContext=1132
11 https://lovdata.no/pro/#document/HRSTR/avgjorelse/hr-1992-60-b?searchResultContext=1889

6 The enforcement of CITES in Norway from the perspective of CITES control agencies

According to the Norwegian Eco Crime Unit's overview of 87 cases involving keeping and smuggling of exotic species from 2000 to 2010, 28 were concluded with a fine and 31 were dismissed for various reasons, including because too much time had elapsed for the case to be prosecuted. These cases are unlikely to be all such cases in this time period, since they are inconsistently coded. The confiscation reports indicate nonetheless, that regardless of how cases are coded, a fine is the usual response to the smuggling of wildlife to Norway. The fines ranged from 2,000 to 20,000 NOK, although 9,000 was the average. The data indicate that there has been an increase in the level of fines imposed, which may demonstrate that law enforcement agencies are taking these crimes more seriously. Even when the crimes in question concern large number of animals of endangered species, however, prison sentences are short and usually suspended. Such lenient punishment does not reflect the potential of the law and the increased priority such crimes should merit. In order to see how these crimes are prioritized by Norwegian police and Customs, I now turn to my interview data.[1]

Enforcement, priorities and knowledge about CITES crimes

In a consultancy report about wildlife trafficking commissioned by the European Commission and carried out by the Ecologic Institute, it is stated that 'the crux of effectuating an EU enforcement strategy at a national level and making it work would be to ensure that mechanisms are in place (at a national level) for collaboration and coordination among the different agencies' (Sina et al. 2016: 32). The NGO International Fund for Animal Welfare (IFAW) found, for example, that in many EU Member States, cooperation mechanisms are lacking or not as effective as they could be (Interpol/IFAW 2013).While lack of cooperation between agencies across borders may be a problem, trade agreements and porous borders have also frustrated law enforcement effects (Maher and Sollund 2016a). This raises the question of how effective cooperation between relevant enforcement agencies is, primarily between police and Customs in Norway. A Customs officer at Oslo Airport who is also *the* CITES expert, described how Customs handled CITES when he started his job:

> No one had control over anything, everything was floating and no one knew what to do. Very, very few are negative about doing CITES control, but you don't know what, how to handle it, what to look after, etc., and so then one rather avoids that kind of control.

Regarding current priorities of CITES, he explained that Customs has more than 200 laws and regulations to enforce. As result, CITES is but one small portion of many Customs concerns. There are no dedicated positions to deal with CITES – the Customs officers are generalists like the judges are. In an interview with an Eco Crime Unit supervisor concerning the lack of consistent coding of CITES cases, and in response to my comment that it seemed the Animal Welfare Act was applied rather than the CITES regulation, the superior stated that he thought the main reason was that in the police districts, there is generally little knowledge about the regulation. 'Consequently they pick what is easiest, I think the answer is that simple . . . and they don't regard it [CITES] so seriously.' He elaborated on how this also affects the investigation of CITES cases:

> I think that these cases are not those taken most seriously in the police districts, because they have so many other cases and then these cases end up in the bottom of the pile, and they work their way through the cases and reach the CITES case, but again they will prioritise this and the CITES case ends up in the bottom again because it is a new field and difficult for them.

This corresponds with my impression after tracking the parrot cases through the judicial system. Regarding the African grey parrot case described in Chapter 3, the case was on the desk of three different prosecutors who all said that other cases had priority, and it was obvious they had little knowledge about CITES. At last one prosecutor was unaware of previous CITES verdicts for similar cases. In other words, state prosecutors are unaware of the seriousness of these crimes and of the director general of the Norwegian Prosecutor Authority's call to prioritize environmental crimes (Den Høyere påtalemyndighet. Riksadvokatens rundskriv 1/2013). When confronted with this issue, an interviewee in the Eco Crime Unit responded that the prosecutors handling it should do the groundwork and that the Eco Crime Unit was available to answer questions, but that few prosecutors contact them for inquiries. Another problem he identified was that in order to alleviate the backlog of the judicial system, fines are imposed rather than bringing the cases to court.[2]

Another Eco Crime interviewee stated that a lack of priority also means lenient punishment in general for environmental crimes, which in turn creates little deterrence. A way to remedy this problem would be to have specialist prosecutors in police districts. In this way, the hard work put down by a dedicated police investigator in charge of environmental crimes (as the one investigating the ivory/collector case) would not be counteracted by the following charge as produced by an unknowledgeable police lawyer (or a very lenient sentence). In the strategy document of the general state attorney, however, the requirements that each police district should have an environmental crime coordinator and an environmental crime lawyer could have a paradoxical effect, according to one interviewee from Eco Crime: 'For some police chiefs this could mean that as long as they fill this requirement they do not have to do anything else, and hence priorities will reflect that.' The implication being that the requirements will be formally met, yet in practice no more will be done and environmental crime will not be prioritized.

One environmental coordinator explained that the coordinator has four areas to deal with: work environment crimes, cultural heritage crime, pollution crimes and crimes against the natural environment. He said,

> The commercialization of exotic animals has many features in common with drugs trade and trade in cultural heritage objects. A lot comes from corrupt states with little control, goes via diverse stages in the form of organized crime before it ends up in Norway. But drugs cannot be compared with the other two when it comes to police efforts and priority.

Although he found that cultural heritage crimes and CITES cases have much in common, the field of his responsibility is too broad. Personal interest of the official, therefore, will likely affect priorities. Based on conversations I had with a few environmental coordinators, it is clear that such dedication is in place, but this interviewee complained that the priority of this field in a general sense is lacking in the police. According to him, despite considerable and increasing focus on the natural environment within central authorities, media and society generally, the police lag behind. While the Eco Crime Unit as a centre for competence represents advancement in terms of directions/instructions, etc., the problem is in the daily running of the various police districts. For example, because of scarce resources, the focus on environmental crime in each police district depends a lot on who is police chief and his/her view on environmental crime in relation to other police tasks. This interviewee's opinion was that today's generation of midlevel leaders do not regard environmental crime as being as important as traditional police work, although there are exceptions; for example, certain rural police chiefs with 'green interests' would, in his opinion, be more inclined to deal with environmental crime than leaders who know nothing about it:

> Another problem relates to targets of the police in that they to a large degree are given directions and are measured on easily measureable parameters. There is a way to go before environmental crime is regarded as a 'full member' of daily police work in practice.

In spite of directions concerning priorities from the director general of the Norwegian Prosecutor Authority, police's traditions for discretion may mean such priorities are not witnessed in practice. This is, for example, evident in the implementation of other police strategies, such as problem-oriented policing (Goldstein 1990), which has been documented as being met with resistance from police officers who want priorities to be set in line with what they consider real crime (Sollund 2007), a traditional offender and also usually a victim. A proper crime is, for example, a street robbery (Lynch and Stretesky 2014) or a drug crime with easily targetable offenders (Christie and Bruun 1985). The natural environment and its animals are not regarded as proper victims (Sollund 2012a), and the crimes committed against them, therefore, are not regarded as proper crimes.

A superficial examination of the roughly eight hundred police case files showed, however, that often the illegal keeping of reptiles in Norway was combined with other offences, mostly drugs and violent crimes. A general feature of these cases is that the exotic animal is a 'bycatch.' Often the police search a suspect's home for drugs or stolen items and find an illegal exotic reptile. The reptile is seized and killed, and usually police do not clarify whether the reptile is CITES listed. The crime of having imported or kept an exotic animal is subjugated to other 'traditional crimes' which are perceived as more serious and involving more 'real' police work (Sollund 2007).

When discussing the priority of CITES crimes with a group of Customs inspectors at Oslo Airport, I asked for their opinions on whether CITES crimes should be prioritized. Here, too, resources were the issue. Such priority would require the establishment of new positions and increasing the competence level of the officers. One officer said nothing would be better than CITES being a target field:

> But we cannot do everything, you cannot be Super Customs in drugs, steroids *and* CITES, you need to specialize. . . . Concerning drugs, there are targets for the number of controls, seizures, etc. Because that is where we are measured, right, so that is our challenge all the time, and it [the target for drugs] ties us up.

He was supported by an interviewee at the Customs Directorate:

> You get a bigger star on your hat if you seize drugs, and it is easier to show such seizures. For the management in Customs, seizures within this field [CITES] are also important, but it is harder to verify that a crime has been committed.

How this priority plays itself out in practice was described by an interviewee in the Norwegian Environment Agency: a truck of a firm dealing in aquariums was, after the Norwegian Environment Agency warned Customs about the truck, stopped at the border and searched by dogs. But since the dogs did not react to drugs, the truck was not stopped by Customs and allowed to pass freely 'with the car loaded with CITES merchandise. And that is rather typical.'

At the time of the interviews, the Customs unit at Oslo Airport had only one specialist in CITES, which meant other officers turned to him all the time, even though he was not, in terms of resources, allocated to work with CITES. He was motivated by his personal dedication. This also meant that the unit became vulnerable because they all depended on him for CITES expertise. One officer added, 'If you had designated positions for CITES, that would make the whole difference. We are lucky to have one specialist, but then the other offices in Norway don't.'

In an interview with the Eco Crime Unit, one of the lawyers stated that the priorities established by the general state attorney, such as environmental crime was in 2013, were very important. A way to ensure CITES cases get attention, according to the Eco Crime Unit, would be to establish targets for environmental crimes along with other targets. One of the interviewees elaborated:

> Those of us working within the field of environmental crimes, we would like to have targets in the area, because we know that would lead police chiefs and others in leadership to take this more seriously. Now they will not prioritise this in order to reach their targets in other areas.

As of present, when statistics for CITES cases are not in demand, let alone impossible to produce since they are not consistently coded, the area will become invisible and also fails to be prioritized by investigators, who, if they are not the designated coordinators of environmental crimes, may never have heard about CITES before. So, whether CITES cases are prioritized and how is connected to targets in the different agencies, to personal interest and not the least to qualifications. Also in Eco Crime, the interviewees said considerably more could have been done with a few more positions; for example, intelligence work connected to internet trade of wildlife. Eco Crime decide themselves which cases to prosecute, but since they also have to prioritize, perhaps cases which could have been prosecuted favourably by this high competence unit are rather omitted and left to unskilled[3] state prosecutors. So, both police and Customs inspectors need to increase their skills concerning CITES.

When asked whether the Customs officers would be able to distinguish a genuine CITES export certificate from a forged one, the Customs CITES expert answered,

> No. One of the big challenges with CITES is that there is not a common certificate for all CITES parties, they vary from state to state.

This makes Customs work in relation to CITES a huge challenge, not only in Norway. For example, when dealing with birds from South Africa, in addition to having to be able to distinguish a genuine from a forged CITES certificate, the Customs officers must also be able to see through attempts to 'launder' irregular CITES-listed individuals from individuals who can be legally trafficked, and forgery may not only be linked to the certificates themselves, but also in the dyeing of birds (painful for bird) in different colours to make them look like permitted species (Bargent 2016; Warchol et al. 2003).

The CITES expert in Customs agreed that the lack of resources allocated to CITES inspections was crucially hindering their work and was the reason why they did not make more seizures. According to him, there was an unwillingness to spend money on tools that could help; for example, *Green Parrot*, a database designed to make it easier to identify animals. Not only that, this tool would also in identifying forged permits and certificates.

When asked whether Customs officers would be able to distinguish a genuine CITES export certificate from a forged one, a Customs CITES expert answered, 'No. One of the big challenges with CITES is that there is not a common certificate for all CITES parties, they vary from state to state.'

He further explained how, when the program was demonstrated, one superior had said, 'this would be very beneficial, but let's wait a bit. Perhaps we can make Eco Crime finance it.' The veterinarian from the Food Safety Authority working at Oslo Airport said, in relation to possible forensic control of unidentified meat and other substances, that this problem relates both to will and resources:

> So, neither Customs nor we have funds to cover such expenses, but pardon me, it is typically Norwegian also; yes we shall do this and that and have that inspection, and then we pretend to do it, to inspect, but then we don't because we don't have those resources to do inspections as we should. And constantly we receive capsules, with all kinds of things, from animals, and we have tried to ask; 'Should we not run some analysis of this? Find out what they contain?' But then it is expensive, and so we don't have the money.

This indicates that both the Food Safety Authority and Customs lack the necessary resources to efficiently control CITES imports at the airport.

In summing up the interview, the Customs officers at Oslo Airport stated,

> Your questions are easy to answer; we don't know anything about this. But it is not because of a lack of will, but there must be a desire from the Customs agency and the Norwegian state that we should prioritise this, it should not depend on single individuals who are passionate about the topic, for generally, that will not help. You need a system that works. For example, like the targets we have for drugs, if there had been targets for CITES. . . . And we need thorough training. It cannot be like today.

One of the interviewees at the Customs Directorate acknowledged that the priority of drugs indeed prevents the Customs officers from seeing CITES cases: 'As long as they look for blue Valium they are blind for everything else.'

Concerning the seizures that are made compared to what actually comes into Norway, the CITES expert in Customs estimated that they seize 3%–5%, in a good year up to 10%, of actual contraband drugs; however, concerning CITES, he figured they were far from this at 1%.

On a busy day, CITES cases fail to be reported because they are not regarded as sufficiently important. The lack of priority these cases are given in the judicial system and the leniency with which they are punished contribute to this. It appeared in interviews it is easier to disregard such crimes because of this, although not when these crimes concern live animals, but stuffed animals and products. There is little reason to react to such cases and file reports for front-line inspectors if they are not followed up in the judicial system.

A recurring issue in the interviews was the lack of resources to carry out the inspections connected to CITES. But equally important was the misdistribution of resources, as it appears combating drug trade is highly prioritized by Customs, due to political will. This is likely connected to the prevailing enemy image relating to drugs and the ways in which illegal drugs (not prescribed drugs or alcohol) are regarded as the big evil of society, causing unnecessary deaths, suffering and increased crime levels (Christie and Bruun 1985). A consequence of regarding drugs as the big enemy is that interest, resources and priorities are moved from other areas of importance, such as the WLT. The Customs agents are rewarded for detecting drugs, they are trained to detect drugs and they have the resources and equipment to detect drugs, consequently they have more motivation to look for drugs and more drugs are seized.

Like Customs, police have targets and police chiefs are also measured according to penal cases and time used for procedures, according to the Eco Crime unit. One of the Eco Crime investigators described the painstaking work involved in solving environmental crime. You can work for a year without solving a single penal case, which makes resources hard to get. Priorities must therefore be identified on all levels: detecting the crime, investigating the crime and ensuring that the case receives proper treatment in the judicial system. This would also mean an altering of priorities by Customs inspectors who would need to develop discretion, not only relating to potential drug traffickers but also concerning wildlife traffickers. As an example of how control may be conducted on the border, one of the advisors in the Customs Directorate with long front-line experience explained that what they control is based on discretion, which again relies on previous experience as well as strategy. For example, Customs know that from a few countries in Europe, more amphetamine is smuggled to Norway than from other countries. So, if a vehicle arrives registered in any of those countries, it will be stopped, and if the driver seems nervous and what he claims to be the purpose of the trip does not seem very convincing and perhaps contradicting, then it will be a basis for a control, and things can be revealed. So Customs inspectors apply a 'radar' that has been developed over time in Customs control; calling it a 'routine control' when relating to the public, and more specifically to potential offenders (cf. Runhovde 2015). Acting on 'gut feeling' to perform a 'routine control' is well known also among the police (e.g., Sollund 2007; Chan 1996); it may also be developed to include CITES crimes and work well in tandem with deliberate strategies to prioritize these crimes. While discretion and 'gut feeling' may be hard to specify, it will be caused by a reaction to something being 'out of place' (Douglas 2003). While it is hard to give specific directions to Customs inspectors or police in this regard, and perhaps also not right since it may entail undue discrimination, it is a method both experienced Customs inspectors and front-line police officers rely on (Sollund 2007; Runhovde 2015).

One of the environmental crime coordinators summed up the situation concerning CITES in Norway this way:

> So, it is not sensational in any way to state that Norwegian authorities have very little control, knowledge and focus on this field. The few persons in Norway who are able to establish which species an animal belongs to are in offices far away from the control situations. Those who do the controls neither possess very impressive knowledge nor resources to uncover such crimes, establish species or handle them, for that sake. We have the Norwegian Environment Agency and the Food Safety Authority but things could be far better.

Generally then, CITES crimes are insufficiently prioritized. As the priorities for both police and Customs come from the political authorities, it may be that the general awareness concerning CITES crimes, reflected, for example, in the UN resolution from 2015 and the EU action plan against wildlife trafficking and awareness campaigns, has not reached Norway. In Norway, except for the formal strategy document prioritizing environmental crimes, the focus remains on traditional crimes. This despite special units and positions and the passionate dedication of some individuals who work within the field.

On cooperation and compartmentalized responsibility among control agencies

That responsibility concerning CITES is compartmentalized in Norway is a problem. On the one hand, the Norwegian Environment Agency is formally the owner of all seized wildlife/wildlife products, but the welfare of the animals is the responsibility of the veterinarians of the Food Safety Authority. This responsibility also covers trafficked animals who are apprehended at Customs. Cooperation between the Customs officers who detect and confiscate animals and the veterinarians who are called on to take care of them is also needed, but this is not always the case.

The Norwegian Environment Agency is to be consulted routinely if there is a risk that a seized animal is CITES listed according to the Customs Directorate. One of the interviewees from the Eco Crime Unit stated that, nonetheless, the veterinarians in the Food Safety Authority fail to report possible CITES cases to the Norwegian Environment Agency. The border veterinarian would like to cooperate more closely with the Norwegian Environment Agency, but the veterinarians are in touch with the Norwegian Environment Agency only on an ad hoc basis when an animal is seized. When asked about what should be done to improve the situation, the veterinarian responded that in addition to coordination among the Eco Crime Unit, Customs, the Norwegian Environment Agency, the veterinarians of the Food Safety Authority, and EU entities, more resources are needed.

A problem in allocating resources, as pointed to by this veterinarian, is the fact that the four entities that are involved in the control of wildlife trafficking into Norway are located in four different ministries: Customs answers to the Ministry of Finance, police is under the jurisdiction of the Ministry of Justice, the Food Safety Authority is part of the Ministry of Agriculture and Food and the Norwegian Environment Agency is part of the Ministry of Climate and Environment. In other words, not only the work but also the resources need to be coordinated. She also wanted project groups to be established for various issues being worked on because, as she said, in order to cooperate she would at least need to know the names of the persons in the other agencies working on the same issue, to know whom to contact. When I asked interviewees in the Eco Crime Unit whether there were clear lines of responsibility within the different agencies, the response was that because all of the entities have their own regulations, there are no clear lines:

> So, we are many, and there are complex regulations.
>
> *Q: Who is responsible for what?*
>
> This is also important to clarify, right? And Customs send cases to the police, but to whom and what shall they contain? The Food Safety Authority states that cases are reported to the police, but perhaps they will think that this is already done by the police, and then they don't.

In another interview with the Eco Crime Unit three years later, the problem of compartmentalized responsibility was discussed again, and a lawyer said that cooperation was discussed regularly in the meetings:

> We emphasize that it is important that each control agency has knowledge about who does what, to ensure the right persons are contacted, and also that each person must know what is her/his role. But each one has different concerns. And this, of course, is a challenge in these cases, that so many instances are relevant to contact and are part of the picture.

Attempts have been made to establish regular inter-sector cooperation, but despite good intentions, several of the interviewees said many initiatives had dissolved. One of the interviewees in the Eco Crime Unit described meetings with the other control agencies; however, it was hard to prioritize them on a busy day. The CITES expert in Customs said that the police in Romerike, which covers Oslo Airport, initiated a meeting to establish a forum which included Customs, police and the veterinarians in the Food Safety Authority, but only one meeting took place. At the time of the interview, he regarded the cooperation between Eco Crime, Customs and the Food Safety Authority as nonexistent.

An interviewee in the Customs Directorate said there was a forum for cooperation involving Customs and the Norwegian Environment Agency. 'So, we try to facilitate that the front-line officers can do the best job possible, at the border, so we are a coordinating point in the Directorate.' He further stated there is cooperation with the Eco Crime Unit; the occasion was Operation TRAM, instigated by Interpol, in order to deal with TCM.[4] Customs also arranged for an expert to come from the Netherlands to teach the Customs officers about the Chinese letters on TCM boxes so they would know what to look for. However, a recurring problem was who would pay for the overtime costs for the officers involved. When asked how formalized the cooperation was, he affirmed that the national group (the Food Safety Authority, Eco Crime and the Norwegian Environment Agency)[5] ideally should meet twice a year. However, at the time of the interview, some time had elapsed since the last meeting. The focus of the group was training, yet the interviewee also considered it key to have established a network and to be connected to an actual person with a telephone number whom he could contact. So in spite of good intentions, the attempts to establish regular cooperation involving all the stakeholders/control agencies has ran out of steam.

One example of an agency that does cooperate effectively with other agencies is the Oslo police Special Environmental and Finance Crime Unit. They regularly cooperate with the other control agencies, although on an ad hoc basis, concerning ongoing investigations. Customs also has an officer who can put police officers in contact with the right people and who can direct police to the relevant regulation immediately and make the work of the investigator much easier. In that way, when police interrogate suspects, they know what to focus on. It was said further that as a rule, the appropriate control agency should have the right to make a statement before prosecutorial charges are made in these cases.

The CITES expert at the Norwegian Environment Agency was the lead figure of the aforementioned cooperation forum and also a key person with CITES expertise. The advantage of having access to such expertise cannot be underestimated, but it also signals the vulnerability of the group, with so much expertise being concentrated in one person. This vulnerability was remedied somewhat by his training another CITES expert at the Norwegian Environment Agency. The Customs Directorate interviewee contrasted this person's availability to the ordinary 9–4 availability of public employees in Norway and credited this person's dedication to the issue. Likewise, the interviewees in Eco Crime claimed to be personally interested in and dedicated to environmental crimes, including CITES, finding these both important and legally challenging. One of the interviewees updated herself on the topic regularly and because of this, cases were handed over to her. A comment by a lawyer in Eco Crime confirms that environmental crime gets investigated largely due to officers with a special interest in it: 'My impression is that the field is very characterised by enthusiasts around in the different police districts.'

While cooperation seems insufficiently developed among the relevant entities, there is some regular cooperation between the Customs directorate and the Eco Crime unit of the police. Every Sunday the week's seizure reports are sent by fax to Eco Crime, according to interviewees in the directorate. The Customers at Oslo airport and other border control points must also consult with the

Norwegian Environment Agency concerning possible CITES listing of animals (and products). Customs themselves will report the crime to the police or alternatively impose a fine, and the Norwegian Environment Agency also reports such crimes to the police.

However, that the responsibility is spread among different agencies and thereby financed by several sources creates conflict. According to Customs, who will cover the costs related to housing seized animals is an area of tension. Disagreement about this has produced a sour relationship with the veterinary care at the airport, because they do not want to cover the costs. Although it is the responsibility of the owner of the animal to pay, if s/he does not, the Food Safety Authority must cover the cost.

The CITES expert interviewee in Customs at the airport provided a concrete example of the difficulties of inter-sector responsibility. A couple had contacted the district veterinary about bringing in an African grey parrot from Spain. They had been assured that everything was in order, but as the expert passed by the inspection, he saw the bird (who was then CITES II listed, now CITES I) and asked the Customs agent involved whether he had seen any CITES certificates, to which the agent responded that the import of the bird was okay because permission had been given by *Statens Dyrehelsetilsyn* (now the Food Safety Authority):

> So I ended up in a lengthy discussion with the veterinarian, and said that since this is a CITES species, it has nothing to do with a veterinarian. So, they had to give in. Since I withheld it, the border veterinarian had to take care of her, and it all took time. And eventually they produced a permit, but this was not acceptable, not being accompanied by an export permit from Gran Canarias. Because, surely s/he was smuggled from Gambia or somewhere else. So then my report was withdrawn and they got to keep him/her, but that was after 40 days during which there was 'war' more or less. And then the boss over there sent an instruction to the veterinarians that they should not accept animals from Customs.

It is clearly Customs' responsibility to control what comes into the country, but when live animals are involved this responsibility, in practice, falls on the border veterinarian. It appeared, from the interview with the border veterinarian at Oslo airport, that the line of responsibility may also be blurred when lives are at stake and due to confusion regarding the regulations concerning animal trafficking. For example, in the parrot case, the veterinarian was about to allow the import of the bird, and s/he would have been trafficked to the country without delay had not the Customs officer accidentally appeared. In this case, eventually, the traffickers succeeded in providing Customs with an export permit from Gran Canarias (Spain).

The veterinarian further elaborated on how a dubious import may go through, for example in the case of aquaria fish. According to her, when the aquaria salespeople import ornamental fish, they may be unaware whether the fish are listed by CITES. There will be many pages with packing lists, and the veterinarians have absolutely no chance to know about these species. So when they have some kind of certificate from veterinarian authorities, it will be taken at face value. When asked about the conditions of the fish in such cases, she said they would arrive in plastic bags; often half of them would be dead. A lot of such arrivals come in with direct flights from Bangkok. She added,

> But when corals arrive, this gives me a bad feeling, because there arrive quite a lot of corals, almost weekly, and they are often threatened.

The border veterinarian gave yet another example of how sector lines can be blurred, this time regarding trophies. The victims of trophy hunting are often CITES listed, and these dead victims usually come accompanied with CITES certificates. When the carcasses come accompanied with CITES papers and if the traffickers have the necessary veterinary papers, such controls will be a sort of clearance, valid also for Customs. If a trophy has been cleared by the Food Safety Authority, she suspected this clearance would be accepted by Customs without further inspection since they had cleared the first inspection. If in doubt about a CITES certificate, they would call Customs, but if the veterinarian suspected nothing, then most likely the CITES documents would not be subject to proper inspection and a CITES-listed animal would be allowed into the country. She reiterated that thousands of fish, coral, etc. arrive every week, as do trophies, and that the paperwork is usually accepted without further inquiries. Confronted with this information from the border veterinarian, the Customs CITES expert admitted this could happen, especially if an inexperienced Customs inspector was involved. Such cases would end up at the goods to declare zone, which is also where the inspectors begin their career, meaning that the least experienced inspectors would work where most skills are in demand.

One of the interviewees in the Customs Directorate also supported the veterinarian in her description of procedure and elaborated on how this took place in the case of an Amazon parrot at the Svinesund border crossing, which involved reoffenders who had been involved in parrot trafficking before. The case shows both that responsibility is blurred and that Customs does not always perform the inspection, which the Food Safety Authority sometimes does, and also that CITES invites forgery of documents and facilitates illegal trafficking through its regulatory permit system. That verification of CITES permits is a problem and that invalid documents accompany animals is confirmed also in relation to export from the EU to Norway. For example, people bring copies, rather than originals. If Customs inspectors are confronted with such documents, and the Food Safety Authority says this animal may be imported, interviewees said that Customs can 'easily push the button and say okay,' which was what happened in the above case. The procedures when an animal arrives is that s/he should arrive with an original document stamped and approved and forwarded to the Norwegian Environment Agency. However, people increasingly want to keep the certificate – 'like a diploma on the wall' – and then they only have a copy. What

Customs is supposed to do is to confiscate the animal and retain the original documentation; otherwise, it can be used to bring in another animal. Still inspectors allow such incidents.

The CITES/Norwegian Environment Agency interviewee was also critical of the Food Safety Authority. He regarded that there is a lack of competence concerning rules. Further, he stated that while Customs and the Norwegian Environment Agency report offences to the police, the Food Safety Authority generally fails to do so:

> We have experienced that the Food Safety Authority can make mistakes. You can do almost anything with animals in Norway without them reacting. So, we see they make mistakes because they are not coordinated with us. They can go to action and take animals, and things are fine with them, but not with us. So it is a challenge we have pointed out, and we need to increase the sharing of information in that regard also.

An advisor in the Customs Directorate gave an example of how a breach of the CITES can fail to be registered if it is also a breach of other regulations. A Chinese doctor was 'curing' his patients by means of TAM that included endangered species, when several became seriously ill. He was charged with breaching regulation about medicines, but not CITES. In this way, various regulations served to conceal CITES, which would only be a 'by catch,' and in the report system of Customs only the main find would be reported.

Another frequent, already mentioned example is when CITES animals are concealed under the regulation prohibiting the importation of 'exotic species' under the Animal Welfare Act, and consequently whether the animals are CITES may be ignored in the paperwork by the police.

The same interviewee explained that they would appreciate increased effort by Customs in inspecting for CITES, but respect for professional boundaries prevents them from interfering with Customs because they want to maintain a good climate for cooperation. At the same time, they must respect the limits for their work. Although acknowledging deficiencies in control practices, they 'secretly' hope for improvements; however, it is up to Customs to do border inspections. Concerning the police, the Norwegian Environment Agency must provide them with tools for their work, so this is what was done with the revision of the CITES regulation.[6] For example, he said, this would make it easier for the police to document illegal possession of a cheetah pelt, which it is easy to get away with now.

To sum up what data indicate in Norway so far: The interviews show that cooperation between Customs and the Food Safety Authority at Oslo Airport is not satisfactory, and that cooperation between different agencies is not sufficiently formalized. To know whom to contact would be the minimum requisite to facilitate cooperation. The fight over scarce resources concerning the care for seized animals is also a problem, consequently sufficient money must be allocated to this end if Norway is to live up to its responsibility. It is stated in CITES, annex 1, concerning guidelines for the 'disposal of confiscated live animals,'

> When live animals are confiscated by government authorities, these authorities have a responsibility to dispose of them appropriately. Within the confines of the law, the ultimate decision on disposal of confiscated animals must achieve three goals: 1) to maximize conservation value of the specimens without in any way endangering the health, behavioural repertoire, or conservation status of wild or captive populations of the species; 2) to discourage further illegal or irregular trade in the species; and 3) to provide a humane solution, whether this involves maintaining the animals in captivity, returning them to the wild, or employing euthanasia to destroy them.[7]

In Norway, as shown previously, little effort is expended to save animals, and the last 'solution' is the regular solution.

It is also evident that much of the work concerning CITES in Norway depends on the dedication of a few individuals in different agencies. These persons do an extremely valuable job, but at the same time their hard work indicates that the inspections as a whole suffer tremendously when they find other employment. Despite there being some voluntary postgraduate courses available at the Police University College, some training offered by the Norwegian Environment Agency, brief training courses in Customs and Eco Crime's yearly environmental crime seminars for environmental crime police coordinators and prosecutors, there is a general lack of competence and awareness about the seriousness of CITES crimes. This is seen by the constant postponing of cases in the judicial system, evinced in the different verdicts, by the lack of knowledge on part of judges and Customs officers, and the dysfunctional cooperative efforts between the various agencies. One of the interviewees from the Eco Crime Unit summed up what should be done in the field:

> Several things could be done. You could improve the cooperation between the police and Customs, and with other organisations in Norway, you could do more intelligence work, more investigations into this, and of course, cases should be followed up and the speed in which they move through the judicial system increased. Finally, you can work to increase the level of punishment and thereby increase general deterrence.

In the next section, I will address a topic that could make Customs increase priority of CITES cases. In brief, money speaks. In contrast are the different individuals in Customs, the Eco Crime Unit and the Norwegian Environment Agency who, because they are personally dedicated, make specific efforts both in terms of training colleagues and to ensure CITES is respected.

When economic value increases priority

An exception to the lack of cooperation was when the CITES expert in Customs was contacted by the Eco Crime Unit because they wanted to move forward on

Russian caviar. The argument was that the price of caviar was greater than cannabis and, as the interviewee said, 'everything is measured in economic terms.' Caviar is an example of the large gains which can be made in the IWT and hence why it is attractive to many people who want to profit from the popularity this luxury item has achieved (van Uhm 2016b). But this also makes it more appealing to counteract by control agencies. The Customs officer further illustrated the importance of the economic value of the illegal wildlife trade, elaborating on how this effort is one that is welcomed by his superior in the Ministry of Finance:

> That these are goods with high economic value, all of a sudden makes it interesting. That x number of endangered animals are killed, that is not so important. But as the *product* actually has a high value, that one has not paid VAT even [laughs], then one must take action.

He also called for harsh sentences for rhino horn traders, arguing that the level of punishment should be determined in relation to the economic value of the crime. However, he also himself found frustrating that drugs overshadowed other illegal goods, whether or not CITES related. He elaborated on the demands from above, in relation to a seizure made of unidentified meat from Thailand, that he thought this was a big case, as a seizure is a seizure, but what counted for his superiors and was later reported was not the meat, but some Valium tablets, as for drugs what count is the monetary value, something he himself found disappointing:

> The demand from the Ministry of Finance is that we shall get money, right. But we are pressured on resources, and also on manpower, and we must get such and such amounts of money for the state. Everything is measured in results. And to perform such controls don't get us money. [So, then you omit the controls?] Sometimes, or we accept the things as they are, without doing the control we should have done.

One of the interviewees in the Eco Crime Unit emphasized the economic value of the trade in endangered species, and admitted they often perceived such crimes as unimportant, since 'it is just an animal, and it is just an egg.' However, he emphasized also the economic value of the animal and egg. For example, in the Finnish case described above, the economic value amounted to 50,000 NOK (€5200) for an egg. Such economic value could then, in his opinion, be used to argue for increasing the priority of IWT. At the same time, he regretted that economics drew attention to the issue, rather than the loss of biodiversity.

As shown previously, the great economic gains of wildlife trafficking, especially ivory and rhino horns, has contributed to growing awareness of the problem, particularly in the past decade. Part of the awareness is connected to the fact that these economic gains attract organized crime and rebel groups (Elliot 2012; Schneider 2012; Sina et al. 2016; Sollund and Maher 2015; Wyatt 2013; van Uhm 2016a). While the rhetoric surrounding wildlife trafficking as organized crime serves to create awareness among national and international bodies, in reality, in many contexts it represents an erroneous picture of the trade and encourages the wrong strategy to combat it (Duffy 2014). Regretfully, from an animal rights and species justice perspective, the organized crime rhetoric in tandem with economics rhetoric is more successful in achieving an increased focus and garnering economic resources to combat the trade internationally than the fact that wildlife trafficking drives species to extinction and causes tremendous suffering and harm at individual and ecosystem levels.

As shown through my examination of Norwegian penal cases, the intrinsic value of the victims of trafficking is rarely the topic in the verdicts. Rather, it is the criminalization of the trade (when it is criminalized). The overall treatment these cases receive in Norway also shows that the IWT is not regarded as a serious offence. It is sad, then, that while the offenders are consistently treated leniently, the animal victims are killed. The idea of emphasizing the economic value of the animals and of the trade as an argument for why fighting the trade should be prioritized is to give into a capitalist logic in which animals are resources for humans (Vetlesen 2015), even though it is possible that within capitalist societies, this argument may actually serve to protect animals through an increased prioritization. The efforts in place to combat wildlife trafficking is apparent, for example, through international cooperative efforts like the \$1.3 billion that was committed by 24 international donors between 2010 and June 2016, funding 1,105 projects in 60 different countries and various regional and global projects (The World Bank 2016). The top five donors were the Global Environment Facility (GEF), Germany, the United States, the European Commission and the World Bank Group, who together contributed \$1.1 billion of the total funding (86%). There are also many regional and global networks like the International Consortium on Combatting Wildlife Crime (ICCWC), with Interpol being an important actor. (For details concerning international collaboration, both at the NGO, GO, regional and global levels, see Fajardo del Castillo 2016; Sollund and Maher 2015; Wyatt 2013: Chapter 7).

Freight companies: a serious challenge

Wildlife products and animals are taken across borders by car or ferry or they are transported by freight companies. These constitute the largest challenge in detecting illegal wildlife trafficking and represent a problem, according to my interview with Norwegian Environment Agency and Customs staff. The CITES Customs officer at Oslo Airport emphasized the great numbers that cross borders as freight and how easy goods can pass uninspected. For example, the forwarder of a freight company will quickly realize what passes automatically in the computer system – 90% of what is declared is passed through the system automatically – and what ends up being inspected by Customs. This makes it appealing to incorrectly declare what kind of goods are passing through, especially if the customer is waiting and the freight company is under pressure to save time and make money. So, whether accidently or deliberately, goods pass through illegally. CITES permits, however, are regarded as a restriction (in the case of a permit, Customs is obliged to check) and alert Customs to check whether requirements are fulfilled. Still, as the Customs officer said, there Customs 'fail hugely.'

He added, concerning a seizure of a container that arrived from Africa full of stuffed animals, including lions, that he had thought at the moment that this would be a big case, as it was not accompanied by the right paperwork. However, eventually, the CITES permits were produced. He added, 'So all of the sudden, it arrives in such quantities right, and it is the same with traditional Chinese medicine, if you sell at large scale, it arrives in containers.' While accidently at times large seizures may be made, usually Customs make only minor seizures while the large shipments pass undetected. This is confirmed by an advisor in the Customs Directorate who sums up the CITES seizures as being an under-prioritized area and that most seizures are done of single offenders crossing borders:

> Of course, this makes one speculate that those [individuals] who try to bring something home are the easiest to catch. And those who profit from this kind of trade, perhaps using other means and smuggling routes, are the hardest to catch.

As confirmed in van Uhm's (2016b) analysis of EU TWIX data, freight companies play a large role in the IWT, especially when it comes to corals and reptiles. His study also revealed that containers are shipped with TCM from Hong Kong, which is the main hub, to ports in Europe. That many illicit goods, including CITES-listed animals, are trafficked through European ports is also confirmed by Europol (2013).

Another problem is the continuous arrival of lorries crossing the Norwegian-Swedish border at Svinesund, where according to this interviewee, 1.2 lorries arrive per minute. Although in theory everything is subject to inspection, in reality, Customs performs a risk analysis. When a load of aquaria CITES-listed fish arrived from Netherlands, the Customs inspector alerted the border control, after he himself had been warned by the Norwegian Environment Agency. Unfortunately, the system was down that day and Customs at Svinesund erroneously assumed it concerned drugs and, as mentioned, the sniffer dog, being trained to detect drugs, found nothing.

When containers arrive at Oslo harbour, they are only randomly inspected, said an interviewee in the Customs Directorate. However, starting in 2012, scanners have been used for entire containers. According to the Port of Oslo (2012), in 2011, 110,000 containers arrived at Oslo harbour. Between January and June 2012, 3,600 seizures were made from 48,000 scanned objects. These include 2.1 tons hash, 350 kilos amphetamines, 40 kilos cocaine, 13 kilos heroin, 34,000 litres liquor, 58,000 litres beer, 2.9 million cigarettes and 3.1 million NOK in cash.

The listing clearly indicates the intention behind the scanners is to look for illegal alcohol and drugs, and as the Customs interviewee said, one must know what to look for. Sniffer dogs are trained to sniff for drugs and cash, not animals or plants, and here one must also assume that Customs will find what they are looking for and that CITES 'goods' will easily be overlooked. That the freight companies constitute a large threat is also confirmed by the interviewee from CITES/Norwegian Environment Agency, who said they had warned Customs that this is the largest loophole concerning import of CITES goods/products. He said they can document that over time, customers receive goods and then re-export it commercially, a sign of laundering, but that there is no trace of paperwork. 'Everything is gone, if it ever existed.' For example, if a truck arrives at the Svinesund border from Sweden, the driver has his papers stamped concerning the kind of goods he is declaring. The goods codes will then be itemized by the freight agent online. This makes it easy to enter the wrong code to avoid tax or inadvertently make an error. If a tourist arrives at Oslo Airport, they might have their luggage checked, but the risk of being inspected when taking a trailer across the border is minimal. When asked about what kind of goods they transport, the officer said plants and corals, and that zoo shops buy most of what they sell from Sweden, suggesting that illegal CITES contraband can be laundered through legal enterprises.

Concerning trophy hunting, the extent to which trophies are brought into Norway is unknown. This is confirmed by my interview with a veterinarian from the Food Safety Authority:

> What I think is a loophole is what happens at cargo, what comes in from South Africa, these prepared pelts, the trophies. Because I think it is very easy to get things like that into the country.

Q: So, they arrive in containers?

Yes, the South Africans have no order, the boxes are nailed so we need a full set of tools to get them open, it is a nightmare so we don't do that each time, but we are obliged to open between 10% and 20% physically. And what they do in Customs I don't know, if they trust they (the goods) are correctly declared and don't check, I don't know.

The Customs officer explained that in order to improve inspection, the Norwegian Environment Agency has offered to be present when Customs inspect trailers,

> because when they open them it causes a lot of screaming and shouting because of plants and animals, right? But we can do it and we have offered to. They have never invited us though, because we are not Customs, and I suppose they don't want to have amateurs around them. But at the occasions we have been with them, we have found a lot, so it is unlikely that this is accidental. So, I am a bit surprised, that . . . we have Norwegian Customs yes, but I must say that we have adapted a lot to the free flow of the market. Because the risk of being inspected is minuscule, also for individuals travelling.

Again it was suggested that compartmentalization of responsibility and lack of proper cooperation facilitates trafficking. Although freight companies and lorries crossing the border constitute a threat in terms of the potential they have to conceal illegal CITES products (and animals), little effort is made to enhance the inspection of such means of transport.

While wildlife trade is a profitable crime causing considerable harm, people also profit from it in other ways, taking advantage of potential consumers. The interviewees from the Food Safety Authority, Customs and the CITES/Norwegian Environment Agency have come across cases showing that swindlers use the pet trade in endangered species on the internet to scam people. The CITES/Norwegian Environment Agency interviewee gave the example of a Nigeria scam: '"You can have a parrot for free, just send 1,500 dollars and I can bail out the parrot who was stopped in Customs in Cameroon" or "meet me at Stortorget and you can get a monkey, all you have to pay is the veterinary certificate."' Such scams are frequent. The positive side is that no animal is hurt in the process. It shows, however, that there is a huge degree of willingness to pay to acquire an endangered animal and also that many are unaware of the rules that govern this trade. The pet trade provides ample possibility for creating parallel legal and illegal markets, a topic explored in the following.

Legal versus illegal trade, parallel legal and illegal markets and ways of offending – Norway

The verdict from 1998, concerning 99 cases in total, indicate that the legality of breeding and selling parrots in Norway makes it tempting to import parrots and sell them as locally bred. This is a phenomenon witnessed on a large scale in the Solomon Islands from where more than 68,000 wild-caught and reportedly captive-bred CITES-listed individuals were exported in the 2000s, mostly imported to Malaysia and Singapore. They were then often re-exported, particularly in the case of Singapore. This took place despite the fact that no breeding facilities were found by TRAFFIC on the Solomon Islands. This led TRAFFIC to the conclusion that

> given the official confirmation of a lack of suitable bird breeding facilities in the Solomon Islands, these data lead to the inescapable conclusion that large numbers of wild-caught birds have been laundered into the global wildlife trade through being declared as captive-bred.
>
> (Shepherd et al. 2012: VII)

In this way, offenders can use their legal (or claimed legal) business to disguise wildlife trafficking. An example mentioned in the interview with the border veterinarian was a reptile salesman in Sweden (where the sale of exotic reptiles is legal in contrast to what was the case in Norway up to August 15, 2017) who takes over reptiles:

> And how serious he is, I don't know, but I think it is better than to euthanize them. So, he will come and pick these up, and he sells reptiles in Sweden. We

> have received a sort of permission to do this, but I don't think myself that it is quite all right.

The consequence of this is that in spite of the animals being seized in Norway, they continue being trafficked but are now laundered through the Norwegian control system and sold to customers in Sweden, which may also well be Norwegians travelling to Sweden to purchase a legal reptile there (see below, Sollund 2013a).

Zoos also pose a problem. When animals are confiscated at the airport, sometimes a zoo will take them in, but confiscation happens so frequently that zoos have become saturated with certain species. The border veterinarian described the Kristiansand Zoo's enthusiasm for chameleons but its unwillingness to take Greek land tortoises.

As in the case in laundering reptiles, this re-homing of chameleons and other animals of threatened species is problematic because zoos indirectly profit from the IWT, and consequently, a legitimate but critique-worthy business sustains itself partly on such crime, and the animal must endure a life in captivity.

The interviewee from the Norwegian Environment Authority, implicating zoos in wildlife trafficking, explained that the system of re-homing seized animals to zoos has been abused by traffickers:

> There are examples of persons in Norway, within the zoo industry, who are friends, and they agree that one asks the Food Safety Authority whether s/he can take over the animals that were seized.

He said this had been going on for years and was only discovered by coincidence. However, from the animal's perspective, this way at least they are able to continue their lives, although far from the lives they should have had.

The same interviewee from the CITES/Norwegian Environment Agency said, in relation to offenders who traffic animals for the zoo trade, that while there are serious traders who do everything according 'to the book,' there are also ways of undermining the legal trade. There have been a few cases in the past years in which the offenders provide order lists, and when they have received sufficient orders, they rent a truck and go on tour in Europe to fill their orders. Upon return to Norway, they contact customers and say, 'today I am in Elverum, today I am in Kongsvinger,' etc. Their customers meet up with them to pick up the animals they ordered. This is also a modus operandi in parrot trafficking:

> There were two firms last year and the year before, with the same modus. They produce lists, saying they can provide all kinds of birds, 'just order and we will fix it'. And as we are aware of this, we send them a letter or warn them that they must comply with CITES. But that does not really interest them, probably because they want to evade taxes, it costs money to get a CITES permission in other countries. And then they don't stop to declare CITES, to say 'Here I am and I have a car loaded with birds worth a

> 100,000'. That saves them money. And then again they undermine the legal businesses by selling birds for half price.

In Norway, it is easy to identify examples of persons who breed and sell parrots who also use the internet (especially Finn.no) to sell birds. As there are no requirements that parrots must be ID-chipped,[8] it is likely that wild-caught parrots are distributed over the internet. For example, a random search for *papegøye* (parrot) on Finn.no on January 7, 2016, yielded 25 hits, including three macaws, several Amazon parrots and an African grey parrot, which is a species that is heavily trafficked from DR Congo and Uganda, where they are nearly extinct.

Based on the interviews with staff of inspection agencies in Norway, there seems to be only a limited effort in monitoring the internet for IWT. In my interview with the Oslo police district's special unit of environmental and financial crime, it became clear that they do not investigate the internet for trade in wildlife, as they regard this to be the responsibility of the Norwegian Environment Agency. The CITES/Norwegian Environment Agency interviewee said that although they are aware of the problem, their surveillance of the internet is minimal. If they see firms advertising, they inform the Eco Crime Unit at once or alert the Food Safety Authority so they can do an inspection. But generally they rely on information from the public and the zoo industry to inform them.

A reason why it is difficult to address the internet trade is that servers are often operated from abroad, making it hard for the police to do anything about it. The CITES/Norwegian Environment Agency interviewee also stated that when it came to internet surveillance, criminals are far more advanced technologically. However, if they see an advertisement, such as

> 'I have received a load of ten amazon parrots that I will sell for 5,000 a piece,' then we can ask the Food Safety Authority and Customs to act and check. And we have often succeeded that way, for example, last winter, we seized a turtle shell. So we do pay some attention, but I cannot claim we are very active in that regard.

Interviewees from the Oslo police district's special unit of environmental and financial crime said that only if they received a tip about a concrete case in their police district would they start investigations. This includes internet cases. The police, like they traditionally do, work reactively, rather than proactively, even though emphasis on analytical preventative policing (Goldstein 1990) has been a strategy within the Norwegian police force since 2003 (Sollund 2007: 45–46). Such a turn in policing is easier to implement in street policing (albeit it has met with problems also in this area [Sollund 2007]) than in investigations and prevention of environmental crimes, especially wildlife trafficking. That professional discretion within police and Customs allows them the liberty to choose *not to* control and investigate, rather than to *choose to prioritize*, is documented in the Norwegian context also in a study by Runhovde (2015, 2016).

Notes

1 Interviews were conducted between 2010 and 2015, most of them took place in 2013. References to the current situation concerns the situation at the time the interviews took place.

2 Both police and customs in Norway have the authority to impose fines as an administrative sanction.

3 As a way to offer police officers competence in environmental crime, it is possible to take a postgraduate course and specialize in environmental crime as a continuation of the education program at the Norwegian Police University College. The course is directed at police officers and employees of the state prosecutor with several years of experience who are intended to work with environmental crime, coming from different parts of Norway, and the course is open also to cooperating control agencies. It is only a one-day course and concerns legislation, experience from cases and national and international cooperation. They have CITES and investigation of CITES crimes in the course: Combatting environmental crime (Module 2 of nature and pollution crimes). This according to personal communication with Henny Irene Bech, Police Superintendent, Head of the Environment and Fisheries Crime Studies at Norwegian Police University College, Post Graduate Studies/Investigation.

4 INTERPOL co-ordinated operation targets illegal trade in wildlife medical products. www.interpol.int/News-and-media/News/2010/PR014

5 He also mentioned that someone involved in fisheries is involved, but without specifying whom.

6 Referring to the revision of the CITES regulation in 2013.

7 Disposal of illegally traded and confiscated specimens. https://www.cites.org/eng/imp/Disposal_of_confiscated_specimen

8 The Norwegian CITES regulation was revised twice during this research, in 2013 and on January 1, 2017. According to §7, the Norwegian Environment Agency can permit import or export of specimens included in the CITES regulation if the owner can prove that the animal was born in captivity or is pre-Convention. Counter to what was suggested, there is no demand that CITES-listed animals/products must be chipped, but in practice in order for breeders to sell their parrots, they are now required to document they were actually bred by them, rather than having been trafficked.

7 The keeping of exotic reptiles in Norway

While importing and owning exotic reptiles with very few exceptions were prohibited in Norway through the regulation concerning exotic reptiles under the 1976 Animal Welfare Law, in 2017 owning reptiles was decriminalized through a decision made by the Food Safety Authority. As of August 15, 2017, 19 reptile species can be kept as pets, and thus are made exempt from the prohibition of §2 of the regulation against the import and keeping of exotic reptiles.[1] Norway had, together with Iceland, been the only country in Europe that generally prohibited importing and keeping exotic reptiles, and this change has resulted in challenges for Customs (see Sollund 2013a), and in the future it may also impact trafficking in endangered reptile species.

Fifteen of the 19 species are either CITES listed or listed as vulnerable on the IUCN list. These also involve species that are already heavily trafficked.

The Food Safety Authority argued that these reptiles and amphibians could be kept in private homes without greater animal welfare risk than other permitted species, and that they considered this the best way to address the challenge of the many illegally kept reptiles in Norway (estimated to be more than 100,000 [Sollund 2013a; Sunde 2010]). They claimed this would make it easier to ensure reptiles receive veterinary care, safeguard infection hygiene and prevent the harms inflicted on animals through illegal trafficking. The Food Safety Authority further claimed to have considered that reptiles include species with different demands to their environments. In order to be suited as companion animals, the species in question must be adapted to a diet and an environment that can be re-created in a private home. The species must also accept necessary handling without being stressed. Other criteria are that the species must not be particularly aggressive, poisonous or in other ways dangerous to people. Species that can establish themselves in the Norwegian wild that violate the CITES rules are not allowed. Neither are wild-caught individuals.[2]

However, nothing that is said in the Food Safety Authority's statement clarifies or addresses how trade in wild-caught individuals can be avoided when the above reptile species are allowed to be traded in Norway, nor does it address the challenges of police and Customs in enforcing the ban that still affects species other than those listed. Because so many of these species are CITES listed, this means further challenges for Customs in terms of assessing the validity of the documents, a problem which is already acknowledged by Customs in Norway

Table 7.1a Snakes permitted as pets

Name	*Norwegian name*	*Species*	*Status*
Green tree python	grønn trepyton	*Morelia viridis*	CITES II
Garden boa	hagetreboa	*Corallus hortulanus*	IUCN listed
Boa constrictor	kongeboa		CITES II
Ball python	kongepyton	*Python regius*	CITES II
King snake	kongesnok	*Lampropeltis getula*	IUCN red list
Corn snake	kornsnok	*Pantherophis guttatus*	IUCN red list
Milk snake	melkesnok	*Lampropeltis triangulum*	
Rainbow boa	regnbueboa	*Epicrates cenchria*	CITES II
Carpet python	teppepyton	*Morelia spilota*	CITES II

Table 7.1b Lizards permitted as pets

Name	*Norwegian name*	*Species*	*Status*
Spiny-tailed monitor	dvergvaran	*Varanus acanthurus*	CITES II
Crested gecko	kranset gekko	*Correlophus ciliatus, Rhacodactylus ciliatus*	IUCN red list
Leopard gecko	leopardgekko	*Eublepharis macularius*	
Ocelleated lizard	perlefirfisle	*Lacerta lepida*	IUCN red list
Eye-dabbed lizard	pigghaleagam	*Uromastyx ocellata*	CITES II
Central bearded dragon	skjeggagam	*Pogona vitticeps*	
Giant Madagascar day gecko	stor daggekko	*Phelsuma madagascariensis*	CITES II

Table 7.1c Tortoises permitted as pets

Name	*Norwegian name*	*Species*	*Status*
Greek land tortoise	gresk landskilpadde	*Testudo hermanni*	CITES II
Chinese prepond turtle	kinesisk trekjølskilpadde	*Chinemys reevesi*	
Red-footed tortoise	rødfotet skogskilpadde	*Chelonoidis carbonarius*, previously *Geochelone carbonaria*	CITES II

(see above and Sollund 2013a) and elsewhere (Warchol 2004). When confronted with the issue of possible legalization of exotic reptiles in Norway, the Customs inspectors I interviewed perceived this as highly problematic, meaning it would cause numerous difficulties: (1) Customs officers would find it difficult to know which species were legal and which were not, (2) Customs officers would be afraid of handling reptiles, risking the possibility that reptiles would pass through control without a thorough inspection, (3) the Customs official would take the claims about the legality of species and individuals at face value, (4) Customs officers already find it hard to assess the authenticity of CITES certificates and, most importantly, (5) it is much easier to enforce a ban than a partial legalization.

These statements reveal the difficulties of parallel legal and illegal markets. For example, it is potentially a big problem concerning species that are bred (CITES listed that can be traded legally with the necessary permits) and species that are wild caught and thus cannot be traded at all (as per the 2017 Food Safety Authority regulations), but which can be traded according to CITES provided the necessary permits exist. This is made even more complicated because species that are illegal to trade may look like species that are permitted. In relation to the global reptile trade, a study focusing on the role of European markets established that laundering crimes such as selling a reptile pretending it is locally bred while in reality it is wild caught, are widespread, and this is a strong argument for why CITES fails in protecting endangered species (Auliya et al. 2016). The problems of fraud and corruption come in addition to this (see Warchol 2004; Warchol et al. 2003). Another problem revealed by Auliya et al. (2016) is that there is widespread trade in endemic reptile species which are never CITES listed; consequently, trade in these species is neither regulated nor banned and trade may proceed until extinction. As stated by the authors of this study,

> More than 90% of the world's reptiles are not regulated by CITES and EWTR [European Union Wildlife Trade Regulations]. This implies that non-CITES species, nationally threatened or newly discovered taxa (that commonly represent endemic taxa of charismatic species groups that have triggered international demand) are not protected from over-exploitation. (113)

Yet another problem reported is that listing a species as CITES drives up demand because collectors want to own an individual of a species nearing extinction.

In view of the logic of CITES which allows trade in species until they become endangered, whereupon trade is generally banned – and considering that many of the species now permitted in Norway are already CITES II or IUCN listed due to trade – (see Sollund and Maher 2015; Maher and Sollund 2016a; Wyatt 2016), it is likely that permitting trade of species that are CITES II listed and IUCN listed will threaten them further.

The Food Safety Authority legalization of trade in foreign reptile species sends a message of normativity that keeping reptiles in terraria in private homes for the pleasure of the owner is acceptable, even though these are species that have not been domesticated and thus adapted to humans and their environments, like dogs and cats (see Serpell 1996). What is in this for the animals involved? Is it to their benefit that keeping them in captivity should be further expanded? This will be explored in my discussion of the interviews with reptile keepers, where I ask them about their experiences of keeping such animals in Norway, why they have them and what it means for them to be committing an offence through their keeping of reptiles, since interviews were done prior to the legalization.

Reptile keepers' motives for keeping their reptiles

In my interviews with reptile keepers ($N = 5$),[3] we talked about their experiences with reptiles, their views of and relationships with them, how and why they acquired their first reptile, and how the ban on exotic reptiles affected their daily lives. A general impression after talking with these persons is that they are responsible reptile keepers who make great efforts to provide their animals with good conditions, not the least concerning their living environment (advanced temperature and humidity systems in their terrariums), and with veterinary care, appropriate food, etc.

That said, as mentioned, through this research I have also accessed 810 penal case files that concern the illegal possession of reptiles or trafficking of animals, usually reptiles. The general impression from these files is that these offences concern people who do not have the same kind of responsibility towards their animals, as is reflected in my interviews. For example, the typical penal case file of this category concerns a male offender whom the police visit because of other crimes, often drug crimes. A boa or two might then be found in a terrarium (or aquarium) in the kitchen of their home. While I have not done a thorough examination of these cases in this book, suffice it to say that the interviews with the reptile keepers may not be representative of reptile keepers in Norway. On the other hand, the stigma often associated with reptile keepers in Norway – a tattooed muscle man involved with drugs who keeps a snake for status – may be far from representative of ordinary reptile keepers who are, judging by the tales of the interviewees and except for their reptile keeping, law-abiding, ordinary citizens who happen to like reptiles rather than cats and dogs (Sollund 2013a). It is likely that precisely because many reptile keepers are often involved in other crimes that they, rather than other reptile keepers who otherwise are law-abiding citizens, are reviled as the typical reptile keeper. My informants serve to nuance a picture of reptile keepers in Norway, and their narratives provide the basis for a rich qualitative analysis of reasons why people acquire these animals.

To explore these issues, I will start by presenting the relationship these people have to their extraordinary pets.

The human-reptile relationship

When people keep dogs, cats and birds, strong bonds often develop with the companion animal (Sollund 2011), which may be both affectionate and mutual (see Anderson 2003; Arluke and Sanders 1996; Beck 1999; Beck and Katcher 1996; Serpell 1996; Sollund 2009, 2017a). There may be something to gain from such a relationship, not only for the human, but also for the animal, if s/he is treated well. Touch is central to this, in part because of the production of the hormone oxytocin, and it is documented that human-animal interaction reduces stress and anxiety (Beetz et al. 2012). When it comes to the human-reptile relationship, touch is in many cases not an option because it causes the animal harm, and therefore other dimensions may be present in this kind of human-animal relationship.

One of the interviewees (male, early 30s) described his relationship to his reptiles:

> I do absolutely have an emotional relationship to my animals. After all, I have a kind of provider role for them, and without emotions it would have been easy to neglect that role. My fascination for them makes me wish to take good care of them, but it cannot be compared to the relationship one has with a dog. There is no 'comradeship' and reptiles' feelings for their owners are probably more or less absent. Reptiles are preponderantly instinctive, to greater or lesser degree. I can, however, underline that my animals can and do not mind being handled. The leopard geckos have a defense mechanism through which they drop their tail if they feel unsafe or threatened; they never did that.
>
> (Interviewee 1)

Another of the interviewees (woman, 23) said this about having snakes as pets:

> It's a bit like having aquaria fish really, the same principle.
>
> *Q: You don't get a relationship in which you can pet and – ?*
>
> No, you don't. It is very easy as a reptile owner to sort of anthropomorphize your animals, especially those who keep them because they want an animal pet too. There are others who have them for other reasons, pass time, to build nice terrariums and so forth. But still, it does far less harm to anthropomorphize your reptiles than your dog. Anthropomorphizing of dogs can lead to huge harm.
>
> *Q: What do you mean by anthropomorphizing, then?*
>
> That you in a way feel that you have a lot of contact: 'Oh she loves me sooo much,' you know. I don't really do much stuff like that, sit on the coach with them, etc.
>
> *Q: So, you don't think these reptiles are fond of you?*
>
> No, I don't think that they have social antenna. I don't think they have that thing.
>
> *Q: Neither the snakes?*
>
> No.
>
> *Q: No reptiles are social animals?*
>
> A few lizards may be social. The green iguanas can enter into some kind of social interaction with you; they are reckoned to have intelligence at level with cats. And central bearded dragons are also lizards with whom you can interact socially; they look at you, you notice that they know you are there. You don't know that with snakes. Snakes are like . . . you hold them, and you might as well be a branch for them.

> *Q: But, what kind of relationship is it you have then, to your snake and your geckos?*
>
> It is fascination, largely. I must admit I find things that are exotic more exciting – concerning everything, really. Dog breeds, I prefer greyhounds to cocker spaniels. The same for cats; Siamese is much cooler than Norwegian forest cat. I like those who are special. I think that is natural for me.
>
> (Interviewee 2)

Watching the reptiles seems to be central for this woman and for the others. She described how she took pleasure in trying out different forms of food for her geckos and how she loved to watch them eat the different fruits, thus serving as their provider, in much the same way as described by the first interviewee. Yet another man emphasized that he keeps his animals in his office at home, where he is most of the time: 'It is important that they are not in a room by themselves.' The fifth interviewee (a male) said that he keeps his anoles mostly in order to watch them, just like an aquarium, even though he can make them eat from his hands; 'but it is like talking to goldfish' he clarified. Even so, it appears he has had some kind of a relationship with a fish:

> *Q: But, you who have had so many fish, could you communicate with them?*
>
> Yes, with a moray eel, it wanted to be petted. . . . So, with two fish I have had a kind of closeness, but it isn't like, for example, a parrot. The parrot will come because it wants you to pet him, or something like that. The moray eel, it comes because it wants to be scratched under here, right, but it didn't have a relationship to me.
>
> *Q: But, that sounds rather fantastic. Are you fond of them?*
>
> I have had a couple of animals who have died for me, they were little kids, and it's shit every time, it's really no fun. But it isn't like if my cats had died.

It is interesting the way he describes the animals who died as 'little kids,' implying affection but without acknowledging the meaning the scratch might have for the eel. I am no judge of why the eel approached him for petting, but it is interesting that he disregards the possibility that there could be more in this for the eel than just being scratched. The way he describes this is different from how a parrot would approach a person to be scratched, but is not the act of coddling/scratching someone, whether between humans and humans and other animals, also often a sign of affection and trust? Is he belittling his relationship with the eel and vice versa? Perhaps his perception of the difference is caused by a possible prejudice against fish as being cognitively and emotionally different from birds and mammal species. For example, it is still a commonly held belief that fish do not feel pain, something which is refuted by Børresen through her large literature review into the cognitive capacities of fish (2007). Research on fish cognition suggests fish show a rich array of sophisticated behaviours; they have excellent long-term memories, develop complex traditions, show political intelligence or social intelligence (so-called Machiavellian intelligence), cooperate with and recognize one another and are capable of tool use. In addition, the fish brain is much more similar to that of humans than previously thought (Brown 2015: 3). One cannot, for instance, but be fascinated by the Japanese puffer fish who by throwing up sand with his fins in an intricate, artistic pattern seeks to attract a female,[4] just like some birds sophisticatedly decorate their nest to attract partners. So, perhaps, it is the challenge of questioning prevailing prejudice that led the interviewees to diminish their animals' cognitive and social skills, while empirically their perceptions of their animals counteract such prejudice, leading to the contradictions that appear in the interviewees' descriptions of relationships with their animals.

Interviewees who kept reptiles usually watched them through the distance of the glass of a terrarium, yet they are together through the physical closeness and also from the nearness produced by the fascinated glance, constituted by looking at (the animal), acknowledging him/her (Berger 2009):

> I have five anoles, they live together, they sit one on top of the other, they have a family life, they are extremely entertaining animals.
>
> (Interviewee 2)

> I love all kinds of animals, but I have had a strange fascination with reptiles since I was a child. They are impressive and fascinating in many ways, from appearance to their physiology and bodily functions.
>
> (Interviewee 3)

In a terrarium the animals are on display, like animals in a zoo (Berger 2009), even though, as one of the interviewees commented, boas can be hard to see sometimes because they hide in their artificial nests. This suggests a kind of objectification as opposed to the anthropomorphism the young woman accused other reptile and dog owners of. It is interesting how several of the interviewees underlined the lack of intelligence of their reptiles, that they were instinctual more than intelligent and emotional, which may imply that despite their fascination and also genuine affection for their reptiles, some of the interviewees still feel a degree of alienation to their compans. For example, while the woman quoted above claimed iguanas possess the intelligence of a cat, another interviewee claimed they were unintelligent, and anoles were also described by several owners as instinctual more than intelligent and rational. However, both anoles (Leal and Powell 2012) and iguanas (Blrghardt 1977) have been found to have high cognitive and social skills. A study into the social lives of newly hatched reptiles, including iguanas, had Blrghardt (1977: 188) warning against prejudices against reptiles:

> Brain size, intelligence and social complexity are often mistakenly viewed as necessarily covarying. While brains of reptiles seem universally smaller than those of equal sized endotherms, neither in social behavior . . . nor in learning ability . . . is the inferiority of reptiles to all birds and mammals supported.

While fascination describes the core of the relationship reptile owners have with their animals, both the woman quoted above and another woman described their relationships to their boas as an ordinary human-compan relationships, exemplified by effectuate relationships between dogs and cats and their respective owners (Sollund 2011):

> I brought my snake with me out, in the early nineties. It[5] was allowed to hang around my waist, and it thought it was quite okay. Because, it was a very special snake. So, if you wrapped it around your waist, it actually hung there, and occasionally would surge up from the waist to have a look out.
>
> *Q: Okay, so, it was inside your clothes?*
>
> Yes, yes, they need to keep warm. So, that's important. But I have not had any other snake which has been like that, mentally. So, it was very special. It was a boa, that was my first, so.
>
> *Q: So, did it have a relationship to you, or was it just the warmth?*
>
> It was very special! When I was sad, it would come up to my face, really, it was very special. And, I have never had a Boa after this, which has been like it was. So, I have several pairs of glasses that broke, because it absolutely wanted to climb over there [over her glasses], I thought it was great. It was really special. It wasn't possible to keep it in an aquarium; it just pushed its way out, so it slept under my pillow. It was not what I now would describe as a good way to keep a boa.
>
> *Q: But one learns?*
>
> Yes, but I think that this was what made its personality the way it was, because it was *handled* in a totally different way [from how she treated other Boas]. So we got a relationship we would not otherwise have had.
>
> *Q: For how long did you have it?*
>
> Oh, for very long.
>
> *Q: It had a name?*
>
> I called it Tine, Serpentine [laughs].
>
> (Interviewee 1)

Interviewee 2, in describing her snake, seemed inconsistent with how she described her relationship to snakes (and other reptiles), simultaneously expressing fascination and perhaps even alienation (Sollund 2008a) to the animals as well as love:

> The first snake I bought, I am going to keep it my whole life. I will. It's just because, she is in a way this very special form, she is. Because she was the first, she is the first in everything. The first one managed to accept my feeding,[6] that is something special. I like her the very, very best, even though, in

> a way she is a bit dull. I mean, there are different types, many different types, and this one isn't very special for those who really are dedicated to reptiles. It is a boa constrictor, it isn't very exciting. It isn't. But for me, that does not matter, because Cleo, that's her name, she is the best of the best, if I may put it that way. So, I am going to keep her all my life.

The third interviewee, also a man in his 30s, said about his tortoise:[7]

> So, I get chased by that tortoise, every time I enter the kitchen, it comes running after me, and runs in between my feet, and it's like. . . . No, I have to push it away because it gets scared when I walk, when I move my foot. But at the same time, it wants to get onto my foot all the time. He literally stands on my foot. . . . It has a lot of personality, more than most others I have met of its kind. So, it's a true little bully. I am very fond of them [all his reptiles].

In sum, these five interviewees seem to carry conflicting feelings about their relationships with their reptiles. While they all describe their fascination with them and that they like to watch them, they also describe the reptiles as purely instinctive and unintelligent, particularly in comparison to other species like dogs and cats, they still have affectionate relationships with reptiles. While on the one hand, the interviewees objectified their reptiles, in other respects they also appreciate the company of fish, tortoises and snakes in ways that represent more than just a gaze. It is also interesting that two of the interviewees stressed their roles as providers for the reptiles, that they make great efforts to get them special food they enjoy and take pleasure in watching them eat. To feed someone, whether nurturing a baby, cooking for children or a lover, or feeding a beloved pet, may be fundamentally satisfying in a way that stands in contrast to one's reaction when someone cares for rejects one's offer of food, whether due to illness or dislike. The interviewees expressed love and affection in making good homes with nutritious food for the dependent reptiles. In this manner, these interviewees' relationships with their animals do not seem to differ much from those of other pet keepers. The pleasure interviewee 3 found in acquiring delicacies for her anoles and watching them eat them may, as suggested in an essay by anthropologist Fox (2003), be an expression of altruism, and of genuine love. Their love and fascination for reptiles, however, are not without consequences.

Being criminalized and labelled

The fascination the interviewees spoke of was also partly the reason why they first acquired reptiles. This was a lifelong fascination for them, and some, when they first were introduced to reptiles, were 'sold.' Interviewee 2 explained that initially, she had no plans of getting a reptile; she was only accompanying her boyfriend to a reptile fair:

> It was at a Danish reptile fair. It was funny actually, how we got there, because it was my partner who was most into that reptile stuff. And he received two

> leopard geckos from his sister, and then he found this fair. So, we had to go, not to buy, no definitely not to buy. Because, I was going to study abroad, in the US, and if you have a criminal record, then you cannot get in.

Still, when they got there, she could not resist buying a boa, and later she went several times to Sweden and Denmark where she purchased reptiles in pet shops.

While she was caught the first time (her partner took the blame so she would avoid a criminal record), she explained how they got more sophisticated in the ways in which they trafficked the reptiles to Norway. They would not cross the Norwegian-Swedish border at night because that would be more suspicious; it was better to blend in with all the other Norwegians who had gone to Sweden to shop. They would also travel in two cars; the second car, with the reptiles, would only follow if the first was not stopped, an indication that border control was lax that day. So the ban did not prevent them from commencing reptile keeping, they rather tried to find ways to avoid being caught.

Similarly, interviewee 3 said:

> The ban did not stop me from starting this past time. Otherwise I am very law abiding and as A4 [straight, ordinary] as one possibly can be. But I have little understanding for the herptile ban, the way I see it, it lacks a reasonable and professional foundation. The ban is just based in prejudices and xenophobia. That makes it difficult to respect the law.

All the interviewees stated that their lives changed when they started keeping reptiles because it was illegal. They said they were careful about whom they saw and usually kept to people with the same interests, who were in the same situation and in whom they could trust. They did not invite other people home and lived quiet lives:

> I fear the authorities, and I must admit you become overly paranoid about getting caught. I don't want my animals to be confiscated and killed. I therefore live a very sober life, behind drawn curtains. I take all the precautions I can. The door is always locked. I am very careful about who I invite. I don't open the door if the doorbell rings and I don't expect visitors. It is a shame for my partner, who can never bring friends. I recently became a father, and I fear the day when the boy starts in kindergarten, for what he might reveal there. The plan is to tell him that they [the reptiles] are something other than what they actually are.
>
> (Interviewee 3)

> Everybody who knows about it is people we know we can trust, who have animals themselves. It is a rather closed little circle, so few people are allowed to come to our place. . . . I know many get burnt, who invite people to parties, and then they are reported.
>
> (Interviewee 4)

> I think the paranoia is what we have in common. We all share that.
> (Interviewee 2)

Interviewee 4 contrasted the Norwegian ban to the situation in the US, where importing wild-caught reptiles is allowed:

> I don't think the reptile keepers in Norway should be criminalised, because they are just ordinary people with an interest in animals. I think it is wrong to criminalise that people like animals. And I understand very well the problem with wild-caught animals. I have a friend in the US whose partner was importing wild-caught reptiles legally. She has shown me pictures of the animals that die during transport, and there is just row after row of dead little lizards. And I think it really isn't worth it.

The last quotation may appear contradictory in that she criticizes the criminalization, while at the same time acknowledges the problems with the wildlife trade. 'Liking' animals is a priority which has had devastating effects on many reptile species (Gibbon et al. 2000). Generally, the impression from the interviewees is that reptile keepers are ordinary people with a special interest and passion albeit one that is criminalized. While keeping exotic reptiles was banned and legalized for a some specific of species, the keeping of another category of animals, tropical birds, such as parrots from South America, was never banned. This is illogical. And there was no reason why they should be exempt fromthe regulation against the import of exotic species. Parrots e.g. canaries and budgerigars' needs for flying and stinlui cannot be covered if they have to live in a cage. As shown in the parrot cases, however, there are no restrictions preventing anybody who wants to from breeding and selling parrots, and such an enterprise can be used to traffic the birds under disguise of the breeding business. Parrots can also legally be imported with CITES certificates, even when they are wild caught. There is no reason to think that keeping parrots and other birds in cages is any less abusive than keeping reptiles in terrariums, especially if the reptile species do not move much in the wild. Keeping parrots in cages, using them as presents, keeping them in menageries, are all practices with a long tradition (see van Uhm 2016b), and therefore trafficked parrots are not regarded as wildlife, but, as shown in Chapter 3, as illegal goods, as 'cage birds.' When compared to parrot keepers, the criminalization of reptile keepers made no sense, thereby suggesting that both practices should be permitted, which they now to large degree are also in Norway.

One could take the opposite perspective, though, and argue that rather than extending and legalizing a practice which puts even more animals at risk and thereby possibly increasing traffick and species extinction, one could do the opposite and ban the keeping of both exotic reptiles and birds, who presumably suffer far more in cages than do snakes.

I realize the injustice in criminalizing some form of pet ownership and not others, which may also be abusive due to owners' ignorance, neglect, carelessness or wickedness (Agnew 1998; Beirne 1999; Sollund 2009, 2011). However, judging by the large number of reptiles seized in connection with other crimes, there is a probability that these species are attractive to people for other reasons than those displayed by the interviewees who take their reptile keeping very seriously.

When talking with the police and Customs, there was an oft-repeated observation, one reflected in the 810 penal cases as well, that people who live on the social margins find reptiles fascinating, for reasons of self-presentation – status (Goffman 1978). And when the animals to an even greater degree are used instrumentally, there might be less concern for their welfare and for the conditions under which they are kept. There may thus be a correlation between the reasons for keeping banned dog breeds – so-called status dogs (Maher and Pierspoint 2011) – and dangerous-looking reptiles, when the animals are used, extrinsically, to achieve the esteem of one's significant subcultural others.

That reptiles in the media are often associated with criminals also contributes to the 'reptile stigma' that is attached to otherwise law-abiding reptile keepers. Interviewee 5 reflected on this:

> Yes, I think it gives status, particularly in criminal social environments, even though I think that such people actually keep few reptiles. But they are the focus. When this is dispersed through media, for people who have no idea, then they think that all reptile keepers are criminals, and associated with, for example, cannabis. But it is not like that at all. And that is good to know. And when people are caught with cannabis and reptiles, people get very angry. I mean, why mix cannabis and reptiles? If you have reptiles, then you must stay away from [other] illegalities. Keep clean, sort of. Please. Because we don't want that stigma, that we use drugs and all that fuzz. It is no good.

Being viewed as criminals because of media representations that associate criminals with reptiles is only part of the problem. Another part of the stigma concerns the animals themselves. While individuals pertaining to criminal subcultures may choose to keep a reptile to display status or to appear frightening, thus enhancing prejudices against reptiles, labelling of reptiles may reflect on all reptile keepers.

> It would have been fun to be able to talk with other people about it [reptiles]. If people ask. But at the same time, you notice, that if you mention reptiles, then people keep a distance, because these are 'dangerous' animals.
>
> I think that if you look normal, then it is better not to talk about such things [reptiles]. Because, then people may think wrongly of you.

There is both the stigma connected to reptiles being linked to other crimes/criminals and the stigma connected to the animals themselves that reflect on the reptile keepers and indirectly stigmatize them too. This is not unlike the experiences of owners affected by the Dangerous Dogs Act (Lie 2017). Lie found that owners of banned dogs experienced people crossing the street to avoid meeting them and their dogs, that their dogs would be excluded from dog training courses, that veterinarians would not treat their dogs and that other dog owners would not let their dogs play with dogs of the banned breeds, as well as with dogs who were assumed to be illegal.

That reptiles are not offered veterinary care because they are illegal was an argument put forward by the Food Safety Authority, but this was, however, not supported by the interviewees. For example, the interviewees listed several specific veterinarians who had specialized in reptiles. This may thus have been used as a pretext by the Food Safety Authority, rather than reflecting a genuine problem that veterinarians refused to attend to reptiles.

The more general stigma associated with reptile keepers may, however, be reduced with the decriminalization of the 19 species, but it still will not make all the reptiles my informants keep legal, since several were not on the legal list.

This connects to the problem of partial legalization/criminalization. While a total ban has not worked effectively to prevent people from keeping reptiles in Norway, and while it has led to criminalization of otherwise law-abiding animal lovers/aficionados, for a long time the ban sent the message that exotic reptiles must not be kept in private homes in Norway. It is also likely that people who would have wanted to buy reptiles abstain from it because it is illegal. The ban may have produced a stigma both of the animals and their owners, but it has not been open to any misinterpretation, the message has been clear: Owning reptiles is against the law.[8]

With the partial legalization, this message becomes blurred and confusing (Goyes and Sollund 2016). Importing some species is legal, others not. People who have reptiles that are not on the legal list will still be subject to prosecution. On one hand, lifting the ban implies that because the ban did not have general support, it was not respected. A common consequence of a general disrespect for a law is that it may eventually be suspended, due to the relationship between public opinion and the law (Aubert 1954). On the other hand, the reaction legalization may go too far in the opposite direction, suggesting that it is perfectly fine to keep exotic reptiles in Norway. This involves an extension of pet-keeping practices, meaning that there is no limit to what kind of animals can be kept in private homes to serve human interests, as long as it is practically feasible. People without experience with reptiles – animals with specific environmental needs – can now acquire them legally, increasing the likelihood of animal abuse. As stated by my interviewees, no one *wants* a wild-caught reptile since these carry diseases and parasites and may not live long (Herbig 2010). Breeding them is preferred (and easy in the case of many species). Lifting the ban may still increase pressure on vulnerable species because people who are unaware of the risks associated with wild-caught animals will still purchase them.

When CITES-listed animals are seized at Norwegian borders, as shown, very often the animals are killed by the Food Safety Authority after Customs have surrendered them. This does not mean that the Food Safety Authority will not attempt to save them. Interviewee 3 told of one such incident. She had been caught by Customs with two boa constrictors on the Norwegian-Swedish border. Customs first saw the terrariums she had bought for them, and then found the snakes in the cotton bags in the trunk. The interviewee had documents for them, but according to her, the Customs agents, who appeared to be afraid of and prejudiced towards the snakes, calling them 'repulsive animals,' threw away the documents. The animals were seized on a Friday, and then the offices of the Food Safety Authority were closed for the weekend. She feared that if the snakes were to remain in those premises, they might get ill and die because of lack of warmth. So, she started calling people she knew to find someone whom she could suggest as a potential caretaker of the snakes to the Food Safety Authority. Eventually, she succeeded in finding a friend who had recently started a zoo in the south of Norway who was willing to take the snakes. She referred to this discussion as a 'big battle,' but eventually the Food Safety Authority gave in, and it was arranged that another friend of hers would pick up the snakes and deliver them to the zoo. She added, '*He* could fetch them, but I couldn't because I was a criminal, "bad, mean, me," sort of. So, that was very odd, but I managed to save the snakes.'

Decisions concerning the fate of the animals may be ad hoc as in this instance, but usually the animals are killed for lack of suitable rescue facilities. Given that this is the usual outcome, one could argue that in order to avoid the killing of animals, the ban should be lifted to save more lives, as it was. Conversely, legalizing the commercialization of reptiles in Norway may put more animals at risk of abuse.

Problems with keeping reptiles

As previously mentioned, parrots are often rehomed. This seems also to be the case with reptiles who may be, if not as (literally) outspokenly demanding as parrots are, far more complicated to care for than people envision. They have specific environmental needs which require investment, dedication and skill. Unfortunately, many reptiles who are victims of trafficking suffer from abuse (Royal Society for the Prevention of Cruelty to Animals [RSPCA] n.d.).

Interviewee 1 took on the role of 'mom' and provided a rescue home for abandoned reptiles. Ehen I asked her how she obtained her reptiles, she replied she had brought them in from abroad, she has had them left on her stairs and she has bought them in Norway. She has kept reptiles for 20 years. Although she has 'run' a rescue home for other reptiles, she did not always give them names.

> So many animals have been by. I have become a kind of dumping site for reptiles, because I am so frequently at the [reptile internet] fora. I have spent a lot of time teaching people about how these animals should be kept. I think behaviour is very interesting, whether of animals or humans. So, as people get tired of animals, they dump them at my door. So, they knew where to go, and I couldn't say no. If the alternative is euthanasia or that someone else takes them, then the answer is a given. And that's what led to –
>
> *Q: You getting caught?*
>
> No, not really, but that I had all the animals I had when it happened, because I had the house full of iguanas. And iguanas really shouldn't be kept. They are not pets.

She told me about her friend who took over an iguana – an animal she described as 'particularly mean,' thus ascribing him both individuality and personality:

> He has been mean since he was little, so he is not a nice guy. They have personality as all others, and he is not very pleasant. And he has had this behaviour all along. So he bit my friend's thumb into the bone. He had two operations in a week and spent a week in the hospital. So his partner did not allow him to have it any longer, so it ended up somewhere else.

I asked whether it often happens that they end up somewhere else, and she confirmed that iguanas are very difficult animals. But at the same time, they are, like parrots, highly desirable (Pires and Clarke 2011):

> It is a beautiful animal; it is an animal that everybody wants. And it is just like if you have a dog with behavioural issues; it takes time to put it in order. And it gets too much for people. And then it gets worse and worse, because you move it. And iguanas are very sensitive to being moved, they may easily go on a hunger strike for two weeks, without problems or physical harm – just in pure stubbornness. And that says something about what kind of animal it is when it comes to training. So, I had five of these when the police came and I also had many other animals.

She explained how she was caught, which in a way was caused by the iguanas themselves:

> The problem was the iguanas. This was also at the time when a lot of cannabis growing operations were discovered, and it was a lot in the media about it. And then one day, the iguanas were climbing around in one of the rooms, and when I was at work, they somehow managed to pull up the curtains. And then the neighbours saw this room with a lot of green, which was from the terrariums, and fluorescent lighting, and thought that it must be cannabis. And then two big cops came at the door and wondered if they could come in. And I am in my pyjamas and say that, no, actually rather not. I know that is the end of it. But I could not refuse them entry; it wouldn't have made any difference. So, I put my bet on goodwill. 'Yes. Please come in!' And they asked, 'do you have anything illegal, that you are not allowed to have?' And I said yes, and I took them on a tour and explained, and I think they were rather disappointed. I was only a crying girl in her pyjamas. So, this was a really downer for all involved. And they said that because of the extent of it they had to report it. Because they did not want that either, it's a lot of paperwork and bad vibrations all the way. So, they wanted to avoid it, that was my impression.
>
> *Q: So, what happened?*
>
> Several persons from the Food Safety Authority came with a lot of cages.

> *Q: And took all the 18 animals?*
>
> Of course they were free to help themselves.
>
> *Q: Were they killed?*
>
> No, actually not. That is because I have good contacts, and the goodwill intermixed, I think. Because I was nice all along, I gave them full training, offered them equipment, made sure they had food for all the different animals, and told them who should have what. So, it was a lot all along. I kept contact, I sent letters to all the zoos I know of, and because I had worked in one of them I had good contacts.

Like the other case described above when the interviewee was stopped at the border, it appears that the control agencies try to save the animals when solutions are available, but that making seizures of this kind is not a priority for the police. These are, as described by Runhovde (2015) 'seizures of inconvenience.' Because she cooperated and showed goodwill to the police and the Food Safety Authority, it was probably easier for them to allow her to help re-home the animals than to kill them. The interviewee suggested police would rather not enforce this kind of legislation, which may result in the laws becoming 'sleeping laws.' Implying that when legislation is not any longer enforced, it will eventually result in a decriminalization (Aubert 1954). This explains the decriminalization of reptiles. In the 810 penal cases I examined, however, very few animals were saved, which can be explained by who the owners were – usually 'life style criminals' – and who offered no alternatives to the authorities about how to save the animals. The interview I conducted with the Food Safety Authority confirmed that they try to avoid killing seized animals if they can. As stated though, killing 'illegal' animals is more the rule than the exception.

While the reptile keepers interviewed for this book can be described as skilled in reptile care and willing to do a lot to avoid the killing of their seized animals, many reptile keepers are unskilled or quickly lose interest, and this was also the reason why interviewee 1 had so many animals in her care since she took over reptiles that others had abandoned. It seems thus that reptiles, like parrots, have a high potential for getting abandoned, and this phenomenon is unlikely to be reduced with the lifting of the ban. Rather, with the legal expansion of reptile keeping, reptile abuse and dumping is likely to increase.[9]

Feeding reptiles live mice

While reptiles suffer from lack of appropriate care, there is also the risk that reptile keeping contributes to other animal abuse, when reptiles are given 'live feed.' As shown in the reptile trafficking case in Chapter 5, in which the offender was first accused of trafficking reptiles from Norway to Australia, there was also extensive breeding of mice for reptile feed. Even though this is prohibited by the Animal Welfare Act, there is a reasonable risk that 'unserious' reptile keepers, that is, those who keep reptiles to present an image of themselves as tough, might find it attractive to add this to further such self-presentation (Goffman 1978) by feeding their reptiles live mice, with the suffering this will entail for the mice victims. As the stigma of a reptile may tint her/his owner as previously discussed, so also can the image of a reptile taking live feed create an image of her/him as mean, and also tint her/his owner with an image of 'meanness' or 'toughness', this being a desired image for the owner.

One of the interviewees elaborated on how a friend of hers in the US bred rats for food for his many reptiles and subjected these highly intelligent animals to extensive abuse by keeping them in small tubes, where they are totally barred from any natural behaviour and have no stimuli. There is reason to believe that even though feeding animals with live animals is illegal, the Food Safety Authority or the police will not likely make an effort to enter private homes to ensure live mice are not bred and kept under unsatisfactory conditions. To treat mice and rats as mere food for pets also increases the instrumental ways with which these animals are perceived. This, in turn, decreases empathy for these animals. Further, one cannot disregard the possibility that there are people who actually take pleasure in witnessing the torture of mice by being served to reptiles.[10] While reptiles eat other animals alive naturally, there is nothing natural in putting an animal with no means of escape or defence into the cage of a predator.

Interviewee 1 also said that she, despite defining herself as an animal lover, had fed her reptiles live mice.

I asked her how she felt when she fed her snakes with live mice. She responded,

> It wasn't all right. I love all animals, I have had pet rats. So, it is not okay. I felt guilty for several days afterwards. Sometimes it is necessary, though. I had a ball python litter from my ball python. They have very few eggs. So you want to succeed with the babies, it is fun if you make it. And there I had five babies, and when you have snake babies they must be started on live feed, and then you can turn to dead feed. And it can take some time to have them going, and some are difficult. But I mean, if you cannot make your snake eat dead food, then you haven't really tried hard enough. Because it is not that difficult, animals don't starve on purpose. But, yes, then I had to feed live. And I also bred mice for the purpose of them being food.
>
> *Q: That sounds bad, don't you think that is an ethical dilemma?*
>
> Yes and no. We eat cows.
>
> *Q: Yes, but we don't eat them alive.*
>
> I am not a vegetarian, but when I bred they weren't fed live, I killed them.
>
> *Q: How?*
>
> There are many ways, for example, carbon dioxide is the most frequent if you have large numbers. Of course, if you are only going to kill five, you don't make a big system for that, but it isn't difficult to euthanize mice humanely, a rat trap, a mouse trap, does the job very humanely. So in principle it isn't

> hard, it just didn't feel all right. It doesn't. As an animal lover it doesn't feel good. But I didn't decide that this is what they eat. It was, as I usually say, it is His [God's] will who didn't put salad on the menu. And it is my responsibility for the animal that I have acquired, to get it food. Even though it feels shit, it doesn't help. It is my responsibility for bringing it to the house. Against its will.
>
> *Q: But you also brought the mice to the house?*
>
> Yes, and they were fine. They had a good environment and good food, I spent so much money on them, and it didn't pay at all. But it is my philosophy that they shall be fine as long as they live. And rationally, the better the feed – the better the [feed] animal's life is – the better the food it is. Lizards for example, are worth nothing if they are not properly fed.

Her feeding snakes with live mice was not without moral deliberation. Her rationalizations are interesting, though. First, she claimed there are humane ways of killing. This is a statement that implies that being killed may in itself be a humane act. I don't discard such a position in principle, if, for example an individual, human or non-human, is sick, it may be better to be killed in a nonviolent way to stop the pain and prevent further suffering. In this case, however, there is no reason to believe that the mice were old or in any way suffering, as she said, it is important to ensure that the mice are in good health. From the mice's perspective, being killed is inconsistent with faring well (Francione 2014; Regan 1987; Sollund 2014) because they die prematurely. Killing being a humane act is a contradiction in terms. How humane it is to kill someone in a trap would depend on the type of trap but also be open to debate more broadly. To say someone is killed humanely may be more of a pretext on the part of humans to soften and excuse acts that in realty are cruel. Even though she thought that killing mice by means of carbon dioxide was humane, a review article looking into the effects of being euthanized by means of carbon dioxide, concludes that

> while CO_2 has long been used as a method of euthanasia, questions have arisen that this practice may not fulfill the criteria for an easy and gentle death, as required by both ethical concerns and policy. The primary concerns are that exposure to CO_2 gas may be painful; CO_2 may cause onset of asphyxia while the animal is still conscious; physiological effects of CO_2 on nasal mucosae and on the autonomic nervous system may be distressing; the cognitive/perceptual/behavioural effects of CO_2, such as ataxia, may be disturbing to the animal; and the process of CO_2 inhalation may be highly aversive. Some or all of these results may cause pain and distress.
>
> (Conlee et al. 2005: not paged)

When the interviewee said it was God, not her, who created the snakes' need for live food, this may also be seen as a way of shirking responsibility for the acts she is committing against the mice, as well as a denial of the victim (Sykes and Matza

1957). God, should s/he exist did not, under any circumstance, put snakes into terrariums and mice into cages; what takes place naturally is far from what takes place under artificial conditions in houses, cages and terrariums where animals are made captives.

The interviewee's moral concerns, and thereby her consideration for the mice as sentient, not only food, are unlikely to be mirrored by potential new reptile owners, and one could ask whether the need (genuine or claimed) that reptiles have for eating live feed should be a strong argument for why such animals should not be allowed in private homes. A recent verdict from Follo District Court (17–196748MED-Foll) confirms there is a genuine danger that reptile keepers will feed their snakes, now legal, live animals. In this one man was sentenced to 24 days unconditional prison time for feeding his 2 m long boa live animals on several occasions. As part of the sentence, he was also forbidden to keep snakes for five years. He had filmed himself feeding the snake a live rabbit and a live hamster, films he posted on YouTube, indicating that he was proud of this, rather than ashamed.

Notes

1 https://lovdata.no/dokument/SF/forskrift/2017-05-11-597. Norwegian reptiles cannot be kept as pets under the Wildlife Law that establishes that no free-born animals can be taken and kept in captivity.

2 www.mattilsynet.no/dyr_og_dyrehold/kjaledyr_og_konkurransedyr/eksotiske_dyr/mattilsynets_arbeid_med_eksotiske_dyr.20907

3 One of the interviews was in a written form, whereby I sent the questions to the interviewee, who wrote elaborate answers to my questions.

4 www.youtube.com/watch?v=nEQNgxnASjA

5 She used *den* (it) when referring to the snake, rather than she or he, her or him, which also hints towards an objectification.

6 To achieve that the snake eats can be difficult.

7 I do not actually know whether this was a turtle or a tortoise, since in Norwegian the same word, *skilpadde*, applies for both tortoise and turtle. Due to the difficulties in keeping a turtle, I assume it was a tortoise.

8 However, permission to keep a tortoise could be extended to people who have allergies to other pets, upon application to the Food Safety Authority.

9 A search on Finn.no for reptiles on August 3, 2018, revealed several hits for reptiles, indicating that now, since they are made legal, 'second-hand reptiles' may be sold openly and without control of where they come from.

10 A search revealed several videos of snakes being fed live mice, but also warnings against it, since mice sometimes will fight for their lives and may harm the reptiles, unless they freeze of fright.

8 Summary of the Norwegian case study

Offenders

The material analyzed from Norway shows there are different categories of consumers of wildlife. The consumers of wildlife represented in these data, as revealed in the seizure reports and that most frequently have wildlife products seized by Customs fall into six, not mutually exclusive, categories:

1 People who travel and who bring, or arrange to have sent to them, wildlife products back home, often so-called "souvenirs".

This can be in the form of inter alia shoes, belts, purses, wallets and clothing made from reptile skins, dead reptiles, stuffed crocodile/alligator heads, pelts, skins, shawls, seahorses, ivory figures and jewellery, turtle shell jewellery, corals, caviar and liquor made with endangered reptiles. People who travel also bring, or arrange to have sent to them, TAM products, such as s seahorse pills, leopard pills, saga antelope pills and musk in different forms.

This list, of course, is not exhaustive, and people bring all kinds of products home from abroad. A tourist who is caught can be anyone who is unaware of CITES rules because little effort is made in Norway to spread information about the regulations and bans in relation to wildlife trafficking.

Those who bring TAM/TCM will likely belong to immigrant groups. However, TCM is spreading to other parts of the world and globalization makes it possible for new groups interested in testing such products to emerge. There are, however, few seizures of this kind in Norway, which suggests that a lot slips in under the radar.

Because people are allowed to bring in certain CITES-listed products that are banned, such as for personal use or those items that are pre-Convention, and because of the increasing number of people travelling as tourists globally every year, the threat this category constitutes to endangered wildlife should not be underestimated (Sollund and Maher 2015; van Uhm 2016b; Wyatt 2013).

2 People buying on the internet.

The people who buy wildlife products and live animals on the internet constitute a large threat to wildlife. It is impossible to say in the Norwegian context how large, because most parcels arriving in Norway or arriving through cargo are never examined (Runhovde 2016; Sollund 2013b; Sollund and Maher 2015). Whether and to what degree Norwegians buy wildlife products on the dark web is also unexamined, but it is likely, as the dark web evolves and as other kinds of illegal products are purchased there with little risk of getting caught; this will also increase in the case of wildlife trafficking (Harrison et al. 2016). As mentioned in the introduction, the internet offers an easy means for anybody to buy and sell wildlife and wildlife products (Interpol/IFAW 2013; IFAW 2008; Lavorgna 2014, 2015; Sollund 2016c, and see chapters herein concerning ivory collecting in Norway and modus operandi in Colombia).

A lot of people gain access to huge markets, both overt and hidden. While many collectors get their items on the internet, this does not mean that they do not also travel to purchase what they collect. Ivory items is an example of products that are frequently trafficked to Norway through mail. Other examples of collector items that are trafficked are stuffed birds/animals.

A frequently seized product according to the seizure reports is jungle cock feathers used in fish flies. Sport fishers are numerous in Norway, and the seizures reflect this tendency. As in the case of tourists, many offenders of this category may be unaware of the illegality of their acts.

3 People involved in the pet trade.

The most frequently seized live species in Norway are reptiles and birds. Because all exotic reptiles were prohibited in Norway between 1977 and 2017, reptiles were also seized. Frequent seizures of reptiles might have been the result of the ban (because they were illegal, they would all be seized when discovered) and also suggest an increase in reptile- keeping, despite the ban. Those who are stopped with reptiles are usually trafficking the animals, and even in this group, there are people who may have been unaware of the ban, for example tourists buying a terrapin baby at a market. How the lift of the ban will affect the legal as well as illegal reptile trafficking to Norway must be examined at a later occasion.

Ornamental fish/aquaria fish are often trafficked to Norway, according to the interview data, but they seldom figure in the seizure reports. One reason for this might be that Customs is unaware of whether they are CITES listed, so they do not confiscate them and reports are not produced.

4 Several cases in the material included people who trafficked many individuals in order to exploit them as part of a business. Not all of these can be categorized as being professional; rather, it appears in several cases that they were men with a dodgy business trying to profit on wildlife trade, because it is low risk, high pay.

5 Taxidermists.
Taxidermists buy carcasses of endangered birds and other animals both in Norway and from abroad. This is a category that is closely connected to collectors who aim to build up 'dead-animal menageries' or who, by stuffing animals, assist other collectors in building up their collections.

In addition to these categories, there is also trade in bird eggs and birds by collectors, which is both internal and external. While the above categories usually refer to micro trade – individuals bringing products or animals for their own consumption or having them sent to their address by post – no less serious are the categories that include traffickers who act on a wider scale:

6 Freight companies constitute a threat, but because containers/lorries largely pass unexamined by control agencies, it is impossible to assess how much wildlife contraband arrives to Norway this way. The confiscation reports do not include seizures made from containers, but as shown, freight companies were considered a very serious problem by the CITES/Norwegian Environment Agency interviewee. It is possible, though, that large shipments of coral have come by freight.

Animal victims in Norway

The animal victims who suffer from Norwegians' involvement in IWT are often described as 'illegal goods' by law enforcement agents and in the legal context. Behind every 'illegal good', however, is an individual who has been victimized. As mentioned in relation to the case analyzed in Chapter 5, thousands of animals were killed in order to form part of the offender's collection. In their case, when trafficked they were already dead and no *more* harm could be done to them. They were deprived, however, of the life they should have had, and in which they had vested interest, just as every human, if healthy, has an interest in life and the pleasures and good experiences that may come with it (Regan 1987). Within the categories of endangered species that are victims of the Norwegian wildlife trade, as exemplified above, there are large numbers of fish, reptiles and birds, birds of prey and parrots, but they also include, 'big cats such as tigers, leopards, and lions, in addition to wolves, bears, musk ox, elephants' ivory and many others.

Because of lack of rescue facilities for trafficking victims in Norway, live animals often remain in the facilities of the Food Safety Authority at Oslo Airport for a long time. According to the airport veterinarian, there have been several free-born parrots among them. One example was an African grey parrot who remained there for an entire summer. The veterinarians realized that s/he must be free born because if they approached her with a distance less than a meter, s/he would scream hysterically. The veterinarians tried to convince a zoo take her, but without success, and eventually s/he was killed. S/he was bought on a market in Indonesia, suggesting s/he may have been caught in Africa and trafficked to an Indonesian bird market, from where s/he was trafficked to Norway.

This must have been a terribly traumatizing journey, and likely the bird's life would have been destroyed either way. The veterinarian added that there were many such stories. One concerned a Vietnamese man who had packed several birds in a tube and stuffed them in his suitcase. Most were dead, but those that were still alive were euthanized by the veterinarians.

Most of the animals who are trafficked alive are reptiles and birds. In many cases, they are killed because of the trafficking to which they have been subjugated, thus doubly victimizing them. Ironically, paradoxically and perversely, these theriocides are often committed by an agency enforcing the CITES, which is designed to protect endangered species.

Although Norwegian involvement in the IWT in many cases might seem like minor offences committed in relation to travelling, in sum, these offences are not minor, but contribute significantly to endangering many species.

Punishment in Norway

In the years that I have been working on this project, the two revisions of the CITES regulation in Norway in 2013 and 2017 have increased the potential punishment for various violations. During these years I have also witnessed what might appear like an increase in the actual punishment for CITES crimes, especially concerning the amount of the fines imposed, which is in line with a general increase in punishment by the Supreme Court for crimes against the environment (Høviskeland 2017). While incidents of trafficking in CITES products a few years ago usually resulted in insignificant fines (e.g., 1,500–2,000 NOK for tortoise trafficking), more recently fines up to 20,000 NOK have been imposed. (For parrot trafficking offences, see Chapter 3.) These cases still are low priority in terms of investigation, prosecution and the extent to which judges prioritize looking into previous cases and the topic more generally. And there is a lack of consistency; punishment appears to be random and overall very lenient compared to the harm committed (Runhovde 2016; Sollund 2013a, 2015c; Sunde 2010). Nevertheless, there appears to be a more deliberate priority of environmental crimes, which include animal abuse, at higher levels of prosecution (Høviskeland 2017). On March 14, 2014, the Eco Crime Unit was given the national responsibility for combatting animal welfare crimes from the Police Directorate (Høviskeland 2017). In addition, special units have been established in three police districts that will concentrate specifically on crimes against animals (Hermansen 2018).

It is nonetheless a common feature of these cases that when they are brought to trial, the investigation has been so lengthy that this is regarded as a mitigating factor for the offender, and sentences are reduced because of it. The strictest prison sentence for CITES crimes to date, in Norway, is still the 1998 sentence of four months in prison for trafficking a large number of live animals for the pet trade.

Although a fine may hurt, when imposing *only* a fine, the judicial system loses a great opportunity to establish clearly, through the public event of a trial, that partaking in IWT is a criminal, punishable offence of importance. The communicative effect of punishment would be greatly enhanced through the consistent use of trials in these cases. By not going to trial, a chance is lost to convey clearly a message to the general public which could deter people from committing such crimes. Few people like to stand as the accused in a courtroom, but this ritual is important in order to establish that a crime has been committed and it is also likely to have the effect of deterring crime more than having to pay a fine does. When only a small fine is imposed on people who regularly commit such offences, such as in the parrot cases described previously, this matter is merely a nuisance and has little deterrent effect at the individual level. As mentioned earlier, one of the parrot traffickers boldly stated to the Norwegian Environment Agency's CITES expert that he saw no point in stopping the trafficking because profit was great and punishment insignificant.

This is evidence of a discrepancy between the seriousness of these crimes and their consequences for offenders. In sum, the potential that lies in the deterrent effect of punishment in Norway is negligible in relation to wildlife trade crimes. Because the potential punishment for such crimes is seldom made known to the public, the crimes continue.

From Norway, I turn the lens to a country with very different political, social, geographical and zoological features from Norway, but where wildlife trade has been regarded as a natural source of income and consumption as well as a part of daily life and practice for centuries.

9 Wildlife trafficking in Colombia

As shown in Chapter 2 on methodology, the case study from Colombia is based on interviews with experts in different fields and organizations, from environmental authorities to NGOs and universities, but all with an expertise concerning wildlife and wildlife trafficking in Colombia. Colombia is a nation rich in biodiversity and regarded primarily as a source country for wildlife trade, but as we shall see, the majority of the animals are trafficked within its borders or to neighbouring countries. Before I enter into the specifics of the trade as presented through my data, I will provide a glimpse into the historical and cultural foundations of WLT there.

Colombian trafficking in a historical and cultural perspective[1]

Like wildlife trade generally, wildlife trade in Colombia has deep roots and extends back into history. Rodríguez and García (2008) describe how today's practices are culturally, as well as commercially, based on tradition. These authors state that the consumption and exchange of wildlife go back thousands of years, with the commercialization of wildlife dating from at least the 15th and 16th centuries, thus largely coinciding with colonialism. Species that were driven almost to extinction include the manatee, which was used to feed slaves. European royalty used parrots as decoration and in collections, and their heads and tongues were favoured as a delicacy (Rodríguez and García (2008: 4621). Skins and furs, tortoises and turtles, have also been and are still used for decoration and in collections and are consumed as food. Historically, the export of wildlife was an important source of income for Colombia. It constituted 30% of all exports in 1870 (Vergara in Rodríguez and García 2008: 4621). In 1913 and 1915, the most trafficked species were birds (79.2%) and mammals (18.48%), while reptiles constituted 1.69%. Later, the export in wildlife was registered in weight, and between 1922 and 1924, 652 tons of animals and animal products were exported. In 1964, the percentage of earnings from wildlife trafficking was 11.9% of the GDP. According to Rodríguez and García (2008), in 1963 restrictions were put on the hunting of a number of species, including icotea turtles, caimans, primates and carnivores, and in 1977, a resolution prohibited the hunting for sport of mammals, birds and reptiles was passed. This did not stop the exploitation of llanero caimans; estimates show that at least 250,000 individuals were killed by the mid-60s. Between 1951 and 1980, 11,649,655 units of skin/fur were exported (Medem in Rodríguez and García 2008).

Although exports were reduced, Rodríguez and García (2008) explain that 'the reduction was not due to lack of demand but exhaustion of resources' (Rodríguez and García 2008: 4622). Despite this, based on licenses that were given for the hunt of caiman, in 1987 and 1988 Colombia exported 7,800 and 14,000 skins, respectively. In addition, the furs of felines were exported on a large scale between 1940 and 1970, as were exotic birds, primates and ornamental fish. Aquatic mammals were hunted so intensely that they have never recuperated (Rodríguez and García 2008)).

Problems have varied. For example, between 1940 and 1970, coinciding with the caucho (rubber) boom, a lot of illegal hunting took place, not the least of tigrillos, known as *las tigrilladas*.[2] People who were in the jungle to work in the extraction of caucho would hunt a tigrillo and bring the pelt, claws, etc. home as a trophy, and the pelts were sold for their value until, in 1978, hunting was restricted (Decreto 1608).

That the IWT has deep cultural roots, and that this also constitutes a problem in its eradication, is underlined by Ortiz-von Halle (then director of the regional office for TRAFFIC, South America, who was interviewed in Colombia for the research):

> First of all, there is the cultural basis, because this was legal until recently, in contrast to homicide and robberies which always have been crimes. This was what everybody did, and people made fortunes taking fauna from the Amazon and from everywhere. Animals were exported and everybody had one at home, we did. And from one day to the other because of a change in paradigm and change in legislation, it became illegal. I think what first of all characterises this is that it is a strongly culturally embedded tradition.

An anonymous expert also pointed to the cultural roots and dispersal of wildlife consumption and exploitation, describing such practices as hard to combat, partly because of the cultural aspect, the violence in the country, the lack of agricultural production and the forced displacement of people to big urban centres. Since these people are used to keeping wild animals as *mascotas* (pets), they bring them to the cities.

They are also accustomed to eating meat of free-born animals and carry these habits with them. He reckoned that 60%–70% of the people in Bogotá originate there and the rest come from other places; in Bogotá there is a colony from Los Llanos, a colony from Paisa, and each one of these colonies bring their gastronomic cultures; the *llaneros* eat meat of *chigüiro* (capybara), of *ñeque* (agouti, a rodent, *Dasyprocta punctate*) and of *borugo* (paca, a rodent). Those from Pasto bring *cuy* (guinea pig) meat; the people form the coast eat turtles, etc. Similarly, there are traditions of keeping pets, as stated by one interviewee:

> For example, in the coast you cannot do business without a canary in a cage; if the canary doesn't sing there is no business. Really such practices are against human logic and against collective interests, but these cultural practices, for example, in the coast, are deeply rooted. To break them is very difficult.

As an example of the implications of such practices, each year 4,000,000 individuals from different species are taken from the Amazon region, representing 40,000 tons of meat (Gómez et al., in Rodríguez and García 2008: 4622), a harm which is categorized as bushmeat trade, through which free-born animals are traded for food consumption.

Bushmeat consumption and trade in the meat of free-born animals is widespread in South America, as well as in West and Central Africa and tropical Asia. While the main reason behind the trade in bushmeat is to augment protein requirements, other reasons for wildlife consumption are related to cultural practices, local religions and traditional medicines (Angelici 2016: 503).

Species that are taken for food as cultural practice include icotea turtles (and their eggs) and iguanas. This was emphasized by several of the expert interviewees, such as Claudia Luz Rodriguez from the Ministry of the Environment and Claudia Brieva Rico from the Universidad Nacional de Colombia (National University of Colombia), the latter in charge of the rescue unit for wildlife there. It is also demonstrated through the large presence of seized icotea turtles both there and at the Centre for Reception and Rehabilitation of Wildlife in Bogotá (CRRFFS) of the District Secretariat of the Environment in Bogotá. Ortiz-von Halle elaborated on this topic:

> Just now, for example, they seized a thousand iguana eggs, in these 'fucked' [*jodidos*] markets associated with Easter, connected to some particular species: *la icotea*, *la iguana* or the meat of *chigüiro* [capybara] that are killed in great numbers and taken to Venezuela. But this is expanding and for example, there are coast families living in Bogotá and for them it is a cultural practice eating it every so often, so distribution webs are created for these products that go far beyond the income generated by the demand for these products [only] during Easter. And this is also the case with migrating ducks which are killed. So it begins like a *seasonal* thing but it then becomes *a generalised practice*, and they continue with people who make a living from this.

According to TRAFFIC, there are numerous bus routes that leave from Putumayo and Caquetá for the interior of the country and which pass through Villavicencio; these are bus lines that arrive at the most important markets. These bus lines and markets are used by people who travel bringing animals with them. Ortiz-von Halle elaborated on how the widespread migration from the countryside into the big cities, which is happening all over Latin America, contributes to the dispersal of such practices, and how these therefore have become the biggest centres of consumption of these species. Initially it was legal, and then it became semi-legal in that prohibition was not enforced. When that finally started happening, the trade went underground and there it continues.

There is a two-step process in the increase and dispersal of animal exploitation that drives people to this as a profit-making business. This, in turn, makes the animals more available to new groups and increases demand. Consequently, there is a spiral causing increased victimization.

Interviews conducted show that while culturally contingent food practices harming different animal species used to take place only at specified times of the year, these practices have been dispersed, increasing the pressure on the animals being consumed. That people bring their food traditions with them when they migrate, and also tend to increase the frequency of their consumption, must be seen in relation to the importance food has in the formation and confirmation of a person's social identity and the ways in which this depends on social upbringing and traditions. Every traveller will know that during long stays abroad, one craves familiar food. For migrants this has a strong impact on their lives, and as documented in connection to female migrants working as au pairs in Norway, their loss of sovereignty concerning what to eat and the absence of their traditional food proved problematic for many (Sollund 2012b).

The above quotation from Ortiz-von Halle further highlights information that is extremely important. While wildlife exploitation may have cultural roots, the escalating exploitation cannot be legitimized (Goyes and Sollund 2016) in it being culturally founded, first because it is unnecessary, second because these practices are spreading among people who formerly were unacquainted with them and third because these meats are being consumed throughout the year rather than for special occasions only.

There is an increased demand for bushmeat, not only by poor or relatively poor forest people, but, as implicitly suggested by Ortiz-von Halle, also by people who want to eat 'exotic' food. For example, during the Sandinista revolution in Nicaragua, a popular restaurant was established in central Managua, mostly frequented by the large contingent of *internationalistas*, foreigners who were there to support the revolution. The restaurant specialized in meat from free-born species, such as anteater (personal observation in 1987). Similarly, bushmeat can be found in markets in London and other West European cities (Angelici 2016; Sollund and Maher 2015; Wyatt 2013). Consequently, when cultural customs spread globally, animals who were previously exploited as part of local cultural traditions are put at further risk by being exploited globally.

The consumption of wildlife is not without its hazards in that it carries zoonotic diseases. In relation to a seizure of African snails at El Dorado Airport, CRRFFS received four kilos of African snails that were on their way from Ecuador to Spain. These are well-known carriers of various diseases; for example, they are infected with parasites that can be transferred to consumers (Pavanelli et al. 2017). That the spread of Ebola was caused by people eating primates is also well known (Alexander et al. 2015).

Not only people eating bushmeat, but also people who keep free-born animals as pets are exposed to diseases that can transfer from animals to humans. This point was emphasized by professor and veterinarian Brieva Rico in an interview:

> They [free-born pets] can transfer several pathogens. A person who has a parrot is exposed to 20 different diseases they would not be exposed to if they bought a canary legally, whom they know where was bred. He who keeps a monkey will be 100 times more exposed to diseases than he who keeps a dog, because the dog is vaccinated and is attended to by a veterinarian. And because the monkey is kept so close it is at risk of exchanging pathogens with humans.

One well-known example of a disease that easily transfers to humans from parrots is *chlamydophila (chlamydia) psittaci*, which can lead to pneumonia.

The capture of free-born animals is facilitated by logging, oil and mining industries that create roads through and extract timber from virgin forest (Boekhout van Solinge 2008a, 2008b; Mowbray 2015). Deforestation, rather than animal trafficking, was described as the main problem in the Northeast Amazon by interviewee Wilfredo Pachón, from the government organization Corporación para el Desarrollo Sostenible del Norte y el Oriente Amazónico (Corporation for Sustainable Development of the North and East Amazon). He said,

> The animals, as they have no places of refuge are searching for these small parts of land that are conserved, so la Serranía de la Lindosa, as it is a zone of rocky outcrop, it provides protection, so there they find a place to stay. In the case of the felines they need a large area to survive and to manage their territory, [but] they are concentrated in less than 18 hectares so the issue of deforestation is rather complicated.

The most frequent confiscations of animals in the region was not of animals destined for sale, but rather of people taking animals for their own use, either as pets or to eat them. In his jurisdiction, they had seized armadillos and *lapas*, whom the locals eat. Pachón expanded on the topic saying that the Northeast Amazon is an area being colonized by people from all over Colombia who want to improve their living conditions. They work from Monday to Saturday, and on the Sunday they go out to hunt for their weekly food. They hunt anteaters, rodents (*lapas*), armadillos and deer. Bushmeat practices include killing pregnant *lapas* and then cutting them open to take the babies, as well as abducting them and domesticating the offspring.

This human colonization of the Amazon thus severely displaces animals as well as resulting in theriocides in areas where animals should be sovereigns (Kymlicka and Donaldson 2011), a point I return to.

Similar developments taking place in Ecuador, a country neighbouring Colombia (Suárez et al. 2012; Suárez et al. (2009) claim that an expanded bushmeat trade created by the roads built for the oil industry in Yasuni National Park in Ecuador depended on four important factors: '1) an increase in population size; 2) improved hunting and fishing technology; 3) loss of local jobs or income sources from other activities; 4) a higher and unsaturated demand for wild meat' (369). The increase in hunting there is due to middlemen who offer indigenous people economic rewards for bushmeat. Indigenous people who have not previously engaged in wildlife trafficking start doing so when they are encouraged to, because of deforestation and because their previous livelihood is being destroyed by 'progress' and industrialization.

Loss of habitat and the abuse of animals facilitated by exploitation of resources in the forest, whether of minerals, oil or lumber, causes a serious threat and drives species to extinction all over the world, as in the well-known case of orangutans in Indonesia (Boekhout van Solinge 2008b; Gaveau et al. 2009). Their habitats are destroyed for palm oil production, and habitats are being destroyed in Colombia for the same reason (Mol 2013). Mol (2013) describes how the industry has left the Colombian Pacific coast, its inhabitants and the environment with contaminated soils, groundwater and rivers, habitat destruction, ecosystem disturbances and loss of aquatic and animal species (254).

As emphasized by Ortiz-von Halle, the problem is not one-dimensional but constituted by a number of intertwining factors, including the loss of habitat. For example, parrot, parakeet and primate species used to be abundant in Colombia because they had many habitats. Trafficking parrots was not a threat to species survival at that point because they existed elsewhere. Today, their habitats are but a fraction of what they were (cf. du Plessis 2000: 21). In addition, he underlined the role of international enterprises in habitat destruction, like the role of Chinese businesses:

> Chinese investments generate a lot of new infrastructure which opens access to zones hitherto unexploited, for example, by use of hydroelectric, roads, all this is a global dynamic, but it is at the same time very local. . . . So, there is a huge amount of different interplaying factors, because here is a relationship to neighboring countries; the illegal dynamic between Colombia and Peru, and between Paraguay and Argentina, and in such a large continent [as this is] what should be prioritised?

While many animals are trafficked within borders or to neighbouring countries, the international aspect of wildlife trade in Colombia is much downplayed in modern times. An article from *Centro de Investigación de Crimen organisado* states that 58,000 trafficked animals are seized in Colombia every year – 160 per day (Southwick 2013). On July 11, 2016, the Colombian police stopped a notorious group which for years had been trafficking animals to Ecuador and Mexico. When arrested, members of the group *los Pajeros*[3] were caught with 83 animals, including parakeets, parrots, toucans, storks, seagulls, turtles and capybaras. Between January and July 2016, the Colombian police had seized 8,300 free-born animals and arrested 1,553 persons 'for crimes against nature.'[4]

Since the pet trade constitutes a large and problematic part of the market for wildlife trade in Colombia, this will be further addressed in the following, before I turn to how trafficked animals are rescued.

The trade in free-born animals for the pet trade

As shown concerning the Norwegian data, to keep an animal as a pet is a widespread and deep-rooted practice. Historical documents reveal that indigenous peoples frequently captured young animals and reared them, and then either sold them or presented them to colonizers and visiting naturalists as curiosities (Alves 2012). Indigenous people traditionally kept and used animals in South America, and when Columbus first arrived in the New World he and his crew were met by natives offering skeins of spun cotton and wooden spears tipped with stingray tails, as well as live parrots. Since that first contact, parrots and macaws have featured in the domestic and international trade in live birds (Thomsen and Brautigam 1991). Analyses of historical documents indicate that indigenous people have kept song and ornamental birds since ancient times because of their beauty, songs and companionship, and bird keeping is firmly entrenched in local cultures and traditions (Carvalho in Alves 2012). Native birds and other animals were sent from colonial Brazil to Portugal for amusement or study throughout three centuries of continuous commercial transactions (Ribeiro in Alves 2012). The commercialization of wild animals was not viewed as illicit in the colonial period, and there are records in official correspondence of many commercial orders being placed (Ribeiro 2006 in Alves 2012). Not less than 72 non-European bird species were offered in the bird trade in Central Europe in 1794 (Bezzel and Prinzinger in Alves 2012).

In South America generally and in Colombia specifically, this practice to large degree involves the abduction and capture of free-born animals. This constitutes a serious problem. Like people who migrate bring their food practices with them, they also bring practices related to pet keeping: This was elaborated upon by Wilfredo Pachón, who said that when people who settle in unorganized settlements in the Northeast Amazon leave, they take their animals with them.

> Several of the confiscations the environmental police have done have been from people who live in such sectors of society. Others who are displaced to outside the county [*departamento*] do the same. So when they pack and leave, they pack also the parrots in a box and the other animals, and sometimes they manage to pass the permanent control posts of the environmental police. We as a corporation do sporadic inspections, but this happens, and also in routes where there is no inspection.

That the keeping of free-born animals as *mascotas* is widespread in Colombia and should be seen in relation to the migration wave is also elaborated upon by Javier Cifuentes of CRRFFS. He said that in 1966, Colombia was a country where 70% of its population was rural, whereas today, 70% are urban. There are still generations who think it is essential to have animals at home. All the interviewees underlined the seriousness of the pet trade. It was said that while open markets for wildlife trade have been shut down in central areas, in many very small villages in Colombia, in the Amazonía, in El Chocó, in Los Llanos, there are still markets for pets, because pets are in high demand, as stated by Ortiz-von Halle:

> Several monkey species can be found, some song birds and always more pericos [small parrot species] than larger parrots, because they go after what remains, because the others are disappearing and are harder to find.

Cifuentes also said that in the interior of the country, 'everyone dreams of having a parrot because they are beautiful, and because they repeat words.' Collectors want them, and they are desired as pets and for ornamental reasons. For example, it was said that the scarlet macaw (*Guacamaya bandera*) costs 300,000 pesos (150 USD) 'because many engineers working for the mining companies in Cerrejón or Pacific Rubiales have *fincas* (small farms/cottages) in la Guajira and they want the birds for ornamental reasons, to keep them on their *fincas*.' Many collectors collect all kinds of parrots; consequently, this is a big business. As it is a cultural tradition to keep a parrot in a cage, monkeys are used in the same way. They are kept chained or on a leash as pets in private homes. However, animals and birds who are adorable when young may become troublesome as they mature:

> What we most frequently confiscate are animals who have been kept as pets [*mascotas*] when people leave for the cities. Once we had tigrillos [oncillaor, margay], one confiscation and one voluntary delivery, from people who think they are cute when they are small, but then as they grow up they become difficult. This is generally a problem also with birds, such as parrots and macaws, and with monkeys.
>
> (Wilfred Pachón)

This quotation reiterates the lines of victimization and the interconnectedness of different environmental crimes (Goyes and Sollund 2016). In Guajira, many are poor and need to make a living, thus they turn to animal abductions. Harmful mining in the area results in settlements of people who also contribute to the demand of parrots and thus environmental destruction in several ways. During our visit to Unidad de Rescate de Animales Silvestres (Unit for the Rescue of Wild Animals) at the Faculty of Veterinary Medicine at the Universidad Nacional de Colombia (hereafter URRAS), Claudia Brieva Rico reiterated that the most affected species are icoteas, then birds, primarily *Psitaciformes*: parrots, parakeets, macaws, all those with hooked beaks and spectacular colours. Then come the primates, especially the *titi gris*, that live in the heavily colonized area of el Magdalena. She described how after logging has destroyed their habitats, they are captured and sold as *mascotas*. Again, this underlines the connection between different forms of eco crimes. Songbirds like *turpiales* and *cardenales* are sought after, as are reptile species, turtles, snakes, boas and iguanas. Finally, people also buy and keep mammals like the *tigrillo* (ocelot, margay), bush dogs (*los perros de monte*) and *cusumbos* (*nasuas*, coatis, a racoon species, also called nose bears).

In order to understand this trade, one must consider the people who comprise the pet markets. Ortiz-von Halle points to the buyers as either being rural, or people who have rural roots:

> You will not find a person with a large apartment with a parrot flying free in Bogotá, you will find it in the poorest barrios where they bring everything with them. So, they don't only have a small parrot [*perico*], they also have a big parrot [*loro*] and a *toche* [yellow-hooded blackbird, *Psittacidae*]. If the animals are . . . confiscated or die, simply, since they have this tradition, they continue to buy them because it is their habit to keep them in the patio.

Keeping free-born animals in homes is also a class issue. While the civil war has had a huge impact on internal migration in Colombia (Goyes 2016), the poor migrate to the cities. Poverty is also connected to lack of education, which provides a further challenge in creating awareness among these segments of society. One interviewee claimed the legislation introduced after Colombia joined CITES was counterproductive because it did not address the fundamental problem, that many of the people involved in taking the animals are poor and that this is why they do it. In his view, the introduction of legislation against wildlife trade increased the criminalization of the poor.

However, such practices are also being spread to people who decades ago would not have thought of acquiring a pet from the forest, as word spreads through social media. The different motives also point to the paradoxical relationship humans have with animals; while some are used for food, like icotea turtles who are brutally slaughtered, other animals, including icoteas, are companions. But the term 'companion' or 'pet' oversimplifies a phenomenon which is more complex (Sollund 2009, 2011). When parrots or songbirds are caged and fed with inadequate food (Leberatto 2016; Sollund 2011), or when monkeys are tinted and chained, it is hard to dignify these practices with words that imply mutuality and social relations, as the words 'companion' and 'pet' do.

According to one interviewee, the reason why rural people buy and transport wild animals to keep as pets is that it makes them feel closer to the forests they have left. In that way, the animals provide consolation in a situation of distress and alienation from nature in an urban environment. Although I acknowledge that such maltreatment stems from ignorance rather than cruelty, 'enslavement' might be a more accurate term than 'companionship.'

The practice of keeping free-born animals as *mascotas* or pets is so widespread that, according to Wilfred Pachón, at least 50% of the *fincas* in the Southeast Amazon have a pig, a monkey, a parrot or another animal who is held captive. The worst, he finds, is that animals are kept in cages or on a leash. These are circumstances, which when they receive complaints about them, lead to confiscation of the animals, if possible. When animals are confiscated, however, this is emotionally hard for the owners[5] of the animals. He emphasized that this is a cultural issue; they have heard of owners developing health issues when their animals are confiscated. One such case concerned a woman who kept a parrot:

> She came here, but we said we could not give him/her back to her because it is illegal to keep parrots in houses and it should be returned to its environment. So the woman was taken to the hospital and they had to provide her with medical care. It was a very difficult situation due to the issue of her health versus the issue of [il]legality.

Evidently this woman was very attached to the parrot, as many parrot owners are (Anderson 2003; Sollund 2011, 2017a). The story is also a good example of the unfortunate effect of people's desire to keep a parrot in their house, which leads many parrot species down the road of extinction (see Annorbah et al. 2016; Gastañaga et al. 2011; Guzmán et al. 2007; Sollund 2011; Tella and Hiraldo 2014; Wright et al. 2001). As previously mentioned, in the case of the African grey parrot, it was in 2016 enlisted in the Appendix I of CITES due to being heavily exploited for the pet trade. The blue Spix's macaw was thought extinct in the wild due to being vicitimized in the IWT, but has recently reestablished in very small numbers.

In the next section, I will present a more detailed overview of the animals who are seized from trafficking, including statistics of seized/received animals in two central institutions for the reception and care for free-born animals in the Bogotá area: CRRFFS and URRAS. Based on statistics from these organizations, I will provide a more nuanced picture of the different categories of wildlife exploitation in Colombia today.

The Centre for the Reception and Rehabilitation of Wild Fauna and Flora, Bogotá, and the animals they receive

In 1993, Environmental Law 99 was implemented, through which the Ministry of the Environment was established. All previous institutions were concentrated in a national system constituted by environmental authorities administering the natural resources with specific jurisdiction for the entire country. In Bogotá, the environmental authority is the aforementioned Secretaría Distrital de Ambiente (District Secretariat of the Environment). It controls all the taking/use of natural resources as well as noise, water, soil and flora and fauna, the latter under the Sub-dirección de Flora y Fauna Silvestre (Division of Wild Flora and Fauna). In Bogotá, liaison offices control three transport terminals: Terminal de Transport de Sur, Terminal de Transport Salitre and El Dorado Airport.

The Secretaría Distrital de Ambiente has functioned since 1990 (before the law was enacted) and in 1995 was reorganized as the environmental authority in the Bogotá area (Interviewee Javier Cifuentes).[6]

According to Javier Cifuentes, former head of CRRFFS, it was in recognition of the importance of preserving the fauna in a country counting for 10% of the earth's biodiversity that CRRFFS was established. CRRFFS was the first reception and rehabilitation centre and was established in cooperation with people from the Universidad Nacional. At the Centre, they receive on average of 4,000 animals annually. When animals are seized at any of the transport terminals, they are first subject to treatment and an assessment of their condition before they are sent to CRRFFS.

When asked about which are the most trafficked species in the country, several of the interviewees said turtles/tortoises, used both as pets and as food; birds (macaws, parrots, canaries and other songbirds); reptiles for the pet/collector trade (chameleons, iguanas, small lizards); insects and fish (including ornamental river fish); crocodile skins and mammal skins trafficked out of the country. In addition come mammals, such as the monkeys, like the *titi gris* and spider monkeys, and also tigrillos and other mammals trafficked for the pet/*mascotas* trade. One interviewee detailed,

> There is the parakeet; perico bronceado [*Brotogeris jugularis*], that is trafficked a lot because it is small, so it is easy to keep anywhere, there is the icotea turtle [*Trachemys scripta*] carried alive but also used as meat and eggs during Easter. Then there are the parrots [*Amazona ochrocephala*, yellow-crowned Amazons] which are the most trafficked. There are various species and certain times of the year some species are more heavily trafficked, like turtles during Easter.

Javier Cifuentes listed the parrot species:

> In the first place [the most trafficked] are the *Psittácides* – parrots, parakeets and macaws. Of the latter [macaws]: *Ara ararauna* and *Ara severa*. In the case of the parrots: *Amazona ochrocephala* and the *Amazona amazónica*. And concerning parakeets: *Brotogeris jugularis, Garganta de fuego*. Some *Algunos forpus, los Forpus conspicillatus*, the latter are the smallest *Psittaciformes* in the neotropics.

Parrots, in his view, are followed by reptiles, boas and freshwater turtles, especially the *Trachemys* (most of all the *Trachemys callirostris*) and *charapas* (turtles) and *morrocoy* (tortoises). Then come the mammals, above all primates the *titis* (*Saguinus oedipus* and *Saguinus leucopus*) that are endemic to the northern coast and Magdalena Medio respectively. Other primates are the *Mono ardilla* (spider monkey), which is the most commercialized and with the greatest national distribution in the Amazon, Meta, Casanare and Arauca.

The various expert interviewees differed somewhat in terms of which species was the most trafficked, but generally agreed that birds, particularly *Psittácides*, monkeys, reptiles, fish and frogs were most heavily trafficked. Other animals that did not come so often to the Centre were sloths, foxes and mountain dogs.

Statistics from CRRFFS in Bogotá show the number of animal intakes, releases and deaths during the period from January 1, 2011, to July 2017.[7] I do not possess statistics that show figures systematically throughout this period. Still, the

Figure 9.1 Yellow-fronted Amazon parrots (Amazona ochrocephala) trafficked for the Colombian pet trade, which are among the most trafficked species

Source: © David Rodríguez Goyes with permission from CRRFFS

Table 9.1 Top species brought to CRRFFS, January 1, 2011 to June 28, 2012

Taxa	*Species*	*N*
Reptiles	icotea tortoise/icotea del caribe (*Trachemys scripta callirotris*)	468
	tortoise morrocoy (*Chelonoidis carbonaria*)	358
	tortoise charapa (*Podocnemis unifilis*)	106
	boa constrictor	36
	rattlesnake/culebra cascabel (*Crotalos durissus*)	16
Birds	perico bronceado (*Brotogeris jugularis*)	477
	yellow-fronted Amazon (*Amazona ochrocephala*)	247
	cotorra carisucia (*Aratinga pertinax*)	169
	canario costeño (*Sicalis flaveola*)	125
	turpial amarillo (*Icterus nigrogularis*)	110
Mammals	titi gris (*Saguinus leucopus*)	40
	spider monkey (*Saimiri sciureus*)	24
	mono maicero (*Cebus apella*)	13
	zariuella (*Sidelphys marsupialis*)	11
	mountain dog (*Potos flavous*)	6
Amphibians	harlequin frog/rana arlequín (*Dendrobates histrionicus*)	48
Invertebrates	caracol manzana (*pomacea bridgesii*)	109
Total		2,363

Source: CRRFFS: Informe final de Ejecución 2012

ones available provide an indication of the number of animals who were either delivered to the Centre or who were seized during this period, although they, unfortunately, do not give me a systematic overview of the whole period, and consequently less can be said about increases or decreases over these years.

The parrot (*perioco bronceado*) was the most trafficked species followed by the icotea, trafficked for the pet and bushmeat trades. These numbers indicate that many animals are trafficked to the Bogotá area; but it is impossible to say how many are trafficked in total. As pointed out by TRAFFIC, the confiscations are the tip of the iceberg. If the numbers of animals confiscated increase, this could be an indication of an increased effort to control the trade, rather than an actual increase in trafficking. That only a small minority of the trafficking is ever uncovered is supported by another interviewee (anonymous), talking about the seizures by the environmental authorities in Bogotá:

> Every day a parrot is seized, every day. So, if one is seized every day, there are so many more in trade. If one is confiscated at the terminal Salitre, in the terminal Sur, the police may seize another, so that is three. Not to mention all the private cars and those that are brought by people who know about the inspections and who get off [the bus] before they arrive at the terminals. And finally, the animals that die on the way. So there are huge quantities of animals involved.

While many die during the journey, many also die after they have been seized. The Tables 9.2a and b illustrate mortality at the CRRFFS.

Concerning more positive figures, the report from 2011 also shows what happened to the animals who left the Centre. Of a total of 427 animals, 328 were liberated (76.8%), six were relocated (1.4%), while 93 (21.7%) were euthanized (CRRFFS 2012: 26).

In 2015, more than 2,500 animals were registered as incoming at CRRFFS. All received veterinary attention as well as a zoo technical and biological evaluation.

Table 9.2a Mortality figures of animals at CRRFFS (2012)

	Initial inventory per month	*Incoming animals per month*	*Number that die or are euthanized**	*Total population*	*Mortality %*
April	2,049	176	490	2,225	22.02
May	1,749	258	97	2,007	4.83
June	1,315	231	121	1,546	7.83
July	1,330	248	127	1,578	8.05
August	1,400	294	164	1,694	9.68
September	1,305	153	70	1,458	4.80
October	1,097	256	75	1,353	5.54
November	1,207	234	98	1,441	6.80
December	1,184	385	93	1,569	5.93
Total 2011		2,235	1,335		

Table 9.2b Mortality figures of animals at CRRFFS (January–June, 2012)

	Initial inventory per month	*Incoming animals per month*	*Number that die or are euthanized*	*Total population*	*Mortality %*
January	986	320	93	1,306	7.12
February	1,154	194	108	1,348	8.01
March	1,072	157	87	1,120	7.77
April	1,024	313	82	1,337	6.13
May	1,146	243	79	1,389	5.69
June	1,148	222	71	1,370	5.18
Total		1,449	520		

Source: Informe de gestion centro de recepcion de flora y fauna silvestre CRRFFS informe final contrato 0738 sda-udca: 102

*The numbers refer to animals who have survived until they arrive at CRRFFS, but die there or are euthanized because of their condition. It is unknown how many animals would have died were they not seized. Therefore, the interviewees repeated statements that up to 90% of animals die before reaching their final destination is incompatible with the statistics from the Centre.

The total number of intake animals for the period was 3,684 animals; the total number of deaths for the period was 1,855 animals, more than 50%.

Table 9.3 Monthly CRRFFS animal entries 2015

	Voluntary entries	*Confiscations*	*Rescues*	*Total**
January	332	109	5	446
February	269	94	7	370
March	117	73	9	219
April	113	98	28	239
May	104	39	20	163
June	122	58	18	198
July	81	110	20	211
August	93	82	18	193
September	72	40	25	137
October	115	31	7	153
November	112	82	4	198
December	186	33	2	221
Total	1,716	849	163	2,748

*Excluding births at the Centre

The peaks of 2015 were in January and February due to the migratory routes of the *tinguas pico rojo* (new world purple gallinule, *Porphyrio martinicus*) who pass over the Bogotá savanna. Most of the animals were delivered voluntarily to the Centre.

The most trafficked species in 2015 were *Porphyrio martinicus* (new world purple gallinule), *Brotogeris jugularis* (orange-chinned parakeet/tovi parakeet), *Chelonoidis carbonaria* (red-footed tortoise), *Trachemys callirostris* (Colombia slider turtle), *Sicalis flaveola* (saffron finch), *Eupsittula pertinax* (brown-throated parakeet/St. Thomas conure) and *Amazona ochrocephala* (yellow-crowned Amazon parrot).

For 2017, I received limited figures for January–September from CRRFFS. Also for 2017, most animal entries concerned voluntary deliveries. In total, 1,709 were registered during these months, of which 1,407 were voluntary deliveries, 273 were confiscations and 23 were rescues. Species were not specified. According to the CRRFFS report for 2017, the majority of the animals who came to the Centre were from Bogotá and the departments of Tolima, Arauca, Cesar, Córdoba and Magdalena. There were also confiscations of animals from Madagascar (60), Venezuela (8) and the US (5) in 2015. Concerning species that are threatened with extinction, such as the tigrillo, CRRFFS will also secure genetic material before returning the animal.

The figures I have obtained and from which the above is derived are not complete. Nonetheless, the reports still contain information concerning what happens to the animals who do not die prior to their entry or during their stay because of injuries inflicted upon them in trafficking.

Rehabilitating and repatriating animals who have been victims of abductions is an important part of the work of the Centre, and in 2017, the cross-disciplinary teams of the Centre freed 1,257 individuals after their rehabilitation process. Seven individuals who had become human dependent and therefore could not be returned to a natural habitat were relocated to other more natural environments. The number of animals who were returned to natural habitats, 1,257 for January–September, is thus significantly increased from 2011, when only 328 were liberated. This may indicate that the Centre enjoys more success in the rehabilitation and liberation processes, but as said, the figures I have received are too random to form a complete picture. It is to be expected that the situation for animals who are confiscated in trafficking will significantly improve at the Centre due to it recently receiving more than 6 million USD to improve its facilities.[8] In the next section, I turn to the rehabilitation and liberation of trafficking victims undertaken by another important institution in the Bogotá area, the National University of Colombia, Unidad de Rescate de Animales Silvestres (URRAS; Unit for the Rescue of Wild Animals) in the Northeast Amazon.

Influx and rehabilitation of free-born animals at URRAS and in the Northeast Amazon

Any romantic illusions that URRAS can free captivated animals quickly evaporated once I began interviewing staff. One interviewee said rehabilitation could take five years. If, for example, a migratory bird has been caught and s/he does not suffer from injuries or has injuries that have healed quickly, s/he may successfully be released. But if s/he is injured, s/he may easily die when released if not sufficiently prepared or released in the wrong or unfamiliar habitat. This is also reflected in the work of URRAS, where parrots from the pet trade, especially yellow-crowned Amazons, are among the most numerous species. During a visit to URRAS where we were guided by professor and coordinator of the Faculty of Veterinary Medicine, Claudia Brieva Rico in September 2017, we witnessed Amazon parrots, turtles, various monkey species and red squirrels in the different stages of reception and rehabilitation. As at CRRFFS, people can voluntarily deliver their pets to the Centre and URRAS is obliged to receive them. This means that if someone, for example, inherits a parrot from their grandmother, or if their animal gets ill, they can bring the animal to the Centre, but this, unfortunately, may be too late for the animals to be saved. Consequently, they will be euthanized. Many of these previous pets have been subject to malnutrition and maltreatment: Turtles remain the size of juveniles, tortoises are drowned because people erroneously believe they must be kept in water, and parrots are fed with meat, chocolate, biscuits and rice. URRAS also receives birds of prey, specifically eagles who are shot as pests by locals.

The animals go through various stages where they receive less and less human contact, have to get accustomed to the flock with which they will be released and must learn to forage. The Centre also ensures that the flock/group contains males and females to enable them to breed. The rehabilitation process of birds takes several years on average, depending on when there is an available location to release them and when they receive the permission of the environmental authorities. In order to track them, animals are equipped with tracking devices and also followed through observations (Capera n.d.; Mateus and Brieva 2010; Camargo-Rodríguez et al. n.d.). According to Claudia Brieva Rico, 70% of the liberations are successful, which must be regarded as a very good result.

Rehabilitation can be complicated when, for example, monkeys and parrots have not learnt how to manage in a natural environment because they were abducted as babies. Despite success stories of rehabilitated and released animals, another veterinary interviewee underlined that many parrots who have been in human custody too long – five, six years – are no longer capable of surviving in their natural habitat. This was the case, for example, for many of the birds at CRRFFS who were kept there, because they were not regarded as fit for release.

The rehabilitation centre will first make an assessment, not only of the physical state of the victim, but also of his/her species, although sometimes this is difficult. The animal's place of origin must also be established, as animals cannot be released into habitats unknown to them and where they may not be able to fend for themselves. Further, during rehabilitation parrots will be exposed to danger to force them to fly, such as putting a boa in the tree where they are.

Another of the interviewees, Wilfredo Pachón from the Corporación para el Desarrollo sostenible del Norte y Oriente Amazónico described what is done when animals are confiscated in this jurisdiction. As in URRAS and CRRFFS, veterinarians will first assess the health of the animals. If an animal is seriously injured, s/he will be euthanized and buried. If s/he is sufficiently well to recover, s/he will be taken to a centre for rehabilitation to receive treatment. Then s/he will be released, unless s/he is too accustomed to human contact, in which cases s/he will be taken to one of the *bioparques* (reserves).

There are several *bioparques* in Colombia. Several of their websites state that their aim is to protect the environment and animal species, while being places to educate people about the environment. What kind of requirements are in place if someone wishes to establish a *bioparque* is unknown. While I was in Colombia in September 2017, I visited one, Bioparque La reserva Cota.[9] While the guide there said it was a sanctuary for animals apprehended in trafficking, Claudia Brieva Rico described the place as a zoo. What kind of conditions are in place for the animals in *bioparques* are therefore likely to vary depending on the commitment and resources of the reserve; for example, in Cota most of the birds were kept indoors. The Corporación para el Desarrollo sostenible del Norte y Oriente Amazónico has two sites for liberation, but Wilfredo Pachón did not elaborate on how they assess whether these provide the right environment for the animals released. Both of the locations are in the zone of the Serranía de la Lindosa, which still has a considerable amount of forest and is important for preservation, according to Pachón. Volunteers bring the animals to where they are released and assist in the animal releases.

Ninety percent of the animals who are seized/delivered here are released, as the majority of the animals arrive in good condition. The reason why so many can be returned is that, in contrast to animals who are seized/delivered in Bogotá, the animals here have not been brought long distances, and therefore have suffered fewer injuries and less stress, dehydration or starvation. During their breeding season, many mammals, such as tigrillos, come to the humid areas around San José del Guaviare and come in direct contact with people. These are caught, rehabilitated and returned to their natural habitats, rather than letting them remain in human-made surroundings.

Not all interviewees were unanimous regarding the success of releases. Without detailing whom, an interviewee from ProAves accused rescue/rehabilitation centres of liberating animals, who were not fit for release, into unsuitable locations. This person's opinions were in line with what interviewees with URRAS and CRRFFS staff said about the requirements that must be in place for an animal to be released, indicating that these centres were not the ones he had in mind:

> It is usual to observe confiscations of 2–300 parrots or primates, and the units [e.g., police] that are in charge of handling these, as they are short of resources and skills in handling them, make inadequate liberations and without any supervision in the localities they think are good. Because, if you don't know, you may think that any forest is fine for the animal, but they don't know that these species have been commercialised in certain areas, but are brought to another place which is totally different. So very frequently in such zones where there are many liberations, the animals die of hunger within a few days, or are caught again, both parrots and monkeys.

He also said that if police confiscate an animal in a remote part of the country, they irresponsibly liberate animals who do not meet the necessary requirements for liberation. This suggests that CRRFFS and URRAS have different standards than some other reception centres in Colombia, and also that elsewhere animals may be released who have not been sufficiently rehabilitated.

Ortiz-von Halle said repatriation efforts at returning trafficking victims to their habitats were useless propaganda and not effective enough to compensate for the damage done. Only if the animal is one of the last belonging to her species did he see it as worthwhile to save the animal for conservation purposes, otherwise he viewed taking tissue, feathers from them, etc. as an adequate response. With such statements, he was much more in line with the previous chair of the standing committee of CITES, cited in the Norway chapters. Such perceptions disregard, however, that animal trafficking victims have intrinsic value and interests of their own in living their lives. Such statements from an anthropocentric viewpoint, corresponding to the CITES logic, imply they are merely 'specimens.' This is an issue which will be further debated in the Chapters 13 and 14 concerning animal victimization and rights.

It is hard to assess whether releases in the Northeast Amazon follow the same requirements for releases as in the two centres in Bogotá, and consequently would be the kind of releases that were criticized by the interviewees from ProAves and TRAFFIC. In Bogotá, they seemed very careful to ensure the animals were fit for release and fully rehabilitated. They also did post-release follow-up. It does appear, however, that there are many destinies for trafficking victims and also that *bioparques* may have dual motivations: providing a sanctuary for animals who cannot be returned to their natural habitat and educating the public. But they may also make a profit and function as ordinary zoos with animals on display.

Figure 9.2 Night monkey (*Aotus*) trafficked in Colombia both for the pet trade and for malaria experiments

Source: © David Rodríguez Goyes with permission from CRRFFS

In the Colombian interviews, broader implications for the ecosystems were also emphasized by most interviewees. For example, not only will only one of 15 individuals remain alive during a trafficking incident, but in order to catch one animal, traffickers often cut down trees or set fire to the forest to drive out the animals, resulting in the destruction of entire ecosystems, the same way as areas are deforested during the yearly Peruvian parrot abductions (Gonzales 2003). In this way, the habitats of the targeted species are also destroyed, causing twofold victimization. Such harm is an issue I return to in the next chapter, in the section discussing the Patarroyo case.

Notes

1 Parts of this section have previously been published as Sollund (2017d).
2 Analogous to *la loreada* in Peru, where people abduct the parrots seasonally (Gonzales 2003).
3 Derived from *pajaro*, 'bird' in Spanish.
4 http://sostenibilidad.semana.com/medio-ambiente/articulo/cayo-la-mayor-red-de-trafico-de-especies-silvestres-de-colombia/35551
5 'Abductors' is a more accurate term since the ownership follows from an illegal abduction.
6 See also a brief history of the Secretariat at www.ambientebogota.gov.co/web/sda/algo-de-historia
7 INFORME DE GESTION CENTRO DE RECEPCION DE FLORA Y FAUNA SILVESTRE CRFFS INFORME FINAL CONTRATO 0738 SDA-UDCA. Bogotá (2012). (Secretaria distrital de ambiente SDA 2012: 30) Dirección de evaluación y seguimiento ambiental. Subdirección silvicultura flora y fauna Silvestre. I have annual statistics for 2016, and half the year for 2017. This tentative, but limited picture of wildlife seizures in Bogotá and its surroundings these statistics serve to paint is complemented and supported by the interview data, specifically from the Centre and the interviews with Claudia Brieva Rico at the National University of Colombia.
8 Personal communication with Javier Cifuentes and Jorge Enrique Hernandez Lopez, September 2017.
9 www.inspirock.com/colombia/cota/bioparque-la-reserva-a2185599715

10 The animal victims in Colombia and how they are abused

The most obvious result of victimization through trafficking is death. Luz Maria Cuadros of CRRFFS said that often 100 birds would come in who had recently been captured on the coast, but still they would all die. They also die during capture, when they are sent/shipped from their place of origin, during transport and when they arrive at their destination. The length of the journey is crucial. Tarantellas and turtles, when they arrive, often come in great numbers. The mortality rate is 80%–90%. The deaths continue during quarantine because of the injuries they have suffered.

Clearly abusive techniques are applied to catch animals. Small birds like canaries and small parakeets are caught by trappers who put glue on the trees and branches where the birds gather to eat. They will be brutally removed, often causing fractures and other injuries, before they are stocked. Trappers also use cage traps with a mechanism which closes the cage when the birds enter, meaning they are without food until the trapper returns. Small birds, including parrots, need to eat frequently because of their high metabolism. Consequently, being left without food and water for hours can have catastrophic effects on the bird's health and survival.

Bird trappers also use nets, known as *red de niebla*, that biologists use when trapping birds for scientific reasons. These nets can be bought by anybody, and therefore they can be set up to catch large quantities. After catching the birds with nets, according to ProAves, they are stuffed into PVC tubes and taken on the bus. This is a joint operation of the settler (who catches the birds), the trafficker and the buyer. It is not hard to imagine the fright and suffering that a bird being treated in such a way goes through, and it makes sense that the majority of the birds die during transport (see Wyatt 2014a concerning the falcon trade).

Primates, especially the *titi gris*, which is one of the most trafficked animals in the pet trade, are also caught using cruel methods. In order to capture them, it is necessary to kill the mother because they carry their babies with them. The traumatized babies can then be abducted. Claudia Luz Rodríguez described how primates, who have been abducted to become pets, are subjected to degrading treatment, such as having their teeth filed down and their fur tinted.

Another way to catch primates is to get them used to being fed, and then halting the feeding to lure them into the abductor's open house where there is food. The monkey can then be captured.

Claudia Brieva Rico and Claudia Luz Rodríguez underlined the cruelty of the methods used to capture animals. Some species are very vulnerable to these kind of situations; for example, infant sloths die in 89% of the cases. In transport, the more you cook, the more you get, so 50 individuals are crammed into a box, and some are sedated to prevent them from screaming. Interviewees said that out of a hundred, ten arrive alive, which is why so many are abducted. Of those who arrive, 80% die in the cities because of the climate. The very few who remain alive are never able to breed because they will live their whole lives in a cage, so there is also a biological loss.

As shown, among the most trafficked species are turtles who are taken as white meat. These animals are also killed in extremely cruel ways. The prevalence can be suggested by the fact that when doing a Google search for icotea turtles, the first to appear was a YouTube video explaining how a turtle should be slaughtered.[1]

One interviewee elaborated on how animals are harmed both when they are captured and during captivity. For example, parrots don't know they are parrots because they only relate to humans; *titi grises* arrive at the Centre with deep wounds or without hands; parrots cannot fly because their flying feathers have been cut or they have been mutilated to prevent them from flying; they come without feet which may have been torn off when they were captured; or their beaks are deformed due to malnutrition.

The largest exports from Colombia concern babillas (interview data; Sinovas et al. 2017). A search for photos[2] of babilla farms in Colombia revealed overcrowded conditions, dirty water, etc. Although it is impossible to say how representative the *zoocriadores* (breeding facilities for species in demand) in these pictures are, I have witnessed the conditions for the animals on a crocodile breeding facility in Cuba, and if babilla farms in Colombia are anything similar, there is definitely a risk of animal abuse here as well.

The injuries and abuses inflicted on animals make plain that wildlife trafficking is violence in its most grotesque form, whether directly inflicted upon the animals when they are abducted or killed, when they are transported, or when they are chained, encaged and/or mutilated, followed by negligence of their physical, psychological, nutritional and social needs. The great variety of species in the reception centres, include various *Psittacide* species (parrots), other birds (caseriformes, eagle, owl, pavos), mountain dogs, nose bears, tortoises and turtles, and several primate species (lanudos monkeys, maiceros monkeys, marimonda monkeys, night monos).

Overview of main categories and motives for abuse and theriocide of free-born animals in Colombia

The interviews in Colombia and seizure data provided a foundation for a typology relating to the various motives for the exploitation of animals, whether they were trafficked alive and meant to be kept alive or whether they were subsequently killed. As shown, bushmeat trade is also important. Today, much animal trade and consumption take place within national borders, although transnational trafficking from Colombia is not excluded, whether to the Caribbean, Venezuela or Europe. This is parallel to the situation in Peru where the majority of WLT is internal and deeply culturally ingrained (Leberatto 2016). Several of the interviewees suggested that animals were likely to be trafficked until their species became extinct or were at the brink of extinction, whereupon traffickers would turn to other species (see Gastañaga et al. 2011; Guzmán et al. 2007; Pires and Clark 2011; Wright et al. 2001 for specific predictions about the parrot trade). As mentioned, Ortiz-von Halle from TRAFFIC said,

> There is now increasingly [more trafficking in] small parrots than in big parrots, because they turn to what is left, because the big ones are lost and it becomes all the time more difficult to find birds of these species.

Leberatto found that his interviewees lamented both the loss of species and the forests where they had thrived, and they regretted their own contribution to the loss of animals. A study into the decreasing parrot populations found also that the illegal trafficking for the pet trade now constitutes the largest threat to parrot species survival (Berkunsky et al. 2017).

The interviewee from ProAves had also observed that many species, not only of birds, were decimated by trade. For example, a fish known as *las cuchas*, that adheres to stones, was trafficked extensively in the 1980s–90s and is now practically gone from the Magdalena River.

There are twelve main categories of reasons/motives people have for getting involved in wildlife use/consumption/destruction in Colombia. I will first sketch out the categories, then elaborate on the various practices related to the use of free-born animals. I will later return to the motives of abductors and traffickers and their modus operandi.

1 **Pet trade:** As shown, parrots and other bird species, primates like the *titi gris* and turtles/tortoises are the most trafficked species for the pet trade. The pet trade also deals in other species, such as tigrillos (ocelots), sloths and squirrels. Fish and poisonous frogs are trafficked from Colombia to be used for ornamental purposes in Germany, Japan and the Netherlands.
2 **Collectors:** Frogs and fish are also attractive for collectors, and poisonous frogs are so heavily trafficked that species have suffered from trade. For example, the *Phyllobates terribilis*, the most venomous frog, is attractive because it is poisonous and generates an enormous interest and high prices, especially in Asian countries (Japan, Thailand and Taiwan). It has therefore become endangered (Nijman and Shepherd 2010).
3 **Animal experimentation and biopiracy:**[3] Non-human primates have frequently been trafficked for experimentation because they bear a physiological resemblance to human primates. Primates have been trafficked in large numbers to Western laboratories for biomedical research (Maldonado and Waters 2017; Zimmerman 2003). According to interviewee Luz Rodríguez, this use has declined as there has been a development in other experimental

methods[4] that do not require the use of animals, and Colombia banned the export of primates in 1974 (Maldonado and Waters 2017). All primates are listed in Appendix I or II of CITES. Despite this, in Colombia, the *Aotus vociferans* (night monkeys) have for decades been trafficked from the Amazon basin, including from Peru and Brazil, to be used in malaria research experiments by Manuel Elkin Patarroyo in Colombia (Goyes 2015; Maldonado et al. 2009; Maldonado and Lafon 2017; see section below for elaboration). Animals are abducted in order to extract the biological/chemical components of their bodies, amphibians in particular are used to find toxins and metabolites by the pharmaceutical industry in the Andean region. Despite stringent legislation concerning the access to 'genetic resources,' little work has been done to throw light on this biopiracy. Others species exploited by foreign scientists and companies that come to Colombia in search of metabolites and proteins is the venomous coral snake. The increase in the trafficking of such species for pharmaceutical purposes also changes the dynamics of WLT for experimental use in Colombia (interviewee Claudia Luz Rodríguez, Goyes and Sollund 2018).

4 **Furs and skins:** Skin and fur from reptile species, including crocodile species and felines, such as panther and *tigrillo* (margay and ocelot)[5] are sought after. Reptile skins that are exported illegally have been seized in Spain, Germany and the US.
5 **Food:** Icotea turtles, iguana eggs, the *Capybara* (chigüiro) and eagles are hunted and used in Colombia and Venezuela because they are considered white meat and are thus 'allowed' in festive seasons, when 'red meat' is not allowed. Locals hunt armadillos, large rodents and monkeys for consumption.
6 **Handicraft:** Turtles, conchs and corals are used for jewellery, combs and musical instruments.[6]
7 **Ritual magic:** Serpents are used in ritual magic.[7] The tail of the rattlesnake is used in amulets. Owls are trafficked extensively for such purposes, as they are considered to bring good luck and are therefore used as *mascotas.*
8 **Traditional medicine:** Meat from raptors such as eagles and hawks is regarded as aphrodisiacal or believed to possess special properties. Vultures' blood is believed to cure asthma and cancer. In addition, the grease from bear and the penis of the river dolphin are used in traditional medicine (see Alves and Rosa 2008).
9 **Breeding purposes:** *Zoocriaderos* also buy free-born animals for breeding purposes.
10 **Selfies:** Another category that has exploded, judging by media reports, is the use of free-born animals for people to pose with in their selfies. Snakes are used for this purpose in Bogotá, and animals, such as sloths and macaws, are abducted in the Amazon for this purpose (Daily 2017). In addition to these harms, animals are drugged and trees are felled in forests to get access to sloths. Internationally, there are frequent reports of animals, such as dolphins and sharks, who have died during people's endeavours to be photographed

with them, and examples of lion cubs who are drugged for photo sessions are legion. I saw one myself in Ibiza, Spain, in the 1990s.

11 **Theriocides committed against animals regarded as enemies.** Among the animals hospitalized in rehabilitation centres are eagles, who are regarded as pests by peasants. Felines are also hunted as enemies by people in the Southeast Amazon who regard them as a threat to their pigs or cows. Monkeys are hunted when they destroy crops. The pressure on their habitats make the maize and fruits that are cultivated by the farmers appealing to animals. When the farmers shoot a feline, they can also gain financially by selling the skin, so even though this may happen only sporadically, there is a dual motive.

12 **Hunting for fun:** A final motive for killing free-born animals is hunting as a recreational pastime, not unlike in the Norwegian context (Sollund 2017b). Such hunting affects lapas significantly because they only have one offspring per year. Armadillos are also hunted, but without the same effect on the species because they reproduce four times a year. Hunting is a phenomenon which can be found all over the planet where there is tradition of hunting and where farmers keep animals whom free-born animals prey on. As discussed earlier, hunting is also, in many cultures, regarded as an aspect of masculinity (e.g., Bye 2003; Kheel 1996; Maldonado and Waters 2017; Nurse 2015; Sollund 2016b, 2017a)

The above categories are not mutually exclusive. Frogs and rare parrots are attractive both for people desiring a special and charming pet but also for collectors, breeders and biochemists. A bear might be killed for the grease, the baby of the killed bear might then be sold as a pet or to a zoo, or the bear might be killed because s/he is destroying crops.

While my interviewees identified the above as the most common reasons for animal trade, use and theriocide, the list of species is not exhaustive. The trade in crocodile skins is big even today, and when the animals originate from *zoocriadores*, it is legal, according to interviewees. The trade in feline skins was big in the 1960s and 70s.

While much of the export descried earlier was of dead individuals or products made from them (e.g., skins, furs and corals), the trade within Colombia today very often involves live animals. Regarding the most trafficked species, Ortiz-von Halle from TRAFFIC said that in addition to the already mentioned icoteas, the capybara in Los Llanos and the babilla (a crocodile species) are extremely important in terms of volume.

In addition to food, the pet trafficking category of the trade appears to be the most important in the Colombian context, based on the interviews. In the coming section, I will focus on *how* the trade takes place and the actors involved.

Modus operandi in Colombia

Wildlife trafficking is by interviewees identified as a major crime in Colombia. Representatives from CRRFFS stated, ‘We are totally aware that the illegal wildlife trade in the country follows drug trafficking as the most lucrative illegal activity in the country.' Yet, counter to the drug trade, far more 'ordinary people' are involved. Concerning the illegal trade, interviewees uniformly stated that most of the animals who are trafficked, whether dead or alive, are taken from the northern coast area. Over the past 15 years, in 95% of the cases, the animals/products have originated far from Bogotá, the majority from the Atlantic coast and south of Tolima, Cundinamarca and Los Llanos. Birds and reptiles (turtles, tortoises) are most affected. One interviewee described the patterns of trafficking as follows:

> The trafficking is heavy in the Caribbean coast, and also primarily in the Middle Magdalena region, because the central route goes through here and this is where people travel to do business. Then they get involved in the trafficking of fauna. Dorada is the place where most of the wildlife trade takes place, above all because the region is very biodiverse and it is easy to take the animals.

According to another interviewee, animals often pass through Bogotá, with either national or international destinations, whether for food, as personal property, or for commerce, although the illegal international trade has been significantly reduced. Nowadays, there are seldom seizures of cargos with 1,500 or more animals, which was the case a few years ago, venomous frogs who are exploited by the pharmaceutical industry being one such 'bulk cargo.' Other big seizures involve the *Strombus gigas* (giant snails) and crocodile skins that people were smuggling out of the country without the necessary CITES documentation.

The coastal area (el Bajo Cauca, el San Jorge, el Magdalena, la Sierra Nevada) is very important because of its rich biodiversity and wetlands, but this also means that wildlife has traditionally been exploited there, in particular species such as manatees and sea turtles. The towns on the coast have been and still are lucrative markets, which also include leather markets. The wildlife trade in the coastal area, therefore, is regarded as more important for the national economy than is Amazonía's. This, according to Ortiz-von Halle, was the case until fauna could be flown in from Leticia in Amazonía, which indicates a professionalization of the trade. The importance of these markets has increased because of the availability and abundance of fauna from the coast and the wetlands and by the large migration from these areas which has spread, for example, practices concerning meat consumption.

There are numerous reasons for individuals to participate in the IWT in Colombia, and their motives depend on where in the chain they fit, whether they are consumers, middlemen or abductors/killers. With the exception of consumers, there are three types of people involved in acquiring and selling animals: (1) people who live in the vicinity of the animals near forests, abduct them for financial gain or to use/keep the animals for themselves; (2) people who act upon pecuniary encouragement from buyers who depend on locals who have knowledge about the animals, their habits and how to catch and/or kill them;

and (3) people who are part of the chain in a more organized way. (2) and (3) often overlap.

Below are quotations from interviews with several of the expert interviewees.[8] They illustrate how abduction and trafficking take place.

The first quotations show how people act opportunistically for financial benefit, using their local and biological knowledge about the animals' whereabouts and when they breed:

> It often happens, a person would say, 'it had not occurred to me, but I can sell this parrot,' so he goes and takes it from the forest or he takes a monkey or any other animal, and sells it at times when a lot of people – tourists – pass on the highways. People know that if they take an animal – the parrots or other birds to the national market – they know a lot of people pass through there during vacations, and they know they will succeed in earning some pesos.
>
> It is free access, so people think that 'rather than others taking it I prefer to take it myself' and earn some money. So, in that way go skins from deer and tigrillo [ocelot/margay] and arrive at a market where someone is willing to pay.

That it is free access is also partly because it is so *easy* to access animals (birds):

> The easiest way, obviously, is to take the nests, in the forests. The people know when the birds breed, the parrots, the songbirds, etc. So they just wait and take them, and it is by far the easiest way.
>
> Regarding the birds, the settlers will take the nests, and then look for the easiest way of commercializing the birds, and here there are no intermediaries so they take the parrots and sell them along the road.

Three groups are behind this type of abduction, although none is solely dependent on wildlife trade: *campesinos* (farmers), *colonos* (settlers) and indigenous people. Because they know the breeding patterns of birds, they capture the animals in these periods. The quotations illustrate that even though living close to nature and non-human animals, they are not necessarily respected. Even the small sums that are earned make a difference in their view, and the animals living in their surroundings are regarded in economic terms, rather than in any relational way. It appears that local knowledge about the animals is crucial in the abduction of them.

> It almost becomes a daily sustenance, an easy way to obtain money. Climb up in a tree, take the nest and they will give you 20,000 or 30,000 pesos,[9] an insignificant sum. Or, 'I see that where I live there are a lot of tourists, so it is easy to take a monkey, put in on my shoulder and stand in the street, signal to the cars that pass, and say, "buy this monkey from me."'

The following quotations describe the chain that is part of the trafficking and what happens to the animals along this chain. They indicate that a certain level of organization is necessary to bring the animals to the cities where, if they survive, they eventually reach the consumers' hands.

> It may take place the same way as with drugs; you pay someone to cultivate and after the process someone else will take the profit. So in this case some persons will catch the animals in their habitat, they sell them for a very low cost to some other persons. There can be four, five or six persons in the chain until the animals arrive to a person who commercialises this species in large quantities, who collects the volume he needs to make a profit. Then they arrive in the city, and it is observed that there are storehouses where all the animals are accumulated. They are sold in large numbers, or small.
>
> Concerning the trafficking to the cities, we know that people specialise in going to places rich in bird diversity where they employ the settlers to trap the birds.
>
> There are networks where intermediaries buy the animals and bring them to urban centres, like Medellin and Bogotá. These small networks constitute families and friends and they place the animals in markets and pet shops. Since there has been an increased public control lately, they have developed new methods, for example, selling the animals by means of catalogues. Those who make a living from this may be defined as illegal networks, many of them have pet shops where they sell legal species, like pigeons, and then they sell the wild animals in the backrooms of the shop.
>
> Always in the first part of the chain is the poor farmer or indigenous person. From them the animal passes to the first intermediary who will have a contact in some kind of enterprise, and from him to someone who may take the animal out of the country and negotiate the sale at the border. Finally, is the receiver of the animal.
>
> This [trafficking in parrots, monkeys and other animals for the pet market] becomes all the time more complicated because they will be seized on the bus, but like in all kinds of illegalities, there are people specialising in answering the demand in these markets. And suddenly there may be large volumes, like with sloths that are offered to tourists. And . . . they [the buyers] remain with this 'thing' that grows.

Professional traffickers take advantage of the locals' knowledge, and they also possess the means to traffic the animals in larger quantities and have contacts which make it possible to conceal and launder the trafficking by means of opportunistic abductors who sell the animals on the road. The methods by which the animals are then sold/trafficked vary; some are placed in legal zoos and remain in the country, but others are trafficked abroad, which involves a more extensive apparatus to organize and hence a greater degree of professionalism. The networks in question vary from family enterprises to professional trader networks.

The interviews in Colombia, as in Norway, reveal a distinction between micro trafficking and professional profit trafficking (see also Runhovde 2017, concerning Uganda). The first category covers people who catch animals on their *finca*, receive the animal as a gift or buy the animal at a local market to keep her/him as a *mascota*. They are able to transport the animal in their own vehicle to where they live or if they move, which makes this difficult to control. No intermediaries are involved.

The second category – intermediaries – involves collectors who have someone abducting animals for them, whether an indigenous person or a peasant. The abductors do not necessarily know this is illegal. The intermediary often accumulates several animals, for example 15 parrots brought by 15 abductors. In this case, the intermediary and the person behind him knows this is illegal and therefore will sell them through catalogues and the internet. In these cases, of the 15 parrots, often only two survive.

> So, there are various mechanisms. A person may say I am only interested in *Perico bronceado* [*Brotogeris jugularis*, orange-chinned parakeet]. So he wants ten, and will say: 'Let me know when you have ten,' and then the man will accumulate them until he has ten and they will be delivered to an intermediary, because the intermediary will not transport only one animal. The intermediary will not go himself but will use a cargo truck, or acquaintances will go where indicated to get the animals. For example, many of the *titi gris* are sold at *Central de Abastos de Bogotá*, a principal market place in Bogotá, because trucks come in there from everywhere.

Another interviewee emphasized the various actors involved in the trade:

> There is the person who works in the market, and his family has always done that, so since he was a baby he has known that this was how to get food on the table. So there's the farmers, the traders, the transport companies of the buses, because they also know that people carry animals in boxes. Often it is due to ignorance because if you ask them, they will say they didn't know.

This underlines that not only are the abductors in the first link of the chain unaware that they are committing a crime, but the bus drivers who contribute to the crime by providing transport without asking questions are also unaware accessories. When asked about the motives people have for engaging in wildlife trade, Claudia Brieva Rico summed up various categories, adding a previously unmentioned motivation:

> It is easy, you don't have to make any investments, just ask a local who knows where the animals are, who, for example, will kill the monkey mother and sell the baby, so that is easy. The demand is varied, many like to keep a wild animal at home, for example, a few years ago DIJIN [La Dirección de Investigación Criminal e INTERPOL de la Policía Nacional – the Direction of Criminal Investigation and Interpol of the National Police] made a seizure in the home of a collector, living in an elegant apartment with many birds flying around; the man was ignorant of the illegality of this. Another category is the drug trafficker who wants to have a mini zoo, then comes the lady whose

> family has always kept parrots, so she wants to keep the tradition going. The last category is those who buy an animal for pity. Seeing a caged parrot, they will think: 'Poor birds, I will save them' but fail to realise that when they do, new birds will be captured and slotted into the trade.

The latter category is easy to sympathize with, seeing parrots suffering in small cages along the road will awake compassion in many (Sollund 2017a), although with disastrous results. The right reaction would be to report the crime to the environmental police and other responsible authorities, like CRRFFS. This, however, also underlines that the first category of offenders, the trapper/killer/abductor, has a very significant role in the wildlife trade in Colombia, by *creating demand, filling the market and emptying the forests.*

There are also other actors involved. International trafficking for biopiracy was described as specialized in interviews. Part of this is the way amphibians who are carriers of toxins of interest are identified. Buyers cooperate with indigenous people and farmers who know where the amphibians live, and this is how they are captured. They are easy to conceal because they are small, so traffickers can evade inspection. The poison can be taken out in a tiny tube, which is almost imperceptible. It is a highly specialized modus operandi (Goyes and Sollund 2018).

Another interviewee emphasized that Colombia was lagging behind in this matter. Part of the problem, he believed, was international trafficking. As long as this kind of piracy is not acknowledged more widely (results are published in scholarly journals based on such search for toxins), Colombia could easily open the gate to a situation parallel to that which took place 40 years ago, when many phenotypes were extracted from animals, who are now bred all over the world.

> In the future we will see with sadness that we did not in time look for ways of detecting how these serums, those proteins and those molecules, were taken out. We will simply have to go down the road of dependence by which we can only get access to these molecules through pharmaceutical industries in ways that will cost us a lot of dollars.
>
> (Ortiz-von Halle)

This trafficking is clearly justified from an anthropocentric perspective, by which amphibians and other animals are regarded as resources for Colombia (Goyes and Sollund 2018). This perspective will be discussed further below.

While many abductors suffer hardship which serves to incentivize the taking of animals, not all opportunistic abductors are in dire need; the opportunities may be as ample for opportunistic abductors who have other sources of income as they are for the truly poor (Leberatto 2016). The fact that abducting animals is seen as an opportunity cannot be perceived in isolation; it is part of a larger pattern in which exploiting animals and alienating them as objectified resources becomes an obvious solution to financial need (Sollund 2008a, 2012a). The options that are regarded as acceptable are contingent on the ways in which earnings are made at a broader level. In the Colombian context, as well as worldwide, free-born animals have for many generations been used to supplement income. From the perspective of the abductors, it is seen as unfair that what is condoned on a larger scale should be criminalized at an individual level, although this does not legitimize this kind of animal exploitation (Goyes and Sollund 2016). As Gastañaga et al. (2011) have shown to be the case in Peru, *la loreada*, a tradition in which locals remove parrot babies from their nests to be sold and thus make extra income, has had detrimental effects on entire cohorts, meaning some years no birds will be allowed to grow up in their habitats, thus affecting the total population.

The interviewees highlighted that middlemen are central actors in the wildlife trade (see also van Uhm 2016b; Wyatt 2013). They approach indigenous people and peasants who know about local fauna and where to find them and offer them money for a specific number of animals, often parrots. Important in this chain is the connection between the local people with knowledge and the wholesaler or exporter. Middlemen will go to locations where others will not go for reasons of security, to ensure they have local contacts who can provide them with what they want. Ortiz-von Halle from TRAFFIC further detailed this:

> They come to Guapi or Timibiquí in el Cauca, and make contact with people who have access to the forests and who store the animals and they help them with tools and infrastructure to keep the animals in good shape until they come to pick them up. They will arrive periodically and these days they communicate via internet and telephone, and they know how to stash the animals so they don't suffocate and die like they do in the Amazon. So there is always this person who is connected to the market and who commercialises the animal, and the person who takes them from their environments and stores them. This is the case, for example, with the mata mata turtles and the venomous frogs.

He added that the trade in frogs in the international market is conducted via intermediaries in Medellin who put them in jars which are then brought to international markets – such as in the Czech Republic– by a passenger who carries them on his person.

According to the interviews, after being trafficked to large cities, the animals, and especially young ones who are the easiest to capture, are sold in the marketplaces, including centres of commerce in fruit and vegetables where the traffickers and buyers meet, as well as in nearby bus stations and truck terminals. *Bodegas* (storehouses) are located near the markets where animals are brought. This was confirmed by Goyes, who during the data collection period of this study went to a pet shop in central Bogotá asking for a parrot and was advised to visit the *bodegas* around Plaza de Restrepo. Javier Cifuentes Álvarez and Ortiz-von Halle both stated that there are three to four centralized areas in Bogotá that specialize in wildlife trafficking – Plaza de Restrepo, Avenida Caracas and Corabastos – which is the largest supply centre in the country.

Javier Cifuentes from CRRFFS elaborated:

> These are organised gangs and they do this as a living. What happens now is that their centre of operations is at la Plaza del Restrepo, but the animals

> are not there. We have searched places, but the animals are not there. So what they do now is that they bring the animals on commission, from catalogues. And this is where we have problems entering, so this is where the environmental police and prosecutors must help us, and where it is necessary to infiltrate the communities, among people. And that is how we made the arrest that led to four years imprisonment. Except for this, it is hard to get to the organised groups but we hope to get there.

Selling free-born animals in markets is illegal, as evinced by the pet store experience of Goyes. Thus animals are no longer as openly commercialized as they used to be, yet as pointed out by TRAFFIC, legislation has to a very small degree made people abstain from engaging in wildlife trade. Colombian legislation differentiates three main categories of animals, wild or domesticated: (1) animals, the trade of whom is absolutely forbidden; (2) animals, the trade of whom is forbidden if they were abducted from the wild but allowed if they were bred in captivity; and (3) animals, the trade of whom is legal (Goyes and Sollund 2016: 91). Of particular relevance here is Colombia's Resolution 438 (2001), which stipulates the process that is required to get a permit to legally take animals and plants from their biological and natural habitat; Law 1333 (2009), which stipulates the procedure to follow upon the event of recovering illegally traded animals; Resolution 383 (2010), which lists the wild species that are threatened with extinction in the country and the trade of whom is consequently punished as defined in Law 1453; and Law 1453 (2011), which modifies Law 611 (2000) and punishes the illegal exploitation of renewable natural resources (including fauna) with four to nine years of imprisonment (see Appendix 2 for details concerning legislation in Colombia, where I discuss the expert opinion of the people I interviewed about the enforcement of such crimes in Colombia).

As discussed in the introduction and in relation to the Norwegian data, the internet has become increasingly important in wildlife trade, facilitating contact between supplier and demand (see Lavorgna 2014; Sollund 2016c), but also as a platform for videos of attractive pets on YouTube, Facebook and other social media that increase demand. This correlation between internet exposure and increased demand has been documented in the cases of owls in the wake of the popular *Harry Potter* series (Nijman and Nekaris 2017) and slow lorises, when YouTube videos of them being tickled (read tortured) were posted (Nekaris et al. 2013). There was also an increased demand for reptiles after *Jurassic Park* was released (Militz and Foale 2017). That popular films increase demand and thereby pose a threat to the species involved was nonetheless refuted in a study concerning clown fish, following the 2003 Disney/Pixar motion picture *Finding Nemo* (Militz and Foale 2017). The researchers investigated US trade data (the US is the largest importer of marine aquarium fish) of the clown fish to determine whether there was an increase in trade. Despite media claiming this to be the case, they found *Finding Nemo* had little immediate impact on US imports of the species presented by the film's protagonist (Militz and Foale 2017: 3). However, they warn that the effect of the follow-up film, *Finding Dory* (*P. hepatus*), which is about a species which is not suitable for aquariums, will likely be much more negative. They also point out that catching methods for this species would negatively harm the ecosystem and future generations of fish. These examples of internet/movie activity demonstrate how free-born animals become cultural icons which become an incentive for people to engage in wildlife crimes as consumers (for discussion of culture as impacting consumerism and environmental harm, see Brisman and South 2014).

Undoubtedly, people are encouraged to purchase free-born animals because of media representations of a species. There are an uncountable number of videos of parrots who sing, dance and do funny tricks on the internet, which make people want them as pets. The interviewees, however, revealed how the internet has become a tool/medium that facilitates an illegal trade. Cifuentes Álvarez from the Secretaría Distrital de Ambiente de Bogotá said,

> Everything is sold on the internet, [advertised in] catalogues. So yes, there is a scheme that is becoming quite simple: 'Get me a boa', so they call a person who has boas in the habitat. [The animal] may pass through four or five [pairs of] hands but it is a scheme that takes advantage of social networks.
>
> We do inspections, with the environmental police, with the investigating entities, because they [the traffickers] are really big mafias, and we have established that they move because of our inspections.

Because the Secretaría Distrital de Ambiente together with the environmental police now are patrolling well-known trafficking spots, traffickers have turned to more sophisticated methods, employing the internet and catalogues for people to order the animals they want. A similar feature of the WLT has been observed in Sao Paolo, Brazil, where, like in Colombia, markets that were previously open for WLT have been shut down, resulting in traffickers turning to internet ads on social media to sell animals (Nassaro 2017).

Ortiz-von Halle implicated international networks in the trade and emphasized how they use the internet to make the trade easier for them:

> I think today it is mostly the international networks that work by means of the internet. It is an extremely important factor today, the way in which information circulates through the internet and how the national collectors make contacts with the international collectors, and how this makes it easy.

So, the internet works as (1) a medium through which demand is created, (2) a facilitator of the crime for the different agents involved in the trade and (3) a marketplace where people can buy the animals.

The people identified as the most important actors in the illegal wildlife trade in Colombia are not those living in such a precarious state that animal abductions are seen as their only option. Rather, it is people who do *not* depend on this for a living but for whom abducting animals means extra income. Those who can most readily capture the animals because they are familiar with their habits are people whom one romantically could idealize as having a strong connection to nature and to the beings living in their surroundings. This, however, is not the case, according to the interview material, which would suggest that these same people objectify animals as income and contribute to deforestation (see also Goyes 2015; Goyes and Sollund 2016; Maldonado et al. 2009). I will now further explore how traffickers work in order to take the animals or the products derived from them out of the country and where they take them.

Trafficking from and through Colombia

Colombia is a significant source country for WLT, although animals are also seized who originate in other countries. As shown through the historical overview and as a country that is rich in biodiversity, Colombian free-born animals are trafficked across borders for international markets. A ProAves staff member reiterated that due its biodiversity, there is little need to traffic animals *to* Colombia; Colombia is the country richest in biodiversity in terms of birds, so it is extremely rare that birds are trafficked to Colombia, except some cases in which birds have been trafficked from Peru and Brazil or from the south of the continent. The main concern, in his view, is trafficking to countries abroad.

Frogs that are trafficked for the pharmaceutical industry in Peru are also much sought after by collectors. The interviewee from ProAves said,

> Just like other illegal substances may be taken out of the country, similarly taking wildlife out of the country is not very difficult. For example, the venomous frogs, you remember the black plastic canisters used for film rolls, the traffickers use this kind of canisters, and they take a piece of humid cotton and put it together with the frog in the box, and it can survive for two, three days. So it is very easy to put into a suitcase, and these frogs are sold a lot for ornamental purposes and to breeders.

CRRFFS interviewees stated that in their experience, the most trafficked species from Colombia abroad were frogs. When they do seizures in Bogotá at El Dorado Airport, these are most frequently frogs destined for Switzerland, Spain and Asian countries, such as Japan.

The ProAves and TRAFFIC interviewees said frogs also often end up in the Netherlands and Germany and that this illegal commercialization of frogs is at a peak, having increased during the last decade. ProAves had also experienced that foreigners, particularly from Germany and the Netherlands, approach ProAves for permission to come and find frogs under the pretext of doing research, but this is seen as a guise for trafficking these species abroad. They pay to enter the reserve and then, if allowed, will take a large number home for breeding purposes. Other modus operandi are to pay locals to find the frogs for them, whereupon they are paid the value of €2–5 for each frog.

Another interviewee said,

> There are rumors that there is micro-trafficking in felines and *titi gris* [which is endemic to Colombia]. They have been found in zoos, and individuals

> abroad have *titi gris*, so the question is, how did they get there? No one knows.

At CRRFFS, they also seize animals destined abroad:

> In 2001 there arrived [at CRRFFS] large quantities of seizures that had been on their way abroad. Once there was a seizure of 1,200 very small mata mata turtles. These are only found in the Amazon.

Several interviewees said that even though only 10%–15% of birds survive trafficking, because thousands can be trafficked simultaneously, the surviving few are still enough to make a profit.

Because Colombia is so rich in biodiversity, there are also many species that are endemic, making them attractive to collectors.

TRAFFIC provided details of the frog trade and how the frogs get to the buyers. Endemic frogs are in great demand, especially in the US and Europe, to where they are exported from South America under the CITES regime (see also Sinovas et al. 2017). This is a point I return to below when I discuss the problem related to parallel legal and illegal markets. Collectors will search everywhere for new species, but they are seldom found. However, within a species itself, a great variety exists in terms of colour and pattern, and collectors want as many combinations as possible:

> So, there appeared a frog with a red circle on the back, like the Japanese flag and this received an enormous amount of interest. So what was done was to immediately secure them, since the distribution of these species is very limited. For example, they can be found only in the basin of a river in Nariño. So, then the collector must get in touch with someone who has access to the zone who can explain to him how he can get the frogs without killing them, and this variety of frogs, *Phyllobates terribilis*, is very venomous. And because it is a new variety it will generate an enormous prize, and an enormous interest. So they will channel the frog through these intermediaries in Medellin and who later will take responsibility for putting it into a jar and send it with a traveller who carries it on his person.
>
> (Ortiz-von Halle)

Since Colombia is a country with many inspections upon both departure and arrival, traffickers take animals out through Ecuador and Peru, since these routes are the least suspicious and this allows them to proceed without being punished.

The drug barons in Colombia are involved in wildlife trade as buyers. Pablo Escobar had a private zoo with animals from around the world, including rhinos, hippos, giraffes, large felines, rare parrots, etc. When Escobar was killed, many of his animals were relocated to zoos in Colombia; the hippos, however, settled in the area and dispersed. They are now breeding, more rapidly than in Africa, and the question is what to do with this spread of an alien species that is flourishing in the habitat of the Magdalena River.[10] Expert in birds of prey in Colombia César Márquez said that during the peak of the drug trade, barons kept birds of prey, like big eagles of the jungle, in their haciendas and houses.

Strategic sourcing points of wildlife in Colombia encompass all of Magdalena, the Dorada and Caldas. Another strategic point for wildlife abductions is the zone of Leticia that borders Manaus and Iquitos in Peru, which are central nodes for wildlife abductions and trafficking. Patarroyo's research victims (see below) are taken from this area (Goyes 2015; Maldonado et al. 2009). Other interviewees pointed out that the northern coastline was a frequent source location for animals. Another important sourcing point for insects, like the Escarabajos Hércules (Hercules beetle) that are used in fights and which cost up to a million pesos (340 USD), is the Venezuelan border region, via Casanare.

The seizure data of CRRFFS between January 1, 2011, and June 2012 details where the animals are taken. Of the 3,690 animals who came to the Centre between March 29 and June 28, 2012, they had data concerning place of origin for 1,759 animals. Of these, 570 animals (32.42%) came from Cundinamarca (the department surrounding the Bogotá area). This is explained by the migration of birds of prey who, during this period, return from the south of Argentina to their place of origin in the northern US and who descend in diverse zones of Bogotá to rest during their long migration. Two hundred twenty-five animals (12.79%) came from el Cesar (Informe de ejecución 2012: 27–28). Concerning the available numbers for 2015 and 2017, they indicate that migratory birds easily fall victim to the wildlife trade, just as migratory birds crossing European borders in the Mediterranean countries fall victim to bird catchers who kill the birds for food, to such a degree that species survival is threatened (Bhattacharya 2016; Brochet et al. 2016).

The connection between wildlife trade and the drug trade is a claim often put forward (South and Wyatt 2011) and in the media, but this was not directly confirmed in the interviews. What was confirmed was that the infrastructure which is in place for other illegal trade is taken advantage of by those involved in WLT. The routes through which illegal logs, fauna, cocaine, chemicals, etc. are trafficked are the same, because these are routes where inspection agents can be bribed and cheated, where traffickers know they will not encounter problems. As traffickers, they traffic whatever they can; obviously some are specialized. Cocaine traffickers know very well that logs are ideal for hiding drugs because the volume that is transported makes them difficult to inspect. Criminals involved in different kinds of crimes take advantage of trafficking methods. One day, fauna is put into a vehicle that carries food, just as it can be put into one that carries logs. The dynamic is more about routes than an effective link between wildlife traffickers and professional drug traffickers. According to Ortiz-von Halle, the route is physical, but it has all these other aspects connected to corruption and contacts to insure that the business is not interrupted.

Claudia Luz Rodríguez said that the legal and illegal trafficking in babilla skins had been of interest to the narcotics police who do thorough inspections to prevent these exports being used to camouflage drugs trafficking. Because Colombia has two coasts, much that is part of international trade can be trafficked from the ports, including both drugs and wildlife. An anonymous interviewee said that in the coastal zone of la Guajira, like the case for the drug routes, there are routes that go directly to Panamá. Traffickers leave through ports, through Venezuela and the illegal routes of the oil traffickers; these are also main routes for many kinds of contraband.

In addition, there is anecdotal evidence of a link between wildlife trade and the drug trade. A famous case concerned boas who had cocaine inserted in their bodies. Yet, interviewees asserted that drug traffickers use whatever means available:

> 100% of what flows through the Putumayo Basin, like the logs from northern Peru and from a little part of Brazil and southern Colombia, everything converges in Puerto Asís and all is illegal. Sometimes there is fauna, ornamental fish, much of which also goes out from Colombia because it does not pay to take it through Iquitos or it is illegal in Brazil. So there are things that are laundered through Colombia, which are illegal in the neighbouring countries or they don't pay, so it is taken out via Colombia.
>
> (Ortíz-von Halle)

An anonymous interviewee elaborated about a specific person who combined drugs and WLT:

> For example, in the Amazon during the 70s, there was a foreigner who stayed in the Amazon who observed that this was a place under development. So he started to import stuff to take it to Leticia, and as part of this he started to take animals abroad. So he took a lot of fauna from the Amazon, like nutria, mammals of all sorts, primates, birds; he was a very important person in Leticia. He was sent to prison, but not for the wildlife trade, but because he was involved in the drug trade. But almost always, the commercialization in fauna is combined with other crimes.

Of the different fish species that are frequent victims of trafficking and trading from Colombia, several have been trafficked to extinction. They are destined for aquariums, especially in Japan. Tortoises are trafficked to become pets on an international market, provided they survive, and despite parrot breeding in many countries, parrots are still trafficked to Europe (see also EC 2016a; van Uhm 2016b), but since the bird import ban to Europe following the bird flu outbreak in 2005,[11] parrots are now largely traded to other countries from South America. An exploration of exports in CITES-listed animal species from the South American Amazon countries (Bolivia, Brazil, Colombia, Ecuador, Guyana, Peru, Suriname and Venezuela) shows that on average 12,000 parrots were trafficked per year between 2005 and 2014, mainly to Singapore, Mexico, the Russian Federation and Thailand, which were the largest single importers of nearly half of the live-parrot exports (Sinovas et al. 2017). In the case of fish, export permits may be in order, but the number of fish actually exported far exceeds the permitted quotas, a point I return to.[12]

The export of primates for the pharmaceutical industry in Europe and the US used to be large (Zimmerman 2003), but, as noted above, has declined due to alternatives employed by the industry. However, nocturnal primates are still trafficked heavily for the much critiqued malaria research of Manuel Elkín Patarroyo, and it is claimed this trafficking has failed to comply with the law (Goyes 2015; Maldonado et al. 2009). This topic will be further addressed later.

Colombian reptile skins have been seized in Spain, Germany and the United States, and the interviews revealed that the trade has not followed CITES regulations. Live reptile export from Colombia consists, according to CITES data (Sinovas et al. 2017), primarily of captive-bred iguanas (Iguanidae) and boas (Boidae) destined for the United States. Colombia is also a large exporter of reptile skins, almost all of which are *Caiman crocodilus*, the claim being that they are exclusively bred in captivity.

The legal trade may be used to disguise illegal trade. One interviewee emphasized how the legal commercialization of crocodile skins is used to hide illegal skins, some of which are seized in Santa Marta in the north. Traders will present the legal skins that are produced by *zoocriadores*, but in between them are live animals and also illegal skins. The problems created by the possibilities the *zoocriadores* provide for laundering illegal wildlife trade under disguise of the legal trade is addressed in the next section

Problems concerning parallel markets and laundering revisited

As shown in relation to the Norwegian data, legal wildlife trade invites illegal trade through the creation of parallel markets, by which legal trade is used to disguise illegal trade. Parts of the trade concerning species and numbers may be legal, while others are illegal. A trader may have permission to trade 100 fish or frogs, but instead he traffics 150. Or, illegal species are trafficked together with legal species. Of special concern is the existence of breeding facilities that makes it possible to claim an individual has been captive bred and therefore is legal in trade, whereas in reality s/he has been abducted from her/his habitat (see Webb 2000: 109; Lyon and Natusch 2011; Shepherd et al. 2012; Sollund 2013a; van Uhm 2016b).

Measures that can prevent animals from being put into traffic may be positive; however, *zoocriadores* were heavily criticized by several of the interviewees. They create situations in which animals are bred under abusive conditions and parallel legal and illegal markets are created (see also Lyons and Natusch 2011; Sollund 2013a; Warchol et al. 2003), and the problem of parallel licit and illicit markets has been raised in relation to transnational environmental crimes more generally (Wright 2011). The reason for upgrading the Southern African elephant to CITES Appendix I must be seen in the context of the problem of parallel markets. The legal trade in ivory was providing traffickers with a means to smuggle ivory into markets in Europe, North America and Asia: 'Authorities and consumers were unable to distinguish illegal ivory from legal, which gave the traffickers and elephant killers a least-cost way to market their products' (Dickson 2005: 48).

The TRAFFIC interviewee was very critical of *zoocriadores*, claiming the many actors in Colombia profit from the breeding businesses, including politicians, who indirectly profit from the reptile skin trade through investing in it. According to Claudia Luz Rodríguez, there are more than 40 breeding farms for babilla in Colombia. While such facilities may disguise illegal trade, breeding facilities do not alleviate the market for trade in free-born animals; they are often themselves based on trafficking as well as facilitating WLT. As said, they also provide wildlife traffickers and buyers with a disguise of legitimacy; people who might abstain from buying animals who are illegally abducted buy them believing they are not trafficked, whereas in reality they are. Another point is that when availability of species in demand increases, this in turn increases the demand and hence poses a risk to free-born animals who are supposed to be shielded from trade through the establishment of the breeding facilities.

The breeding business in Colombia was, according to interviewees, regarded as easy money by drug traffickers who withdrew when they did not find it sufficiently profitable anymore. But during years when these breeders worked at the edge of illegality, they would take animals from the wild, claiming they were bred in their facilities'. Drug trafficking was also associated with the export of babilla skins. Ortiz-von Halle claimed in the case of parrots that trafficking provides the breeding facilities and zoological gardens with fresh genes. He regarded such enterprises as laundering facilities for illegal wildlife trade: 'Many of those who today appear like big collectors and who also finance good conservation projects for parrots, at the same time they continue to serve as instigators for the illegal trade, like the Loro Parque in the Canary Islands.'

That zoological gardens are involved in wildlife trade has been confirmed by other sources as well. In Indonesia, the forestry department in 2009 alleged that three zoos were involved in trafficking in endangered animal species, including Sumatran tiger, orangutan, Malayan tapir, sun bear, leopard, bird of paradise and cuscus. The trafficking was connected to corrupt zoo officers (Born Free 2009). The paradox is that the three zoos involved claimed they *protected* endangered species. In the UK, *The Guardian* (Barnett 2004) carried an article about an *Observer* inquiry that revealed that three zoos were involved in wildlife trafficking, selling their surplus animals to a Belgian trafficker who operated with lists of animals for sale through a company called Herne Breeding Centre.[13] The animals trafficked were a black panther for 1,000 USD, an American bald eagle for 6,000 USD, two 13-month-old lions at 1,000 USD each, a three-year-old zebra for 6,500 USD and wallabies for 1,800 USD. The undercover team of the *Observer* bought two rare ring-tailed lemurs using credentials which were never checked. According to *The Guardian*, *The Observer* also had documents that proved that Hamerton Zoo sold the Belgian four rare white-headed marmosets who were later for sale in the pet shop Animal Express near Brussels Airport (Barnett 2004, see also Profauna 2009).

Zoos may maintain that they buy animals of endangered species in order to secure species survival and to create concern for endangered species,[14] while in reality they are draining the ecosystems of the few remaining individuals, driving species to extinction in nature. Zoological gardens also require fresh blood to ensure genetic diversity and therefore also participate in WLT. That animals suffer all over the world in zoos as captives under horrible conditions is indisputable. What to my knowledge is not broadly known is that zoological gardens, like the one in Copenhagen, not only kill the offspring of their captive animals, such as lion pups and giraffes,[15] but also traffic their corpses, which was mentioned in relation to the Norwegian data, by the interviewee from CITES/Norwegian Environment Agency.

The pretext of the breeding facilities is conservation, and some have been successful and because of their knowledge of the species they have been able to offer solutions to save species, meaning that scientists are involved. However, some of them have their own agenda and contribute in taking and bringing the animals to such facilities, who are abducted from their natural habitats. Ortiz-von Halle underlined the grey zones and the overlap between lawful and unlawful activities connected to zoos. Obviously, there are powerful people involved in this only for profit:

> It has always been a problem, that legal zoos connect with collectors under the guise of conservation, and thereby move their threads to continue to get new animals or maintain their genetic stock, as is the case e.g. in Italy, with parrots. (Ortiz-von Halle)

In addition, free-born animals are abducted to be caged in zoos that are not professionally run, like the roadside zoo I came across in the 1980s in Baños, Ecuador, that kept a bear, a maca, a tigrillo and several other animals under horrific conditions, apparently captured in the vicinity, and the roadside serpent zoo I saw in Costa Rica in 2002, where Costa Rican snakes were kept in glass boxes in the baking sun.

Another way of laundering that is preponderantly used in internal markets is the existence of pet shops. Claudia Brieva Rico, amongst others, said that many of these shops sell animals who are legal in trade, but also sell wild animals in the back room. This statement is supported by another interviewee who pointed out that the companies that sell ornamental fish use this as a facade behind which they sell large quantities of native fish, like pirarucu and mata mata turtles (*Chelus fimbriatus*), which are taken illegally.

That legal enterprises frequently provide a cover for illegal trafficking was further detailed by Ortiz-von Halle in relation to the frog trade that involves *zoocriadores*:

> So they meet, the collectors of frogs from the Czech Republic which is one of the main world centres for trafficking in reptiles and amphibians, so, supposedly they come to interchange 'specimens' and talk about techniques for

> reproduction, as a hobby, just like the aquarists. In the context of such gatherings, everything is legal, but in the hotel where the exhibition takes place, that is where the *illegal* negotiations take place, behind the curtain. So this is a parallel trade and they know what they're doing.

A report about CITES-listed animals trafficked legally from South America shows that while the majority of amphibians who are trafficked from the region are wild-sourced from Suriname and Guyana, frogs who are trafficked from Colombia are 'captive-produced' (Sinovas et al. 2017). This means animals of the same species are both legally and illegally traded, and bribery and forged documents are employed to pass them through Customs inspections (see also South and Wyatt 2011).

As shown in the section describing the roots of wildlife trade in Colombia, the export of reptile skins is an important part of Colombia's economy. According to Sinovas et al. (2017), Colombia's CITES exports amounted to USD 50.2 million between 2005 and 2014. The majority of this came from caiman skins and caiman leather products. The interviewees said this trade is also one which provides offenders with the guise of legal trade in order to launder illegally captivated/killed individuals.

Parallel markets are largely the result of CITES, whereby trade in many species is legal, while others are banned from trade, or trade is regulated. This means that a species which is legal to trade in one country may be illegal to trade in another depending on the size of local populations and on whether a species is endemic to one country. For example, certain ornamental fish may be legal to trade Colombia but illegal in Peru, and they may be laundered through Colombia with offenders pretending that they are from Colombia.

Ortiz-von Halle's statement that breeders contribute to the illegality by taking animals from their habitats and pretending they were bred in a *zoocriador*, and the enormous sums of money involved, is the reason why international networks get involved who employ the internet as a means for their crimes. Thereby they establish contact between national and international collectors and ensure the trade proceeds. This leads to the question of whether the WLT in Colombia can be referred to as organized crime.

Is WLT in Colombia organized crime?

Because the organized crime discourse concerning WLT is becoming increasingly more important, I will discuss the concept and how, depending on its definition, it is relevant in the Colombian context based on my data. Clearly much of the trafficking crime described above is well organized. This does not necessarily mean it can be defined as organized crime. Levi and Maguire (2004) argue that organized crime is a notoriously difficult concept to define. One partial reason for this is that how to define the concept of organized crime is not universally agreed upon and the concept may even be applied normatively in order to create attention and moral concern. For example, currently, the UN and EU place WLT in the category of organized crime (EC 2016b; UNODC (2015). The concept may also be applied strategically for investigation purposes.[16]

The UN Convention against Transnational Organized Crime (Article 2a) defines organized crime as:

- A group of three or more persons that was not randomly formed;
- Existing for a period of time;
- Acting in concert with the aim of committing at least one crime punishable by at least four years' incarceration; and
- [Committing crime] in order to obtain, directly or indirectly, a financial or other material benefit.

(UNODC 2015b)

In order to distinguish organized crime groups from others containing three or more people and working in concert for an extended period, the UNODC (2015a) website also states: 'the true defining characteristics of organized crime groups under the Convention are their profit-driven nature and the seriousness of the offences they commit.' The UN definition limits organized crime to those crimes that are punishable by more than four years in prison. Determining whether a crime is organized by its 'seriousness' leaves very much to discretion.

The UN resolution (UNODC 2015b) regarding wildlife trafficking also states the relationship between organized crime and wildlife trafficking makes WT a serious crime. The EC action plan to combat IWT, in accordance with the UN resolution, suggests that wildlife trafficking 'involving organised criminal groups' qualifies 'as a serious crime, punishable with a maximum sanction of at least four years' imprisonment (EC 2016b). It should be noted that in Norway, under §60 of the Norwegian Penal Law, punishment may be doubled if a crime, punishable by more than three years, is committed as part of organized crime, defined as 'conspiracy among three persons or more.'

Organized crime is defined in different ways in academic literature. Schneider's (2012: 52) narrow definition involves more than two people committing crime over time with the capacity to operate outside their national boundaries. According to Spapens (2010), in the 1990s, a school of thought emerged that approached organized crime from a social network perspective; criminal organizations were considered social networks with specific characteristics, such as non-hierarchical, fluid and flexible internal relations, and were seen as collectives rather than as formal organizations (Spapens 2010: 185–186). The modus operandi in Colombia would harmonize with such a definition. However, as shown, much of the trafficking in Colombia is connected to the informal labour market, through which locals take the opportunity to make extra income by abducting and selling an animal. This is parallel to the findings of Leberatto (2016) in his extensive Peruvian field study, where he found that the large majority of the offenders were poor locals who engaged in the trade to make a little profit, to carry them through the day. They would sell animals in season, and other merchandize on the market, depending on what was available. While the middlemen in the present study seem more organized, concerning their application of catalogues, etc., Leberatto found that also the middlemen were opportunistic, working in the informal labour market, in which WLT constituted *additional* income, rather than their main income.

Wyatt (2013) argues that the illegal wildlife trade market is not necessarily consistent with official understandings of organized crime and groups, and instead, she suggests the following definition in relation to IWT: Organized crime 'is violent, long-lasting, structured, rational, and adaptive, with networks to legitimate and illegitimate industries' (Wyatt 2013: 90). While this definition includes violence, and as such would be applicable in the Colombian case given the violence committed against the animal victims and the high mortality rates, likely this definition is about inter-human violence, rather than inter-species violence.

However, rather than looking at statutory (and international) bodies' definitions of organized crime, I suggest that we focus on the methods by which the crimes take place and the level of planning and organization that are required to carry them out, to establish whether the crime is organized. The key word is 'networks,' and, as shown by van Uhm (2016a,b), networks that can be defined as organized crime groups operate in relation to the trafficking of macaque monkeys from Morocco, in the trafficking connected to the market for TCM, and in the killing of sturgeon and the trafficking of caviar in and from Azerbaijan, Kazakhstan and Russia to the EU, consequently also making it transnational environmental crime (White 2011; Wright et al. 2001). Such networks are in place in Colombia. The networks are structured, rational and adaptive when they turn to selling animals by means of catalogues and the internet, and the *zoocriadores* and pet shops function as legitimating illegal WLT. When crimes are committed as network crimes or organized crime, the potential damage to victims is likely to be greater since the trafficking takes place on a large scale. However, there is not one unified kind of organized crime group, but such crimes are conducted by a multiplicity of actors, some of whom are organized groups, including small amateur groups and large-scale organized criminal groups (Wright et al. 2011: 337).

Another question is how to act against these crimes, when targeting the semi-open marketplaces results in the criminals turning to more clandestine markets like the internet. Animals have intrinsic value and are interested in their own freedom and survival. As such, abducting and killing them should be regarded as a serious crime regardless of whether or how perpetrators are punished by the judicial systems in the states where such crimes occur and independently of whether the crime is called organized. Due to the increase of wildlife trafficking on global and local levels, increased use of the internet (including the dark net) for this trade and the opportunities this offers for increasing organization of wildlife trafficking, as well as the resources which may be released to combat these crimes though naming it organized crime, I support a broad definition that can be adapted to individual cases. However, to provide an answer to the question raised in the title of this section, there is no doubt that if applying Spapens's definition, much of the wildlife trafficking crimes taking place in Colombia is indeed organized crime. Before I discuss what impact the war in Colombia has had on WLT in the country, I will present another case with a special character, containing breaches of not only species justice, regulation and legislation concerning free-born animals, but also destruction of ecosystems and human rights abuses.

The Patarroyo case

Non-human primates have frequently and for long been trafficked for scientific experimentation because they bear a physiological resemblance and genetic closeness to human primates. They have been trafficked on a large scale to Western laboratories for biomedical research (Maldonado and Waters 2017; Zimmerman 2003). Primates were abducted and trafficked to be used in experiments, for example, to study the problematic of the colon. They were used as important biomodels, and one interviewee said that a large number of the animals who were trafficked out of Colombia were trafficked through exchanges with zoos that were authorized by the government, because these were already existent networks. Despite the decline in the use of primates in experiments and the ban Colombia imposed on export in primates in 1974 (Maldonado and Waters 2017), the *Aotus vociferans* and Aotus nancymaae (night monkeys) have for more than three decades been trafficked from the Amazon basin, including from Peru and Brazil, to be used in experiments conducted by Manuel Elkin Patarroyo in Colombia (Goyes 2015; Maldonado et al. 2009; Maldonado and Lafon 2017), who since 1984 has been working on a malaria vaccine in his laboratory in Leticia (Goyes 2015; Maldonado et al. 2009; Maldonado and Lafon 2017; Maldonado and Waters 2017). The experiments have not resulted in any vaccine so far. Both study species, *Aotus nancymaae*, trafficked from Peru and Brazil, and *Aotus vociferans*, were considered of little concern by the International Union for Conservation of Nature (IUCN), partly due to their wide distribution. However, according to Maldonado, there has been a lack of appropriate field studies to reveal to what degree the species are threatened.

Maldonado is a primatologist and founder of Entropika Foundation.[17] Entropika, since 2007, has been working with conservation of fauna in cooperation with indigenous communities in the national park Amacayacu on the Colombian-Peruvian border, the area from where night monkeys are trafficked. Maldonado says she does this

> first, to stop the illegal trafficking of fauna in this zone. Secondly, to put an end to the corruption. I know it is a utopia, but all this trafficking takes place because of the existence of permissive and corrupt environmental authorities. So, when I realised this, I said to myself, 'This is going to be the end of the Amazon, it is going to end it all. If this is happening with the monkeys, the same is happening with the timber'. I said 'no!' What I wanted was that the monkeys became the flag species for the protection of the ecosystem in the zone.

Maldonado has been leading an *acción popular*[18] against the trafficking of monkeys for the malaria research of Patarroyo. These protests have resulted in harsh reactions by Patarroyo and his supporters. She conducted a study about the impact of trafficking on the species in Colombia and Brazil, as well as other environmental and social impacts for local indigenous people involved in the trafficking, and has published widely about the case (Maldonado 2011; Maldonado et al. 2009; Maldonado and Lafon 2017; Maldonado and Peck 2014; Parathian and Maldonado 2010; Svensson et al. 2016). Her study went on from 2008 to 2011 and involved observation and interviews in the local communities.

While conducting her research, she tried by legal means to stop the harmful trafficking through gathering documentation, including from the state attorney. In this process, she sought to cooperate and receive and provide information about the case to/from Corpoamazonia, the state attorney and the Ministry of Environment. She said in interview about the process:

> Years went by, no one answered. And at the time, I was sending a petition of rights, so I became an unwanted person for all these people; because they did have to answer me, and they realised that the evidence [of illegalities] I had was overwhelming.

Before the popular action was organized, she had tried all other available legal procedures, and throughout the process she was harassed by Fundación Instituto de Inmunología de Colombia (FIDIC; Institute for Immunological Research)[19] led by Patarroyo. This resulted in Maldonado filing a lawsuit for libel and slander. In 2011, the lawsuit was filed before the Administrative Court in Cundinamarca. In July 2012, Maldonado won her case in this court, and in 2013 in the court of appeal, with a verdict that granted rights to the monkeys, the first time rights have been granted to animals in a Colombian court (Tribunal Administrativo de Cundinamarca 2012). On May 8, 2014, the legal representative of FIDIC sued (writ of injunction) the section of the State Council that gave the second instance ruling that revoked the trapping permits. On December 12, 2014, the Fourth Section of the State Council ruled in favour of FIDIC, nullifying the second instance ruling of the Third Section of the State Council. In March 2015, the State Council received the appeals of the Third Section of the State Council and of Angela Maldonado, as well as the dissenting opinion of one of the judges of the Fourth Section. The case was transferred to the Fifth Section of the State Council, who judged the appeals to be extemporaneous after they had already been received and accepted by the Fourth Section, leaving Corpoamazonia (sanctioned by the popular action) to decide whether FIDIC met with the obligations under the permits granted by Corpoamazonia. A complaint was then filed by Maldonado to the Superior Judiciary Council for lack of transparency of the State Council. Corpoamazonia reported that FIDIC partially fulfilled its obligations and that a study on the population status of *Aotus* spp. was required before determining hunting quotas for malaria research. The case was transferred to the Constitutional Court, which rejected a revision request filed by the Ombudsman Office, arguing that the defence of animal rights was not a priority for this court.[20]

When I met with Maldonado in September 2017, she showed me flyers that had been distributed in Leticia by accomplices of Patarroyo, depicting her as an enemy of the state. This was only one example of a long line of acts of defamation against Maldonado, including in public media. This defaming was particularly outstanding in a resolution (Resolución 2012) from the Azcaita community from 2012, where Maldonado and Entropika were featured as the villain, while Patarroyo was depicted as a hero. These campaigns have the potential to counteract the work she is doing with indigenous peoples in the Amazon to prevent the trafficking and restore the ecosystems with their cooperation.

According to Goyes (2015: 173), Patarroyo's scientific endeavours to find a vaccine against malaria began in 1984 when INDERENA, the then Colombian National Institute of Natural Resources under the Ministry of Agriculture, granted him permission to capture and use 200 individuals of the *Aotus vociferans* species from the Colombian side of the Amazon basin over a two-year period. New permits have been granted by Corpoamazonia in the years 1999, 2002, 2006 and 2010, permitting him to collect 8,200 owl monkeys over a period of 15 years, with the blessing of the Ministry of Environment. According to a statement by Maldonado in an interview, Patarroyo has used between 50,000 and 70,000 monkeys in his research (Defenzoores 2015).

The reason why Maldonado and Entropika seek an end to the *Aotus* abductions is the harm this trafficking does to the ecosystems, to the species and to the indigenous groups who are hired by FIDIC to commit these harms. The harms are also criminal. According to Colombian law, Decree 309 from 2000, commercializing samples of species used for scientific purposes is prohibited (Goyes 2015; Maldonado, in interview). In addition, when animals are trafficked from Brazil and Peru, CITES is breached.

Maldonado explained the procedure by which the animals are caught. When a tree is cut in order to catch the monkey family in its nest, if the abductors are lucky, they catch two of three, since many die in the fall of 15–30 metres. This means that if 4,000 are trafficked in one year, at least twice as many will have died even if they are released after the experiments.

When a line of trees is felled, trappers put a fish net in the last tree, in the line where the monkeys will fall to if the capture is successful. The trappers climb the tree with the nest to startle the monkey, to make them jump. The felling of trees to capture monkeys also results in drastic deforestation, because not only is the tree with their nest felled, all the trees around the nest tree are cut in order to prevent the monkeys from jumping to another tree to escape. Maldonado estimates 65,000 trees are lost annually (Goyes 2015: 174; Maldonado and Lafon 2017).

Maldonado stated that 30.4% of the animals die. Even before they are sent to the local communities that look after them prior to transport to the laboratories, they die from lack of food or water and from the terrible conditions under which they are kept awaiting transport to the laboratories; it can take months (Defenzoores 2015). In the laboratory, the animals are inoculated with malaria. According to Maldonado, the torture here lasts up to two years, on average 270 days (Patarroyo claims they are released after three months). The experiments include being injected with malaria vaccines and removal of the splint. Initially the death rates were at 70% but that has decreased to 40%. Those that survive are released. The survival rate of monkeys who are infected with malaria or who have had their splints removed has not been established by FIDIC. This means also that animals who were forcefully abducted in Peru are released in Colombia. While releasing species where they do not belong (since they are different subspecies), FIDIC also releases groups of several hundred animals at the same time within an area of 500 square metres. This causes overpopulation of Peruvian animals (*Aotus nancymaae*) in Colombia. This may also affect species survival of the very reduced *Aotus vociferans*, since the species may interbreed.

Releasing animals who have been victims of experimentation is, according to Maldonado, both unethical and illegal. It constitutes a risk to the monkeys who are released, as well as to those who inhabit the area, because many of the animals who have been experimented on are released with pneumonia and septicemia. This means all the animals living there, including human animals, can be negatively affected.

It has been claimed by the opponents of Maldonado that catching monkeys is a cultural feature of the indigenous groups who carry out abductions for Patarroyo. However, according to her, it has nothing to do with their culture. She said that FIDIC is paying the indigenous authorities to destroy her because they want to make people believe this practice has cultural, traditional roots. However, before FIDIC entered the Amazon and started paying people to abduct the monkeys, this was not a tradition. She explained that what has characterized the area was first the rubber industry (*las caucherías*) 'The people were enslaved and destroyed, it was a genocide.' Then came *las tigrilladas* (hunting felines for the fur industry; Payán and Trujillo 2006) as well as other fur animal hunting, and then came cocaine production:

> The indigenous people of this zone, for living by the Amazon River, have always been enslaved and exploited. So Patarroyo enters among those who wanted tigrillos, coca, etc. The doctor wants monkey, and the indigenous people refer to all these people as *patrones*. So, the culture was lost, and they know it; they have even lost their language, there are very few communities that have maintained their language.

Amazonían communities have for centuries been victims of colonization by which their cultural heritage is lost. This situation and the ways in which Patarroyo has contributed to the prolongation of it should be seen in relation to decolonization. Colonization is an ongoing process that began with the repression of knowledge production of the colonized. Then the colonizers' patterns of expression were imposed on them, depriving them of their means of expression and their universe, which suppressed the heterogeneity of the subjects of oppression (Goyes 2017: 57). The resolution by the Azcaita community leader in 2012 exemplifies the complete acceptance of the distorted colonialized representation of the benefits of Patarroyo's agenda.

The indigenous people have a long history of being exploited in order to facilitate the drain of natural resources and animals in this area, illustrating the manifold victimization that affects ecosystems, humans and other animals living there (Goyes and Sollund 2016). Indigenous people who work for Patarroyo have died from falling out of trees in the pursuit of monkeys, and they have no form of social security. They are paid per monkey, which is an incentive for them to catch as many as possible, and consequently Patarroyo's quotas are exceeded, and many animals are stored and die for no reason. The abductions and trafficking done to satisfy the needs of Patarroyo also serve to feed the pet market with baby monkeys and pregnant mothers who are not fit for experiments.

The ecogenocide (Higgins et al. 2013; Larsen 2012) that in the worst-case scenario was carried out by Patarroyo and the colonizers who came before him thus concerns both human and animal species, as well as their natural surroundings. The crimes of Patarroyo have had tremendous impact in terms of human-environmental rights, eco/biojustice, as well as animal rights and species justice (Benton 1998; Halsey and White 1998; White 2013). As stated by Maldonado and Lafon (2017):

> this ecocide has been perpetrated by FIDIC under the supervision of the Corpoamazonia and with the endorsement of the Ministry of the Environment, leaving these three entities responsible for the introduction of the *A. nancymaae* in Colombia and the local extirpation of *A. vociferans* in the southern Colombian Amazon.
>
> (274)

One way to address these harms and crimes committed in relation to the Patarroyo case would be the acceptance of their ecocidal character (Higgins et al. 2013). This means addressing these harms as a 'moral category' (Larsen 2012: 50) rather than looking at it from a legal perspective, especially since, according to Maldonado, corruption played an important part in the ways in which the permits were obtained. While the harms against nature and those in the Amazon have gone on for generations, the specific cruelty in the Patarroyo case is the way in which the people, who are themselves harmed by the biomedical activities, contribute in its production and receive only a small pecuniary short-sight award, while the long-term consequences are the destruction of their natural environment, the spread of diseases and extinction of species they used to share the natural environment with.

While Patarroyo should receive adequate punishment for what he has done, he should also be compelled to right, in all ways possible, the harms done. Higgins et al. (2013) see restorative justice as being built on an understanding of 'humans' relationship with nature and the duty to remedy the harm caused,“ addressing 'the needs of the beleaguered party to restore that which has been harmed rather than simply fixating on the punishment of the perpetrator" (255). This would, however, require the cooperation of FIDIC, and if achieved it could imply the administration of environmental justice, implying these indigenous peoples' rights to live in an unharmed natural environment (White 2013), invoking methods and principles of mutual engagement and shared learning (Higgins et al. 2013). This, however, would probably be too much to hope for in this case.

Maldonado sees the cooperation with indigenous groups as essential to prevent further harms, as well as address harms done. While arguments have been put forward by her opponents that thousands of families would be left without employment were they not to continue with the abductions, similar to arguments advanced in the resolution, the reality is that the money they receive for this is only 10%–15% of their total income. Thus to remove this would not have a significant impact on their living standard. As we have seen in relation to other opportunistic trafficking encouraged by middlemen and organizers of trafficking, what is gained by the abductions is *extra* income.

Maldonado wants to engage the indigenous groups in a reforestation project. While some areas are naturally reforested, in other areas more effort must be made to accomplish this. She has also undertaken an extensive study of the *Aotus* population in the area, and lastly, she hopes to initiate an economic project benefitting the monkey abductors. Several other projects are carried out in the region of Entropika that benefit both the environment and its species, whether human or non-human.[21]

However, not only are the animals, the indigenous people and the ecosystems victims, Maldonado has often been prosecuted by powerful actors and could easily be the next environmental movement victim in Latin America, along with Berta Caceres in Honduras who was killed in March 2016 (Goyes et al. 2017; Lynch et al. 2018). She sees her openness and international cooperation as a protection against such fatal victimization.

What impact has the war had on wildlife trade?

Because of the ongoing war in Colombia, the migration caused by poverty is added to by displacement caused by the war. According to a report from the UN, Colombia has 7.4 million displaced persons.[22]

The role these migrants play in the chain of wildlife trafficking cannot be seen in isolation; their role is caused by structural features of Colombian society which have put them under immense hardship. As explained by an interviewee:

> I know that the illegal trade has a foundation in the people. In Córdoba, where the paramilitaries and the land owners took 90% of the land and left the people to live in small, fragmented parts of it, they did not even have a cow or any place to keep one, so the only option that is left for them is trafficking, which comes with the tourists. So the *campesinos* take a sloth and earn 10–20,000 pesos, and in that way they have 20,000 that is needed on a daily basis for the family. As long as this people are left with no other options, the trafficking will proceed exactly the same way.

Another interviewee similarly said:

> Unfortunately, the farmers and indigenous people [are abductors] although I defend them because they have been displaced, and they base themselves

> on what is in demand and where there is a business that gives them something to eat.

In these cases, wildlife trafficking is caused directly by poverty and displacement which in turn is caused by the illegitimate abuse of power by paramilitary groups and big land owners, as well as by the state (Goyes 2016; Goyes and South 2015; Mol 2013). So while the abductions may be opportunistic, they are the result of poor *campesinos* being victimized. We therefore see a chain of victimization, which was seen also in the Patarroyo case.

Several of the interviewees described the involvement of the army in wildlife trafficking, although not for profit. People in the army, like locals living in or close to the forests, also keep wild animals as pets. This was regarded as disappointing because it shows a bad example and contributes to wildlife trafficking:

> It is very common to see soldiers with a monkey or a squirrel or a parrot on the shoulder
>
> They all have a parrot on their shoulder when they descend from the mountains; ALL of them! They are conveying this image to the people that they are heroes of the nation and they take animals.
>
> (ProAves)

Some of the interviewees said there was reason to believe that paramilitary groups in conflict zones, like Nudo de Paramillo National Park, were involved in WLT, but they did not elaborate further on the topic.

The armed forces, however, are implicated in the WLT according to Ortiz-von Halle from TRAFFIC. He said that animals are used as presents and status symbols for the colonels, but also that the army is involved on a larger scale, as air transports have been used to transport mahogany[23] and the army consequently entered into conflict with the authorities of the airports. This, he stated, had happened both in Colombia and Peru: 'Because they have the power to do it, and thus do.' On the other hand, in an article in the military magazine *Díalogo* (Pelcastre 2016), it appears that the armed forces of Colombia are working to counter wildlife trade (including timber) and that this formed part of their strategy in 2013–2015: Pelcastre claims that in 2016 they made great strides against the finances of the criminal groups involved in these activities, and that the 17th Battalion of the Marine Corps Brigade no. 1 confiscated 1,200 cubic metres of timber in Magdalena River in August 2016. They also allegedly prevented the trafficking, sale and exploitation of 11,899 animals of protected species.

Another interviewee said the armed forces would *not* keep animals as *mascotas* because they could slow them down when swift action was needed. This seems logical, and it is hard to establish the involvement of armed forces in WLT without empirical investigation. Nonetheless, the interviewee from ProAves claimed that the armed forces were the most important actors in WLT in Colombia and that the army was deeply implicated, first for its ignorance – not knowing that it is illegal – and also for ignoring the value of wildlife and consequently continuing to take them, sell them and provide the public with the opportunity to buy the animals.

The army may have had a dual role in wildlife trade, and most likely their habits of keeping wild animals as *mascotas* will decrease, both as a consequence of military strategy, but also because the majority of guerrilla soldiers have put down their arms following the peace agreement in 2016. The development of the peace process may determine how the Colombian wildlife may be further impacted by the war.

One should think that the use of wildlife, such as giving commanders tigrillos, would be equally common among members of the guerrilla groups; however, the majority of the interviewees said the guerrillas served as a form of vanguard for the forests, and *prevented* traffickers from coming in to take the animals: 'The guerrilla prohibited both hunting and trafficking in the jungle zones they controlled.'

While the armed forces were identified as participants in wildlife trade, the guerrilla groups were said to have the opposite effect. Ortiz-von Halle said the guerrillas in many places had been the only authority protecting the environment and its species during the civil war. For example in places with cedar trees and turtles, they would be preserved because the guerrilla regulated and prevented wildlife trade. The guerrillas kept an eye on networks to make sure that they did not overfish and prevented or regulated access. They did this with far more efficiency than the state. Obviously, and like the armed forces, the guerrilla also kept pets from the wild, indicating they did not always play the part of the 'good,' but they played the role of environmental authorities in many places and as such were important in places where the state was not present.

The guerrillas would enforce their rules against wildlife trade (and theriocides) by ways of fines; for example, people from Meta and Magdalena have told TRAFFIC that if they killed a puma or a tapir, the guerrillas would impose a fine of 5.6 million pesos, a considerable sum for a local in Colombia (equivalent to 1,702–2,043 USD).

Interviewees accused paramilitary groups of killing mammals for consumption. So, it was said, would the guerrilla groups:

> I was working two years in the national park of Sumapaz, which is one of the biggest in Colombia, and the guerrillas were there. There was not trafficking, but animals were the preferred dish, because it is very cold there, so they were constantly hunting mammals. We were trying to do environmental campaigning, but they said, 'yes, but we need to eat, we need to survive, so we hunt what we need and leave the rest.'
>
> (Yudi Cardenas, CRRFFS)

To briefly sum up, Colombia has been riddled by war and violence for more than 70 years, a situation which has had damaging effects on free-born animals and the environment. The conflicts and the violence have led to poverty and migration to the cities. People have therefore engaged in wildlife trade as a means to make an income, but also as a means to make easy additional income, simply because it is money with little risk attached to it. People have brought their cultural habits of bringing free-born animals with them to the cities, likely because this provides some consolation in a difficult situation.

The armed conflict has had a direct consequence on animals who have been hunted to provide food for the soldiers, whether soldiers of the Colombian military forces or guerrilla groups. Soldiers have also used free-born animals as pets, although it is hard to establish how widespread this practice has been, since interviewees provided contradictory information. Nonetheless, it is clear that the violence has impacted negatively on free-born animals in Colombia. Next, I will look at the success of law enforcement related to wildlife trafficking in Colombia.

Notes

1 www.youtube.com/watch?v=o6KWau2dxJ8

2 www.google.no/search?q=zoocriaderos+de+babilla+en+Colombia+fotos&hl=en&tbm=isch&source=iu&ictx=1&fir=WVpg2Jo0khQwoM%253A%252C7CEWbnzGEdSWXM%252C_&usg=__SxRRASzlL4AfQI6Ic9jRNSdU59U%3D&sa=X&ved=0ahUKEwiK-4zLvtLXAhUkLZoKHSg-DLQQ9QEIQTAL#imgrc=MHV4CcU3onouMM:&spf=1511364259546

3 The concept of biopiracy refers to the appropriation of knowledge and nature, describing the ongoing global and local corporate practice of asserting the right of ownership over genetic materials taken from living organisms (Mgbeoji 2006 in Goyes and South 2015: 3), including the patenting of medicines, seeds, plants and even other forms of life. Adherents of such processes would rather refer to these practices as 'bioprospecting' (Goyes and Sollund 2018). All use of biological material may, from the perspective of the donor or, rather, from the *victim* from whom the genetic material was taken, be regarded as biopiracy, because such activities normally include an invasion of personal integrity, provided the human or animal in question is a sentient being, even when samples may be taken with the donor/victim's consent. Consequently, the term 'biopiracy' should not only include the appropriation of knowledge about how different genetic compositions may be applied to develop medicines, but also refer to the process of taking genetic material directly from individuals. This broader definition of biopiracy helps avoid tacit acceptance of animals as property, and even human beings as exploitable resources, who are used for that purpose.

4 These are known as the three Rs: reduction, replacement and refinement, and include computerized modelling and audiovisual alternatives. http://norecopa.no/about-norecopa

5 It appears in Colombia both margays and ocelots are referred to as tigrillo. They are similar, but not the same species, differing in weight and the length of the tail (Haemig 2012).

6 Another example from Bolivia is the use of armadillo to produce the stringed instrument charango.

7 In an article from 1991, Guillermo Trujillo confirms the use of animals in witchcraft and the superstitious use of animals in medicine in Colombia. There are numerous academic articles referring to the traditional use of witchcraft in Colombia, including Franco (2001) and Uribe (2003). The categories of traditional medicine and witchcraft overlap. A Google image search reveals several photos of shamans using feathers of endangered Amazon parrot species. Presumably, these birds have not been trafficked but killed for use as adornment that forms

part of such cultural practices. www.google.no/search?q=cascabel+magia+negra&biw=1280&bih=597&source=lnms&tbm=isch&sa=X&ved=0ahUKEwiT5JHLr__LAhUrGZoKHeSTDK0Q_AUIBigB#tbm=isch&q=chamanes&imgrc=JkYw4CE2SIJ-EM%3A

8 Claudia Luz Rodríguez (Grupo de Gestión de Especies Silvestres, Dirección de Bosques, Biodiversidad y Servicios Ecosistémicos [Ministry of Environment and Sustainable Development in Colombia]), Javier Cifuentes Álvarez, Luz María Cuadros, Yudi Cárdenas, and Carolina Rangel from CRRFFS, Bernardo Ortiz-von Halle, director of the regional office for TRAFFIC, and Professor Claudia Brieva Rico from URRAS.

9 About 6–9 USD according to the conversion rate on March 14, 2016.

10 www.bbc.com/news/magazine-27905743

11 www.eurosurveillance.org/ViewArticle.aspx?ArticleId=2819

12 As shown in relation to Norwegian data, a similar case involved parrots who were trafficked to Norway; eight 'surplus' birds who could not be accounted for through the permits were seized and eventually killed by Norwegian authorities (see also Sollund and Maher 2015: 21).

13 www.hernebreedingcentre.be/page.php?1. The firm claims to apply to CITES, providing welfare to their animals who are under the regular care of wildlife veterinarians. They also state they provide zoos with animals. The stock lists were available on the website on October 14, 2016.

14 See, e.g., http://cincinnatizoo.org/conservation/

15 www.bbc.com/news/world-europe-26734377

16 In Norway, for example, when offenders are suspected of organized crime, the police have more liberty concerning the investigation of a crime, e.g., tapping into phone call conversations (see www.regjeringen.no/no/dokumenter/faktaark-om-nye-etterforskningsmetoder/id88217/; Sollund 2017).

17 www.entropika.org/en/about.html

18 This is a legal instrument in Colombian procedural law, by which the public powers and, in general, any citizen, is legitimized to urge the action of the administration of justice in defence of collective or diffuse interests.

19 www.fidic.org.co/pagina/trayectoria.html

20 www.entropika.org/en/projects.html

21 www.entropika.org/en/projects.html

22 www.acnur.org/recursos/estadisticas/

23 Wildlife is understood by TRAFFIC as encompassing both plants and animals, as in CITES.

11 Responses to wildlife trafficking by the Colombian authorities

The Colombian environmental authorities developed a guide[1] in 2007 for the control and prevention of wildlife trafficking in the country. According to the guide, the Ministry of the Environment and Sustainable Development coordinates this work at the national level. This initiative is called *Convenio Interinstitucional* (Interinstitutional Convention), produced by the following institutions: Ministry of the Environment and Sustainable Development, Ministry of Defense, Ministry of Agriculture and Rural Development, general state prosecutor, general attorney of the nation, Administrative Ministry of Security (DAS), National Direction of Tax and Customs (DIAN), Alexander von Humboldt Institute for the Study of Biological Resources and the National University of Colombia.

With the intention of decreasing the illegal exploitation of wildlife at the regional level, the Comités Interinstitucionales Contra la Tenencia y Comercio Ilegal de Fauna Silvestre (CITECIF; the Interinstitutional Committee against the Illegal Possession and Commercialization of Wildlife) was formed by the following governmental institutions: environmental authorities, the secretariats of the government, the National Institute of Fisheries and Aquaculture (IMPA), the national police, the Colombian army, the Administrative Ministry of Security, DIAN, the DAS, the state prosecutor, Interpol, and universities and institutions, such as NGOs, private centres and centres for investigations who have a vested interested in the work of the committee (Guía para el control al trafico ilegal de fauna Silvestre Colombiana 2007).

Despite this guide being written in 2007, which shows that the harms of illegal wildlife trade has priority at national level, it has been difficult to determine how the cooperation works in practice and how successful such cooperative efforts have been. What the interviewees said about inspections and prevention measures made in Colombia against WLT, however, does reflect points made in the convention and show established cooperation.

All expert interviewees in Colombia were interviewed about *how* wildlife trade and CITES were enforced in Colombia, as well as their views of the success of inspections and enforcement. Before I turn to discussing their views, I will present a brief history of how the Colombian legislation pertaining to IWT came about and of the framework for law enforcement as described by the interviewees.

The development of the framework and organization for law enforcement of wildlife trafficking in Colombia

Concerning the organization of the environmental authorities in Colombia, first is the Ministry of the Environment and Sustainable Development, with 34 *corporaciones autónomas regionales* (CARs, regional autonomous corporations), one in each of the country's departments. For example, in Cali the authority is Corporación Autónoma Regional del Valle del Cauca (CVC), and in Bucaramanga and Santander it is Corporación Autónoma Regional para la Defensa de la Meseta de Bucaramanga (CMBD). It is expected that each one of these CARs will conduct inspections concerning environmental violations. Much is in the hands of the police and the DIJIN[2] (La Dirección de Investigación Criminal e INTERPOL), but it is the environmental authorities that document inspections, while the confiscation of animals can only be done by the environmental police or the DIJIN based on a technical report issued by the environmental authorities.

The formation of the CARs was established by Law 99 of 1993, Sistema Nacional Ambiental (SINA). SINA is a national organization for environmental management. Regionally, the CARs execute the national plan of the SINA in their respective jurisdictions, conducting evaluations and inspections of *inter alia* the exploitation and use of renewable natural resources. They also have the responsibility for national parks. In addition, they organize educational campaigns, which promote sustainable development (Guía para el control al trafico ilegal de fauna silvestre Colombiana 2007).

Large urban centres with populations over 1 million inhabitants, such as Bogotá, have an environmental authority with the Secretaría Distrital de Ambiente (the District Secretariat of the Environment), under which CRRFFS is located.

In 1995, the Ministry of the Environment (DAMA, the precursor of the Secretaría Distrital de Ambiente) decided that fauna was important to protect. Subsequently, a proposition was made concerning a structure based in liaison offices in the one air- and two ground-communication centres in Bogotá. Because of the large numbers of animals who were seized, CRRFFS was established.

The plan was to create specialized centres for wildlife rehabilitation all over Colombia, e.g., in Amazonía, in the Orinoquía, in Chocó. The only specialized rescue and rehabilitation centre for fauna that actually was established by an environmental authority, however, was CRRFFS. This does not mean it is the only centre for reception and rehabilitation of animals. Interviewees said there were 10–12 centres in the country; none, however, was of the magnitude and importance as initially envisioned. Various CARs have rehabilitation centres for wildlife: the Corpoguajira of the Bolívar police, the Corantioquia which has a centre supported by three CARs, and the centre in Orinoquía, according to two interviewees, including Javier Cifuentes.

In 2010, a group of state prosecutors specializing in the environment was established, and this was followed by the police establishing specialized investigation bodies: the Directorate of Criminal Investigation and Interpol (DIJIN) and the Secciones de Investigación Criminal (SIJIN), criminal investigation units that permit the police to intervene in trafficking networks. The results were not apparent immediately, but little by little a strategy has developed that may result in the reduction of trafficking, according to Javier Cifuentes of CRRFFS.

Laws governing environmental issues and trade in plants and animals in Colombia, and law enforcement in practice

In Colombia, a wide range of laws and regulations are relevant to the trafficking in plants and free-born animals. They do not all directly concern trafficking in free-born animals, but they are interconnected. The laws most often applied in relation to trafficking in free-born animals are:

1 Decreto 1608 de 1978 (Código Nacional de los Recursos Naturales).
2 Ley 599 de 2000 (Código Penal) Artículos 328 y 329.
3 Ley 84 de 1989 (Estatuto de Protección a los Animales).
4 Ley 99 de 1993, Artículo 1.

A more detailed overview of the relevant legislation concerning WLT in Colombia is included in an appendix to the book.

Several interviewees noted the extensive legal framework that is in place to protect the animals after they are trafficked as a direct result of Colombia signing the CITES. This, however, says little about if and how this is enforced, and how many animals pass under the radar of law enforcement agencies. This topic will be explored below.

CITES is enforced by regional environmental authorities. The responsibility for this in Bogotá is the Secretaría Distrital de Ambiente. Because of the large number of animals arriving at CRRFFS from other parts of the country, the opinion of CRRFFS staff was that the CARs are inefficient. Ortiz-von Halle from TRAFFIC was also critical of law enforcement in Colombia: 'If I am caught with cocaine, I will get 20 years, but if I am caught with fauna, the only thing happening is that the animal will be confiscated. This will be more profitable, this is how it is.'

Ortiz-von Halle described the training of the environmental police and the environmental authorities in Colombia as pioneering and acknowledged that they can make life difficult for traffickers. On the other hand, he claimed there was much corruption in relation to the lucrative cocaine trade where the police turn a blind eye. The control and enforcement of wildlife trade benefits from this because the police are eager to show that they are doing a good job, which they do by prioritizing environmental crimes; for example, they confiscate some parrots or turtles. When big money is involved, however, he said corruption also impacts WLT control. The problem of corruption was also mentioned by other interviewees: 'Obviously, if someone pays for a permit, they will get it.' When I asked who was involved, an anonymous interviewee answered:

> They are powerful people. There are politicians who have animals on their *fincas* and who benefit from this, so if anyone is going to fix this problem it must be a person with sufficient power and resources to do it.

Wildlife trafficking used to be regarded as a minor offence; today it is an environmental crime. However, such criminals can be released without any punishment. Even when concerning endangered species, the criminals can avoid prison.

Although imprisonment is envisioned in the legislation, with for example 48 to 108 months according to Article 331 of the Penal Law (see Appendix 2), seldom does anybody get a prison sentence. Additionally, offenders, who are convicted to less than four years in prison and if it is their first offense, can serve the sentence at home. According to Javier Cifuentes, a maximum of 20 persons are convicted per year for wildlife trafficking. This is because the specialist prosecutors are still in a process of being trained and the penal law in this matter is very lax, so, consequently, there is little preventing wildlife trafficking from expanding.

César Márquez, expert in raptor birds, expanded on the topic:

> There are very few convictions. For example, there was a project about the reintroduction of the Andean condor in Boyacá, where a farmer shot one of these condors, and he was convicted to prison. Another case concerned an endangered species: an eagle from the wet rainforests in Colombia. The woman had to present herself before the judge, but he decided not to convict her. It is only now that this legislation is starting to get known. In a country as complex, with so many social problems, violence, kidnappings etc., it is 'normal' that that these crimes are regarded as secondary.

A ProAves interviewee agreed that because of the lax control and law enforcement and very lenient punishments, there is little deterrence for traffickers and buyers.

There is also lack of inspection of land transport, and although some operations end in confiscation, these do not take place regularly. Often the confiscations result from local communities alerting the police, but if this does not happen, very little is done to stop the trafficking. If a person is caught trafficking animals, authorities confiscate the animals, but there are few other consequences for the offender. Apart from confiscation (which is regarded as punitive, especially when people are reported for keeping animals as pets and have them confiscated), the main form of punishment is, like in Norway, a fine: 'Roughly speaking; the proportion is 98% fines and 2% like a penal offense' (Javier Cifuentes).

According to Cifuentes, the sanctions that can be imposed by the environmental authorities, according to Law 99 of 1993, vary from fines to the closing of establishments and the confiscation of animals. Fines range from one to 1,000 minimum month's salary (a minimum month's salary in Colombia is 570,000 pesos (€238)) and in addition to this, the judicial system can impose further punishments of fines or prison. The extent of the punishment is assessed based on the vulnerability of the species as outlined in the red books of the Ministry of the Environment.

When a person is stopped with an animal in his/her possession and the animal is confiscated, the seizure is registered in the central database used by all the CARs' (*Registro Único de Infractores Ambientales*, the register of environmental offenders). The offender is registered and if s/he recidivates, s/he will receive a stricter punishment. If an endangered species is involved (in accordance with Resolución 383), stricter sanctions are applied, like fines, and there are tables establishing the amount of the fine depending on the impact of the crime.

As shown, a lot of trafficking and other wildlife crimes take place in the Amazon. Wilfredo Pachón from Corporación para el Desarrollo Sostenible del Norte y el Oriente Amazónico elaborated upon what his organization does to counter wildlife trafficking in the area. A designated group called Subdirección de Normalización y Calidad Ambiental (Subdivision of Normalization and Environmental Quality) is in charge of the control and monitoring of natural resources: flora, fauna and mining. In Calamar and in El Retorno, for example, a group of professionals, sometimes coordinated with the environmental police, target exit points like airports and bus terminals to avoid the commercialization of wildlife. In addition, they plan environmental awareness campaigns to make people conscious about the scale of deforestation and wildlife trade and its consequences.

No one has been incarcerated for such crimes in the district of Northeast Amazon, according to Wilfredo Pachón. Only if someone reoffends or if a crime concerning endangered species is committed would there be incarceration. Such cases would be transferred to the state prosecutor, and if they concern fines, these would be imposed by the Corporación. Usually the police handle cases concerning offenders who have been detained for a day or two while investigations are carried out to the Corporación. The prosecutors then decide what happens, but usually offenders are released. Normally, the only sanction is the confiscation of the animals, but in roughly 3% of the cases, a fine is imposed.

CRRFFS interviewees talked about a change in how environmental crimes are perceived by the judicial system. One case concerned an offender who was trafficking in Plaza de Restrepo and who was convicted to four years' prison. According to Javier Cifuentes, similar cases are increasingly seen all over the country:

> And the state prosecutors are starting to show signs that this is definitely a crime and these gangs are as criminal as the drug and arms traffickers, and so these criminals will start to realise that 'it really is not that easy.'

Every week CRRFFS carries out operations with the environmental police and they have been successful in pushing traffickers from Plaza de Restrepo. As mentioned, this does not mean the trade stops. Rather, professional traffickers find other means of trafficking, like catalogues and the internet. CRRFFS and the environmental police also have operations in other plazas in Bogotá, at bus terminals, and near pet shops and meat markets. Because of these operations, at least four persons have been incarcerated.

For the most part, there is very little control of ports and departure points in Colombia, according to Cifuentes. However, because El Dorado Airport, Terminal de Transporte Salitre and Terminal de Trasnporte de Sur are within CRRFFS's jurisdiction, they do inspections there frequently.

One of the interviewees pointed out that the establishment of the Ministry of the Environment in 1993 and the 'environmental systems' and CARs that went along with it was an important step in terms of legal strategies. He emphasized that the smooth operation of these institutions and enforcing the legislation would result in adequate control. This, however, is not happening because of a general lack of consciousness about the legislation, among both ordinary citizens and those responsible for the control and prevention of WLT. Even when legislation is in place, its effect will be minimal if people are unaware of the legislation (Goyes and Sollund 2016).

If WLT is as prevalent among the population in Colombia as seizures and interview data suggest, then it is even more urgent to enforce the legislation which is meant to change deep-rooted practices – to educate people on the illegality of certain acts – and in this way, gradually change the normative foundation of the people.

CRRFFS does an important job creating awareness among people via interviews given to newspapers, advertisements[3] and social media, letting people know about animals who have been rescued and rehabilitated. For example, on November 20, 2017, *Noticias* carried an article about 122 animals who were returned to their natural habitats in Guaduas, Puerto Salgar y Caparrapí, in an action called *Retorno a casa* (The return home).[4]

The assistant director of Silvicultura, Flora y Fauna Silvestre de la Secretaría de Ambiente (Secretary of the Environment, Wild Flora and Fauna) Yaneth Buitrago, was quoted as saying that the operation was impressive:

> It is really fantastic to have the opportunity to see these animals be given the opportunity to return to nature. We hope this will be a significant event and that it will help us turn the minds of the children who will accompany us, and that the community will be sensitised and acquire a new consciousness regarding the treatment and protection our wild animals deserve.

The return operation was accompanied by personnel from the Secretaría de Ambiente, the government of Cundinamarca and the CAR of Cundinamarca. The publicity about the return operation in media also has the potential to make people aware that their pets may be illegal to keep and encourage them to deliver them to the authorities, even if they are emotionally attached to them.

The autonomy of CARs is an issue. CARs in each region are responsible for ensuring that the regulations concerning wildlife trade are enforced, but this means that information about numbers of animals who are trafficked is dispersed nationwide, and the Ministry of Environment will not have the entire picture because it relies on numbers being provided by regional CARs and they may or may not provide the Ministry with the data. This does not mean that the CARs do not cooperate, and the Ministry of the Environment will periodically bring together CAR staff to strategize how to address and control trafficking of various prioritized species such as titi gris, icotea turtles, Andean bears, sloths and migratory birds.

One of the interviewees from the environmental authority considered the cooperation between the various branches of police, the DIJIN and the SIJIN to be good, in terms of processing the paperwork necessary to open a judicial case against a person. However, often cases would die for lack of proof and the CARs would simply receive the animals. He blamed this on a lack of cooperation between the environmental sector and the police, resulting in a lack of coordination of the work.

Concerning international cooperation in the case of seizures destined abroad or coming from abroad, one interviewee said that any communication would go through the Ministry of the Environment, which is in charge of international communication. For example, if a cargo of bullfrogs would come from Ecuador en route to the US, the CITES paperwork would be checked, and if there were irregularities, the Ministry would be informed.

At present, legal strategies are not as effective as they could be because some of the people involved in WLT are uneducated or/and illiterate; the message of the law is hindered from reaching such offenders with a normative message, as elaborated upon by one interviewee:

> There are several laws, but they are not very clear. Often the people who keep *mascotas* don't know how to read or write, they are people from the countryside, so to use the legal system against them does not make much sense. A person might say, 'Someone just gave me this parrot.' So the application of the normative message of the law is complicated.

Other problems concerning legal strategies are presented by the interviewees.

1 The law itself is ambiguous. For example, it does not prohibit the trafficking of animals, it simply prohibits 'use of resources of fauna and flora,' so from that judicialization could be entailed by a person trafficking ('only') one turtle, or one hundred parrots, indiscriminately. The problem of ambiguous laws in relation to Colombian wildlife trade is discussed by Goyes and Sollund (2016), who conclude ambiguity is a general problem in relation to the legislation of such crimes there.
2 Only Bogotá has environmental prosecutors. This means that too much of a burden is placed on too few people. On a day when authorities undertake 52 seizures, 52 prosecutions must be made, and for one prosecutor, this is an astronomical amount of paperwork. For each confiscation, the environmental authorities must produce a technical document which is sent to a lawyer of the Secretaría de Ambiente to impose fines, make a list of offenders and assess the harm to the environment. Such a heavy workload has meant there are years' worth of delays in meting out fines to offenders.
3 The DIJIN and the police do not always have the technical competence to assess what crime has been committed, and if the environmental authorities are not there to assist, confiscations can end up with no punitive response; i.e., the proofs which are necessary to prosecute are not acquired.

4 Other times the environmental police and the DIJIN will go for small cases in order to establish the impression that they are successfully enforcing WLT. If they have not had any prosecutions in three months, they will look for whatever excuse to make one and prosecute a person carrying one parrot, rather than going for the big traffickers, according to interviews.

One interviewee argued for differentiated law enforcement because indigenous groups involved in wildlife trafficking should be shown concern for their specific situation. From a legal, ecojustice or species justice perspective, this would mean that some groups of people would be allowed to exploit animals, while others would not. This would run the risk of confusing for which circumstances, for whom, and if and which law should be applied. It would entail unjust and partial legalization of a crime, adding further to the existent ambiguity of the law. Such differentiated law enforcement would thus, in terms of animals and the ecosystems, represent a step backwards. It is also difficult to distinguish between people who engage in wildlife trafficking because they are in dire need and those who do this opportunistically to generate extra income (Goyes and Sollund 2016; Mowbray 2015). This can be discussed in relation to the concept of 'folk crime' (Holmes 2016; Sollund 2017b; White 2016b), whereby crimes against free-born animals linguistically, conceptually and euphemistically are regarded as being 'not so serious.' For example, when endangered animals are killed, these theriocides are regarded as being 'merely' tokens of protest and dissent against environmental authorities (Holmes 2016; von Essen and Allen 2015) or 'only' for subsistence. By accepting such a perspective, one delegitimizes the victims of the crimes. This is a dangerous path to take when individual life and well-being, ecosystems and species are at stake. However, obviously, professional traffickers should be fined more heavily than micro traffickers, and the offender's income, legal as well as illegal, and economic situation should be taken into account.

One interviewee pointed out how enforcement produces counterproductive effects for the animal victims, despite legislation to prevent trafficking in Colombia having been introduced. For example before the legislation, if parrots were seized at El Dorado Airport, they would be immediately released, but with the new system the judge must first *see* the animals, and sometimes 10–15 days can pass before this happens and thus 90% of the birds die. It appears to be more important to prosecute the offender than to save the victim, not unlike the killing of the African grey parrots in Norway in order to enforce CITES. This is a paradoxical and tragic effect of the legislation and its enforcement meant to protect free-born animals and endangered species.

Colombia's fulfilment of its obligations to CITES

Whether estimates concerning numbers of recorded animals subject to trade are accurate and do not exceed the number that would cause a threat to species depends first on whether the species is listed (Natusch and Lyons 2012) and second on whether Colombia fulfils its CITES requirement to report all exports.

In the Patarroyo case, for example, the trade in night monkeys from Brazil and Peru for malaria research was not tracked (Maldonado et al. 2009). On the other hand, Claudia Luz Rodríguez asserted that in relation to export from breeding facilities, *zoocriadores*, Colombia always fulfils its obligations. She claimed Colombia submits the information on time, shows which breeding facilities have been approved, which mechanisms have been adopted to guarantee that the production quotas are filled in an appropriate way, and that the facilities are not used illegally:

> Colombia is trying all the time to adopt the recommendations made by CITES in order to remain in the international market with credibility, because this has been questioned historically. So what CITES has done, is to pay attention to the recommendations and tell the responsible sector in the member states, that either it adapts to the recommendations or this international market will be closed [for them].

In relation to CITES, Ortiz-von Halle also stated that Colombia fulfils its obligations to CITES, but he also asked rhetorically:

> What would it be to fulfil them well? A lot has been done to sort out the forgery of permits, but local control is a problem. For example, it is not established, which are the legitimate and which are the illegitimate breeders and sanctions are not imposed on those who err. Legal authorities never sanction these, close their businesses or confiscate their cargo.

Ortiz-von Halle raised the concern that WLT is treated as a problem of natural resources, whereas he regarded it as a problem of organized crime. WLT consequently should be treated with the same seriousness as is an investigation of a drug cartel. But, according to him, crimes against the environment are treated superficially because there are not enough resources. Sometimes the police and the environmental authorities will collaborate, other times not.

His statement is noteworthy, not the least because the general rhetoric concerning wildlife trade internationally is that it is indeed organized crime, and this rhetoric is also what has generated priority at EU and UN levels (Fajardo del Castillo 2016; Sollund and Maher 2015; Sina et al. 2016; Runhovde 2016, see introduction). However, as Runhovde (2016) shows, such claims are not always rooted in empirical reality, nor does this rhetoric fit the majority of Colombian WLT, as represented in my data.

Ortiz-von Halle is also critical of seeing CITES as the solution, emphasizing that CITES is only as effective as the environmental authorities in each of its member states:

> But what is CITES? It is a secretariat in Switzerland where a few persons administer this matter, but CITES is also the Colombian authorities, and is only as good or as bad as these authorities. CITES cannot be better than the

> Ministry of the Environment in Colombia, or better than the Corporación Autónoma Regional de la Amazonía, so CITES is like the country itself, it is not external or supranational. So the reports of the national authorities that are brought to the conferences of the parties to the Convention is the version of the national authorities that should have control. CITES does not have any mechanisms, CITES is easy to fool, as easy as it is to intimidate or marginalise the Colombian authorities. So CITES is the same as the Ministry of the Environment and as efficient as this Ministry. And this is where we stand, because one tends to think that CITES is an organism, like the UN trying to solve the problem of endangered species, but CITES can only do what the authorities in the different countries do, with all their strengths and weaknesses, this is what CITES can do.

The lack of measures available to CITES to enforce decisions have been treated in the literature (e.g., Challender et al. 2015), which has called into question CITES's effectiveness (see section concerning CITES below). One issue is the moral and ethical foundation of CITES, which through regulation prolongs and encourages trade in endangered species (Goyes and Sollund 2016; Maher and Sollund 2016a, 2016b; Sollund 2011; Sollund and Maher 2015). Another issue is that even if accepting the anthropocentric premise of CITES, CITES and its member states have few means of punishing the member states that do not comply, other than restricting their trade. This, however, can hurt the country economically if the trade in a specific species is one on which the country is reliant.

An anonymous interviewee, an expert in CITES, put forward another critique of CITES:

> CITES, which is an international agreement, is also a voluntary agreement. This means 'Yes, we are friends, but we take small steps.' So, in the moment of implementing a sanction, it is on level with pulling an ear, and nothing happens. And one of the conclusions is that CITES is turning into a cover of or distraction from the problems of international wildlife trade, but it is without teeth; it is more like a salute to the flag [something more symbolic than real] because when it comes to imposing sanctions there is no way.

As a party to the Convention, a country must have legislation in place which will ensure the country acts according to the Convention, but legislation alone has no effect. As shown, there is no lack of legislation concerning wildlife trade and animal abuse in Colombia.

The interviewee's point, that CITES works to distract attention from the problem, is also an important socio-legal observation. It corresponds with similar observations made by interviewees concerning the implementation of other legislation. Implementing laws gives political credibility, making it appear that something is being done, but nothing really happens to combat the problem (Aubert 1954; Mathiesen 1990). This is true in Colombia. Legislation makes it appear as if the problem is being addressed, whereas in reality the problem is so profound and widespread that legislation is not the right tool in many cases of wildlife trade.

Just like the Norwegian Customs inspectors who feared that the legalization of exotic reptiles in Norway would make it difficult to distinguish between CITES-listed and non-CITES-listed species, in Colombia the control agents in charge of preventing wildlife trade and enforcing the existing legislation have similar problems. As elaborated upon by Javier Cifuentes of CRRFFS:

> The problem is the skills that the various authorities have in determining whether a species is CITES listed, and discerning between different CITES species. Often also, the regional authorities cannot distinguish a native from an exotic species, whether or not it is an endangered species, and consequently how to follow up on the offense in the judicial system.

The lack of adequate enforcement is associated with the ignorance and lack of interest in the matter among state prosecutors, according to interviewees. The areas specialized prosecutors are supposed to cover in relation to the environment are many and diverse, like mining, oil extraction *and* wildlife trafficking, which is only a small part of their responsibility. Therefore, there should be specialization in wildlife trafficking to address the problem seriously.

While the environmental police are considered to be doing a very good job, they are few and the staff of the CARs are said to have little training. The interviewees listed a lack of continuity among personnel responsible for control and enforcement as another problem. New people get involved all the time who, e.g., were unaware of previous practice: 'They have no body of knowledge and experience, because everything changes all the time, so there is no control.'

Several interviewees also complained about the lack of qualifications concerning wildlife trafficking among street police. One interviewee involved in rescue and rehabilitation of animals recounted episodes when they were involved in procedures to get cages with boas, parrots and mammals to safety and had met the police, and the police officers would say, 'How sweet, can you sell me one?' And they would say, 'Mr. police, do you not know that this is illegal?' to which the police would respond, 'no.' This ignorance is why traffickers will not be stopped by ordinary police officers.

Awareness campaigns and control measures combined

A softer and probably more fruitful way than by using law enforcement to prevent IWT, at least micro trafficking and pet keeping, would be by means of awareness campaigns. One such campaign is '*En tu casa no se sienten como en su casa*' ('In your home they do not feel at home').[5] Awareness is also created by the Ministry of Education with messages concerning flora and fauna on programs in public media. This way the young generation can unlearn the mistakes of previous generations and learn that animals should be allowed to remain in their habitats.

However, to prevent abductions and trafficking, combined efforts and a diversity of tactics must be used (Ayling 2015; Maher and Sollund 2016a; Sollund and Maher 2015). As an interviewee said,

> The environmental authorities in Bogotá have successfully cooperated with SIJN, with the carabinero police or with Interpol, because the origin of the problem is not in Bogotá and therefore control strategies must be addressed to where the problem is.

To this end, environmental authorities in Bogotá use dog patrols to detect wildlife in airport and other terminals. If this is successful, it will be replicated at the national level, exactly when was not specified. CRRFFS is working hand in hand with the CARs CorTolima and CorpoCesar to spread the campaign to those areas and to ensure that it includes species from those areas.

However, as long as there is demand there is supply, and as long as men eat iguana eggs for potency and people eat icotea turtle because it is white meat and is much cheaper than to eat than other meat is, the wildlife trade will continue. Trafficking is well connected to people's level of education, consciousness and sensitization. Therefore, with increased resources and successful operations by the CARs in the most important sourcing locations, wildlife trafficking may be counteracted, provided the CARs receive the necessary training and resources and also educate people. Unfortunately, interviewees complained about the lack of resources to prevent and control; several of the CARs are not funded specifically to deal with the problem.

Creating awareness is not only essential among citizens, but also among the people in the judicial sector – prosecutors and judges. Interviewees emphasized they have to acknowledge that this is a crime that needs to be punished. Unfortunately, there are very few specialists in this area among state attorneys/prosecutors, so they also need training, but finding the resources for this constitutes a problem in a country with so many other problems.

Another important area of work for the environmental authorities and the CARs is prevention. These institutions educate people about trafficking and its cruelty to animals, that trafficking is illegal, and warn them that it can get them into trouble. They go to schools and universities to inform about trafficking and advise people that if they hear strange noises from their neighbours' houses, they should report it, as it could be a titi gris or another illegal animal. They also communicate with airlines and transport companies about illegal transport of animals, that it must be reported to the environmental police, and that they should check all paperwork. They also cooperate with Customs, tax authorities, with Instituto Colombiano Agropecuario (ICA; the farming institute) and DIJIN to follow up on cases, demanding documents if anything suspicious is reported or discovered. As was said by the interviewees at CRRFFS:

> As an example, last year we trained more than ten thousand persons who work at the airport and the bus terminal. There are the cleaners, the guards,

> the people at the post service, the people at the courier companies, the stewardesses, the pilots, the bus conductors, telling them that wildlife trade is illegal, and about the implications this has on ecosystems and on human health.

Many interviewees said that the main problem is a general lack of environmental consciousness in the country. An animal rights activist told me in 2017 that Colombians would purposefully drive over opossums because they regard them as big rats. Such speciesist crimes highlight the problems Colombia faces in protecting its free-born animals. As said by Ortiz-von Halle, control and enforcement will remain insufficient unless the basis of the problems is addressed so that people protect the fauna where they live.

Police and the environmental authorities also work with voluntary deliveries. Often the police discover an illegal parrot being kept and demand that s/he be delivered to the authorities voluntarily, rather than processing a confiscation. Whether this is truly voluntary is debatable, but it indicates that other measures than punishment can be applied. Undoubtedly, such measures are more effective deterrents than a minor fine would be.

In sum, in Colombia there is a good formal organization for the control and enforcement of broad legislation related to wildlife trafficking. In practice, however, there is a lack of training at various levels of the enforcement agencies, as well as a lack of resources. This means that enforcement is lax, and usually results only in the confiscation of the animals, or sometimes a fine. The job of enforcement agencies is further complicated by the generally broad acceptance for wildlife trade in the country, in which very many Colombians, as in the rest of Latin America (e.g., Leberatto 2016; Nassaro 2017), are involved as consumers.

To briefly sum up the problems concerning the control of wildlife trafficking in Colombia and enforcement of bans, as these were described by the interviewees: The ordinary police, prosecutors and judges lack the necessary knowledge about the seriousness of the crime, resulting in lax enforcement. The general population is to a large degree ignorant of the harms of wildlife trade or fails to consider these in their daily lives.

From this detailing of how WLT is met by enforcement agencies in Colombia at present, in the next chapter based on knowledge gained from the interviews, I proceed to ways in which WLT can further be counteracted.

Notes

1 The text of this document was produced by the different regional environmental authorities: *corporación autónoma regional* (autonomous regional corporations).
2 The DIJN is a national corpus under the national police of Colombia, overseeing the SIJNs (*Seccionales de Investigación Criminal*) [the local judicial police].
3 www.eltiempo.com/colombia/cali/fauna-mas-de-200-animales-de-distinta-especie-en-viaje-a-la-libertad-95678;www.elheraldo.co/cesar/liberan-287-animales-silvestres-en-ecosistemas-estrategicos-del-cesar-373133
4 http://ambientebogota.gov.co/ru/archivo-de-noticias/-/asset_publisher/5PPa/content/retorno-a-casa-operacion-que-llevara-a-122-animales-al-entorno-

natural?redirect=http%3A%2F%2Fambientebogota.gov.co%2Fru%2Farchivo-de-noticias%3Fp_p_id%3D101_INSTANCE_5PPa%26p_p_lifecycle%3D0%26p_p_state%3Dnormal%26p_p_mode%3Dview%26p_p_col_id%3Dcolumn-2%26p_p_col_pos%3D1%26p_p_col_count%3D2

5 The campaign took place in 23 municipalities under the leadership of the Group for the Protection of the Environment in the Police in Colombia. www.policia.gov.co/noticia/en-tu-casa-no-se-sienten-como-en-su-casa

12 How to respond to the harms of wildlife trafficking

In this chapter, I will discuss the ways in which the trafficking of animals should be addressed, as well as what can be done to improve the situation in Colombia and Norway. While criminalization may be an answer in some areas of the wildlife trade, in others, other preventative measures must be sought. There is a risk that criminalization of all wildlife trade may affect people differently, or even have adverse impact on some people. Criminalizing the poor may not be the right instrument to prevent them from hunting or abducting animals, whereas for people who engage in the trade for profit, the picture may look different, and the options must be there for more serious sanctioning. Depending on the risk of detection, the certainty of being punished quickly and the severity of penalties, punishment may have a deterrent effect. This could be the case in relation to organized crime. It should be noted, though, that given the multiplicity of offenders and consumers, there cannot be a single solution but many targeted to the specific groups. This is also the case in relation to other environmental crimes, as Wright (2011) observes:

> Thus the perpetrators of TEC [Transnational Environmental Crime] include large-scale criminal organisations, loosely organised networks, small and ad hoc groups of associates, opportunistic criminals, corrupt officials and corporations. It is clear that this multiplicity of actors has a bearing upon the development of effective countermeasures, as a diverse range of perpetrators is likely to require a diverse range of policing methods and other policies. (338)

The different categories of offenders, whether opportunistic micro-abductors/traffickers (semi)professional organized middlemen/contractors, or those organizing/directing the trade, call for diverse responses.

In regards to micro-trafficking of animals or products of parts thereof in Colombia and Norway, generally there should be no exceptions. For example, pre-Convention ivory and sturgeon caviar for personal use should not be allowed. The total amount of products made from endangered species for personal use represents the death of very many animals. Personal use exceptions are also difficult to enforce as they create a grey zone and require expertise. No free-born animals or animals who are not adapted to humans through long-term coexistence should be allowed in the pet trade.

Concerning those who engage in WLT on a professional level and who take advantage of the willingness of locals to commit the crimes for them for low pay, stricter punishments must be in place. Minor fines have little effect. If fines are levied, they should be so considerable that they deter offenders from repeating such crimes. As shown in relation to the Finnish bird/egg trafficking case and as demonstrated in the EFFACE studies, many countries impose considerable fines for environmental crimes, including WLT, although responses vary greatly (Chin et al. 2014). Imposing strict fines may be effective in deterring people from engaging in WLT.

The potential that exists in law to punish should be used to its full extent, because for people who can afford to pay a fine, it is only a nuisance, whereas a prison sentence of significant duration will deter them and others from committing such crimes, especially if they have to face trial and the punishment is publicized. WLT is a serious crime, and those who make a profit from it should fear the prospect of prison sentences (Wyatt 2013).

As discussed by Runhovde (2017) and as shown in the international responses to organized WLT, there has been a militarization in law enforcement reflecting the militarization involved in WLT, with heavily armed actors on both sides (Ayling 2013), specifically in relation to the iconic species of elephants, rhinoceroses and big felines (Wyatt 2013). Such responses, which include draconian punishment, may still not be sufficient to make such offenders desist from their crimes, due to the resilience of such networks. In order to address this, first-hand information about how such groups work in each specific context is crucial (Ayling 2013). Elephant and rhino massacres and the subsequent trafficking of their body parts invokes a totally different modus operandi from that, which is presented in relation to the WLT in Colombia or in Norway (although the transnational and global character of WLT means few countries are not implicated in some way). More research is needed to establish who comprises the networks described by the interviewees in Colombia, how they work and whether WLT is their primary activity or something in which they engage, in addition to other criminal activities.

The implications of criminalization, on the other hand, may make it harder to establish how many animals are actually trafficked (Cooney and Jepson 2006). As seen in relation to drug and alcohol prohibitions, banning trafficking will not necessarily mean the end of it. Rather, black markets may emerge and become harder to identify because they are underground (Hansen et al. 2012; Harrison et al. 2016; Lavorgna 2014; Sajeva et al. 2013; Sollund 2016c). Criminalization may have unpredicted consequences. In regards to the Norwegian alcohol prohibition that lasted from 1917 to 1927, Johansen (2013) writes,

> The authorities were overwhelmed by a series of escalating and to some extent insoluble problems such as smuggling, illicit distilling, prescription swindles, organised crime, 'unconventional' police methods, and indications of corruption.
>
> (62)

Similarly, Christie and Bruun (1985) found that the costs of criminalizing drug users were dramatic and failed to reduce the drug market.

Although the trade in wildlife and drugs may be comparable in some ways and attract similar organized groups (South and Wyatt 2011), there is still a huge difference between trafficking drugs/alcohol and wildlife; drugs and alcohol are substances harming humans through (self-imposed) addictions and additional social costs,[1] while animals (and humans) may suffer *indirectly* when ecosystems are destroyed in cocaine production (Santana and Chin 2015). The large majority of animals are sentient beings, rather than illegal goods/substances, and they suffer directly as victims when they are abducted or killed in the WLT. A more valid comparison than drugs and WLT would be to compare WLT with *human* trafficking, which is an international crime (Sollund 2013a). Just like one would not argue for *regulating* human trafficking and enslavement, one cannot argue for the *regulation* of wildlife trade. Whether trafficking in humans or animals, it is an abominable crime.

In both Colombia and in Norway, the pet trade is a big part of the problem, and in Colombia, the practice of pet owning has deep roots. Micro-trafficking for this purpose represents a large problem. Criminalization of this group of consumers/traffickers cannot be the only solution to the problem, although its criminality should be made more widely known, because for many people keeping pets is ordinary, rather than extraordinary, and what determines whether this is criminal is the type of species and the origin of the animals.

The opportunist offenders who engage in the abduction of animals need to be educated through awareness campaigns to appreciate the richness of their natural environment and why they should abstain from this kind of crime. For example, the biodiversity that surrounds them may offer benefits, such as the opportunity to serve as guides for tourists who would enjoy seeing animals in their natural habitat.

One may expect that as (if) the war in Colombia approaches an end, the violence will cease and the country will be more attractive to tourists who want to see the country's beauty and biological diversity. Because it was the guerrillas protecting the environment and impeding nature destruction and trafficking, however, there is now carte blanche for all kinds of enterprises to exploit natural resources like timber and animals (Watts 2017). This has caused an increase in the killing of environmental protectors, not the least among indigenous groups. In 2017, 197 were killed, of whom 32 were killed in Colombia in the power vacuum caused when FARC laid down its weapons (Lynch et al. 2018; Watts 2018).

Ecotourism is one way to address WLT in Colombia, especially the part of it that is fuelled by local/national demand, where individuals make extra income through opportunistic abductions/trafficking or when they are encouraged to commit such crimes by middlemen and organized criminals. Important habitats could be allocated to ecotourism by the environmental authorities, and locals could be involved as expert guides to protected reserves. Their special competence concerning the whereabouts of the animals could serve to guard and protect them, rather than causing their demise. In this way, former abductors/traffickers could make an income by protecting animals, rather than abducting or killing them. This could be done in a way similar to in Costa Rica, but as emphasized by Javier Cifuentes, it must be done in a way that genuinely respects ecosystems and those living there.

While ecotourism may sound appealing, it is not necessarily a quick fix. There is reason to be cautious about this option. Tourists may fail to respect the wildlife that a reserve is supposed to protect, and the government may be too eager to make a profit from it, which can result in excessive pressure on vulnerable ecosystems. If the state where the ecotourism is supposed to take place suffers from corruption, this may entail another risk of failure (Isaacs 2000). Corruption and the power of organized crime, which, historically, have been strong in Colombia, may prevent rule of law (Wyatt 2013). If governments do not use their power to address problems related to insecure property rights, misdistribution of resources and economic inequity, then, given the current situation in Colombia, people will despoil natural areas, and the power of ecotourism to enhance environmental protection will be curtailed (Isaacs 2000). Isaacs further warns that ecotourism may foster a reliance upon recreational areas as a method of conservation that is inadequate if not delusive (Isaacs 2000: 65). Consequently, Colombians, environmental authorities and NGOs would need constant reassurance that ecotourism was carried out in an environmentally, ecojust way, and this would need ongoing monitoring by authorities, such as the environmental police, which would need to be strengthened.

An interviewee said that ecotourism would have to be better than what is currently in place. While it began well 15–20 years ago, with education programs and the establishment of alliances between national parks and communities, this changed approximately 10 years ago. Tourism in national parks was privatized and monopolized by a company called Aviatur.

> It appears Aviatur is leveraging among many interests, some rather obscure, like in the Parque Tayrona. There appears to be strong influence by a group of paramilitaries, and also multinationals, and it was turned into a business. This is a business for which conservation is not important, but to generate resources that end up in the hands of one or two persons. And this development interrupted the social process and did not involve communities.

The overall evidence of the outcomes of ecotourism in the world shows mixed results (Das and Chatterjee 2015). There are many success stories, but the list of failures is long. Owing to structural, operational and cultural problems, ecotourism in many places has become a predicament. Therefore, ecotourism should be introduced with proper monitoring, evaluation and management of ecotourism sites in place so that long-term conservation is a reality (Das and Chatterjee 2015: 4). Presumably, the situation caused by Aviatur is the consequence of failing to comply with the requirements established in the Quebec Declaration on Ecotourism (2002): It must contribute actively to the conservation of natural and cultural heritage, include local and indigenous communities in its planning, development and operation, and contribute to their well-being, and interpret the natural and cultural heritage of the destination to visitors (4).

In theory, ecotourism can be very profitable. In such enterprise, however, as in any country that through generations has fought against violence and corruption, such endeavours are jeopardized if the wrong people get involved. To counteract this, the state and the environmental authorities must control and be responsible for the national parks and their protection through alliances with the local communities living in them or in their vicinities. Scheyvens (1999), likewise, emphasizes the importance of the involvement of local communities when ecotourism is developed, to ensure that it does not harm their social and cultural fabric. It is thus vital that they are made stakeholders in any such development if it is to be successful, rather than allowing the establishment of wildlife reserves to be seen as a threat (Duffy, 2013).

As suggested by Wyatt (2013), consumers in the wildlife trade also have different levels of culpability, which should determine any penalization. Several scholars have pointed out that a ban increases the value of the animals in the black market, making them more desirable for traffickers (Lemieux and Clarke 2009; Rivalan et al. 2007) and for collectors (Auliya et al. 2016; Courchamp et al. 2006; Hall et al. 2008; van Uhm 2016b). This would suggest that if researchers discover animals from species that are believed to have gone extinct and publicize this, collectors would immediately arrange to have these rare animals procured. Immediately after the Roto Island snake-necked turtle (*Chelodina mccordi*) and the gecko (*Gonirosaurus luii*) from Southeastern China were identified as rarities in the international pet trade, they became so heavily traded that today the turtle is nearly extinct in the wild, while the gecko has been extirpated from its locality. Consequently, many biologists refrain from publicizing where endangered animals are located (Auliya et al. 2016: 106). Collectors drive the hunt for the last living individuals of many rare species, and such offenders should be punished accordingly (Wyatt 2013) – after all, it is not stamps they are collecting!

While traffickers may be encouraged by the value collectors place on rare species, it is likely that the open market will be more apt to refrain from engaging in wildlife trade as consumers when bans are introduced and the act criminalized. This would again give a clear-cut message (Goyes and Sollund 2016; The EU Wild Bird Declaration) Dickson (2005: 50–51), however, using the example of the parrot trade from Australia, argues that bans do not reduce trade, and that if bans are introduced, traffickers will stop laundering and find alternative routes/means. This, nonetheless, does not mean that the wildlife trade as a whole cannot be banned. As previously discussed, no one has suggested that human trafficking should be legalized because law enforcement of this crime may be difficult (Sollund 2013a). How bans are enforced will also depend on political will, which is often lacking with respect to WLT (Reeve 2002; Sollund and Maher 2015).

While I support banning wildlife trade from a species justice perspective, I acknowledge that participation in WLT must be addressed differently when it is motivated by high profits, as in the rhino horn, elephant tusk and tiger bone trades and other organized theriocides, than when it is carried out primarily due to ignorance or dire need. The measures that need to be set in place to prevent people from taking parrots from their nests are different from the measures that must be used to prevent people from buying them at their destination. In this instance, information campaigns, such as those used in Colombia can be effective.

Several of the bird trafficking cases in Norway concerned crimes committed prior to the European ban of free-born birds in 2006, and according to an airport veterinarian, bird seizures were much more frequent prior to the ban. van Uhm (2016b: 92) found in his analysis of EU TWIX data that seizures of live birds (N = 877) dominated the 1,490 bird-related seizures listed. These consisted primarily of parrots and falcons, of whom the most frequently seized species were the African grey parrot (*Psittacus erithacus*), the eastern rosella (*Platycercus eximius*) and the rose-ringed parakeet (*Psittacula*). As shown also in the EFFACE case study (Maher and Sollund 2016a, 2016b; Sollund and Maher 2015) and elsewhere (Sina et al. 2016), the EU is well-known for its on-demand market of wildlife, including for CITES birds. Between 2000 and 2003, the EU imported 2.8 million wild CITES birds (van Uhm 2016b: 92). This makes the EU the largest such market worldwide, representing 93% of registered imports (FAO 2011, here in van Uhm 2016b: 92). Because of the ban following the outbreak of avian flu, however, legal wild-bird imports to the EU have been reduced drastically (Nijman 2010), and this may also be why the Norwegian veterinary witnessed fewer bird trafficking cases.

Whether bans lead to a reduction in bird trafficking, however, is debatable (Burton 2006; Cooney and Jepson 2006). In their broad study of parrot trafficking, Wright et al. (2001), found, that while transnational trade may be reduced by means of bans, local and national trafficking is not necessarily reduced, as shown in to the case of Colombia. Most bird trafficking is domestic. van Uhm (2016b) states in regards to transnational trade that the trafficking of wild-caught birds to the EU was not affected by the ban, rather it went underground and traffickers found other ways to conduct their trade, such as trafficking eggs rather than birds. While bans may ruin the foundation of the legal trade, it is claimed it also increases the illegal trade (Cooney and Jepson 2006), especially if this is connected to rare species (e.g., Courchamp et al. 2006).

While WLT is generally under-criminalized and under-policed, the criminalization of reptile keepers in Norway has resulted in prosecutions that may be considered as unjust, because the offenders were not guilty of doing anything different from other pet keepers, except for their choice of species (Sollund 2011, 2013a). In other countries, and as shown in the case of Norway, reptile keeping can be criminalized and decriminalized, just as other acts are. Even though owning pets can create an incentive for WLT and harm animals (Sollund 2011), this category of consumers, whether in Norway or Colombia, need to be treated with more leniently than professional traffickers, and should be targets of education/awareness campaigns.

One of the Norwegian interviewees in the Eco Crime Unit emphasized the lack of political will in Norway, indicating that as long as there was no room for increased punishment in CITES cases, CITES crimes would remain low-priority crimes and would receive lenient punishment. If punishments were increased – convicted drug traffickers receive 21-year prison sentences in Norway – it would also signal that this was a crime that society regarded as serious.

In addition, one of the interviewees in the Environmental and Finance Crime team of the Oslo police underlined the importance of employing the entire range of possible regulations/legislation to ensure the cases are treated seriously by the penal system. For example, while CITES itself provides a limited legal framework from which to prosecute, in addition to applying legislation concerning organized crime or money laundering, if relevant; punishments could be stricter and deter people from engaging in wildlife trade for profit (DLA Piper 2015).

In Norway, there is a need to establish a special unit with formal coordination responsibility, a forum where all enforcement agencies meet on a regular basis, since the ad hoc nature of the current cooperation between agencies falls short. In both Norway and Colombia, specialist judges who preside over trials concerning wildlife trafficking and other environmental crimes are needed. As shown in relation to the Norwegian cases, judges lack competence, experience and interest in these kinds of cases. The lack of enforcement in Colombia suggests that the same is true there. Moreover, it is crucial that enforcement agencies give priority to WLT and that targets are set for CITES cases, just as they prioritize drugs because there are set targets for drug crimes. This is not just a question about the priorities of law enforcement agencies, but a political issue, and it is necessary that politicians take the necessary steps to ensure WLT prosecution is prioritized. While I do not underestimate the importance of individuals who are working passionately to prevent IWT, this harm must have a much greater official and structured priority, from the judicial system to the political level.

Both in Colombia and Norway, there is a need for specialists, from police investigators to state prosecutors, from lawyers to specialist judges/courts. At present, the environmental coordinators in Norway have too broad an area of responsibility, as has the Eco Crime Unit. Their specialist areas should be narrowed to concern crimes against the environment and its beings, including animal abuse.

In Norway and Colombia, more research is needed to uncover the modus operandi of freight companies that transport large cargos of wildlife. One important corrective to environmental and wildlife crimes is the role of NGOs (Nurse 2015; Chin et al. 2014; Smith and Klaas 2015). In the following section, I consider the role they play in Norway and Colombia in this regard.

The role of NGOs

Internationally, NGOs like TRAFFIC, WWF Norway, World Animal Protection (2014) and IFAW (e.g. 2008) play a very important role in the fight against wildlife trade, liaising with CITES, Interpol and Europol, the World Bank, UN, and other governmental entities. While in Norway there are NGOs that work to protect free-born animals, their work is primarily focused on protecting endangered Norwegian species from hunters, not the least being state-licensed hunts: *Foreningen Våre Rovdyr* (Working to protect the large carnivores),[2] *Naturvernforbundet* (Norwegian Association for the Conservation of Nature),[3] and *Norsk Ornitologisk Forening* (Working to protect birds and their habitats). In addition, there are animal rights/welfare organizations that address IWT, of which *NOAH for Dyrs Rettigheter* (NOAH for animal rights)[4] is preeminent. WWF Norway[5] works to conserve Norwegian species, of which 3,000 are threatened, along with Norwegian forests, mountain terrains and waterways. Together with other environmental and animal rights organizations, WWF Norway, has filed a lawsuit against the state in order to stop future state-licensed wolf hunts following the mass theriocide of Norwegian wolves that took place in the winter of 2017–2018, in which more than 70% of the Norwegian wolf population was killed. This lawsuit was unsuccessful.[6]

None of the NGOs present in Norway is concerned about IWT in the Norwegian context, although though there is some effort to create awareness of the effects of IWT. While WWF is engaged in combating wildlife trafficking and saving species that are endangered due to trade and habitat loss internationally, in Norway they concentrate their efforts in protecting Norwegian endangered species, like the grey wolf, lynx, wolverine, brown bear and golden eagle and their habitats.

In Colombia, organizations such as TRAFFIC,[7] ProAves and Entropika, play a more important role in regards to WLT than they do in Norway. For example, Cesar Márquez of Instituto de Investigación de Recursos Biológicos' Alexander von Humboldt (The Alexander von Humboldt Institute for Research on Biological Resources)[8] is involved in the conservation of birds of prey. In addition, there are many animal welfare/rights organizations in Colombia, and some were also involved in the establishment of CRRFFS (Lozano-Ortega et al. n.d.).[9]

According to Cifuentes of CRRFFS, there are many NGOs working in Colombia that do important work in the area of IWT, such as a handful of persons in Cundinamarca (whose organization was not specified), and Iván Lozano, from the Centro de Primatología Araguatos, who with colleagues has written a document describing how animals who are confiscated should be treated (Lozano-Ortega et al. n.d.). These NGOs are important centres for education and research. Regrettably, according to Cifuentes, NGOs are isolated forces.

While Cifuentes may regard NGOs as isolated forces, in my view they are still very important. Entropika's essential role in counteracting and bringing attention to the harms perpetuated by Patarroyo's malaria research is evidence of that (Maldonado and Lafon 2017).

Fundación ProAves[10] was founded in 1998 as a UK-registered charity to protect the yellow-eared parrot (*Loro orejiamarillo*). This NGO receives support from IUCN and Bird Conservancy, and also from Loro Parque,[11] a zoo criticized by Ortiz-von Halle for contributing to species extinction, since they constantly need to feed their zoo with fresh genes. ProAves plays an important role in the protection of habitat and the conservation of birds and amphibians. The aim of ProAves is to carry out conservation activities, such as the creation of natural reserves in Colombia, of which they have succeeded in establishing 22, in order to protect the most threatened bird species in Colombia.

The foundation has four basic areas of activity: education, conservation and investigation, which are directly connected to IWT, and the administration of the foundation. The investigations, for which donations are sought, are described as the most important activity. It works out and plans the conservation strategies. If a species is endangered in a specific zone of the country, the surroundings are surveilled, to see if, for example, there is implemented cultivations of palm oil or mining. Through conservation, ProAves seeks ways to mitigate the harms done by mining, palm oil plantations, etc. Education is important because it sensitizes communities to the importance of conservation.

TRAFFIC, is a strategic alliance of IUCN and WWF. It receives support from a wide range of organizations and countries, including CITES and the EC. Like CITES, the goal of TRAFFIC is to make wildlife trade sustainable, not to ban it. TRAFFIC employs more than 150 people in five continents who produce research and aim to create awareness about WLT. TRAFFIC cooperates with Interpol, Europol, The World Bank, CITES, UNODC and many other intergovernmental, non-governmental and business organizations worldwide. TRAFFIC documents IWT worldwide and feeds international bodies with crucially important information gained from their research and report activities.

As observed by Nurse (2015: 120–121), NGOs are important in the policing of wildlife crimes when governmental action is inadequate. In so far as they can assess the situations of endangered species, develop conservation measures and create awareness in Colombia and elsewhere. As cautioned by Nurse, however, they cannot replace proper policing even if they can pass on invaluable information to police and enforcement agencies. When policing fails or when crimes are permitted by corrupt enforcement agencies, NGOs are able to draw attention to injustices and crimes that take place and can bring states and corporations to justice, as they are doing in Norway, concerning the wolf hunts, and in Colombia concerning night monkey trafficking for malaria research (Maldonado and Lafon 2017). NGOs provide essential information about species and the harm done to them, and can liaison with enforcement authorities in the protection of endangered species, as well as in establishing typologies of offenders.

While arguing that CITES crimes should be prioritized and accepting that CITES currently is essential as an international instrument in relation to wildlife trade, it is also problematic. As the framework of CITES was presented in the introduction, I will here only briefly address some of the critiques raised against the Convention and point out its main weaknesses.

Critique of CITES and its anthropocentric logic

Before entering into a critique of CITES, I briefly describe how it works, according to the CITES website. CITES works by subjecting international trade in individuals, or products of endangered plants or free-born animals listed on the three CITES appendices to certain controls. All import, export, re-export and introduction from the sea of species covered by the Convention has to be authorized through a licensing system. Each Party (country/state, including the EU) to the Convention must designate one or more Management Authorities in charge of administering that licensing system, such as the Norwegian

Environment Agency, and one or more Scientific Authorities to advise them on the effects of trade on the status of the species. As shown, the species covered by CITES are listed in three appendices according to how endangered they are and the degree of protection they need. Appendix I includes species threatened with extinction. Trade in products or individuals of these species is permitted only in exceptional circumstances. Appendix II includes species not necessarily threatened with extinction, but in which trade must be controlled in order to avoid utilization incompatible with their survival. Appendix III contains species that are protected in at least one country, which has asked other CITES Parties for assistance in controlling the trade. Changes to Appendix III follow a distinct procedure from changes to Appendices I and II, as each Party's is entitled to make unilateral amendments to it.

The Conference of the Parties (CoP), which is the supreme decision-making body of the Convention and comprises all its Parties, has agreed in Resolution Conf. 9.24 (Rev. CoP17) on a set of biological and trade criteria to help determine whether a species should be included in Appendices I or II. At each regular meeting of the CoP, Parties submit proposals based on those criteria to amend these two appendices. Those amendment proposals are discussed and then submitted to a vote.[12]

The success of CITES is debated:

> Some have explained the apparent failures of the treaty in terms of a failure to effectively enforce its regulations, while others have seen the CITES approach to conservation as fundamentally misconceived.
>
> (Hutton and Dickson 2000: XV)

The failure in enforcement is but one of the problems related to the Convention. Some regard it as an insufficient or inadequate measure to address wildlife trade (Goyes and Sollund 2016; Sollund and Maher 2015; Reeve 2002; Sollund 2011). Reeve (2002) lists a number of weaknesses related to legislation and penalization: the lack of economic incentives; the lack of a provision for scientific advice for administrative and enforcement personnel; the lack of trade monitoring and analysis; the lack of education and awareness raising aimed at traffickers and the public; the lack of support for the judiciary in providing adequate responses to crimes and to deter offenders; and the lack of interagency cooperation and exchange of information at national, regional and international levels (Hutton and Dickson 2000; Reeve 2002: 245).[13] Reeve considers the lack of enforcement as the Achilles heel of CITES. A study by DLA Piper (2015) that investigated the success of CITES in 15 jurisdictions (Angola, Cambodia, The Republic of the Congo, Gabon, Indonesia, Laos, Mongolia, Mozambique, Myanmar, Namibia, Pakistan, South Africa, Sri Lanka, Zambia and Zimbabwe), found that with few exceptions, weaknesses existed in the principal legislation of all countries analyzed. These included significant loopholes, variations on provincial implementation of national laws, inadequate penalties and, in some cases, extremely antiquated legislation or legislation that expressly contradicted the country's obligations under

CITES (DLA Piper 2015: 1). Corruption within government agencies and the court system was a serious problem for most of the jurisdictions examined (6). Lenient sentencing below minimum penalties established in legislation was a further problem. While countries may be parties to the Convention and even have implemented legislation to respond to CITES obligations, this is no guarantee that the country will comply. Many of these weaknesses also appear in the contexts of Norway and Colombia.

The perspective one takes on the success or failure of CITES also depends on one's ideological convictions. While some support trade to secure income for poor people and nations, others who are guided by other ethical values, take the animals' perspective, seeing WLT as meaningless animal abuse (Dickson 2005: 24; Sollund 2011; Goyes and Sollund 2016; Maher and Sollund 2016a,b). According to Dickson (2005), such ethical stands have influenced decisions made in CITES, often strengthening the support for restrictions in wildlife trade. This has resulted in parties to the Convention, which benefit greatly from wildlife trade, to portray the anti-use perspective – the perspective of those against wildlife trade – as an illegitimate imposition of specific moral values on the wider conservation community (25).

While CITES can be criticized for not sufficiently protecting endangered species, others claim the restrictions put on trade go too far: 'By restricting trade in wild species, and so limiting the benefits that humans can derive from them, CITES has actually reduced the incentive to maintain wildlife habitat' (Hutton and Dickson 2000: xvii). Such an argument is highly anthropocentric and also reduces all people s' motives to protect habitats as being only economic, that is, as if they can see no other value in preserving habitats for animals than the economic gains that can be produced by trafficking the animals. This reductionist view implies that all people regard animals who surround them instrumentally as resources.

CITES has been critiqued for offering more protection to 'charming' species, such as sea turtles, than the biologically similar and equally threatened crocodile (Kievit 2000; Webb 2000), thus relying on speciesist principles. Whether it fails to protect the species that are listed may be debatable, CITES offers little in the way of protecting species that are seldom traded, and therefore not listed, or species that are traded under the radar. Other species may not be CITES listed because they are regarded as no concern, but then are traded into extinction (Lyons and Natusch 2011; Nijman and Nekaris 2017). Many species will also go extinct due to loss of habitat, so individuals of such species should therefore also be banned from being traded, yet are not mentioned in any appendix of CITES because trade has not been perceived as a problem concerning the species.

Fuchs (2008) sums up the critique of CITES, stating that CITES's effectiveness in regulating global trade is doubtful due to the large amount of money involved in the illegal trade. According to Fuchs (2008), not only are quotas exceeded, quota setting is done without biological data and without proper peer review of field studies, and there is a lack of uniform standards for non-detriment findings, as well as a lack of follow-up of recommendations. Importing states fail to comply with trade suspensions, and a final problem is that reviews consider only a limited number of species while the majority of species are ignored. The quota system is criticized for being uncontrolled, unscientific and open to abuse (Fuchs 2008: 1588).

CITES is also criticized from a legal perspective. Upgrading or downgrading species on the appendices creates a lack of transparency and an ambiguous message concerning the criminalization versus the legalization of wildlife trade (Fuchs 2008; Goyes and Sollund 2016)., My main concern about CITES, however, is its constant and profound failure in acknowledging the interests, inherent value and capacities of non-human animals, making it an antiquated convention relying on outdated scientific ideas about non-human species.

Often when the value of CITES is debated, the focus is on whether it succeeds or fails according to its own anthropocentric logic. The fact that animals are considered resources is doxic (Sollund 2012a). The interviewee from TRAFFIC, the interviewee from CITES/Norwegian Environment Agency and an interviewee from the environmental authority in Colombia concurred that trade should proceed because of the resources it generates. They viewed it as problematic when genetic resources were taken from source countries to be used in the breeding of these species elsewhere because the source countries, often poor, no longer benefit from this 'resource.' It follows from such an opinion that it would be better to abduct and traffic free-born animals than to breed animals for trade. From an animal welfare point of view, this is difficult to accept, because of the atrocities free-born animals experience when they are abducted, trafficked and caged for life.

Ortiz-von Halle suggested that zones should be established where local communities can hunt, while other areas (and species) should be protected to allow them to recover. In this way, people would agree that it would be in their own interest not to overexploit species. In other words, the trafficking in fauna could be converted into a sustainable business alternative. For example, he said, trafficking parakeets could be subject to legal trade; the birds would be registered and enter into legal national or international trade. In this way, the species would be 'managed' and the abductions 'sustainable.' This would ensure conservation and at the same time, people lacking other alternatives could make a living. Ortiz-von Halle further argued that this had been done in Argentina, where, according to him, it worked 'wonderfully.' This was jeopardized, he said, by animal rights groups who regarded trafficking as cruel and damaging to biodiversity and therefore blocked shipping of animals abducted from nature. Oriz-von Halle was critical of this because he argued that it resulted in parrots being trafficked illegally, rather than legally and in a controlled manner.

The historical impact of wildlife trade on the security of biological resources has largely been negative, but the utilitarian value of wild animals, plants, their products and derivatives continues to fulfil important human needs. 'This value may in some circumstances provide direct incentives for protection of natural habitats and systems' (Broad et al. 2005: 3).

If CITES were to truly protect endangered species, the first thing that would have to be done would be to introduce a total ban of trade in all free-born animal species, rather than seeking its prolongation. All member states should commit financially in order to change the Convention from regulating to preventing trade, rich countries contributing much more than would poor countries that now depend on wildlife trade for economic reasons. The better the states accomplish the protection of their wildlife, the more they should be awarded, financed by membership fees determined on the member states' GNP. This would also turn the Convention into a convention providing aid to protect the environment and endangered species, rather than facilitating their trade, and focus could be on encouragement for protection, rather than penalties for failure. CITES could thus have a dual role that would benefit the countries rich in biodiversity from where much wildlife is sourced, and which therefore sell their endangered species in the wildlife trade and offer another motivation for conservation and protection, rather than exploitation.

The pet trade is a large market of the wildlife trade, demonstrating that while people regard some animals as commodities, there is also a human-animal relationship that exists independently of commodity value. Next, I discuss the consequences of wildlife trafficking for the direct victims through the empirical data provided by the case studies of Norway and Colombia.

Notes

1 Animals, however, have been widely used in experiments involving drugs or other medicinal procedures (e.g., Jentsch et al. 2002; Pickens and Thompson 1968). Such experiments, of course, are extremely unethical and rejectable.
2 http://fvr.no/fvr_page/om-fvr.html
3 g=en_GB
4 www.dyrsrettigheter.no/
5 www.wwf.no/
6 In a trial on May 18, 2018, concerning whether Norway had breached with the Nature Diversity Act for these wolf hunts, the judge's decision was in favour of the state. Whether it will be appealed remains to be seen. www.domstol.no/contentassets/de4f2fbd41a345c9aafcc3efc4f8e2ce/wwf–staten–felling-av-ulv–dom-fra-oslo-tingrett-18.05.18.pdf
7 www.traffic.org/overview. Apparently, the South American office in Ecuador has closed down since the interview with Ortiz-von Halle took place.
8 www.humboldt.org.co/es/
9 https://manosqueflorecen.wordpress.com/about/
10 www.proaves.org/about-proaves/?lang=en
11 www.loroparque.com/index.php/en/?view=default. According to the Loro Parquet website: 'Since its inception in 1972, Loro Parque has created the most diverse genetic reserve of parrots in the world, attaining more than 4,000 specimens of 350 different species and sub species which have been entirely donated to Loro Parque.'
12 https://www.cites.org/eng/disc/how.php
13 These studies are not new, and possibly exchange of information has improved. Since this study is not an empirical study of the functioning of CITES, I cannot confirm or refute this.

13 Animal victimization in Norway and Colombia

Most animals who are seized at Norwegian borders are killed as directed by the Norwegian Environment Agency. Yet, the recommendations to the parties of CITES (1998) is that an action plan should 'identify approved facilities and programmes located within the country that have agreed to provide adequate care, including veterinary or phytosanitary care, and that are willing to accept confiscated live specimens [sic] of particular taxa.' In Norway, such locations are few and far between, whereas in Colombia, this CITES requirement is implemented both legally and practically through rehabilitation centres. CITES (Conf. 9.9) establishes further the responsibility of parties in cases of wildlife confiscation and that the seizure and confiscation of animals are generally preferable to the definitive refusal of the import of them. Hence, it should be ensured that the animals are not re-entered into illegal trade, and their repatriation should be monitored (Sollund and Maher 2015: 21).

CITES (n.d.) has rules for how to treat animals who are seized in trafficking, under Resolution Conf. 10.7 (Rev. CoP15): With reference to

> Article VIII, paragraph 4 (b), of the Convention confiscated live specimens [sic] shall, after consultation with the State of export, be returned to that State at the expense of that State, or to a rescue centre or such other place as the Management Authority deems appropriate and consistent with the purposes of the Convention.

The conference of the parties to the conventions RECOMMENDS that:

a Management Authority before making a decision on the disposal of confiscated live specimens of species in the Appendices consult with and obtain the advice of its own Scientific Authority and, if possible, of that of the State of export of the confiscated specimens, and other relevant experts such as IUCN/SSC Specialist Groups;

b each Scientific Authority in preparing its advice take note of the guidelines in Annexes 1 and 2;

c the Secretariat be informed about any decision taken on the disposal of confiscated live specimens of species that are either in Appendix I or, if in Appendix II or III, involve commercial quantities;

d in the case where live specimens arrive in an importing country without the proper export permits or re-export certificates, and where an importer refuses to accept a shipment of live specimens, the shipment be confiscated and the specimens disposed of in accordance with the guidelines set out in Annexes 1 or 2; and
e priority be given to the care of seized or confiscated wild-collected specimens of Appendix-I species and of Appendix-II species that may be at risk;

URGES Management Authorities, in consultation with Scientific Authorities and other bodies concerned, to develop action plans to deal with seized and confiscated live specimens consistent with the guidelines set out in Annex 3.

In deciding on the disposal of confiscated animals, managers must ensure both the humane treatment of the animals and the conservation and welfare of existing wild populations of the species involved. Options for disposal fall into three principal categories: (1) maintenance of the individuals in captivity; (2) returning the individuals in question to some form of life in the wild; and (3) euthanasia. The last option often proves the most appropriate and most humane, it is said.

The general rule in Norway is that the animals who are seized are killed. The interviewee from the CITES/Norwegian Environment Agency confirmed that 80%–90% of the animals are euthanized:

> And it will depend on the species, where they come from and the regulations, and if it is the regulation of the Food Safety Authority and veterinary concerns. And if not it may depend on the Wildlife Law that prohibits the keeping of various species. And also there is a saturation problem in Norwegian zoos. I mean, how many crocodiles and pythons do they need? And it is the same with birds. So, when it is full, it is full, and we have a dilemma.

This does not mean the Norwegian Environment Agency does not on occasion try to re-home seized animals, and they have even tried to return some. The CITES/Norwegian Environment Agency interviewee elaborated on efforts made to save animals, and why killing them often is the result:

> We recently had a case where we tried to return an animal to another country. And both on this and other occasions, we experience that it is very hard. First you need to find out who can receive him/her, and it needs to go to an accepted quarantine, and costs escalate, ten thousand, just to build a cage that is an acceptable way of transport. . . . It was a serval [cat, natural to Africa]. And before that it was a sea turtle, and we had to go all the way to the top of the Ministry of Environment in Portugal to return it. They had a rescue centre for sea turtles, but the bureaucracy is enormous.

In the case of the serval cat, it was kept in Norway for six months, before finally being killed, as it proved too difficult to return him to the UK.

That animals are killed as procedure is not what the interviewee would have wished. He started his career in the Norwegian Environment Agency by working to establish a rescue centre for CITES animals. He even had a place for it and had received funding from the then Environment Directorate (Now the Norwegian Environment Agency). Unfortunately, the remainder of the funding was not raised, because the Ministry of Agriculture did not want to contribute its portion due to Norway's adaptation to the European Economic Area (EEA)[1] agreement. He said that, The Ministry of Agriculture thought they would no longer have a problem with these kinds of animals from the EU. So the attempt stalled there and chances are slim it will ever be resurrected, according to him.

Like the airport veterinarian, the Customs Directorate found the continuous killing of seized animals in Norway frustrating:

> Yes, and it has been irritating me for a long time, that when Customs seize endangered animals the first thing that occurs is that they are euthanized. And it does not look very good in the press either, when Customs seizes 70 snakes and the first thing happening is that they are taken to the freezing storage of the Food Safety Authority where they are killed because there is no one to take care of them.

The situation in Colombia is different, but the work undertaken to save trafficking victims through rehabilitation and re-homing was not appreciated by TRAFFIC's Ortiz-von Halle:

> To release a seized animal to nature is impossible. Forget it! If it is taken from nature, it is finished. It can only live in captivity. And I would not have tolerated any relapses of wolf or whatever in Norway without knowing 100% about what it is. It is gambling, right.

In so saying, he is misinformed concerning the possibilities of re-homing trafficking victims, but this is a view shared by many environmentalists, in part because they view each victim as unimportant as long as the species survives (see Svärd 2008).

In Norway, theriocides are regarded as a solution to a problem of what to do with the animal victim (see also Runhovde 2015). Confiscating and killing the animal makes a point to the offender concerning the illegality of wildlife trafficking, as well as may serve to deter possible other offenders. In this way, the killing of an animal is used instrumentally, through which the authorities seek to accomplish a series of goals. Still, rather than having carefully planned for such a solution – the theriocide – it seems more likely that this is the *simplest* solution; attention is not paid to the interests of the animal, because animals are not viewed as having victim status (Sollund 2017b; White 2018).

While in Norway animals are only rescued by zoos if they are rare, when animals in Colombia cannot be rehabilitated and freed, they are often sent to sanctuaries, or as in Norway, to zoos. This means that such establishments, at least theoretically, profit from wildlife trade under the pretext of doing ideological work for animal victims. While zoos often sail under the flag of conservation, there are ample examples of the contrary, that zoos partake in the illegal wildlife trade and profit from it.

Zoos and breeding centres often breach the five freedoms considered important under the animal welfare paradigm: (1) freedom from hunger, thirst and malnutrition; (2) freedom from disease and injury; (3) freedom from physical forms of discomfort due to inadequate thermal, resting or environmental conditions; (4) freedom from fear, distress and negative psychological states, and not least; (5) freedom to carry out normal behaviours (Engebretson 2006; Nekaris et al. 2015).

The border veterinarian interviewee said that other veterinarians decide to euthanize too quickly; that if they have a 'problem' with an animal, they will kill her/him. It is also a resource issue; they are told to keep budgets down, so it is cheaper to kill the animal. These animals are killed under the pretext of animal welfare, but welfare is, by definition, incompatible with being killed. When animals are killed, the animal is deprived of the possibility of experiencing welfare ever again (Francione 2014; Sollund 2014).

In most of the literature addressing wildlife trade, legal or illegal, the animal victims are forgotten. When falling prey to legal trade they are regarded as goods, specimens or resources, rather than being acknowledged as victims of abduction, abuse, forced captivity or theriocide. When taken illegally, again they become *illegal* goods and stolen property. The victims are then the states and people who lose their resources.

I argue here, as elsewhere (Sollund and Maher 2015), that many resources need be channelled into taking care of the animals victims who have been subject to trade. Indeed, the trade in free-born animals needs to stop. While this may be seen as a radical step to many, the consequences of pursuing this evil are much worse – if we continue they may soon not be there anymore to enrich the world.

As exemplified in the case of Colombia, much work is put into saving trafficking victims. This is also the case in many other places rich in biodiversity where animals suffer greatly from this trade; sanctuaries can be found in many countries: Brazil (Nassaro 2017), South Africa (elephants),[2] Botswana (rhinos),[3] Borneo (orangutans),[4] and many more.

There is still little focus, however, on saving animals who are victims to WLT. I thus echo Gray et al. (2017) when they argue that

> the care and rehabilitation of confiscated animals is a critical, but often missing, aspect in approaches for disrupting the illegal wildlife trade. The importance of such a comprehensive approach is clear. Law enforcement without care or consideration for confiscated wildlife is likely to create additional problems and may be as irresponsible as doing nothing.
>
> (4)

Gray and colleagues argue that a holistic approach to dealing with live animals must be considered in conservation planning and high-level intergovernmental dialogues on combatting wildlife trafficking. This is what was argued in the

EFFACE report (Sollund and Maher 2015), which revealed that while the UK has rescue facilities for trafficking victims, Norway addresses this inadequately. Consequently, this issue was highlighted in an EU consultancy response concerning IWT (Maher et al. 2014).

Victimization versus animal 'resources' and rehabilitation

As previously shown in the literature review and in relation to the Colombian data, the practice of abducting and trafficking birds and mammals is abusive and the mortality rates high. For parrots, fatalities of up to 50% occur during capture (Gonzales 2003) and between 75% and 89% during trafficking (Guzmán et al. 2007). They suffer from premature deaths due to malnutrition in captivity (see Sollund 2013a). In Colombia, it has been said that only about 5%–10% arrive in the hands of the buyer. It does not take much imagination or empathy to recognize the horror, pain and suffering the animals go through when they are taken so brutally from their habitats, stuffed into tubes and boxes, and, in the case of the titi (marmoset) and other primates and sloths, the anguish suffered by both mother and child when the mothers are killed, or for the parrots, the horror when their babies are taken from the nest. Parrots and primates are highly intelligent and social beings, which are aspects of their personalities that are abused by the animal abductors, for example, when they capture one parrot and use her as bait – when she screams – to attract the whole flock into a trap (see Nassaro 2017 for a more elaborate discussion about methods).

While people desire pets who are intelligent, the more intelligent the animal is, the harder it is to rehabilitate her/him after s/he has been abducted from the wild. One interviewee said that turtles would be easier than parrots and monkeys to rehabilitate and release them, e.g., because they can change their diet. Parrots who have learnt to speak a human language will not get very far in the jungle saying 'I want cocoa,' and it is very hard to make them stop repeating words. As shown by Pepperberg et al. (1997, 2007), parrots use words intelligibly. Her African grey parrot Alex had a large vocabulary, and her studies on her other parrots Griffin and Arthur prove that Alex was not a 'parrot Einstein,' rather that these are general capacities of parrots when they are trained by humans. *Alex learned to accurately use over 100 English words to describe objects, shapes, colours and materials; he did simple math and he understood concepts of 'none,' 'same/different,' 'bigger/smaller.' Grey parrots see optical illusions as do humans and engage in various forms of inferential reasoning (Alex Foundation website).*[5] Alex posed the question: 'What colour am I?' when seeing his reflection in a mirror. His confusion regarding his colour can be explained by the fact that African greys do not easily see the colour grey. It shows, however, that he clearly knew who he was, that he knew that the animal in the mirror was him, and that he knew the concept of 'colour' and that he was able to pose a question using a human language. This shows parrots are highly intelligent. Many more examples could be given, but suffice it to say that locking such beings into cages for decoration or entertainment is extremely cruel, because in such circumstances they will not be stimulated in ways that intelligent individuals need to be.

Very few animals in captivity enjoy the aforementioned five freedoms especially if they have been abducted for the wildlife trade. While some parrots are abducted from their nests as eggs and brought to people's *fincas* where they are not kept in cages, most pet birds are caged. In many cases, wing feathers of parrots are cut to curb flight. In addition to the emotional trauma this causes to the birds, it also has disastrous consequences. One interviewee described how helpless parrots had been found on the street, trying to fly. Of course, without the ability to fly, they have no way of escaping predators or other threats.

In green criminology, such acts of harm and abuse are defined as crime even when they do not constitute breach of law (see Beirne 1999, 2007, 2014; Brisman and South 2014; Sollund 2011, 2013a, 2015c; South 2008, 2014; White 2013, 2018). Concepts like animal rights and species justice refer precisely to the place of non-human animals within their environments and their intrinsic right not to suffer abuse. Inevitably, they will suffer when they are victims of trafficking, regardless of whether or not they are in excess of the permitted CITES quota. Furthermore, whether the animals are taken legally or illegally according to CITES quotas, these acts of harm would be breaches of animal welfare legislation, if this were to be taken seriously (see Beirne 1999, 2009; Benton 1998; Francione 2009 for discussions of the functions of and relationships between animal welfare legislation and animal rights).

Animals as beings with intrinsic value versus animals as resources

The data of this study indicate that even in the cases when indigenous groups get involved in WLT, they are often enticed into it with the promise of additional income. Often WLT is not something they engaged in traditionally or depended on historically, but they turn to it for profit. As in the Patarroyo case, when encouraged to engage in trafficking, they take far more animals than they would take for their own use[6] (Goyes 2015; Maldonado et al. 2009; Maldonado and Lafon 2017). Many argue (e.g., Cooney and Jepson 2006; WWF/TRAFFIC 2008) that indigenous groups should be secured special rights to exploit their natural environment and that this should be regarded as part of their environmental rights, as an extension of their human rights (White 2013). While one can assume that indigenous groups who exploit wildlife for their own consumption will be more cautious in preventing their 'resources' from going extinct, this remains mere speculation. Human history has shown that our species has driven many other species to extinction, such as megafauna and other human species than homo sapiens (Harari 2014; Kolbert 2014). When indigenous groups with local knowledge are encouraged to get involved in the trade for profit, it becomes even more unsustainable in terms of species survival, because it is dispersed more broadly, involving more animal victims.

That local communities should be entitled to partake in wildlife trade is, as mentioned, also the opinion shared by TRAFFIC director Ortiz-von Halle. He claimed the only way of preventing unsustainable wildlife trade is to promote *in situ* management of species so that the communities affected can enter a discussion concerning what to do with the fauna and how to secure their interests through generating economic incentives for preserving the fauna. There is no incentive for local communities to protect the animals, he claimed, implying that all incentives must be economic. He objected to *zoocriadores* being seen as a way to preserve wildlife, because they only serve to generate business for people with sufficient capital on their own to start such business.

The comparison he made between wildlife trafficking and other crimes reflects an anthropocentric rather than an ecojustice and species justice perspective. Cannot the killing and trafficking of animals be seen on par with homicide when applying a non-speciesist perspective? Could not these crimes be regarded as abductions (Sollund 2011), theriocide or murder (Beirne 2014)? At least, even from an anthropocentric point of view, could it not be seen as robbing nature (Goyes et al. 2017)? Rather than contrasting wildlife trafficking to crimes against humans, like robberies and homicides, as suggested by Ortiz-von Halle, both categories could be perceived in conjunction as harms that are *mala in se* (Sykes and Matza 1957; for a discussion see Sollund 2012a, 2016a).

To perceive animals merely as resources is obviously not only his opinion, rather it is doxa (Sollund 2012a). This view is also conveyed in an ethnographic study of bird trafficking in Mexico (Roldán-Clarà et al. 2017). The authors argue that the abducting, 'acclimatizing' and trading birds are an important part of the *pajajeros*[7] identity. They regard the critique raised by NGOs against this form of trafficking as unjust:

> Mexico is one of the countries in which the use of wild fauna in general (and the use of wild birds in particular) is a culturally and economically important subsistence activity. Ecologists and non-governmental organisations (NGOs) have demonised the capture and confinement of wild birds; this reaction is, in part, due to misinformation regarding the ethnographic origins of the activity.
>
> (Roldán-Clarà et al. 2017: 1)

The authors take the view of the people they are studying to the degree that makes one suspect they have "gone native" in the course of their research. They fail to adopt a more holistic perspective: What it is like for *birds* to be captivated, abducted and confined in limited space for the rest of their lives? The authors emphasize the skills the bird traffickers have developed, for example, constructing and employing the devices they use to capture and abduct the birds, and the meaning this trade gave to the traffickers and communities. In so doing, the authors disregard that the birds who these devices are used against are prey to old traditions, which are glorified as extremely valuable. But traditions are not good merely because they are traditions. Considering that Mexico faces species decline because of such traditions and the individual harm to animals (du Plessis 2000; Gonzales 2003; Guzmán et al. 2007; Weston and Memon 2009), this is a perspective that must be taken into account. In this study, it also becomes clear that just like in the parrot trade in countries such as Peru and Bolivia (Gonzales 2003; Herrera and Hennessey 2007; Weston and Memon 2009), and as shown to be the case in Colombia, traffickers do this as a *supplementary* means of income, showing again that this harm is not something upon which they are ultimately dependent. The trade of the *pajajeros* also includes endangered species, such as the yellow-headed parrot. Describing the abductions, the authors write that 'in mid-September, wild birds of all ages are captured, although the pajareros insist on protecting the females, because they prefer retaining only the fledglings and males' (Roldán-Clarà et al. 2017: 8).

No attention is paid to the harms done to the birds by breaking up their families and flock structures. Regarding the procedures by which the birds are 'acclimatised,' the authors buy into the wording and the worldview of the traffickers, which shows a significant lack of sensitivity to the harms they are doing to their victims.

They state that the birds must be accustomed to a new diet, which means they are forced to eat food other than that for which they have developed and to which they are adapted. This means that the birds are fed the *wrong* food, causing malnutrition and disease, and ultimately premature death.

In order to 'tame' the birds, they are kept in isolation. The authors state that the birds during such procedures become depressed from stress, a natural consequence of being captured and deprived of their usual food. This is referred to as the birds being 'spoiled and sad' (*'se chiquean, se ponen tristes'*). Birds who refuse to eat the new food are force fed directly into their beaks.

Natural reactions, such as depression and refusing to eat, are responded to by feeding the birds antibiotics and covering their cages with a cloth. While the harms the birds are subjected to are abusive, the authors describe the traffickers are caring: 'The above description of the acclimation [sic] tasks performed by specialists in the trade demonstrates their deep knowledge *and extreme care*' (Roldán-Clarà et al. 2017: 11; emphasis added).

Rather than describing them as romantically caring, one could say that these traffickers protect their income, that is, they cannot make money from dead birds. From the descriptions of how 'close they feel to nature,' and that this, in part, is why they love their part-time metier, it does not logically follow that part of loving nature is to capture and abduct the beings within it, give them antibiotics and inadequate food, and sell them to make extra income. The perspective in the article, however, encourages respect for the traffickers who in traditional and knowledgeable ways profit from the resources the birds constitute for them.

This is a view that parallels Ortiz-von Halle's position that free-born animals and nature should be 'managed,' just like Norwegian authorities claim to 'manage' Norway's endangered species. Management is in reality a euphemism for animal murder (Sollund 2017a). No attention or care is paid to the individual interests of these animals.

Likewise, Claudia Luz Rodríguez from the Ministry of the Environment and Sustainable Development stated that the Ministry's policy is to position biodiversity as a potential, a natural richness that must be valued, but most importantly, it should be used in a sustainable way. If not, it would be like having lost the goose who lays the golden egg.

Rodríguez also stated that it is not only the responsibility of the Ministry of the Environment or the environmental authorities, but also of all Colombians because it is a 'richness that belongs to all, it is the national patrimony, and everybody must take care of it.' This includes negotiating the use of these resources at an international level, so that all can benefit from it. 'And if the people are not conscious about this, they will not help to save this heritage, these assets, each animal is a public good, each tree is a public good, each ecosystem is a public good.'

Based on my interview data, the exploitation of animals in wildlife trafficking in Colombia is more a matter of selfish exploitation than theft of a public good, the problem being that it is unsustainable; '[t]he favoured environmental strategy of anthropocentrism is neo-environmentalism or sustainable development' (Halsey and White 1998: 350).

Rather than taking such an anthropocentric and egoistic approach as is demonstrated by TRAFFIC and the Ministry of Environment and Sustainable Resources, one could apply a less anthropocentric, more moral philosophical and ethical approach, whereby animals are accorded rights in their own capacity, instead of treating animals as a common good through which they are accorded no moral rights. This would mean acknowledging that they are individuals with interests in living their lives unharmed (Regan 1987). First, one must recognize that animals, just as humans, are victims when atrocities are committed against them, regardless of their 'use value' for humans. White (2018: 11) suggests that a major challenge for green criminologists is to develop conceptual and scientific tools whereby 'value' and 'harm' can be measured, compared and evaluated. This could possibly lead one into some kind of utilitarian debate in which the gains of humans are balanced against the suffering of the animals, such as trafficking victims. As observed by White, there may evidently be conflicts of interest and when one stands to gain and another may lose. But undoubtedly and most importantly, taking (or destroying) the life of any individual is in reality a denial of her/his intrinsic value, and denying such value should not be taken lightly (Bennison in White 2018: 13). There is little hesitation among traffickers to harm animals or consideration for the intrinsic value of their victims. Even when abductors are in need, taking the animals or killing them will do little to alleviate their misery, and usually, it is merely extra income, so their needs do not justify their acts, even when balancing their anthropocentric interests against the interests of the animals.

In this regard, I will now discuss the rights of free-born animals, taking as a point of departure the theory of Kymlicka and Donaldson (2011), who sketch out a political philosophical proposal for animal rights.

Free-born animals as sovereigns, rather than property or common good

Kymlicka and Donaldson (2011) acknowledge that the three basic frameworks for animal rights – the 'welfarist,' 'ecological' and 'basic rights' approaches – have all failed. Therefore, they aim to provide a framework that connects the treatment of animals more directly to fundamental principles of liberal democratic justice and human rights. Within this framework, they categorize animals depending on their independence/dependence on humans and their proximity to us, that is, their capability of acting autonomously.

I will not enter into the debate concerning the different approaches in depth here, but instead offer a brief introduction and some observations. I will first consider the ecological approach. This is relevant for the animal victims in this study – the free-born animals – as this approach also has repercussions for them. The ecological approach has severe deficiencies, because the overall concern is not individual rights and interests, but the health and well-being of the ecosystem. Svärd (2008) criticizes green movements for sustaining speciesist hegemony and not taking into account individual animals. Such views can indeed lead to animals being killed in culls (Chapron and Treves 2016), in order to 'protect' ecosystems, which in reality, means killing free-born animals under the pretext of management (Sollund 2017b). An example of this is from Norway. A breeding program of polar foxes was initiated to address the diminishing of the species brought on by climate change. Other foxes who had interbred with the 'pure breed', were systematically killed for not having the right genes (Sollund 2012c). The ecological approach has much in common with the anthropocentric nature view represented by CITES and TRAFFIC. With the same logic, as mentioned, in Norway in 2017, the Ministry of the Environment determined to kill 42 wolves, 75% of the total wolf population, 16 of whom lived within designated wolf zones. Authorities were confident that this critically endangered species would survive; no attention was paid to the individual wolves' wishes and their pack's existence, nor the harms they were subjected to when they were wounded but not killed or when they were chased with helicopters before they eventually fell from the hunters' bullets.

What the Norwegian wolves face can be defined as ecogenocide (Larsen 2012), and environmental organizations contest the assurance of the government that the species will survive after this. In response to the culling, WWF Norway took the Norwegian state to court for failure to comply with the Nature Diversity Act and the Bern Convention. In Oslo District Court on November 21, 2017, the judges halted the licensed hunting of 24 wolves which had been going on since October 1 (12 had been killed by then). Rather than appealing this court decision, the Minister of Climate and Environment altered course and decided that 42 wolves should be killed. This regime is not 'nature management'; it is mass theriocide of free-born animals that serves (some) human interests. Evidently, an ecological approach, at least as interpreted through nature management regimes, is worthless when it comes to animal rights, since animals are appreciated only as part of a species, and only the latter is accorded any value. As stated by Regan (in Svärd 2008),

> The reason we ought to save the members of an endangered species is not because the species is endangered, but because the individual animals have valid claims and thus rights against those who will destroy their habitat, for example, or who would make a living of their dead carcasses through poaching [sic] and trafficking in exotic animals, practices that unjustifiably override the rights of these animals.
>
> (172)

While not disagreeing with Regan's argument for, and defence of, the individual, it is possible to employ a *dual* argument here, providing more weight: Individual animals should have the right not to be molested in their habitats in any way, but so should their species and consequently their ecosystems. This would add a second and third dimension, and thus emphasize the importance of not separating rights and justice, but seeing them in conjunction with each other (Benton 1998; Halsey and White 1998; White 2013, 2018). Individual animal rights, species justice and biocentric/ecocentric rights and justice must be brought together for a holistic care approach of humans towards the natural world. *Her er du!*

Animal rights theorists (Francione 2009; Regan 1987) argue that animals should be accorded the right not to suffer from harm inflicted upon them by humans because they are individuals with interests in continuing their lives, e.g., with their flocks in their habitats. These are negative rights, which may be sufficient for free-born animals (Kymlicka and Donaldson 2011: 9). For all the animals who are under human control, such a hands-off approach is insufficient. One can argue the best way to ensure free-born animals' rights is to leave them alone, not to molest or kill them and not to destroy their habitats. But many animals are in a different situation, like the animals humans have exploited for meat or other products through the millennia (Nibert 2013; Noske 1989) and all the species that live near humans and that have accompanied human settlements (Tønnessen 2013).

As argued by many animal rights scholars, the main problem when it comes to animal rights is that they are regarded as the property of humans (Francione 2009, 2014; cf. Beirne 2009); the animals we keep as companions may also easily be victims of abuse and premature death (e.g. Agnew 1998; Beirne 1999; Sollund 2011). As shown in this book, not even free-born animals escape the property status; Norway, after all, owns all wildlife within its borders, according to the wildlife law. While animal rights theorists highlight the need for negative rights – animals 'rights to *not* be 'tortured, experimented on, owned, enslaved, imprisoned, or killed,' – Kymlicka and Donaldson extend this, arguing for a theory of citizenship. Concerning the animals whom we claim to be 'domesticated,' they opine that they should be regarded as members of society. We are responsible for having brought them into a situation of dependent slavery; therefore, it is also our responsibility to include them justly in political and social arrangements. As members of society they are also to be citizens, which entails three elements: their right to be here; that their rights are interests that must be incorporated into our conception of the common good for society; and they themselves shall define the rules for cooperation (2011: 100). This may sound radical; however, as discussed by Regan (1987) the mentally disabled, Alzheimer's patients and infants who cannot as mentally capable, adults act in society, all have rights since human rights are universal (see also Benton 1998). Likewise animals should have moral rights. And while most animals do not communicate as we do, they are able to 'voice' their opinion. Few people can misunderstand why a mother cow cries when her calf is taken away from her, just as we know what the calf wants in that situation (Larsen 2013). By truly seeing (and listening to) an animal who is caged (Sollund 2009, 2017a), one knows through her voicing, posture and body language, and the look in her eyes, that she wishes to be released. We might have to work a bit harder to understand what they want than when we communicate with another human, but we can still understand (Kheel 1996). In order to do so we will need to be compassionate (Donovan and Adams 1996; Sollund 2017a), rather than reject them and subordinate them to us because they are different (Noske 1989; Sollund 2008a).

Kymlicka and Donaldson (2011) find that citizenship presupposes a level of sociabilitythat makes reciprocal engagement possible. Both humans and so-called domesticated animals need to be socialized into their role of co-citizen, just like migrants and host society inhabitants need to mutually adapt. This requires trust and cooperation (Kymlicka and Donaldson 2011: 214; see also Sollund 2012d). An explanation must be offered about the concept of 'domestication.' Kymlicka and Donaldson 's use of the term 'domesticated citizens' does not convey enslavement and torture, which, as discussed in the first chapter, is what domestication usually means for animals (Nibert 2013). This form of domestication is what an animal rights theory like Kymlicka and Donaldson's aims to change. When using the concept 'domesticated,' the image of barns, crates, cages, etc., come to my mind, whereas, in reality, these represent the instruments and facilities by which they are enslaved (e.g., Nibert 2013; Spiegel and Walker 1996).

Kymlicka and Donaldson (2011) refer to as animals as "liminal", whoare those adapted to living among humans without being under direct human care, such as pigeons, rats, crows, foxes, sparrows, badgers, raccoons, gulls, bats, etc., many of whom are 'flexible opportunists' (219). Many of these animals are also frequently regarded as vermin (Hallsworth 2008), and, as such, targets of 'lethal campaigns to limit their numbers' (Kymlicka and Donaldson 2011: 220). Often, they are descendants of parent opportunists who migrated to the city, but they have no way of themselves returning to the wild; corridors may be closed, habitats may be lost.

Among these liminal denizens, the concept Kymlicka and Donaldson reserve for this category of non-humans is that they are 'niche specialists – species that have become dependent on a specific ecologic niche created by human activity, such as the corn crake. Many habitats created by human activity face destruction due to modernization and farming methods. Among the liminal species are also those referred to as 'invasive species.' Often they are imported and released by humans, and then they settle in human areas. Ring-necked parrots in cities of Europe are one such species. These species are often regarded, not only as 'alien', but also as enemies who must be destroyed. Liminal animals also include those defined as feral, domesticated animals who have escaped human control, usually, dogs and cats. In Australia, feral animals include millions of pigs, horses, cattle, goats, buffalo and camels (Kymlicka and Donaldson 2011: 224; see also White 2018).

Liminal animals – the denizens – should, according to Kymlicka and Donaldson (2011), have rights as co-residents, rather than co-citizens. This means we should recognize the legitimacy of those already present as residents of a community and devise strategies for coexistence which recognize animals' rights as well as our own, rather than regarding and treating them as aliens (250). We owe it to them to acknowledge their basic rights to life and freedom, and to take into account their interests in living in a human-dominated environment. We also owe them our assistance when this can be offered without undermining their freedom.

I have some reservation about the concept 'liminal species.' 'Liminality' is defined from the human perspective, whereas these animals might consider themselves neither as denizens nor liminal, but rather as being in the perfect place, in fact *in* place, rather than 'out of place' (Douglas 2003), or half-in-place. These species could theoretically regard humans as liminal, rather than themselves. Why should humans have the right to define who belongs and who is accepted as a citizen or co-citizen with their particular rights? After all, many animal species have developed and spread in tandem with the dispersal of *Homo sapiens.*

One must not forget that it is us – humans – who consistently invade and destroy their habitats, indeed their homes. We should feel obliged not to inflict harm on free-berm species and not to invade their territories. Kymlicka and Donaldson (2011) compare the situation of free-born animals with that of other colonized people who have lost their lands due to European colonization and more modern imperialist colonization (Mol 2013). Kymlicka and Donaldson suggest free-born animals be accorded sovereign territorial rights, thereby protecting them against such human actions as hunts, abductions and destruction of habitats (Kymlicka and Donaldson 2011: 169–170). This is seen in contrast to a 'stewardship model,' setting aside habitats for free-born animals in sanctuaries or national parks. This model implies humans 'manage' the animals' habitats, whereas a sovereign model would imply that humans have *no rights to govern* that territory. A sovereignty model regards the animals *not* as passive recipients (Regan's [1987] as 'moral patients'), but as individuals with the will and capacity to pursue their own good and to shape their own communities autonomously. Free-born animals have legitimate interests in maintaining their own social organization on their territory, they are vulnerable to the injustice of having alien rule imposed on them and their territory; and sovereignty is an appropriate tool for protecting that interest against injustice (Kymlicka and Donaldson 2011: 174). That animals are regarded as sovereign does not imply that we cannot *assist* animals in need: 'When we can help animals without usurping their autonomy or causing greater harm, we should be moved by the plight of suffering animals' (187). This means humans have obligations both in terms of free-born animals' negative rights, not to suffer abuse inflicted upon them by humans, but also in terms of their positive rights, as stated in the Norwegian Animal Welfare Law, that humans have the obligation to help animals who are suffering. This clause may not have much practical value, because the Norwegian state simultaneously arranges mass theriocides through hunts. Nonetheless, having this established in legislation can be regarded as a step in the right direction.

This raises some interesting questions concerning how to perceive animals who have been domesticated and then liberated (repatriated) and human responsibility towards them. For years, they may have been under human control and 'care' and thus according to Kymlicka and Donaldson have had rights as members of society/citizens, just as humans have responsibilities towards them. But when they are repatriated and have been 'dedomesticated,' how far does human obligation reach if they cannot fend for themselves, if they are not properly 'rewilded,' and if repatriation into a state of sovereigns cannot be defined as successful? With help from humans, who could assist them with food supplies, they could be regarded as sovereigns of their territory, their animal rights to live unharmed in their habitat could be fulfilled and their lives significantly improved compared to a life in a cage or in a sanctuary with restricted freedom of movement. Consequently, they will largely benefit from a life as 'citizens' and a life as 'sovereigns,' not the least because in reality, very few people acknowledge that their pets are members of society, even if they are accepted as members of the family (Anderson 2003; Serpell 1996; Sollund 2009).

Another take on the treatment, or lack of treatment, of free-born animals is compassionate conservation (Bekoff 2013), which I turn to in the next and last chapter.

Notes

1 https://eeas.europa.eu/diplomatic-network/european-economic-area-eea_en
2 www.elephantsanctuary.co.za/
3 http://www.khamarhinosanctuary.org.bw/
4 www.orangutan-appeal.org.uk/about-us/sepilok-orangutan-rehabilitation-centre
5 https://alexfoundation.org/
6 Concerning the night monkeys, they would not have taken them at all, since they regard them as too distasteful to eat (Goyes 2015; Maldonado in interview).
7 The word is derived from *pájaro*, bird. The meaning then concerns the bird traffickers, which is rooted in long traditions and their 'skills' as bird captivators.

14 Mirror, mirror on the wall, who's the wildest of them all?

An overall problem arising from the interviews is the issue of demand among all categories of consumers, whether in Colombia or in Norway or other countries. The responsibility for the conservation of biodiversity and protection of endangered species lies not only in source countries, but also throughout the world, and the authorities in demand countries, like the EU, play an important part in reducing that demand. As shown in the introduction, this seems to be a responsibility the EU, the UN and Interpol/Europol are responding to WLT through different means of action. However, whether such cooperative efforts also result in improved prevention and law enforcement of WLT at national levels is more dubious. They provide, nonetheless, a signal that WLT is a problem, which again may produce indirect results. Actions to create awareness largely lack in Norway, while in Colombia much remains to be done, despite legislation and more attention to the problem given by the authorities.

The measures taken, however, are often a response to anthropocentric interests; species must be conserved to prolong the exploitation of them for human benefit. In this final chapter, I lay and discuss another theoretical foundation that can guide our treatment of free-born animals.

As a prolongation of the previous chapter, one question is whether a UN declaration of animal rights[1] could move the normative climate in the right direction, even though human rights doctrines are often not respected (Benton 1998; Pellow 2013). A UN animal rights declaration would, if it were to be enforced, turn the present world with its heavy reliance on animal exploitation upside down. For example, in Article 6 of the proposed animal rights declaration, it is stated,

> Animals are not the property or commodity of humans, and are not theirs to use for their benefit or sustenance. Therefore, they are to be free from slavery, exploitation, oppression, victimization, brutality, abuse, and any other treatment that disregards their safety, own free will and dignity. They should not be slaughtered for food, killed for their skins, experimented on, killed for religious purposes, used for forced labor, abused and killed for sport and entertainment, abused for commercial profit, hunted, persecuted or exterminated for human pleasure, need, or other ends.

Given the revolutionary consequences of such a declaration and the resistance most people have against giving up their privileges, a realistic question is therefore how far such rights should stretch –relative or full rights to a life in freedom without being victimized by human abuse/exploitation? Positive rights or negative rights? A declaration of 'animal' rights would still convey a strong signal that hopefully, with time, could drizzle down to legislation and the socio-legal climate in society. As mentioned in relation to the Patarroyo case, monkeys were granted rights, and a Supreme Court decision in Colombia established that animals are subjects with rights to habeas corpus.[2] According to the newspaper *El País*, the judge in the Supreme Court stated that animals are sentient subjects with non-human rights, such as their prerogative as protected fauna with their role in saving the natural equilibrium of all species and nature. Therefore, they should be objects for conservation and protection against suffering abuse and unjustified cruelty. The case concerned a bear called Chucho, who for 18 years was held in a zoo in Barranquilla, trafficked from the reserve Río Blanco de Manizales.

However, this right can only be exercised when it does not threaten agricultural development, medical development and people's access to food, according to the judgment. It is thus a right to be considered a subject, which is only relative to humans' 'needs.' Nonetheless, the judge in the Supreme Court said that this was about recognizing and assigning rights and legal status to determine epistemologically, ethically, politically, culturally and legally the irrational destruction of our planet and of all nature that afflicts the generation of our time in a shameful and tragic way.

Legal progress in terms of animal rights and habeas corpus has been made in several places on earth, such as in the US, Colombia, Brazil and Spain, and concerning different species such as chimpanzees, elephants and tigers in the US,[3] and orangutans in Argentina.[4] Another element that comes into play, which is why many people on earth engage in the animal rights movement, is their empathy, which is evoked by watching the overall animal abuse for various purposes worldwide.

Further, parallels are drawn between different forms of structural oppression. Feminists writing about human-animal relations have pointed out the connections between animal abuse and harm and other forms of oppression, such as that of women, people of colour and the disabled (see Cazaux 1999; Donovan 1993, 1996; Donovan and Adams 1996; Gruen 1993; Kheel 2008; Nibert 2002; Nussbaum 2009; Sollund 2008a). Adams sees the interconnectedness of different isms as related to difference from what constitutes white, male manhood: 'Man' (read white, male man) exists as a concept and a sexual identity through negation; 'not woman, not beast, not coloured' – that is 'not the other' (Adams 1996: 174).

Caring theory is central for much of the feminist animal welfare movement (Engster 2004). It was first developed by Gilligan (1982) and is rooted in a relational ontology that does not privilege the rational individual nor require rationality as a 'means test' for ethical treatment. It was developed out of a recognition of unequal relationships where the carer had more power than the cared for (or than the one who failed to be cared for). Caring theory values emotions and considers sympathy, empathy and love as central, as they should be to any ethical theory. Gilligan contrasts what she considered as a female concept of morality "concerned with the activity of care, responsibility and relationships," with the male conception of "morality as fairness, concerned with rights and rules" (Donovan and Adams 1996: 13). The feminine conception implying a morality of responsibility, underlining the maintenance of relations, was then brought forward by animal care ethic feminists, such as Donovan and Adams (1996; Kheel 1996, and see also Beirne 1999; Sollund 2008a). It means that one should engage oneself in trying to understand and feel what it is like to be in the skin of another individual, and allow those emotions to guide your actions (Kheel 1996).

Donovan and Adams are critical to animal rights theorists, such as Peter Singer and Tom Regan, for rejecting emotions as guiding principles for our actions towards animals: "This means that a major basis for the human-animal connection – love – is not encompassed" (Donovan and Adams 1996: 15). One can draw a parallel between human-animal relationships, as they should ideally work, with the ways in which we treat people with whom we have care obligations, whether children or the elderly. In such relationships, compassion is a central element. While children and humans generally have legal rights, this does not mean that care, emotions, love and compassion are not central in determining how we treat them and that these do not guide our actions towards them. A relationship in which one is carer and the other cared for, therefore, in the view of Donovan and Adams, includes a psychology more relevant for our relationships to animals than a rights-based equal relationship discourse. According to Engster (2004), in his development of care theory where he also meets the criticism raised against it, amongst others, for being vague,

> Care theory derives our moral obligations not from some abstract quality such as autonomy or self-consciousness but rather from our relations with others as dependent social creatures. We have duties to care for others because we have appealed to others for care, and other individuals have duties to us because they have appealed to still others.
>
> (2004: 4)[5]

Consequently both demands *of care*, as well as obligations to *care for* is something with which most humans, perhaps all, are familiar, since some degree of care will be necessary to develop as a human being. It is thus a tool, which is near at hand for us all if we choose to acknowledge it and use it, for our relationships with animals as well – whether near or distant.

Care ethics was not new with the ecofeminist care-ethics theorists cited above; rather, it has long theoretical roots. Gålmark (2016) elaborates upon how Olympe de Gouges' rejection of the contemporary broad use of violence in France around the revolution was an issue her opponents could not accept, and that for de Gouges,

> the most beautiful trait in the human being, [is] its humanity, its sensitivity and its capacity to empathy. Humans become no more human, gain no more rights, when they kill or order others to kill. De Gouge's thinking suggests

> a humanitarian feminism that includes the weak and excluded groups while limiting the governing power's measure of control the violence.
>
> (29)

De Gouges was not only an early care-ethics feminist, she also saw the human as an animal, not as superior to him/her, but different from other animals (as the other animal species are different from each other). According to Gålmark (2016), inter-human equality departs from the insight that all humans share belonging to the same heterogeneous group of animals: We are all beings of nature – the human in all her beautiful nuances and differences. The special condition of humans is to create a compassionate and just society in harmony with limits of nature (55).

In the era of Olympe de Gouge, several other thinkers also meant that humans would be hardened through committing violence against animals or witnessing it; consequently, the idea that empathy should guide our acts did not reside with de Gouge alone. William Blake, for example, suggested a direct connection between the quality of a society and its treatment of animals, just as Mahatma Gandhi was credited with later (Gålmark 2016: 30).

Nussbaum (2009) argues also that we must *act upon* our compassion for suffering animals:

> duties of compassion involve the thought that it is *wrong* to cause animals suffering. Where that suffering is caused by a wrongful act, a duty of compassion would involve acknowledgement of that wrongfulness. That is, a duty to compassion would not be just a duty to have compassion, but a duty, as a result of one's compassion, to refrain from, inhibit and punish acts of the sort that cause the suffering occasioning the compassion.
>
> (336; emphasis original)

Not only is it wrong of us humans to cause suffering to animals, but animals also have a moral entitlement not to be inflicted with such suffering (Nussbaum 2009: 337). While feminists have argued for empathy with animals and for actively employing this capacity (rather than oppressing it), we differentiate not only between which animals we regard with empathy, but also between which humans. The possibility of empathizing with a victim can be read into Christie's (1986) elaboration of the ideal victim. Who is perceived as the ideal victim would not only depend on the victim her/himself, her innocence and respectability in terms of her activities. It would also depend on the degree to which she invokes a feeling of empathy with the bystander and consumer. Christie's ideal victim is an old lady who is attacked when she is on her way to help her sister. *Her* activities are respectable; she is weak and does no harm. But while this may be recognized by most humans, concerning animals and their activities, *who* they are and *what* they do may not be clearly grasped, far less respected. Perhaps because of the paradox in the human-animal relationship (Sollund 2009), they are seldom regarded as ideal victims. Rather, because animals are regarded as resources and property (Beirne 1999; Francione 2009), empathy for them may be hard to invoke in the potential and actual contributor to animal exploitation. Should s/he empathize with the victim, s/he would also have to be critical of her/his own complicity in animal abuse. Consequently, there are several barriers preventing humans from empathizing with animals, for example the objectification of animals, the social distance and the challenging inherent self-critique this would imply for most humans (Sollund 2008a).

One of the interviewees conveyed a compassionate approach to animals, an approach she sees as generally lacking in Colombians' relationships to animals:

> To see a bird in a cage, it is like putting a person in a cage without her being guilty of anything wrong. So I think people lack consciousness. Colombians are uncultivated in relation to the environment.

To see an animal, not just glance at her, is to *know* an animal, because you can own an animal without knowing or seeing her, without establishing a personal relationship with her. Through *seeing* her, you become someone for her, and she someone for you – you are a person for her, as s/he is a person for you (Francione 2009; Smuts 1999).[6] To *see* the other is not to anthropomorphize the animal, as little as to *see* another human is to ascribe her/him characteristics/properties that person does not possess. On the contrary, it is seeing that animal person (Francione 2009) for who s/he really is, with her needs and capacities, as an individual pertaining to a specific animal species. It is the opposite of the objectification (as property) they are usually subject to. It can help reduce the social distance and alienation between humans and non-humans that facilitate abuse (Sollund 2008a). An animal and her caretaker can become something *more* than just the two persons; they add to each other, through which, when this exists, they can achieve a mutual relationship just as human-human relationships are mutual (Sollund 2017a).

An approach related to care ethics is offered also by compassionate conservation (Ramp and Bekoff 2015). This direction suggests evolutionary underpinnings, for the ethical behaviour of compassion can be practically defined as reflecting empathy in humans for non-human animals and a desire to alleviate harm and suffering. This is especially important in the area of WLT. Unlike the dominant utilitarian approach to conservation which puts the cost of conservation on the shoulders of other animals, a compassionate ethic for conservation brings empathy into decision making.

Engster (2006) argues that we have obligations to care for animals under our dominion, such as our companion animals and animals raised for meat. The latter is incompatible with care theory since even when animals are raised and treated in ways which provide them with necessary room for nutrition, freedom from pain and the liberty to move and act in ways natural to them, the ultimate killing of them is *uncaring*, since they are killed counter to their interest. Engster concludes that the positive contribution care ethics makes to the animal welfare movement is to focus our attention on the way we actually treat the animals that are dependent upon us. Care ethics, he states, returns our moral attention to the relationships we have with animals and the quality of life we provide for them (2006: 4). I argue, though, that our obligations to care apply just as much for those animals who are not under our care, those free-born animals who we either kill or put into traffick, since also for them to be killed is counter to their interests, and putting them into traffick, we set them forcefully under our dominion in situations in which they are bound to suffer, which I have demonstrated in this book.

Compassionate conservation implies first to *do no harm*, which is important not only because of what we now know about the cognitive and emotional lives (consciousness and sentience) of other animals (Bekoff 2013; Bekoff and Pierce 2009), but also as a moral imperative for providing modern solutions for sharing space with nature and for fostering the possibility for diverse species to live in peaceful coexistence (Ramp and Bekoff 2015: 33). The compassionate conservation field is critical to the ways in which free-born animals are exempt from individual animal welfare concerns, in that what matters in conservation is species and ecosystem welfare: 'the grounding of conservation in species welfare has, perhaps unintentionally, subjugated individuals for collective benefits' (Ramp and Bekoff 2015: 2). Such practice is understood by Ramp and Bekoff (2015: 2) as being caused by negativity toward individual welfare which has become entrenched, because it has been viewed as an impediment to holistic decision making. Compassion must be encouraged, generated and applied so that it involves individuals, whether human or non-human, their species, their living conditions in the ecosystems to where they pertain, and their future prospects for well-being and survival. Wildlife trade, whether legal or illegal, is a breach of all such considerations, and therefore should be banned. In our treatment of other animals, those we define as 'wild,' as well as those who are subjugated to our power in other ways, it is perhaps the human species that remains the wildest – the most savage – of all the animal species. If we do not alter our ways, there is a great risk that this will result in us being alone – very, very soon.

Notes

1 One such animal declaration has been proposed. See http://declarationofar.org/textSign.php#sign
2 www.elpais.com.co/colombia/la-corte-suprema-establece-que-los-animales-son-sujetos-con-derechos.html
3 www.nonhumanrights.org/blog/category/cases/
4 www.scientificamerican.com/espanol/noticias/sandra-la-orangutan-cuyos-derechos-basicos-son-reconocidos-en-argentina/
5 Paging from downloaded pdf: https://onlinelibrary.wiley.com/doi/abs/10.1111/j.1467-9833.2006.00355.x
6 And see Saint-Exupéry's (2015) story of the little prince and his encounter with the fox who instructs the prince about how to 'tame' him, by which they become someone to/for each other.

References

Adams, C. (1996). Caring about suffering: Feminist exploration. In J. Donovan & C. Adams (Eds.), *Beyond animal rights: A feminist caring ethic for the treatment of animals* (pp. 170–197). New York: Continuum.

Adams, C. J. (2015). *The sexual politics of meat: A feminist-vegetarian critical theory.* USA: Bloomsbury Publishing.

Agnew, R. (1998). The causes of animal abuse: A social-psychological analysis. *Theoretical Criminology, 2*(2), 177–209.

Alacs, E., & Georges, A. (2008). Wildlife across our borders: A review of the illegal trade in Australia. *Australian Journal of Forensic Sciences, 40*(2), 147–160.

Alexander, K. A., Sanderson, C. E., Marathe, M., Lewis, B. L., Rivers, C. M., Shaman, J., . . . Eubank, S. (2015). What factors might have led to the emergence of Ebola in West Africa? *PLoS Neglected Tropical Diseases, 9*(6), e0003652.

Alves, R. R. (2012). Relationships between fauna and people and the role of ethnozoology in animal conservation. *Ethnobiology and Conservation, 1*(2), 1–69.

Alves, R. R., & Rosa, I. L. (2008). Use of tucuxi dolphin *Sotalia fluviatilis* for medicinal and magic/religious purposes in North Brazil. *Human Ecology, 36*(3), 443–447.

Alves, R. R., Washington, L. da S. V., & Giundomar, G. S. (2008). Reptiles used in traditional folk medicine: Conservation implications. *Biodiversity and Conservation, 17*, 2037–2049.

Anderson, P. (2003). A bird in the house: An anthropological perspective on companion parrots. *Society and Animals, 11*(4), 393–418.

Anderson, L. (2006). Analytic autoethnography. *Journal of Contemporary Ethnography, 35*(4), 373–395.

Angelici, F. M. (2016). Problematic wildlife at the beginning of the twenty-first century: Introduction. In *Problematic wildlife: A cross-disciplinary approach* (pp. 3–20). Heidelberg: Springer International Publishing.

Animal Defenders International (2009). Primate testing in Europe. http://www.navs.org.uk/downloads/stpreporten.pdf

Annorbah, N. N., Collar, N. J., & Marsden, S. J. (2016). Trade and habitat change virtually eliminate the grey parrot Psittacus erithacus from Ghana. *Ibis, 158*(1), 82–91.

Arluke, A., & Sanders, C. R. (1996). *Regarding animals.* Philadelphia: Temple University Press.

Aubert, V. (1954). *Om straffens sosiale funksjon.* Oslo: Universitetsforlaget.

Auliya, M., Altherr, S., Ariano-Sanchez, D., Baard, E. H., Brown, C., Brown, R. M., . . . Hintzmann, J. (2016). Trade in live reptiles, its impact on wild populations, and the role of the European market. *Biological Conservation, 204*, 103–119.

Ayling, J. (2013). What sustains wildlife crime? Rhino horn trading and the resilience of criminal networks. *Journal of International Wildlife Law and Policy*, *16*(1), 57–80.

Ayling, J. (2015). *A regulatory approach to demand reduction in the illegal wildlife market*. RegNet research paper, no. 82, Regulatory Institutions Network. Accessed on January 17. https://papers.ssrn.com/sol3/papers.cfm?abstract_id=2634303

Bargent, J. (2016). Colombia investigation reveals workings of wildlife traffickers. *InsightCrime*. Accessed on July 18, 2016. www.insightcrime.org/news-analysis/colombia-investigation-reveals-workings-of-wildlife-traffickers

Barnett, A. (2004). Revealed: UK zoos caught in rare wildlife trade with dealer. *The Guardian*, https://www.theguardian.com/environment/2004/mar/28/animalrights.conservationandendangeredspecies

Beck, A. (1999). Companion animals and their companions: Sharing a strategy for survival. *Bulletin of Science, Technology and Society*, *19*, 28–295.

Beck, A., & Katcher, A. (1996). *Between pets and people: The importance of animal companionship*. West Lafayette, IN: Purdue University Press.

Benton, T. (1998). Rights and justice on a shared planet: More rights or new relations? *Theoretical Criminology*, *2*(2), 149–175.

Beetz, A., Uvnäs-Moberg, K., Julius, H., & Kotrschal, K. (2012). Psychosocial and psychophysiological effects of human-animal interactions: The possible role of oxytocin. *Frontiers in Psychology*, *3*. doi:10.3389/fpsyg.2012.00234

Beirne, P. (1997). Rethinking bestiality: Towards a concept of interspecies sexual assault. *Theoretical Criminology*, *1*(3), 317–340.

Beirne, P. (1999). For a nonspeciesist criminology: Animal abuse as an object of study. *Criminology*, *37*(1), 117–148.

Beirne, P. (2007). Animal rights: Animal abuse and green criminology. In P. Beirne & N. South (Eds.), *Issues in green criminology* (pp. 55–87). Devon, UK: Willan Publishing.

Beirne, P. (2009). *Confronting animal abuse: Law, criminology and human-animal relationships*. Lanham, NJ: Rowman & Littlefield Publishers.

Beirne, P. (2014). Theriocide: Naming animal killing. *International Journal for Crime, Justice and Social Democracy*, *3*(2), 49–66.

Beirne, P., & South, N. (2007). *Issues in green criminology: Confronting harms against environments, humanity and other animals*. Devon, UK: Willan Publishing.

Bekoff, M. (Ed.). (2013). *Ignoring nature no more: The case for compassionate conservation*. Chicago and London: University of Chicago Press.

Bekoff, M. (2006). Animal emotions and animal sentience and why they matter: Blending "science sense" with common sense, compassion and heart. In J. Turner & J. D'Silva Eds.), *Animals, ethics and trade: The challenge of animal sentience* (pp. 27–40). London: Earthscan Publishing.

Bekoff, M., & Pierce, J. (2009). Wild justice: Honor and fairness among beasts at play. In *Excerpted from Wild justice: The moral lives of animals*. Chicago: University of Chicago Press.

Berger, J. (2009). *Why look at animals?* Johannesburg: Penguin Books.

Bergo, B. (2006). *Emmanuel Levinas* (Stanford Encyclopedia of Philosophy), https://plato.standford.edu/entries/levinas.

Berkunsky, I., Quillfeldt, P., Brightsmith, D. J., Abbud, M. C., Aguilar, J. M. R. E., Alemán-Zelaya, U., & Barberena, J. B. (2017). Current threats faced by Neotropical parrot populations. *Biological Conservation*, *214*, 278–287.

Bhattacharya, S. (2016). Slaughter of the songbirds. *Nature*, *529*(7587), 452.

Birkeland, J. (1993). Ecofeminism: Linking theory and practice. In Gaard, G. (Ed.). *Ecofeminism: Women, animals, nature* (pp. 13–59). Philadelphia: Temple University Press.

Blrghardt, G. M. (1977). Of iguanas and dinosaurs: Social behavior and communication in neonate reptiles. *American Zoologist*, *17*(1), 177–190.

Boekhout van Solinge, T. (2008a). Crime, conflicts and ecology in Africa. In R. Sollund (Ed.), *Global harms: Ecological crime and speciesism* (pp. 13–35). New York: Nova Science Publishers.

Boekhout van Solinge, T. (2008b). The land of the orangutan and bird of paradise under threat. In R. Sollund (Ed.), *Global harms: Ecological crime and speciesism* (p. 5170). New York: Nova Science Publishers.

Bourdieu, P. (1995). *Outline of a theory of practice*. Cambridge: Cambridge University Press.

Brandth, B., & Haugen, M. S. (2006). Changing masculinity in a changing rural industry: Representations in the forestry press. In H. Campbell, M. M. Bell, & M. Finney (Eds.), *Country boys: Masculinity and rural life* (pp. 217–234). University Park, PA: Pennsylvania State University Press.

Brewer-Hay (2008). eBay to institute global bans on ivory sales. Accessed on November 12. https://www.ebayinc.com/stories/news/ebay-to-institute-global-ban-on-ivory-sales/

Brisman, A. (2014). Of theory and meaning in green criminology. *International Journal for Crime, Justice and Social Democracy*, *3*(2), 21–34.

Brisman, A., & South, N. (2014). *Green cultural criminology: Constructions of environmental harm, consumerism, and resistance to ecocide*. London: Routledge.

Brisman, A., South, N., & White, R. (Eds.). (2016). *Environmental crime and social conflict: Contemporary and emerging issues*. London/New York: Routledge.

Broad, S., Mulliken, T., & Roe, D. (2003). The nature and extent of legal and illegal trade in wildlife. In S. Oldfeld (Ed.), *The trade in wildlife: Regulation for conservation* (pp. 3–22). London: Earthscan.

Brochet, A.-L., van den Bossche, W., Jbour, S., & Ndang'ang'a, P. K. (2016). Preliminary assessment of the scope and scale of illegal killing and taking of birds in the Mediterranean. *Bird Conservation International*, *26*, 1–28.

Brown, C. (2015). Fish intelligence, sentience and ethics. *Animal cognition*, *18*(1), 1–17.

Brownmiller, S. (2013). *Against our will: Men, women and rape*. City: Open Road Media.

Burton, J. A., 2006. The international wild bird trade: a response to Cooney & Jepson. Oryx, 40, p. 261.

Bye, L. M. (2003). Masculinity and rurality at play in stories about hunting. *Norsk Geografisk Tidsskrift-Norwegian Journal of Geography*, *57*(3), 145–153.

Børresen, B. (1996). *Den ensomme apen: Instinkt på avveie*. Oslo: Gyldendal.

Børresen, B. (2007). *Fiskenes hemmelige liv* [The secret lives of fish]. Oslo: Transit forlag.

Camargo-Rodríguez, N. F., Ordoñez, E. Z., & Alvarez, C. R. (n.d.). Informe final rehabilitación y liberación de un grupo de *Saimiri sciureus* (mono ardilla) en la reserve forestal "La Marteja" (Casanare) [Final report of the rehabilitation and release of a group of *Saimiri sciureus* (squirrel monkeys) in the reserve "La Marteja". Bogotá: Universidad Nacional de Colombia.

Capera, V. H. (n.d.). *Informe liberación de loras Amzona Achrocephala ochrecephala en la hacienda Netu, vereda Maraíbo, Municipio de Armero-Guyabal, departemento de Tolima* [Report of the release of amazon parrots *Achrocephala ochrecephala*] in the department of Tolima]. Bogotá: Universidad Nacional de Colombia.

Case, D. O. (2009). Serial collecting as leisure, and coin collecting in particular. *Library Trends*, *57*(4), 729–752.

Cazaux, G. (1999). Beauty and the beast: Animal abuse from a non-speciesist criminological perspective. *Crime, Law and Social Change*, *31*(2), 105–125.

Cazaux, G. (2007). Labelling animals: Non-speciesist criminology and techniques to identify other animals. In P. Beirne & N. South (Eds.), *Issues in green criminology: Confronting harms against environments, humanity and other animals* (pp. 87–114). Devon, UK: Willan Publishing.

Centro de Primatología Araguato. Accessed on November 15, 2017. www.academia.edu/12728133/GUIA_BASICA_PARA_EL_MANEJO_DE_FAUNA_PERIDECOMISO

Centro de recepcion de flora y fauna silvestre crffs. (2012). Informe final contrato 0738 sda-udca. Bogotá 2012. Secretaria distrital de ambiente SDA 2012, p. Dirección de evaluación y seguimiento ambiental. Subdirección silvicultura flora y fauna silvestre.

Challender, D. W., Harrop, S. R., & MacMillan, D. C. (2015). Towards informed and multi-faceted wildlife trade interventions. *Global Ecology and Conservation*, *3*, 129–148.

Chan, J. (1996). Changing police culture. *The British Journal of Criminology*, *36*(1), 109–134.

Chapron, G., & Treves, A. (2016). Blood does not buy goodwill: Allowing culling increases poaching of a large carnivore. *Proceedings of the Royal Society B*, *283*, 20152939. http://dx.doi.org/10.1098/rspb.2015.2939

Chin, S., Veening, W., & Gerstetter, C. (2014). Policy brief 1: Limitations and challenges of the criminal justice system in addressing environmental crime. *EFFACE*. Accessed on March 26, 2018. http://efface.eu/sites/default/files/publications/EFFACE_Policy_Brief%201_29Oct14_1.pdf

Christie, N. (1975). Hvor tett et samfunn?: Oslo: Universitetsforlaget.

Christie, N. (1977). Conflicts as property. *The British Journal of Criminology*, *17*(1), 1–15.

Christie, N. (1986). The ideal victim. In I. Antila (Ed.), *From crime policy to victim policy* (pp. 17–30). London: Palgrave Macmillan.

Christie, N., & Bruun, K. (1985). *Den gode fiende* [The good enemy]. Oslo: Universitetsforlaget.

CITES. (n.d.). Resolution conf. 10.7 (Rev. CoP15) Disposal of confiscated live specimens of species included in the Appendices. *Amended at the 15th meeting of the conference of the parties*. https://cites.org/eng/res/10/10-07R15.php

CITES. (2017). European Union invests 30 million Euro to counter the illegal killing and trafficking of wildlife in Southern, Eastern Africa and the Indian Ocean. Accessed on July 23, 2018. https://cites.org/eng/EU_invests_30_m_euro_to_counter_illegal_killing_trafficking_wildlife_05122017

CITES Secretariat. (1998). *Notification to parties*. Accessed on January 22, 2015. http://cites.org/sites/default/files/eng/notif/1998/54.shtml

CITES Secretariat (2013a). CITES Secretary-General welcomes adoption of UN Commission on crime prevention and criminal justice draft resolution recognizing wildlife crime as a serious crime. Accessed on September 24, 2014. www.cites.org/eng/news/sundry/2013/20130502_ccpcj_resolution.php

CITES Secretariat (2013b). Heads of UNODC and CITES urge wildlife and forest offences to be treated as serious transnational organised crimes. Accessed on October 14, 2014. www.cites.org/eng/news/pr/2013/20130423_CCPCJ.php

CITES Secretariat (2015). Conf. 9.9: Confiscation of specimens exported or re-exported in violation of the Convention. Accessed on January 22, 2015. http://cites.org/sites/default/files/eng/res/all/09/E09-09.pdf

Clifford, J. (2003). Collecting ourselves. In S. M. Pearce (Ed.), *Interpreting objects and collections* (pp. 258–269). London and New York: Routledge.

Cohen, S. (2001). *States of denial.* Cambridge: Polity Press.

Collard, A., & Contrucci, J. (1989). *Rape of the wild: Man's violence against animals and the earth.* Bloomington, IN: Indiana University Press.

Conlee, K. M., Stephens, M. L., Rowan, A. N., & King, L. A. (2005). Carbon dioxide for euthanasia: Concerns regarding pain and distress, with special reference to mice and rats. *Laboratory Animals, 39*(2), 137–161.

Connell, R. W. (2005). *Masculinities.* Berkeley, CA: University of California Press.

Cooney, R., & Jepson, P. (2006). The international wild bird trade: What's wrong with blanket bans? *Oryx, 40*(1), 18–23.

Courchamp, F., Angulo, E., Rivalan, P., Hall, R. J., Signoret, L., Bull, L., & Meinard, Y. (2006). Rarity value and species extinction: The anthropogenic Allee effect. *PLoS Biology, 4*(12), e415. doi:10.1371/journal.pbio.0040415

Cowdrey, D. (2002, December). Switching channels: Wildlife trade routes into Europe and the UK. *A WWF/TRAFFIC report.* Accessed on October 14, 2104. www.wwf.org.uk/filelibrary/pdf/switchingchannels.pdf

Crosta, A., & Sutherland, K. (2012). The white gold of jihad: al-Shabaaband and the illegal ivory trade. *Elephant Action League.* Accessed on April 4, 2018. https://elephantleague.org/wp-content/uploads/2016/02/Report-Ivory-al-Shabaab-Oct2016.pdf

Daily, N. (2017). *Special report: The Amazon is the new frontier for deadly wildlife tourism.* An exclusive National Geographic investigation reveals widespread animal suffering in Amazonian port towns, fueled by "selfie safaris". Accessed on October 20, 2017. www.nationalgeographic.com/photography/proof/2017/10/wildlife-watch-amazon-ecotourism-animal-welfare/#/20-wildlife-watch-ecotourism1.jpg

Danet, B., & Katriel, T. (2003). No two alike: Play and aesthetics in collecting. In S. M. Pearce (Ed.), *Interpreting objects and collections* (pp. 220–240). London and New York: Routledge.

Das, M., & Chatterjee, B. (2015). Ecotourism: A panacea or a predicament? *Tourism Management Perspectives, 14*, 3–16.

Davenport, J. (2014, February 10). eBay traders "are flouting ban on ivory by calling it faux". *London Evening Standard.* www.standard.co.uk/news/uk/ebay-traders-are-flouting-ban-on-ivory-by-calling-it-faux-9119071.html

Decreto 1608 del 31 de Julio de 1978. *Por el cual se reglamenta el Código Nacional de los Recursos Naturales Renovables y de Protección al Medio Ambiente y la Ley 23 de 1973 en materia de fauna silvestre.* Republica de Colombia, Ministerio de Agricultura. Accessed on November 2, 2017. www.sinchi.org.co/files/leyes%20y%20decretos/dec_1608_310778.pdf

Defenzoores. (2015). *El Infierno de los micos de Patarroyo.* Accessed on April 19, 2018. www.entropika.org/documents/defenzoores.270514.article.pdf

Den Høyere påtalemyndighet. Riksadvokatens rundskriv 1/2013. *Mål og prioriteringer for straffesaksbehandlingen.* Accessed on July 19, 2016. http://riksadvokaten.no/filestore/Dokumenter/2013/Rundskrivnr1for2013-Mlogpriforstraffesaksbehandlingen.pdf

Derridá, J. (2002). The animal that therefore I am: More to follow. *Critical Inquiry, 28*, 369–418.

de Saint-Exupéry, A. (2015). *Le petit prince: avec des aquarelles de l'auteur*. Stuttgart: Ernst Klett Sprachen GmbH.

Dickson, B. (2005). What is the goal of regulating wildlife trade? Is regulation a good way to achieve this goal? In S. Oldfield (Ed.), *The trade in wildlife: Regulation for conservation* (pp. 45–54). Abingdon, UK: Earthscan.

Dixon, A., Batbayar, N., Purev-ochir, G., & Fox, N. (2011). *Developing a sustainable harvest of saker falcons (falco cherrug) for falconry in Mongolia*. Paper presented at Gyrfalcons and Ptarmigan in a changing World. doi:10.13140/2.1.1801.2168

DLA Piper (2015). *Empty threat: Does the law combat illegal wildlife trade? A review of legislative and judicial approaches in fifteen jurisdictions*. Accessed on April 19, 2018. www.gtlaw.com/en/insights/2015/2/empty-threat-2015

Donovan, J. (1993). Animal rights and feminist theory. In G. Gaard (Ed.), *Ecofeminism: Women, animals, nature* (pp. 167–195). Philadelphia, PA: Temple University Press.

Donovan, J. (1996). Attention to suffering: Sympathy as a basis for the ethical treatment of animals. In J. Donovan & C. J. Adams (Eds.), *Beyond animal rights: A feminist caring ethic for the treatment of animals* (pp. 147–170). New York: Continuum.

Donovan, J., & Adams, C. J. (Eds.). (1996). *Beyond animal rights: A feminist caring ethic for the treatment of animals*. New York: Continuum.

Douglas, M. (2003). *Purity and danger: An analysis of concepts of pollution and taboo*. London: Routledge.

Duffy, R. (2013). *A trip too far: Ecotourism, politics and exploitation*. London/New York: Routledge.

Duffy, R. (2014). Waging a war to save biodiversity: The rise of militarized conservation. *International Affairs*, *90*(4), 819–834.

Du Plessis, M. (2000). CITES and the causes of extinction. In J. Hutton & B. Dickson (Eds.), *Endangered species threatened convention: The past, present and future of CITES* (pp. 13–28). London: Earthscan.

Ellefsen, R., Sollund, R., & Larsen, G. (2012). *Eco-global crimes: Contemporary problems and future challenges*. Farnham: Ashgate.

Ellefsen, R. (2013a). Den modern pelsdyrfabrikken. Konflikten om legitimiteten [The modern fur animal factory: The conflict over legitimacy]. In R. Sollund, M. Tønnessen, & G. Larsen (Eds.), *Hvem er villest i landet her? Råskap mot dyr og natur i antropocen – menneskets tidsalder* [Who is the wildest in the country? Cruelty against animals and nature in the Anthropocene: The human era] (pp. 205–225). Oslo: Spartacus SAP.

Ellefsen, R. (2013b). *Med lov til å pine. Om bruk og beskyttelse av dyr* [With permission to harm: About use and protection of animals]. Oslo: Fritt forlag.

Ellefsen, R. (2017). Taking sides? Issues of bias and partisanship when researching socio-political conflict. *Critical Criminology*, *25*(2), 231–244.

Elliot, L. (2007). Transnational environmental crime in the Asia Pacific: An "un(der) securitised" security problem? *The Pacific Review*, *20*(4), 499–522.

Elliott, L. (2012). Fighting transnational environmental crime. *Journal of International Affairs*, *66*(1), 87–104. www.jstor.org/stable/24388253

Ellis, R. (2005). *Tiger bone and rhino horn: The destruction of wildlife for traditional Chinese medicine*. Washington, DC: Island Press.

Engebretson, M. (2006). The welfare and suitability of parrots as companion animals: A review. *Animal Welfare*, *15*(3), 263–276.

Enger, C. (2013). Rovdyrranet [The predator robbery]. *Magasinet, Dagens næringsliv*, *4*(5), 2–27.

Engler, M., & Parry-Jones, R. (2007). *Opportunity or threat? The roles of the European Union in global wildlife trade*. Brussels: TRAFFIC.

Engster, D. (2004). Care ethics and natural law theory: Toward an institutional political theory of caring. *The Journal of Politics*, *66*(1), 113–135.

Eniang, E. A., Akpan, C. E., & Eniang, M. E. (2008). A survey of African grey parrots (Psittacus erithacus): Trade and trafficking in. *Ethiopian Journal of Environmental Studies and Management*, *1*(2), 68–73.

European Commission. (2010). *Wildlife trade regulations in the European Union: An introduction to CITES and its implementation in the European Union*. Accessed on January 10, 2014. https://cites.unia.es/file.php/1/files/wildlife-regulation-eu.pdf

European Commission. (2014a). *Communication from the commission to the Council and the European Parliament on the EU approach against wildlife trafficking*. Brussels: European Commission.

European Commission. (2014b). *Commission staff working document: Summary of the responses to the stakeholder consultation on the EU approach against wildlife trafficking*. 26.11.2014 SWD (2014) 347 final. Brussels: European Commission.

European Commission. (2014c). *New EU initiative to protect biodiversity and fight wildlife crime* [press release]. Accessed on September 24, 2014. http://europa.eu/rapid/press-release_IP-14-593_en.htm

European Commission. (2016a). *Analysis and evidence in support of the EU action plan against wildlife trafficking accompanying the document EU action plan against wildlife trafficking*. Accessed on July 1, 2016. http://eur-lex.europa.eu/legal-content/EN/TXT/?uri=SWD:2016:38:FIN

European Commission. (2016b). *EU action plan against wildlife trafficking*. Accessed on July 1, 2016. http://eur-lex.europa.eu/legal-content/EN/TXT/?uri=COM:2016:87:FIN

Europol. (2013). *Threat assessment 2013 environmental crime in the EU*. Accessed on January 19, 2015. www.europol.europa.eu/publications-documents/threat-assessment-2013-environmental-crime-in-eu

Fajardo del Castillo, T. (2016). The European Union's approach in the fight against wildlife trafficking: Challenges ahead. *Journal of International Wildlife Law and Policy*, *19*(1), 1–21.

Faure, M., Philipsen, N., Fajardo del Castillo, T., Farmer, A., Gerstetter, C., Germani, . . . Veening, W. (2016). Conclusions and recommendations: Deliverable no.7.4. *EFFACE: European Action to Fight Environmental Crime*. Accessed on February 1, 2018. http://efface.eu/sites/default/files/publications/EFFACE_Conclusions_recommendations.pdf

Ferrell, J. (1997). Criminological verstehen: Inside the immediacy of crime. *Justice Quarterly*, *14*(1), 3–23.

Fine, L. M. (2000). Rights of men, rites of passage: Hunting and masculinity at Reo Motors of Lansing, Michigan, 1945–1975. *Journal of Social History*, *33*(4), 805–823.

Fitzgerald, A. J. (2010). The "underdog" as "ideal victim"? The attribution of victimhood in the 2007 pet food recall. *International Review of Victimology*, *17*(2), 131–157.

Foley, E. K-E., Stengel, C., & Shepherd, C. (2011). *Pills, powders, vials and flakes: The bear bile trade in Asia*. A TRAFFIC SouthEast Asia report. Petaling Jaya, Selangor, Malaysia: TRAFFIC.

Foreign & Commonwealth Office (2014). *Declaration: London Conference on the Illegal Wildlife Trade*. Available at: https://www.gov.uk/government/publications/declaration-london-conference-on-the-illegal-wildlife-trade. Accessed on September 24, 2014.

Formanek, R. (2003). Why they collect: Collectors reveal their motivations. In S. M. Pearce (Ed.), *Interpreting objects and collections* (pp. 327–446). London and New York: Routledge.

Fox, R. (2003). *Food and eating: An anthropological perspective*. Oxford: SIRC.

Francione, G. (2009). *Animals as persons: Essays on the abolition of animal exploitation*. New York: Columbia University Press.

Franco, F. (2001). Reseña de 'Hechicería, brujería e inquisición en el Nuevo Reino de Granada (Un duelo de imaginarios)' de Diana Luz Ceballos Gómez. *Boletín Antropológico*, *1*(51), 86–90, Mérida, Venezuela: Universidad de los Andes.

Francione, G. (2014). Animal welfare and the moral value of nonhuman animals. In E. A. Cederholm, A. Björck, K. Jennbert, & A.-S. Lönngren (Eds.), *Exploring the animal turn: Human-animal relations in science, society and culture* (pp. 57–72). Lund, Sweden: Pupendorfinstitutet.

Fuchs, C. (2008). Convention on International Trade in Endangered Species of Wild Fauna and Flora (CITES)-Conservation Efforts Undermine the Legality Principle. *German Law Journal*, 9, 1565.

Gadamer, H. G. (1975). Hermeneutics and social science. *Cultural Hermeneutics*, 2(4), 307–316.

Gaard, G. (1993). Living interconnections with animals and nature. In G. Gaard (Ed.), *Ecofeminism: Women, animals, nature* (pp. 1–13). Philadelphia, PA: Temple University Press.

Gould, S. J. (1996). *The mismeasure of man*. New York: WW Norton & Company.

Gålmark, L. (2008). Aristotle revisited: Anthro-andocentrism and meat normativity. In R. Sollund (Ed.), *Global harms: Ecological crime and speciesism* (pp. 87–108). New York: Nova Science Publishers.

Gålmark, L. (2016). *Revolutionens rosenvatten* [The rosewater of the revolution]. Stockholm: Dela förlag.

Gastañaga, M., MacLeod, R., Hennessey, B., Nunez, J. U., Puse, E., Arrascue, A., . . . Engblom, G. (2011). A study of the parrot trade in Peru and the potential importance of internal trade for threatened species. *Bird Conservation International*, *21*(1), 76–85.

Gaveau, D. L., Wich, S., Epting, J., Juhn, D., Kanninen, M., & Leader-Williams, N. (2009). The future of forests and orangutans (Pongo abelii) in Sumatra: Predicting impacts of oil palm plantations, road construction, and mechanisms for reducing carbon emissions from deforestation. *Environmental Research Letters*, *4*(3), 034013.

Gibbon, J. W., Scott, D. E., Ryan, T. J., Buhlmann, K. A., Tuberville, T. D., Metts, B. S., . . . Winne, C. T. (2000). The global decline of reptiles, déjà vu amphibians: Reptile species are declining on a global scale. Six significant threats to reptile populations are habitat loss and degradation, introduced invasive species, environmental pollution, disease, unsustainable use, and global climate change. *BioScience*, *50*(8), 653–666.

Gibbs, C., Gore, M. L., McGarrell, E. F., & Rivers III, L. (2010). Introducing conservation criminology: Towards interdisciplinary scholarship on environmental crimes and risks. *The British Journal of Criminology*, *50*(1), 124–144.

Gilligan, C. (1982). *In a different voice*. Cambridge: Harvard University Press.

Glaser, B., & Strauss, A. (1967). *The discovery of grounded theory: Strategies for qualitative research*. Chicago, IL: Aldine Publishing Company.

Goffman, E. (1978/1956). *The presentation of self in everyday life*. Harmondsworth: Penguin.

Goldstein, H. (1990). *Problem-oriented policing*. New York: McGraw-Hill.

Gonzales, J. (2003). Harvesting, local trade, and conservation of parrots in the northeastern Peruvian Amazon. *Biological Conservation, 114*, 437–446.

Goyes, D. R. (2015). Denying the harms of animal abductions for biomedical research. In R. Sollund (Ed.), *Green harms and crimes: Critical criminology in a changing world* (pp. 170–188). London: Palgrave Macmillan.

Goyes, D. R. (2016). Land uses and conflict in Colombia. In A. Brisman, N. South, & R. White (Eds.), *Environmental crime and social conflict: Contemporary and emerging Issues* (pp. 75–94). Farnham: Ashgate.

Goyes, D. R., Mol, H., Brisman, A., & South, N. (Eds.). (2017). *Environmental crime in Latin America: The theft of nature and the poisoning of the land*. London: Palgrave Macmillan.

Goyes, D. R., & Sollund, R. (2016). Contesting and contextualizing CITES: Wildlife trafficking in Colombia and Brazil. *Journal for Crime, Justice and Social Democracy, 5*(4), 87–10. www.crimejusticejournal.com/article/view/331

Goyes, D. R., & Sollund, R. (2018). Animal abuse, biotechnology and species justice. *Theoretical Criminology, 22*(3), 363–383. Goyes, D. R., & South, N. (2015). Land-grabs, biopiracy and the inversion of justice in Colombia. *British Journal of Criminology, 56*(3), 558–577.

Goyes, D. R., Mol, H., Brisman, A., & South, N. (Eds.). (2017). *Environmental crime in Latin America: The theft of nature and the poisoning of the land*. London: Palgrave Macmillan.

Gray, T. N., Marx, N., Khem, V., Lague, D., Nijman, V., & Gauntlett, S. (2017). Holistic management of live animals confiscated from illegal wildlife trade. *Journal of Applied Ecology, 54*(3), 726–730.

Griffiths, M. (1999). Gambling technologies: Prospects for problem gambling. *Journal of Gambling Studies, 15*(3), 265–293.

Griffiths, M. (2003). Internet gambling: Issues, concerns, and recommendations. *Cyber Psychology and Behaviour, 6*(6), 557–568.

Grønli, K. S. (2004). Hvor mange husdyr tar rovdyra i Norge? [How many domesticated animals are taken by predators in Norway?]. *Forskning.no*. Accessed on November 8, 2016. http://forskning.no/biologi-rovdyr-okologi-politikk/2008/02/hvor-mange-husdyr-tar-rovdyra-i-norge

Gruen, L. (1993). Dismantling oppression: An analysis of the connection between women and animals. In G. Gaard (Ed.), *Ecofeminism: Women, animals, nature* (pp. 60–91). Philadelphia: Temple University Press.

Guía para el control al trafico ilegal de fauna silvestre colombiana. (2007). *Técnicos Fauna Autoridades Ambientales Participantes* [Guide for the control of illegal trafficking in wild Colombian fauna]. Accessed on November 21, 2017. http://cmap.upb.edu.co/rid=1196367690281_1423547947_682/guia%20control%20ilegal%20ultima%20version%20noviembre.doc

Guzmán, J., Saldaña, M., Teyeliz, A., Grosselet, M., & Gamez, J. (2007). *The illegal parrot trade in Mexico: Defenders of wildlife*. Accessed on June 25, 2014. www.defenders.org/mexicanparrot

Haemig, P. D. (2012). Ecology of the ocelot and margay. *Ecology.Info #9*. Accessed on March 5, 2018. www.ecology.info/ecology-ocelot-margay.htm

Hagstedt, J., & Korsell, L. (2012). Unlawful hunting of large carnivores in Sweden. In R. Ellefsen, R. Sollund, & G. Larsen (Eds.), *Eco-global crimes: Contemporary problems and future challenges* (pp. 209–232). Farnham: Ashgate.

Hall, R. J., Milner-Gulland, E. J., & Courchamp, F. (2008). Endangering the endangered: The effects of perceived rarity on species exploitation. *Conservation Letters, 1*(2), 75–81.

Hallsworth, S. (2008). Imaginary spaces and real relations. In R. Sollund (Ed.), *Global harms: Ecological crime and speciesism* (pp. 71–87). New York: Nova Science Publishers.

Halsey, M., & White, R. (1998). Crime, ecophilosophy and environmental harm. *Theoretical Criminology, 2*(3), 345–371.

Hansen, A. L. M., Li, A., Joly, D., Mekaru, S., & Brownstein, J. S. (2012). Digital surveillance: A novel approach to monitoring the illegal wildlife trade. *PLoS One 7*(12), 1–12. http://dx.doi.org/10.1371/journal.pone.0051156

Harari, Y. N. (2014). *Sapiens: A brief history of humankind*. New York: Vintage.

Harding, S., & Norberg, K. (2005). New feminist approaches to social science methodologies: An introduction. *Signs, 30*(4), 2009–2015.

Harding, S. (1995). 'Strong objectivity': A response to the new objectivity question. *Synthese, 104*(3), 331–249.

Harding, S. G. (Ed.). (1987). *Feminism and methodology: Social science issues*. Bloomington: Indiana University Press.

Harding, S. (2004). Introduction. In S. Harding (Ed.), *The feminist standpoint theory reader: Intellectual and political controversies* (pp. 1–16). New York: Routledge.

Harrison, J. R., Roberts, D. L., & Hernandez-Castro, J. C. (2016). Assessing the extent and nature of wildlife trade on the darkweb. *Conservation Biology, 30*(4), 900–904. doi:10.1111/cobi.12707

Herbig, J. (2010). The illegal reptile trade as a form of conservation crime: A South African criminological investigation. In R. White (Ed.), *Global environmental harm: Criminological perspectives* (pp. 110–131). Devon, UK: Willan Publishing.

Hermansen, K. H. (2018). *"Dyrepoliti" i Norge og Sverige. En kvalitativ studie av politi- og tilsynsmyndigheters arbeid mot dyrevelferdskriminalitet* (MA thesis). University of Oslo, Deptartment of Criminology and Sociology of Law.

Herrera, M., & Hennessey, B. (2007). Quantifying the illegal trade in Santa Cruz de la Sierra, Bolivia, with emphasis on threatened species. *Bird Conservation International, 17*, 295–300.

Hessen, D. (2013). Hvor unikt er mennesket? In R. Sollund, M. Tønnessen, & G. Larsen (Eds.), *Hvem er villest I landet her? Råskap mot dyr og natur I antropocen, menneskets tidsalderi*. Oslo: Spartacus SAP.

Higgins, P., Short, D., & South, N. (2013). Protecting the planet: A proposal for a law of ecocide. *Crime, Law and Social Change, 59*, 251–266. https://doi.org/10.1007/s10611-013-9413-6

Hill, J. F. (2015). A systems thinking perspective on the motivations and mechanisms driving wildlife poaching. In R. Sollund (Ed.), *Green harms and crime: Critical criminology in a changing world* (pp. 189–219). London: Palgrave Macmillan.

Hillyard, P., Pantazis, C., Tombs, S., & Gordon, D. (Eds.). (2004). *Beyond criminology? Taking harm seriously*. London: Pluto Press.

Holmes, G. (2016). Conservation crime as political protest. In J. Donnermeyer (Ed.), *The Routledge international handbook of rural criminology* (pp. 309–318). London: Routledge.

Høviskeland, H. T. (2017). Høyesterettspraksis om miljøkriminalitet fra de siste 15 år [The Supreme Court's practice concerning environmental crime from the past 15 years]. *Miljøkrim1*, *17*, 5–24.

Hutton, J., & Dickson, B. (Eds.). (2000). *Endangered species threatened convention.* London: Earthscan.

INFORME DE GESTION CENTRO DE RECEPCION DE FLORA Y FAUNA SILVESTRE CRFFS INFORME FINAL CONTRATO 0738 SDA-UDCA. (2012). Bogotá [Secretaria distrital de ambiente SDA Dirección de evaluación y seguimiento ambiental: Subdirección silvicultura flora y fauna Silvestre].

International Fund for Animal Welfare [IFAW]. (2008). *Killing with keystrokes: An investigation of the illegal wildlife trade on the world wide web.* Accessed on June 14, 2011. www.ifaw.org/Publications/Program_Publications/Wildlife_Trade/Campaign_Scientific_Publications/asset_upload_file64_12456.pdf

Interpol. (n.d.). *Environmental crime.* www.interpol.int/Crime-areas/Environmental-crime/Environmental-crime

Interpol and International Fund for Animal Welfare [IFAW]. (2013). Environmental crime programme: *Project web: An investigation into the ivory trade over the internet within the European Union.* Environmental Crime Program. INTERPOL. https://s3.amazonaws.com/ifaw-pantheon/sites/default/files/legacy/Project%20Web%20-%20PUBLIC.pdf

Isaacs, J. C. (2000). The limited potential of ecotourism to contribute to wildlife conservation. *Wildlife Society Bulletin*, *28*(1), 61–69.

Istad, T. (2008). Trenger vi straffeloven §152b? [Do we need the Penal Law's §152b?]. *Miljøkrim*, *2.* www.okokrim.no/trenger-vi-straffeloven-s-152-b.416453.no.html

Istad, T., & Vigane, A. (2016, May 1). Netthandel med truede arter til eBay og tilbake [Internet trade of endangered species to eBay and back]. *Miljøkrim.* www.okokrim.no/netthandel-med-truede-arter-til-ebay-og-tilbake.416402.nn.html

Jahoda, M. (1982). *Employment and unemployment: A social-psychological analysis.* Cambridge: Cambridge University Press.

Jentsch, J. D., Olausson, P., De La Garza, R., & Taylor, J. R. (2002). Impairments of reversal learning and response perseveration after repeated, intermittent cocaine administrations to monkeys. *Neuropsychopharmacology*, *26*(2), 183–190.

Johansen, P. O. (2013). The Norwegian alcohol prohibition: A failure. *Journal of Scandinavian Studies in Criminology and Crime Prevention*, *14*(supl), 46–63.

Jørgensen, M. W., & Phillips, L. J. (2002). *Discourse analysis as theory and method.* Thousand Oaks, CA: Sage.

Kemmerer, L. (2011). *Sister species: Women, animals and social justice.* Chicago: University of Illinois Press.

Kheel, M. (1993). The ecofeminist challenge. In G. Gaard (Ed.), *Ecofeminism: Women, animals, nature* (pp. 243–272). Philadelphia: Temple University Press.

Kheel, M. (1996). The liberation of nature: A circular affair. In J. Donovan & C. Adams (Eds.), *Beyond animal rights: A feminist caring ethic for the treatment of animals* (pp. 17–34). New York: Continuum.

Kheel, M. (2008). *Nature ethics: An ecofeminist perspective.* Lanham, NJ: Rowman & Littlefield Publishers.

Kievit, H. (2000). Conservation of the Nile crocodile: Has CITES helped or hindered? In J. Hutton & B. Dickson (Eds.), *Endangered species, threatened convention: The past, present and future of CITES* (pp. 88–97). London: Earthscan.

Kolbert, E. (2014). *The sixth extinction: An unnatural history*. New York: Harry Holt.

Kurpiers, L. A., Schulte-Herbrüggen, B., Ejotre, I., & Reeder, D. M. (2016). Bushmeat and emerging infectious diseases: Lessons from Africa. In F. Angelici (Ed.), *Problematic wildlife: A cross-disciplinary approach* (pp. 507–551). Heidelberg: Springer International Publishing.

Kymlicka, W., & Donaldson, S. (2011). Zoopolis. *A political theory of animal rights*. Oxford: Oxford University Press.

Laland, K. N., & Hoppitt, W. (2003). Do animals have culture? *Evolutionary Anthropology: Issues, News, and Reviews, 12*(3), 150–159.

Larsen, G. (2012). The most serious crime: Eco-genocide concepts and perspectives in eco-global criminology. In R. Ellfesen, R. Sollund, & G. Larsen (Eds.), *Eco-global crimes: Contemporary problems and future challenges* (pp. 33–57). Farnham: Ashgate.

Larsen, G. (2013). Kuas tildelte rolle som matobjekt [The cow's attributed role as food object]. In R. Sollund, M. Tønnessen, & G. Larsen (Eds.), *Hvem er villest i landet her? Råskap mot dyr og natur i antropocen – menneskets tidsalder* [Who is the wildest in the country? Cruelty against animals and nature in the Anthropocene: The human era] (pp. 131–165). Oslo: Spartacus SAP.

Lavorgna, A. (2014). Wildlife trafficking in the internet age. *Crime Science, 3*(1), 1–12.

Lavorgna, A. (2015). The social organisation of pet trafficking in cyberspace. *European Journal on Criminal Policy and Research, 21*(3), 1–18.

Lawson, K., & Vines, A. (2014). *Global impacts of the illegal wildlife trade: The costs of crime, insecurity and institutional erosion*. London, UK: Chatham House.

Leal, M., & Powell, B. J. (2012). Behavioural flexibility and problem-solving in a tropical lizard. *Biology Letters, 8*(1), 28–30.

Leberatto, A. C. (2016). Understanding the illegal trade of live wildlife species in Peru. *Trends in Organized Crime, 19*(1), 42–66.

Lee, J. (1996). Poachers, tigers and bears . . . oh my! Asia's illegal wildlife trade. *Northwestern Journal of International Law and Business, 498*(16), 495–515.

Lemieux, A. (Ed.). (2014). *Situational prevention of poaching*. London: Routledge.

Lemieux, A., & Clarke, R. (2009). The international ban on ivory sales and its effects on elephant poaching in Africa. *British Journal of Criminology, 49*(4), 451–471.

Lenth, L., Bøckman, P., & Tønnessen, M. (2018). *Ulvetider: Rovdyret som splitter Norge*. Oslo: Vega.

Levi, M., & Maguire, M. (2004). Reducing and preventing organised crime: An evidence-based critique. *Crime, Law and Social Change, 42*(5), 397–469.

Liberg, O., Chapron, G., Wabakken, P., Pedersen, H. C., Hobbs, N. T., & Sand, H. (2012). Shoot, shovel and shut up: Cryptic poaching slows restoration of a large carnivore in Europe. *Proceedings of the Royal Society of Britain, 279*(1730), 910–915.

Lie, M. S. (2017). "Stepdogs" of society: The impact of breed bans in Norway. *Critical Criminology, 25*(2), 293–309.

Lie, M. S., & Sollund, R. (2017). Speciesism and theriocide. In E. Carrabine, A. Brisman, & N. South (Eds.), *The Routledge companion to criminological theory and concepts* (pp. 386–390). London: Routledge.

Lin, J. (2005). Tackling Southeast Asia's illegal wildlife trade. *Singapore Yearbook of International Law*, *9*, 191–208.

Logan, F. D. (2013). *The Vikings in history*. London: Routledge.

Lowther, J., Cook, D., & Roberts, M. (2002). *Crime and punishment in the wildlife trade*. WWF/Traffic. Wolverhampton: University of Wolverhampton.

Lozano-Ortega, I., Zangen, S., Rojas, S., Suarez, C., Durán, C., Pereira, V., & Nassar-Montoya, F. (n.d.). *Guia basica para el manejo de fauna peridecomiso*. Accessed on March 20, 2018. http://ambientebogota.gov.co/documents/10157/2447683/8.+GU%C3%8DA+B%C3%81SICA+PARA+EL+MANEJO+DE+FAUNA+PERIDECOMISO+EN+EL+CRRFS.pdf

Luke, B. (1998). Violent love: Hunting, heterosexuality, and the erotics of men's predation. *Feminist Studies*, *24*(3), 627–655.

Lynch, M. J., Long, M., & Stretesky, P. (2015). Anthropogenic development drives species to be endangered: Capitalism and the decline of species. In R. Sollund (Ed.), *Green harms and crimes: Critical criminology in a changing world* (pp. 117–146). London: Palgrave Macmillan.

Lynch, M. J., & Stretesky, P. B. (2014). *Exploring green criminology: Toward a green criminological revolution*. London: Routledge.

Lynch, M. J., Stretesky, P. B., & Long, M. A. (2018). Green criminology and native peoples: The treadmill of production and the killing of indigenous environmental activists. *Theoretical Criminology*, *22*(3), 318–341.

Lyons, J. A., & Natusch, D. J. (2011). Wildlife laundering through breeding farms: Illegal harvest, population declines and a means of regulating the trade of green pythons (Morelia viridis) from Indonesia. *Biological Conservation*, *144*(12), 3073–3081.

Maher, J., & Pierpoint, H. (2011). Friends, status symbols and weapons: the use of dogs by youth groups and youth gangs. *Crime, law and social change*, *55*(5), 405–420.

Maher, J., & Sollund, R. (2016a). Law enforcement of the illegal wildlife trade: A comparative strengths, weaknesses, opportunities and threats [SWOT] analysis of the UK and Norway. *Journal of Trafficking, Organised Crime and Security*, *2*(1). www.brownwalker.com/ojs/index.php/JTOCS/article/view/55

Maher, J., & Sollund, R. (2016b). Wildlife trafficking: Harms and victimization. In R. Sollund, C. S. Stefes, & A. R. Germani (Eds.), *Fighting environmental crime in Europe and beyond: The role of the EU and its member states* (pp. 99–128). London: Palgrave Macmillan.

Maher, J., Sollund, R., & Fajardo, T. (2014). Response to the EU Commission's consultation on wildlife trafficking. *Statement on behalf of the research project European Union Action to Fight Environmental Crime (EFFACE)*. Accessed on March 23, 2018. http://efface.eu/sites/default/files/publications/EFFACE_contribution_WLT_consultation_April2014.pdf

Maldonado, Á. M. (2011). Tráfico de monos nocturnos *Aotus* spp. en la frontera entre Colombia, Perú y Brasil: Efectos sobre sus poblaciones silvestres y violación de las regulaciones internacionales de comercio de fauna estipuladas por CITES [Trafficking in night monkeys, *Aotus* spp.: On the Colombian, Peruvian and Brazilian border: Effects on the wild populations and breaches of international CITES regulations of fauna]. *Revista de la Academia Colombiana de Ciencias Exactas, Físicas y Naturales*, *35*(135), 225–242.

Maldonado, Á. M., & Lafon, T. (2017). Biomedical research vs. biodiversity conservation in the Colombian-Peruvian Amazon: Searching for law enforcement where there is lack of accountability. In *Environmental crime in Latin America* (pp. 261–294). London: Palgrave Macmillan.

Maldonado, Á. M., Nijman, V., & Bearder, S. K. (2009). Trade in night monkeys *Aotus* spp. In the Brazil-Colombia-Peru tri-border area: International wildlife trade regulations are ineffectively enforced. *Endangered Species Research*, *9*(2), 143–149.

Maldonado, Á. M., & Peck, M. R. (2014). Research and in situ conservation of owl monkeys enhances environmental law enforcement at the Colombian-Peruvian border. *American Journal of Primatology*, *76*(7), 658–669.

Maldonado, Á. M., & Waters, S. (2017). Primate trade (neotropics). In A. Fuentes (Ed.), *The International Encyclopedia of Primatology*. New Jersey: John Wiley & Sons. doi:10.1002/9781119179313.wbprim0393

Manrod, J. D., Hartdegen, R., & Burghardt, G. M. (2008). Rapid solving of a problem apparatus by juvenile black-throated monitor lizards (*Varanus albigularis albigularis*). *Animal Cognition*, *11*(2), 267–273.

Martinsen, S. (2013). Dyrs verdi i lys av utvalgte fangsttradisjoner [Animals' value in view of selected methods of capturing]. In R. Sollund, M. Tønnessen, & G. Larsen (Eds.), *Hvem er villest i landet her? Råskap mot dyr og natur i antropocen – menneskets tidsalder* [Who is the wildest in the country? Cruelty against animals and nature in the Anthropocene: The human era] (pp. 99–121). Oslo: Spartacus SAP.

Mateus, D. & Brieva, C. (2010). *Informe de liberación de cuatro monos maiceros (Cebus apella)*. Unidad de rescate y rehabilitación de animales silvestres. Bogotá, Colombia: URRAS and Corpoorinoquia.

Mathiesen. T. (1990). *Retten i Samfunnet. En Innføring i Rettssosiologi* [Law in society: An introduction to sociology of law]. Oslo: Pax forlag.

Mathismoen, O. (2018). *Bønder fikk erstatning for 840 drepte sauer. Én svensk ulvetispe sto bak* [Farmers received compensation for 840 killed sheep]. www.aftenposten.no/viten/i/kaw6Ma/Bonder-fikk-erstatning-for-840-drepte-sauer-n-svensk-ulvetispe-sto-bak?spid_rel=2

Mazurek, K. (2017). Fish used in aquariums: Nemo's plight. In J. Maher, H. Pierpoint, & P. Berine (Eds.), *The Palgrave international handbook of animal abuse studies* (pp. 313–336). London: Palgrave.

McIntosh, W. D., & Schmeichel, B. (2004). Collectors and collecting: A social psychological perspective. *Leisure Sciences*, *26*, 85–97.

Miljødirektoratet (n.d.). Handel med trua arter (Cites) http://www.miljodirektoratet.no/no/Tema/Arter-og-naturtyper/Handel-med-trua-arter-CITES/

Militz, T. A., & Foale, S. (2017). The "Nemo effect": Perception and reality of Finding Nemo's impact on marine aquarium fisheries. *Fish and Fisheries*, *18*(3), 596–606.

Milliken, T., & Shaw, J. (2012). *The South Africa: Viet Nam rhino horn trade nexus: A deadly combination of institutional lapses, corrupt wildlife industry professionals and Asian crime syndicates*. Johannesburg: TRAFFIC.

Mills, L. S., Soule, M. E., & Doak, D. F. (1993). The keystone-species concept in ecology and conservation. *BioScience*, *43*(4), 219–224.

Minnaar, A. (2014). The poaching of rhino in South Africa: A conservation, organised and economic crime? In D. Sorvatzioti, G. Antonopolous, G. Papanicoulaou, & R. Sollund (Eds.), *Critical views on crime, policy and social control* (pp. 196–227). Nicosia: University of Nicosia Press.

Mol, H. (2013). "A gift from the tropics to the world": Power, harm and palm oil. In R. Walters, S. Westerhuis, & T. Wyatt (Eds.), *Emerging issues in green criminology: Exploring power, justice and harm* (pp. 242–260). London: Palgrave Macmillan.

Moore, A. N. (2005). Defining animals as crime victims. *Journal of Animal Law, 1*, 91–108.

Mowbray, S. (2015). Oil roads to ecological ruin: Ecuador's bushmeat and wildlife trade. *Mongabay*. Accessed on January 3, 2016. https://news.mongabay.com/2015/10/oil-roads-to-ecological-ruin-ecuadors-bushmeat-and-wildlife-trade/

Nassaro, M. R. F. (2017). Wildlife trafficking in the state of São Paolo, Brazil. In D. R. Goyes, H. Mol, A. Brisman, & N. South (Eds.), *Environmental crime in Latin America: The theft of nature and the poisoning of the land* (pp. 245–260). London: Palgrave Macmillan.

Natali, L., & McClanahan, B. (2017). Perceiving and communicating environmental contamination and change: Towards a green cultural criminology with images. *Critical Criminology, 25*(2), 199–214.

Natusch, D. J. D., & Lyons, J. A. (2012). Exploited for pets: The harvest and trade of amphibians and reptiles from Indonesian New Guinea. *Biodiversity and Conservation, 21*, 2899–2911. https://doi.org/10.1007/s10531-012-0345-8

Nekaris, K. A. I., Campbell, N., Coggins, T. G., Rode, E. J., & Nijman, V. (2013). Tickled to death: Analysing public perceptions of "cute" videos of threatened species (slow lorises: *Nycticebus* spp.) on Web 2.0 Sites. *PLoS One, 8*(7), e69215.

Nekaris, K. A. I., Musing, L., Vazquez, A. G., & Donati, G. (2015). Is tickling torture? Assessing welfare towards slow lorises (*Nycticebus* spp.) within Web 2.0 videos. *Folia Primatologica, 86*(6), 534–551.

Nibert, D. A. (2002). *Animal rights/human rights: Entanglements of oppression and liberation*. Lanham: Rowman & Littlefield Publishers.

Nibert, D. A. (2013). *Animal oppression and human violence: Domesecration, capitalism, and global conflict*. New York: Columbia University Press.

Nijman, V. (2010). An overview of international wildlife trade from Southeast Asia. *Biodiversity and Conservation, 19*, 1101–1114.

Nijman, V., & Nekaris, K. A. I. (2017). The Harry Potter effect: The rise in trade of owls as pets in Java and Bali, Indonesia. *Global Ecology and Conservation, 11*, 84–94.

Nijman, V., & Shepherd, C. R. (2010). The role of Asia in the global trade in CITES II-listed poison arrow frogs: Hopping from Kazakhstan to Lebanon to Thailand and beyond. *Biodiversity and Conservation, 19*(7), 1963–1970.

Norwegian National Research Ethics Committee. (2014). *Ethical guidelines*. Accessed on January 19, 2015. www.etikkom.no/en/

Norwegian Environment Agency (2016). *Autoriserte preparanter i Norge* [Authorised taxidermists in Norway]. Accessed on November 8, 2016. www.miljodirektoratet.no/Global/dokumenter/tema/jakt_og_fiske/autoriserte-preparanter-norge.pdf

Norwegian Social Science Data Services. (2014). *Norwegian Social Science Data Services* [online]. Accessed on January 19, 2015. www.nsd.uib.no/nsd/english/index.html

Noske, B. (1989). *Humans and other animals: Beyond the boundaries of anthropology*. London: Pluto Press.

NOU. (2012). *Utenfor og innenfor. Norges avtaler med EU. Departementenes servicesenter. Norges offentlige utredninger* [Outside and inside: Norway's agreements with the EU: Norway's public inquiries]. Statsministerens kontor [Prime Minsiter's Office]. https://www.regjeringen.no/contentassets/5d3982d042a2472eb1b20639cd8b2341/no/pdfs/nou201220120002000dddpdfs.pdf

Nurse, A. (2011). Policing wildlife: Perspectives on criminality in wildlife crime. *Papers from the British Criminology Conference*, *11*, 38–53.

Nurse, A. (2013). *Animal harm: Perspectives on why people harm and kill animals.* London: Routledge.

Nurse, A. (2015). *Policing wildlife: Perspectives on the enforcement of wildlife legislation.* Basingstoke: Palgrave.

Nussbaum, M. C. (2009). *Frontiers of justice: Disability, nationality, species membership.* Cambridge, MA: Harvard University Press.

Öhman, A., & Mineka, S. (2003). The malicious serpent snakes as a prototypical stimulus for an evolved module of fear. *Current Directions in Psychological Science*, *12*(1), 5–9.

Oslo havn/Port of Oslo. (2012). *Ny mobil tollskanner til Oslo* [New mobile customs scanner to Oslo]. Accessed on March 7, 2017. www.ohv.oslo.no/no/nyheter/2012/Ny+mobil+tollskanner+til+Oslo.b7C_wlfUZL.ips

Ot.prp. nr. 54, innst. O. nr. 111, besl. O. nr. 115 for 1992–93 Lov om endringer i viltloven (faunakriminalitet) (ulv) (redet vilt) [Law preparatory work: Law concerning changes in the wildlife act: Norwegian Parliament]. www.stortinget.no/no/Saker-og-publikasjoner/Saker/Sak/?p=4771

Palmer, C. T. (1988). Twelve reasons why rape is not sexually motivated: A skeptical examination. *Journal of Sex Research*, *25*(4), 512–530.

Parathian, H. E., & Maldonado, A. M. (2010). Human: Nonhuman primate interactions amongst Tikuna people: Perceptions and local initiatives for resource management in Amacayacu in the Colombian Amazon. *American Journal of Primatology*, *72*(10), 855–865.

Pavanelli, G. C., Yamaguchi, M. U., Calaça, E. A., & Oda, F. H. (2017). Scientometrics of zoonoses transmitted by the giant African snail Achatina fulica Bowdich, 1822. *Revista do Instituto de Medicina Tropical de São Paulo*, *59*.

Payán, E., & Trujillo, L. A. (2006). The tigrilladas in Colombia. *Cat News*, *44*, 25–28.

Pearce, S. M. (2003). The urge to collect. In S. M. Pearce (Ed.), *Interpreting objects and collections* (pp. 157–160). London and New York: Routledge.

Pearson, H. (2003). Mouse intelligence measured: Rodent "g" might reveal genes for intellect. *Nature*. doi:10.1038/news030728-9

Pelcastre, J. (2016, November 8). *Armada Nacional de Colombia enfocada en la seguridad y defensa del medio ambiente* [The Colombian National Army focused on the security and defense of the natural environment]. Diálogo, Revista militar eléctronica. Accessed on November 10, 2017. https://dialogo-americas.com/es/articles/colombian-navy-focuses-environmental-security-and-defense

Pellow, D. N. (2013). Environmental justice, animal rights, and total liberation: From conflict and distance to points of common focus. In South, N. and Brisman, A. (Eds), *Routledge international handbook of green criminology* (pp. 347–362). London and New York: Routledge.

Pepperberg, I. M. (2007). Grey parrots do not always 'parrot': The roles of imitation and phonological awareness in the creation of new labels from existing vocalizations. *Language Sciences*, *29*(1), 1–13.

Pepperberg, I. M., Willner, M. R., & Gravitz, L. B. (1997). Development of Piagetian object permanence in grey parrot (Psittacus erithacus). *Journal of Comparative Psychology*, *111*(1), 63.

Peters, C., & Bodkin, C. P. (2007). An exploratory investigation of problematic online auction behaviors: Experiences of eBay users. *Journal of Retailing and Consumer Services*, *14*, 1–16.

Pickens, R., & Thompson, T. (1968). Cocaine-reinforced behavior in rats: Effects of reinforcement magnitude and fixed-ratio size. *Journal of Pharmacology and Experimental Therapeutics*, *161*(1), 122–129.

Pires, S., & Clarke, R. (2011). Are parrots craved? An analysis of parrot poaching in Mexico. *Journal of Research in Crime and Delinquency*, *49*(1), 122–146.

Pires, S., & Moreto, W. (2011). Preventing wildlife crimes: Solutions that can overcome the "Tragedy of the Commons". *European Journal of Crime Policy*, *17*(2), 101–123.

Presser, L., & Taylor, W. V. (2011). An autoethnography of hunting. *Crime, Law and Social Change*, *55*(5), 483–494.

Proctor, R. N. (1991). *Value-free science? Purity and power in modern knowledge*. Cambridge, MA: Harvard University Press.

Profauna. (2009). *Alleged illegal zoo trade in Indonesia*. Accessed on October 14, 2016. www.profauna.org/content/en/pressrelease/2009/international_concern_over_alleged_illegal_zoo_trade_in_indonesia.html

Ramp, D., & Bekoff, M. (2015). Compassion as a practical and evolved ethic for conservation. *BioScience*, *65*(3), 323–327.

Reeve, R. (2002). *Policing international trade in endangered species: The CITES treaty and compliance*. London: Earthscan.

Regan, T. (1987). The case for animal rights. In M. W. Fox & L. Mickley (Eds.), *Advances in animal welfare science* (pp. 179–189). Amsterdam: Springer.

Regan, T. (2004). *Empty cages: Facing the challenges of animal rights*. Oxford: Rowman & Littlefield Publishers.

Renctas. (2001). *1st national report on the traffic of wild animals*. Accessed on December 5, 2014. www.renctas.org.br/wp-content/uploads/2014/02/RELATORIO-INGLES_final.pdf

Risan, L. C. (2003). *Hva er ei ku? Norsk Rødt Fe som teknovitenskap og naturkultur* [What is a cow: Norwegian red cattle as techno science and natureculture]. Oslo: Unipub.

Risan, L. C. (2005). The boundary of animality. *Environment and Planning D: Society and Space*, *23*(5), 787–793.

Rivalan, P., Delmas, V., Angulo, E., Bull, L., Hall, R., Courchamp, F., Rosser A. M., & Leader-Williams, N. (2007). Can bans stimulate wildlife trade? *Nature*, *447*, 529–530.

Rodríguez, N. J. M., & García, O. R. (2008). Comercio de fauna silvestre en Colombia. *Revista Facultad Nacional de Agronomía*, *61*(2), 4618–4645.

Roldán-Clarà, B., Toledo, V. M., & Espejel, I. (2017). The use of birds as pets in Mexico. *Journal of Ethnobiology and Ethnomedicine*, *13*(35). https://doi.org/10.1186/s13002-017-0161-z

Rosen, G. E., & Smith, K. F. (2010). Summarising the evidence on the internationalisation of illegal wildlife. *EcoHealth*, 7, 24–32.

Royal Society for the Prevention of Cruelty to Animals (RSPCA). (n.d.). *Far from home: Reptiles that suffer and die in captivity*. Accessed on October 7, 2014. www.rspca.org.uk/.../LocateAsset%3Fasset=document

Runhovde, S. R. (2015). Seizures of inconvenience? Policy, discretion and accidental discoveries in policing the illegal wildlife trade at the Norwegian border. *Crime, Law and Social Change*, *64*(2–3), 177–192.

Runhovde, S. R. (2016). Taking the path of least resistance? Decision-making in police investigations of illegal wildlife trade. *Policing*, *11*(1), 87–102. https://doi.org/10.1093/police/paw026

Runhovde, S. R. (2017, January). Merely a transit country? Examining the role of Uganda in the transnational illegal ivory trade. *Trends in Organised Crime*, 1–20. doi:10.1007/s12117-016-9299-7

Sajeva, M., Augugliaro, C., Smith, M. J., & Oddo, E. (2013). Regulating internet trade in CITES species. *Conservation Biology*, *27*(2), 429–430.

Santana, G., & Chin, S. (2015). *Can cocaine production in Colombia be linked to environmental crime? A case study into the effect of EU legislation on the trade*. The Hague: Institute for Environmental Security.

Scheyvens, R. (1999). Ecotourism and the empowerment of local communities. *Tourism Management*, *20*(2), 245–249.

Schmidt, C. (2004). Environmental crimes: Profiting at the earth's expense. *Environmental Health Perspectives*, *112*(2), 96–103.

Schneider, J. (2008). Reducing the illicit trade in endangered wildlife: The market reduction approach. *Journal of Contemporary Criminal Justice*, *24*(3), 274–295.

Schneider, J. (2012). *Sold into extinction: The global trade in endangered species*. Santa Barbara, CA: Praeger.

Searle, J. (1995). *The construction of social reality*. New York: The Free Press.

Serpell, J. (1996). *In the company of animals*. Cambridge: Cambridge University Press.

Shapiro, K. (1994). The caring sleuth: Portrait of an animal rights activist. *Society & Animals*, *2*(2), 145–165.

Shepherd, C. R., Stengel, C. J., & Nijman, V. (2012). *The export and reexport of CITES-listed birds from the Solomon Islands*. Petaling Jaya, Selangor, Malaysia: TRAFFIC Southeast Asia.

Smith, L., & Klaas, K. (2015). *Networks and NGOs relevant to fighting environmental crime: Study in the framework of the Efface research project*. Berlin: Ecologic Institute. Available at: www.efface.eu.

Sina, S., Gerstetter, C., Porsch, L., Roberts, E., Smith, L. O., Klaas, K., & Fajardo del Castillo, T. (2016). *Study on wildlife crime*. Brussels: European Parliament.

Sinovas, P., Price, B., King, E., Hinsley, A., & Pavitt, A. (2017). *Wildlife trade in the Amazon countries: An analysis of trade in CITES listed species*. Technical report prepared for the Amazon Regional Program (BMZ/DGIS/GIZ). Cambridge: UN Environment–World Conservation Monitoring Centre.

Smart, C. (1989). *Feminism and the power of law*. London and New York: Routledge.

Smith, D. E. (1974). Women's perspective as a radical critique of sociology. *Sociological Inquiry*, *44*(1), 7–13.

Smuts, B. (1999). Reflections. In J. M. Coetzee (Ed.), *The lives of animals* (pp. 107–120). Princeton, NJ: Princeton University Press.

Sollund, R. (1999). *Kan vold forklares? [Can violence be explained?]*. Oslo: Spartacus.

Sollund, R. (2001). Political refugees' violence in Norway. *Journal of Scandinavian Studies in Criminology and Crime Prevention*, *2*(1), 84–103.

Sollund, R. (2004). *Rammer, rom og mobilitet. Innvandrerkvinners arbeidsliv [Frames, space and mobility: Immigrant women's work lives]*. Oslo: Unipax.

Sollund, R. (2007). The implementation of problem-oriented policing in Oslo-Norway: Not without problems. In K. Froeling (Ed.), *Criminology research focus* (pp. 175–194). New York: Nova Science Publishers.

Sollund, R. (2008a). Causes for speciesism: Difference, distance and denial. In R. Sollund (Ed.), *Global arms: Ecological crime and speciesism* (pp. 109–131). New York: Nova Science Publishers.

Sollund, R. (2008b). *Global harms: Ecological crime and speciesism*. New York: Nova Science Publishers.

Sollund, R. (2009). Menneskers paradoksale forhold til dyr [The paradox in the human-animal relationship]. *Sosiologi i dag*, *39*(3), 42–68.

Sollund, R. (2011). Expressions of speciesism: The effects of keeping companion animals on animal abuse, animal trafficking and species decline. *Crime, Law and Social Change*, *55*(5), 437–451.

Sollund, R. (2012a). Speciesism as doxic practice versus valuing difference and plurality. In R. Ellfesen, R. Sollund, & G. Larsen (Eds.), *Eco-global crimes: Contemporary problems and future challenges*. Farnham: Ashgate.

Sollund, R. (2012b). The essence of food and gender and the embodiment of migration. In R. Sollund (Ed.), *Transnational migration, gender and rights* (pp. 77–98). Bingley, UK: Emerald Group Publishing Limited.

Sollund, R. (2012c). Oil production, climate change and species decline: The case of Norway. In R. White (Ed.), *Climate change from a criminological perspective* (pp. 135–147). New York: Springer.

Sollund, R. (2012d). *Transnational migration, gender and rights*. Advances in ecopolitics, Vol. 10. Bingley: Emerald Publishing.

Sollund, R. (2013a). Animal trafficking and trade: Abuse and species injustice. In R. Walters, D. Westerhuis, & T. Wyatt (Eds.), *Emerging issues in green criminology: Exploring power, justice and harm* (pp. 72–92). Basingstoke, UK: Palgrave.

Sollund, R. (2013b).The victimization of women, children and non-human species through trafficking and trade: Crimes understood through an eco-feminist perspective. In N. South & A. Brisman (Eds.), *Routledge handbook in green criminology* (pp. 317–331). London: Routledge.

Sollund, R. (2014). A comment to Gary Francione: Animal rights versus animals as property and nature. In E. Andersson, A. B., Cederholm, K., Jennbert, & A.-S. Lõnngren (Eds.), *Exploring the animal turn* (pp. 73–88). Lund, Sweden: Pupendorf.

Sollund, R. (2015a). *Green harms and crimes. Critical Criminology in a changing world*. London: Palgrave.

Sollund, R. (2015b). With or without a license to kill: Human-predator conflicts and theriocide in Norway. In A. Brisman, N. South, & R. White (Eds.), *Environmental crime and social conflict: Contemporary and emerging issues* (pp. 95–124). Farmham, UK: Ashgate.

Sollund, R. (2015c). The illegal wildlife trade from a Norwegian outlook: Tendencies in practices and law enforcement. In R. Sollund (Ed.), *Green harms and crimes, Critical criminology in a changing world*. Basingstoke: Palgrave.

Sollund, R. (2016a). Introduction. In R. Sollund, C. S., Stefes, & A. R. Germani (Eds.), *Fighting environmental crime in Europe and beyond: The role of the EU and its member states* (pp. 1–16). Basingstoke: Palgrave.

Sollund, R. (2016b). The animal other: Legal and illegal theriocide. In M. Hall, T. Wyatt, N. South, A. Nurse, G. Potter, & J. Maher (Eds.), *Greening criminology in the 21st century: Contemporary debates and future directions in the study of environmental harm* (pp. 79–99). Abingdon, UK: Routledge.

Sollund, R. (2016c). Wildlife trafficking in a globalised world: An example of motivations and modus operandi from a Norwegian case study. In A. M. Francesco

(Ed.), *Problematic wildlife: A cross-disciplinary approach* (pp. 553–570). New York: Springer.

Sollund, R. (2017a). Doing green, critical criminology with an auto-ethnographic, feminist approach. *Critical Criminology*, *25*(2), 245–260.

Sollund, R. (2017b). Legal and illegal theriocide of trafficked animals. In P. Beirne, J. Maher, & H. Pierspoint (Eds.), *International handbook on animal abuse studies* (pp. 453–474). London: Palgrave Macmillan.

Sollund, R. (2017c). Perceptions and law enforcement of illegal and legal wolf killing in Norway: Organised crime or folk crime? *Palgrave Communications*, *3*. doi:10.1057/palcomms.2017.59

Sollund, R. (2017d). The use and abuse of animals in wildlife trafficking in Colombia: Practices, and injustice. In D. R. Goyes, H. Mol, A. Brisman, & N. South (Eds.), *Environmental crime in Latin America: The theft of nature and the poisoning of the land* (pp. 215–244). London: Palgrave Macmillan.

Sollund, R. (2018a). Umoralsk norsk ulvejakt. Den pågående jakten kan bety slutten for den norske ulvebestanden [Imoral Norwegian wolf hunt. The ongoing hunt could mean the end of the Norwegian wolf population.]. Op.ed. *Dagsavisen*. www.dagsavisen.no/nyemeninger/umoralsk-norsk-ulvejakt-1.1082939

Sollund, R. (2018b, May 14–16). *The Norwegian predator killing regime: Legal and moral issues*. Paper presented at The Scandinavian Research Council for Criminology (NSfK) 60th Research Seminar, Helsinki, Finland.

Sollund, R., & Brisman, A. (2017). Editors' introduction to the special issue, "researching environmental harm, doing green criminology". *Crit Crim*, *25*, 159. https://doi.org/10.1007/s10612-017-9354-

Sollund, R., & Maher, J. (2015). *The illegal wildlife trade: A case study report on the illegal wildlife trade in the United Kingdom, Norway, Colombia and Brazil*. EFFACE. Work package 4 'case studies'. www.ecologic.eu/sites/files/publication/2015/efface_illegal_wildlife_trade_in_united_kingdom_norway_colombia_and_brazil_0.pdf

South, N. (1998). A green field for criminology? A proposal for a perspective. *Theoretical Criminology*, *2*(2), 211–233.

South, N. (2008). Nature, difference and rejection of harm: Expanding the agenda for green criminology. In R. Sollund (Ed.), *Global harms: Ecological crime and speciesism* (pp. 187–200). New York: Nova Science Publishers.

South, N. (2014). Green criminology: Reflections, connections, horizons. *International Journal for Crime, Justice and Social Democracy*, *3*(2), 5–20.

South, N., Brisman, A., & Beirne, P. (2013). A guide to a green criminology. In N. South & A. Brisman (Eds.), *The Routledge international handbook of green criminology* (pp. 27–42). London: Routledge.

South, N., & Wyatt, T. (2011). Comparing illicit trades in wildlife and drugs: An exploratory study. *Deviant Behavior*, *32*(6), 538–561.

Southwick, N. (2013, November 28). 58,000 animales confiscados anualmente en Colombia [58,000 animals confiscated annually in Colombia]. *Insight crime*. Accessed on April 21, 2016. http://es.insightcrime.org/noticias-del-dia/58000-animales-traficados-son-confiscados-anualmente-en-colombia

Spapens, T. (2010). Macro networks, collectives, and business processes: An integrated approach to organised crime. *European Journal of Crime, Criminal Law and Criminal Justice*, *18*(2), 185–215.

Spiegel, M., & Walker, A. (1996). *The dreaded comparison: Human and animal slavery*. New York: Mirror Books.

Steiner, A. (2014). *Putting a stop to global environmental crime has become an imperative.* UN Chronicle Vol.LI No. 2 2014. Accessed on July 23, 2018. https://unchronicle.un.org/article/putting-stop-global-environmental-crime-has-become-imperative

Stoett, P. (2002). The international regulation of trade in wildlife: Institutional and normative considerations. *Politics, Law and Economics, 2*(2), 195–210.

Store Norske Leksikon. (2014, February 6). EØS: Avtalen. Accessed on January 26, 2015. https://snl.no/E%C3%98S-avtalen

Store Norske Leksikon. (2017, September 28). Anke – straffedommer. https://snl.no/anke_-_straffedommer

Stretesky, P., Long, M., & Lynch, M. (2013). *The treadmill of crime: Political economy and green criminology.* London: Routledge.

Suárez, E., Morales, M., Cueva, R., Utreras Bucheli, V., Zapata-Rios, G., Toral, E., . . . Vargas Olalla, J. (2009). Oil industry, wild meat trade and roads: Indirect effects of oil extraction activities in a protected area in north-eastern Ecuador. *Animal Conservation, 12*, 364–373.

Suárez, E., Zapata-Ríos, V., Utreras, S., Strindberg, S., & Vargas, J. (2012). Controlling access to oil-roads protects forest cover but not wildlife communities: A case study from the rainforest of Yasuní Biosphere Reserve (Ecuador). *Animal Conservation, 16*, 265–274.

Sunde, S. (2010). Ett av tusen ulovlige reptiler i Norge blir beslaglagt? [One of a thousand reptiles confiscated?] Miljøkrim. Tidsskriftet for miljøkriminalitet. Accessed on June 30, 2012. www.okokrim.no/miljokrim/nor/tidligere_utgaver/3_desember_2010/artikler/ett-av-tusen-ulovlige-reptiler-i-norge-blir-beslaglagt

Svärd, P. A. (2008). Protecting the animals? An abolitionist critique of animal welfarism and green ideology. In R. Sollund (Ed.), *Global harms: Ecological crime and speciesism.* New York: Nova Science Publishers.

Svensson, M. S., Shanee, S., Shanee, N., Bannister, F. B., Cervera, L., Donati, G., . . . & Mollinedo, J. M. (2016). Disappearing in the night: An overview of trade and legislation of night monkeys in South and Central America. *Folia Primatologica, 87*(5), 332–348.

Sykes, G., & Matza, D. (1957). Techniques of neutralization: A theory of delinquency. *American Sociological Review, 22*, 664–670.

Tella, J. L., & Hiraldo, F. (2014). Illegal and legal parrot trade shows a long-term, cross-cultural preference for the most attractive species increasing their risk of extinction. *PLoS One, 9*(9). https://doi.org/10.1371/journal.pone.0107546

Thomsen, J. B., & Brautigam, A. (1991). Sustainable use of neotropical parrots. in J. G. Robinson & K. H. R Edford (Eds.), *Neotropical wildlife use and conservation* (pp. 358–380). Chicago: University of Chicago Press.

Thorsen, V. G. (2007). *Fangst og eksport av norsk rovfugl ca. 1100-1350. [Capture and export of Norwegian birds of prey, ca. 1100–1350].* MA thesis, University of Oslo. Faculty of Humanities. Accessed on November 14, 2018 from http://urn.nb.no/URN:NBN:no-15808

Thagaard, T. (2011). *Systematikk og innlevelse: en innføring i kvalitativ metode* (3. utg.). Bergen: Fagbokforlaget.

Thorsen, L. E. (2013). Museumsdyr [Museum animals]. *Sosiologi i dag, 43*(2), 61–84.

Thorsen, L. E., Rader, K. A., & Dodd, A. (Eds.). (2013). *Animals on display: The creaturely in museums, zoos, and natural history.* University Park, PA: Pennsylvania State University Press.

Tønnessen, M. (2013). Menneskeveldet [Human might]. In R. Sollund, M. Tønnessen, & G. Larsen (Eds.), *Hvem er villest i landet her? Råskap mot dyr og natur i antropocen – menneskets tidsalder [Who is the wildest in the country? Cruelty against animals and nature in the Anthropocene – the human era].* (pp. 79–99). Oslo: Spartacus.

TRAFFIC. (2008). *What's driving the wildlife trade? A review of expert opinion on economic and social drivers of the wildlife trade and trade control efforts in Cambodia, Indonesia, Lao PDR and Vietnam.* East Asia and Pacific Region Sustainable Development Discussion Papers. Washington, DC: East Asia and Pacific Region Sustainable Development Department, World Bank.

TRAFFIC. (2017). *Wildlife trade: What is it?* Accessed on August 1, 2017. www.traffic.org/trade/

Tribunal Administrativo de Cundinamarca. (2012). Sección primera, subsección A.

UNODC (2015a). *Organised crime.* Accessed on October 15, 2015. www.unodc.org/unodc/en/organised-crime/index.html

UNODC (2015b). UNODC welcomes first United Nations General Assembly resolution on wildlife crime. Accessed on November 15, 2018 from https://www.unodc.org/unodc/en/frontpage/2015/July/unodc-welcomes-first-united-nations-general-assembly-resolution-on-wildlife-crime.html

UNODC. (2012). *Wildlife and forest crime analytic toolkit*, rev. ed. www.unodc.org/documents/Wildlife/Toolkit_e.pdf

UNODC, & Fedotov, Y. (2013). *Wildlife and forest crime.* www.unodc.org/unodc/pt/wildlife-and-forest-crime/index.html

Uribe, C. A. (2003). Magía, brujería y violencia en Colombia. *Revista de estudios sociales, 15*, 59–73.

van Uhm, D. P. (2016a). Illegal wildlife trade to the EU and harms to the world. In T. Spapens, R. White, & W. Huisman (Eds.), *Environmental crime and the world* (pp. 43–66). London: Ashgate.

van Uhm, D. P. (2016b). *The illegal wildlife trade: Inside the world of poachers, smugglers and traders.* Switzerland: Springer.

van Uhm, D. P. (2018). The social construction of the value of wildlife: A green cultural criminological perspective. *Theoretical Criminology, 22*(3), 384–401.

van Wilgen, N. J., Wilson, J. R. U., Elith, J., Wintle, B. A., & Richardson, D. M. (2010). Alien invaders and reptile traders: What drives the live animal trade in South Africa?. *Animal Conservation, 13*, 24–32.

Vetlesen, A. J. (2015). *The denial of nature: environmental philosophy in the era of global capitalism.* London New York: Routledge.

Villamar, A. A., Corona, E., Alcántara-Salinas, G., Santos-Fita, D., Maya, E. M. A., Velázquez, R. S., . . . & Astorga-Domínguez, M. (2015). Historia, situación actual y perspectivas de la etnozoología en México. *Etnobiología, 10*(1), 18–40.

Von Essen, E., & Allen, M. P. (2015). Reconsidering illegal hunting as a crime of dissent: Implication for justice and deliberative uptake. *Criminal Law and Philosophy, 11*(2), 1–16.

Walters, R. (2010). Toxic atmospheres air pollution, trade and the politics of regulation. *Critical Criminology, 18*, 307–323.

Warchol, G. L. (2004). The transnational illegal wildlife trade. *Criminal Justice Studies, 17*(1), 57–73.

Warchol, G., Zupan, L., & Clarke, W. (2003). Transnational criminality: An analysis of the illegal wildlife market in southern Africa. *International Criminal Justice Review, 13*(1), 1–26.

Wasser S. K., Clark, W. J., Drori, O., Kisamo, E. S., Mailand, C., Mutayoba, B., et al. (2008). Combating the illegal trade in African elephant ivory with DNA forensics. *Conservation Biology, 22*, 1065–1071.

Wasser, S. K., JOSEPH CLARK, W.I.L.L.I.A.M., Drori, O., STEPHEN KISAMO, E.M.I.L.Y., Mailand, C., Mutayoba, B. and Stephens, M., 2008. Combating the illegal trade in African elephant ivory with DNA forensics. *Conservation Biology, 22*(4), pp.1065–1071.

Watts, J. (2011). *'Cure for cancer' rumour killed off Vietnam's rhinos.* www.theguardian.com/environment/2011/nov/25/cure-cancer-rhino-horn-vietnam

Watts, J. (2017, October 29). Battle for the mother land: Indigenous people of Colombia fighting for their lands. *The Guardian.* www.theguardian.com/environment/2017/oct/28/nasa-colombia-cauca-valley-battle-mother-land

Watts, J. (2018, February 2). Almost four environmental defenders a week killed in 2017. *The Guardian.* www.theguardian.com/environment/2018/feb/02/almost-four-environmental-defenders-a-week-killed-in-2017?CMP=share_btn_tw

Webb, G. J. (2000). Are all species equal? A comparative assessment. In J. Hutton & B. Dickson (Eds.), *Endangered species, threatened convention: The past, present and future of CITES, the Convention on International Trade in Endangered Species of Wild Fauna and Flora* (pp. 98–106). London: Routledge.

Wellsmith, M. (2010). The applicability of crime prevention to problems of environmental harm: A consideration of illicit trade in endangered species. In R. White (Ed.), *Global environmental harm: Criminological perspectives* (pp. 132–150). Devon: Willan.

Weston, M., & Memon, M. (2009). The illegal parrot trade in Latin America and its consequences to parrot nutrition, health and conservation. *Bird Populations, 9*, 76–83.

Wilson-Wilde, L. (2010). Wildlife crime: A global problem. *Forensic Science, Medicine, and Pathology, 6*(3), 221–222.

White, R. (2008). *Crimes against nature: Environmental criminology and ecological justice.* Cullompton, UK: Willan.

White, R. (2011). *Transnational environmental crime. Toward an eco-global criminology.* London and New York: Routledge.

White, R. (2013). *Environmental harm: An ecojustice approach.* Bristol: Polity Press.

White, R. (2016a). Inter-species violence: Humans and the harming of animals. In J. Stubbs & S. Tomsen (Eds.), *Australian violence: crime, criminal justice and beyond* (pp. 176–193). Annandale, NSW: The Federation Press.

White, R. (2016b). Re-conceptualising folk crimes in rural contexts. In J. Donnermeyer (Ed.), *The Routledge handbook of rural criminology* (pp. 299–307). London: Routledge.

White, R. (Ed.). (2017). *Transnational environmental crime.* London: Routledge.

White, R. (2018). Green victimology and non-human victims. *International Review of Victimology, 24*(2), 1–17. http://journals.sagepub.com/doi/10.1177/0269758017745615

World Animal Protection. (2014). *Wildlife crime in the UK.* Accessed on November 10, 2014. www.worldanimalprotection.org.uk/campaigns/wildlife/wildlife-crimeecrime

The World Bank. (2016). *New analysis shows scale of international commitment to tackle illegal wildlife trade: Over $1.3 billion since 2010.* Accessed on March 6, 2017. www.worldbank.org/en/news/press-release/2016/11/17/new-analysis-shows-scale-of-international-commitment-to-tackle-illegal-wildlife-trade-over-13-billion-since-2010

Wright, G. (2011). Conceptualising and combating transnational environmental crime. *Trends in Organised Crime, 14*(4), 332–346.

Wright, T. F., Toft, C. A., Enkerlin-Hoeflich, E., Gonzalez-Elizondo, J., Albornoz, M., Rodríguez-Ferraro, A., . . . & Brice, A. T. (2001). Nest poaching in neotropical parrots. *Conservation Biology*, *15*(3), 710–720.

Wyatt, T. (2009). Exploring the organisation in Russia far east's illegal wildlife trade: Two case studies of the illegal fur and illegal falcon trades. *Global Crime*, *10*(1 & 2), 144–154.

Wyatt, T. (2011). Illegal raptor trade in the Russian Federation. *Contemporary Justice Review*, *14*(2), 103–123.

Wyatt, T. (2013). *Illegal wildlife trade: A deconstruction of the crime, the offenders and the victims*. London: Palgrave Macmillan.

Wyatt, T. (2014a). Non human animal abuse and wildlife trade: Harms in the fur and falcon trades. *Society and Animals*, *22*, 194–210.

Wyatt, T. (2014b). A criminological exploration of the industrialisation of pig farming. *Critical Perspectives on Green Criminology*, *1*, 12–28. https://docs.wixstatic.com/ugd/b93dd4_ff9a32d73c7248688e01b0d88db23e05.pdf

Wyatt, T. (2016). A comparative analysis of wildlife trafficking in Australia, New Zealand and the United Kingdom. *Journal of Trafficking, Organised Crime and Security*, *2*(1), 62–81.

Zhou, Z. M., Hong, Z., Zhang, Z. X., Wang, Z. H., & Wang, H. (2012). Allometry of scales in Chinese Pangolines: (MAnis Pentadactyla) and Malyan Pangoline (Manis *javanica*) and application of judiclal expertice. *Zoological Research*, *33*(3), 271–275.

Zilli, G. (2011, February 11). RENCTAS: The Brazilian NGO on the frontline of the war on animal trafficking. *Ecologist*. Accessed on April 21, 2018. www.theecologist.org/campaigning/wildlife/767769/renctas_the_brazilian_ngo_on_the_frontline_of_the_war_on_animal_trafficking.html

Zimmerman, M. (2003). The black market for wildlife: Combating transnational organised crime in the illegal wildlife trade. *Vanderbilt Journal of Transnational Law*, *1*(36), 1657–1690.

Åårnes A. (1994). *Den annens humanisme. Emmanuel Levinas; Oversatt og med innledning, noter og et essay av Asbjørn Aarnes: Efterord om Bergson og Levinas av Hans Kolstad* [The humanism of the other. Emmanuel Levinas; translated and with introduction, notes and an essay by Asbjørn Aarnes]. Oslo: Aschehoug.

Court cases

Borgarting lagmannsrett. (2015). LB-2014–92357.

Dalane Tingrett. (2015). 15–156399ENE-DALA.

Gulating lagmannsrett. (2014). 14–049847AST-GULA/AVD1.

Høyesterett. (1990a). Rt-1990–156 (40–90). https://lovdata.no/pro/#document/HRSTR/avgjorelse/rt-1990-156-27b?searchResultContext=1132

Høyesterett. (1990b). Rt-1990–203. https://lovdata.no/pro/#document/HRSTR/avgjorelse/rt-1990-203-25a?searchResultContext=1004

Høyesterett. (2003). HR-291-a-Rt.

Høyesterett. (2016a). HR-2016–2285-A.

Høyesterett. (2016b). HR-2016–295-A.

Kristiansand tingrett. (2013). 13–137704MED-KISA/06.

Oslo tingrett. (2016). 16–107157MED-OTIR/05.

Sarpsborg forhørsrett. (1998). 98–00805 F.

Tønsberg tingrett. (2014). 14–068308MED-TONS.

Appendix 1

Seizure reports from Norwegian Customs

Table A1.1 Details of cases: category 1 – live animals (the table runs over several pages)

No.	*Categories/ subcategories*	*Species/parts/ products*	*Date of seizure*	*Decision**	*Decision concerning animal*	*Modus operandi*	*Gender*	*CITES listing*
1	Reptiles Amphibians	1 tortoise 2 salamanders	06.02.08	Confiscation and fine (amount unknown)		Trafficked from Sweden by car	M	CITES
2	Birds Mammals	1 Amazon parrot 2 canaries 1 American Staffordshire terrier	10.11.08	5,000 fine	Animals confiscated	Trafficked from Sweden	M	CITES
3	Amphibians Fish Birds	2 salamanders (*Ambystoma mexicanum*) 21 fish 2 doves	08.03.10	21 days prison, 15,000 fine, confiscation of driver's license (drove drunk)	Animals confiscated	Trafficked from Sweden Doves meant for breeding	M	CITES II Unknown
4	Reptiles	2 pythons (*Python regius*)	01.03.08	5,000 fine		Trafficked by car from Denmark	M	CITES II
5	Reptiles	2 pythons (*Python regius*)	24.03.08	15,000 fine		Trafficked by ferry from Denmark Detected by drug-sniffing dog (because of drugs)	M	CITES II
6	Reptiles	2 turtles	22.02.09	4,000 fine		Trafficked by plane from Poland Detected by dog	M	CITES

7	Reptiles	2 tortoises	26.02.09	8,000 fine		Bought in Istanbul in a store	F	CITES
8	Reptiles	2 royal pythons	08.02.10	Fine (amount unknown)		Trafficked from Germany by ferry Trafficker working for zoo shop	M	CITES II
9	Reptiles	1 albino tiger python	03.01.11	8,000 fine		Trafficked by car from Sweden	M	CITES I
10	Reptiles	2 swamp turtles	24.10.11	10,000 fine Charged under Animal Welfare Act		Trafficking, origin unknown, arrived by ferry from Denmark	M	CITES
11	Reptiles	1 royal python	24.10.11	Unknown		Trafficked by car on ferry from Denmark	M	CITES I
12	Reptiles	2 tortoises	09.01.12	Unknown		Bought at market in Egypt Trafficked by plane	F	CITES II
13	Reptiles	2 Yemen chameleons	09.01.12	Unknown		Bought in and trafficked from Stockholm	M	CITES II
14	Reptiles	2 leopard tortoises (*Stigmochelys pardalis*)	16.03.12	Unknown	Animals confiscated	Trafficked from Copenhagen	M	CITES II
15	Reptiles	1 Greek land tortoise (*Testudo graeca*)	05.07.13	Owner had valid CITES permit	Animals returned to owner	Trafficked by ferry from Denmark	M	CITES II
16	Birds	1 parakeet (*Agapornis nigrigenis/fischeri*)	05.11.08	Unknown		Found on baggage belt in cage in bag Trafficked from Copenhagen	M	CITES II

(*Continued*)

Table A1.1 (Continued)

No.	*Categories/ subcategories*	*Species/parts/ products*	*Date of seizure*	*Decision**	*Decision concerning animal*	*Modus operandi*	*Gender*	*CITES listing*
17	Birds	4 African grey parrots (*Psittacus erithacus*)	21.11.10	60 days prison of which 45 suspended	Birds euthanized	Parrots trafficked to enter commercial business Trafficked by car (see analysis of parrot case Chapter 3)	M	CITES I
18	Birds	8 African grey parrots (*Psittacus erithacus*)	20.10.11	60 days prison of which 45 suspended. Also convicted for taking a sea eagle egg. Both cases appealed and punishment reduced in the court of appeals.	Birds euthanized	Parrots trafficked to enter commercial business Trafficked by car (see analysis of parrot case Chapter 3)	M	CITES I
19	Birds	25 birds (*Psittacus* and four unknown species)	13.11.11	10,000 fine	Some birds saved, most euthanized	Parrots trafficked to enter commercial business Trafficked by car from Copenhagen	M	CITES I
20	Birds	44 parrots, 8 without export/import permits	30.03.14	20,000 fine	8 surplus birds euthanized	Parrots trafficked to enter commercial business Trafficked on ferry from Denmark	M	CITES I
21	Birds	6 African grey parrots (*Psittacus erithacus*)	12.08.14	20,000 fine	Birds euthanized	Parrots trafficked to enter commercial business Trafficked by car from Netherlands	M	CITES I

22	Mollusca	557/575? (both numbers listed) corals, specification unknown	26.11.13	Unknown			Part of aquaria business	M	
23	Mollusca	174 corals, specification unknown 32 giant clams (*Tridacna gigas*)	05.03.14	Dismissed		Corals and clams sent to National Food Authority for destruction	Sent from Vietnam via Frankfurt to a pet store		CITES II
24	Mollusca	1 coral, specification unknown	20.03.14	3,000 fine			Trafficked from Thailand	M	CITES II
25	Mollusca	1 stony coral (*Scleractinia*)	08.08.16	Unknown			Bought as souvenir in Mogadishu, Somalia	F	CITES II
26	Mollusca	1 queen conch (*Strombus gigas*)	06.04.16	Unknown			Sent from Thailand	M	CITES II
27	Mollusca	14 stony coral (*Scleractinia*) 2 giant clams (*Tridacna gigas*)	17.08.16	4,000 fine		Confiscated and handed over to Food Safety Authority for destruction	Trafficked from Ho Chi Minh Trafficker claimed they were meant for home aquaria, rather than entering aquaria business	M	CITES II

(*Continued*)

Table A1.1 (Continued)

No.	*Categories/ subcategories*	*Species/parts/ products*	*Date of seizure*	*Decision**	*Decision concerning animal*	*Modus operandi*	*Gender*	*CITES listing*
28	Arthropods	1 Chilean rose tarantula (*Grammostola rosea*)	04.06.13	Unknown	Euthanized by freezing	Trafficked by car from Sweden	M	CITES II
29	Mammals	1 Bengal cat	08.12	Convicted to 21 days suspended prison for breach of the Wildlife Law	Animals confiscated and euthanized	Trafficked from Germany without permit	M	CITES I/II
30	Annelids	35 European medicinal leeches (*Hirudo medicinalis*)	15.10.14	6,000 fine		Trafficked from Ukraine Purchased from a pharmacist	M	CITES II

*All fine amounts are in NOK.

Table A1.2 Details of cases: category 2 – animal parts/products and stuffed animals

No.	*Category/ subcategory*	*Species/parts/products*	*Date of seizure*	*Decision**	*Treatment of animal*	*Modus operandi*	*Gender*	*CITES listing*
31	Mammals Birds Reptiles	24 animals: lynx, wolf, bear, turtle, buzzard, long-eared owl, honey buzzard hawk owl, marsh harrier, red kite, Ural owl, gyrfalcon, kestrels	20.11.07 (report dated 17.04.12)	10,000 fine Estimated economic value €19,000	Animals confiscated	Part of seizure of 240 non-CITES-listed stuffed animals Trafficker was a collector	M	CITES I/II
32	Reptiles Fish	1 gecko 1 seahorse (*Hippocampus* spp.) dried in bottle	02.10.08	6,000 fine	Seizure confiscated	Trafficked by plane together with 800 cigarettes	M	CITES II
33	Reptiles	1 sea turtle (*Chelonia mydas*)	27.08.09	Unknown	Seizure confiscated	Found in sailor's cabin.	M	CITES I
	Mollusca	1 conch (*Strombus gigas*)						CITES II
34	Reptiles	2 bottles with cobra (*Naja atra* or *Naja kaouthia*)	22.02.11	12,000 fine	Seizure confiscated	Tourist shopping, Thailand	M	CITES II
	Arthropods	1 scorpion[1]						
35	Mammals Fish	1 ivory bracelet, 1 bottle containing 10 seahorses (*Hippocampus* spp.)	25.05.15	Unknown		Trafficked from China via Amsterdam	F	CITES I/II
36	Mammals	232 tablets in 3 boxes containing fur seal parts (*Arctocephalus* spp.)	25.06.15	Dismissed		Sent from China	M	CITES II
	Reptiles	Chinese pond turtle (*Mauremys reevesii*)						CITES III
	Fish	1 seahorse (*Hippocampus* spp.)						CITES II

(*Continued*)

Table A1.2 (Continued)

No.	*Category/ subcategory*	*Species/parts/products*	*Date of seizure*	*Decision**	*Treatment of animal*	*Modus operandi*	*Gender*	*CITES listing*
37	Mammal	2 oil products containing musk deer parts (*Moschus* spp.)	15.01.16	Dismissed		Sent from UK in boxes labelled 'Indian God Oil'	M	CITES I or II
	Fish	1 seahorse (*Hippocampus* spp.)						CITES II
38	Birds	1 stuffed common buzzard (*Buteo buteo*)	01.12.08	10,000 fine		Stopped in airport security, trafficked from Syria	M	CITES II
39	Birds	1 neck of grey junglefowl (*Gallus sonneratii*)	17.03.09	Dismissed		Sent from UK	M	CITES II
40	Birds	1 stuffed common buzzard (*Buteo buteo*) 1 stuffed northern goshawk (*Accipiter gentilis*) 1 stuffed tawny owl (*Strix aluco*)	24.04.12	Unknown		Trafficked in car	M	CITES II
41	Birds	1 neck of grey junglefowl (*Gallus sonneratii*)	01.08.12	Unknown		Sent from Estonia	F	CITES II
42	Birds	1 neck of northern rosella (*Platycercus venustus*)	10.06.14	Unknown		Sent from UK	F	CITES II
43	Birds	2 jungle cock fish flies with feathers from grey junglefowl (*Gallus sonneratii*)	14.08.14	Fine (amount unknown)		Sent from Sweden to fishing equipment store		CITES II
44	Birds	1 neck of grey junglefowl (*Gallus sonneratii*)	17.10.14	Dismissed		Sent from UK	M	CITES II

45	Birds	1 stuffed common kestrel (*Falco tinnunculus*) 1 stuffed gyrfalcon (*Falco rusticolus*)	28.10.14	No reaction	Found in a bag in the arrival hall at the airport; no owner was found		CITES II
46	Birds	18 jungle cock fish flies with feathers from grey junglefowl (*Gallus sonneratii*)	02.03.15	Unknown	Sent from UK	M	CITES II
47	Birds	1 neck of grey junglefowl (*Gallus sonneratii*)	20.03.15	Dismissed	Sent from UK	M	CITES II
48	Birds	1 neck[2] of grey junglefowl (*Gallus sonneratii*)	13.04.15	10,000 fine	Sent from UK	M	CITES II
49	Birds	284 jungle cock fish flies with feathers from grey junglefowl (*Gallus sonneratii*)	07.09.15	Unknown	Sent from Kenya via Dubai	M	CITES II
50	Birds	1 neck of grey junglefowl (*Gallus sonneratii*)	14.10.15	Fine (amount unknown)	Sent from UK	M	CITES II
51	Birds	1 neck of grey junglefowl (*Gallus sonneratii*)	28.10.15	No reaction	Sent from UK	M	CITES II
52	Birds	1 neck of grey junglefowl (*Gallus sonneratii*)	28.10.15	No reaction	Sent from UK	M	CITES II
53	Birds	1 neck of grey junglefowl (*Gallus sonneratii*)	28.10.15	No reaction	Sent from Estonia	M	CITES II
54	Birds	1 neck of grey junglefowl (*Gallus sonneratii*)	08.12.15	Unknown	Sent from UK	M	CITES II
55	Birds	1 neck of grey junglefowl (*Gallus sonneratii*)	22.04.16	Unknown	Sent from UK	M	CITES II
56	Birds	2 necks of grey junglefowl (*Gallus sonneratii*)	23.06.16	Unknown	Sent from UK	M	CITES II

(*Continued*)

Table A1.2 (Continued)

No.	*Category/ subcategory*	*Species/parts/products*	*Date of seizure*	*Decision**	*Treatment of animal*	*Modus operandi*	*Gender*	*CITES listing*
57	Birds	266 jungle cock fish flies with feathers from grey junglefowl (*Gallus sonneratii*)	10.08.16	Unknown		Sent from UK	M	CITES II
58	Birds	3 necks of grey junglefowl (*Gallus sonneratii*)	30.09.16	Unknown		Sent from UK	M	CITES II
59	Birds	1 bag containing feathers from grey junglefowl (*Gallus sonneratii*)	26.10.16	Unknown		Sent from UK	M	CITES II
60	Birds	1 neck of grey junglefowl (*Gallus sonneratii*)	03.11.16	Unknown		Sent from UK	M	CITES II
61	Mammals	1 primate head	18.02.08	Unknown	Seizure confiscated	Traffickers wanted to make a business selling primate heads	F	CITES I or II
62	Mammals	1 stuffed wolf and 2 wolf pelts (*Canis lupus*)	27.03.08	Unknown.	Not confiscated	Trafficker had import permit, not export permit	M	CITES II
63	Mammals	200 tiger bone pills	14.03.09	4,500 fine		Trafficked by plane from Vietnam Medicinal product	M	CITES I
64	Mammals	8 adhesive plasters from musk deer (*Moschus* spp.)	17.06.10	Unknown	Seizure confiscated	Post from China Discovered by scanning medicinal product	F	CITES II
65	Mammals	1 adhesive plaster from leopard bone	05.05.11	Dismissed		Stopped at the Norwegian-Swedish border Medicinal product	M	CITES I

66	Mammals	1 grizzly bear skin with skull (*Ursus arctos*) 1 black bear skin with skull (*Ursus americanus*)	26.05.11	Unknown Estimated economic value of skins: €5000+		Trophy hunting Trafficked from Alaska by plane	M	CITES II
67	Mammals	4 bear pelts with heads	26.05.11	Unknown	Seizure confiscated	Trophy hunting Trafficked from Alaska by plane	M	CITES I/II
68	Mammals	2 ivory tusks 1 hippo-skin rope	18.04.12	Unknown		Sent from Ethiopia	M	
69	Mammals	1 ivory tusk	01.11.12	15,000 fine 14-day suspended prison sentence		Collector case including ivory bought on eBay (see analysis of ivory case, Chapter 4)	M	CITES I
70	Mammals	1 stuffed Siberian tiger (*Panthera tigris altaica*)	31.10.13	Unknown	Tiger confiscated	Trafficked from a zoo in Sweden and put up for sale on a known website, *Finn.no*, which caught the attention of Customs and the Norwegian Environment Agency	M	CITES I
71	Mammals	4 elephant ivory figurines	03.01.14	10,000 fine			M	CITES I
72	Mammals	1 elephant ivory figurine	10.06.14	Unknown		Trafficked from Portugal Trafficker also carrying 2 illegal guns, for which he was turned over to the police	M	CITES I

(*Continued*)

Table A1.2 (Continued)

No.	*Category/ subcategory*	*Species/parts/products*	*Date of seizure*	*Decision**	*Treatment of animal*	*Modus operandi*	*Gender*	*CITES listing*
73	Mammals	1 spoon with elephant ivory handle	17.06.14	Unknown		Sent from Denmark	M	CITES I
74	Mammals	1 elephant ivory necklace	04.08.14	fine (amount unknown)		Trafficked from Burundi via Sweden	M	CITES I
75	Mammals	1 lion pelt with head (*Panthera leo*)	04.08.14	Unknown		Trafficked from Denmark Trafficker also carrying 34 bags of new clothes and alcohol over the limit	M	CITES I or II
76	Mammals	1 elephant ivory figurine	26.08.14	Dismissed		Sent from Denmark	M	CITES I
77	Mammals	1 sperm whale-tooth figurine (*Physeter microcephalus*)	16.03.15	Dismissed		Sent from Denmark	M	CITES I
78	Mammals	500 tablets containing parts from saiga antelope (*Saiga tatarica*)	08.07.15	Unknown		Trafficked from China via Helsinki Also trafficking a CITES I plant	M	CITES II
79	Mammals	1 narwhal tooth (*Monodon monoceros*) 1 polar bear claw 1 polar bear head (*Ursus maritimus*)	18.08.15	Unknown		Sent from Greenland	F	CITES II
80	Mammals	1 whale bone	13.01.16	Unknown		Trafficked from Ecuador via Amsterdam	F	CITES I/II
81	Mammals	1 baboon head (*Papio ursinus*)	26.01.16	Unknown		Sent from South Africa	M	CITES II

82	Mammals	1 polar bear claw (*Ursus maritimus*)	10.06.16	Unknown		Trafficked from Greenland	M	CITES
83	Mammals	1 elephant ivory figurine	22.06.17	Unknown		Shipped from Belgium	M	
84	Reptiles	2 python billiard cues	23.05.09	Unknown	Seizure confiscated	Trafficked from the Philippines	M	CITES II
85	Reptiles	1 dead snake in liquor bottle	18.01.10	No reaction		Tourist to Thailand for collection	M	
86	Reptiles	1 stuffed Nile crocodile (*Crocodylus niloticus*)	24.01.11	Unknown		Sent by post from Dubai	F	CITES I
87	Reptiles	58 crocodile teeth 1 skin and 2 claws of unidentified species	26.07.11	Unknown		Post package sent from Peru	M/F	
88	Reptiles	3 snake skins monocled cobra (*Naja kaouthia*)	31.07.11	Unknown		Unaccompanied luggage from Malaysia at Stavanger Airport Reptile skins were bought in a souvenir shop in Thailand	M	CITES II
89	Reptiles	1 watchband of viscount alligator	24.11.11	Unknown		Post from UK	M	CITES II
90	Reptiles	1 crocodile head	18.01.12	15,000 fine and suspended 14-day prison sentence		For collection (see analysis of ivory case Chapter 4)		
91	Reptiles	2 crocodile heads (*Crocodylus siamensis*)	19.01.12	Unknown		Post from Thailand	M	CITES I
92	Reptiles	1 crocodile skin wallet	08.01.14	Dismissed		Sent from UK	M	CITES II

(Continued)

Table A1.2 (Continued)

No.	*Category/ subcategory*	*Species/parts/products*	*Date of seizure*	*Decision**	*Treatment of animal*	*Modus operandi*	*Gender*	*CITES listing*
93	Reptiles	Several snake skins, including tiger python, cliff python, royal boa and *Shamanism paraphernalia* rattlesnake skin and tails[3]	01.04.14	Dismissed		Sent by post from US	F	CITES II
94	Reptiles	3 snake skins: boa, tiger python, cliff python	16.06.14	Dismissed		Sent by post from US	M	CITES II
95	Reptiles	1 head of freshwater crocodile (*Crocodylus siamensis*)	23.06.14	Dismissed		Sent from Thailand	M	CITES I
96	Reptiles	1 snake skin bracelet with cobra head	24.07.14	Unknown		Trafficked from Ibiza, Spain via London Suspect was detected by sniffer dog and was found carrying a small amount of drugs and hard alcohol Suspect turned over to the police	M	CITES II
97	Reptiles	2 liquor bottles containing monocled cobra (*Naja kaouthia*)	26.06.15	No reaction		Trafficked from Qatar Meant for a bachelor party	M	CITES II
98	Reptiles	10 crocodile teeth	10.11.15	5,000 fine		Sent from US	M	CITES II

99	Reptiles	5 savannah monitor skins (*Varanus exanthematicus*)	14.04.16	Unknown	Trafficked from Gambia via Brussels Skins intended for drums	M	
100	Reptiles	1 crocodile skin wallet	21.06.16	Unknown	Sent from Thailand	M	CITES II
101	Reptiles	2 yellow python-skin sneakers	29.09.16	Unknown	Sent from US		CITES II
102	Reptiles	200 crocodile blood capsules	17.10.16	Unknown	Sent from Thailand	M	
103	Reptiles	1 crocodile skin bag	18.11.16	Unknown	Sent from Thailand	M	CITES II
104	Reptiles	1 snake skin Monocled cobra (*Naja kaouthia*)	11.02.17	Unknown	Trafficked from Thailand by tourists who claimed they ate the snake at a restaurant and received the skin as a souvenir	M	CITES II
105	Reptiles	1 turtle shell	28.04.17	Unknown	Trafficked from Montenegro along with alcohol and cigarettes	M	
106	Fish	1 swordfish snout (*Pristidae* spp.)	02.11.11	3,000 fine	On ferry from Denmark	M	CITES I
107	Fish	12 tablets containing seahorse parts (*Hippocampus* spp.)	21.01.12	Unknown	Sent by post from the UK Medicinal product/ erectile dysfunction medicine	M	CITES II
108	Fish	249 tablets containing seahorse parts (*Hippocampus* spp.)	22.01.15	6,000 fine	Trafficked from the Philippines via Amsterdam Medicinal product/ erectile dysfunction medicine	M	CITES II

(*Continued*)

Table A1.2 (Continued)

No.	*Category/ subcategory*	*Species/parts/products*	*Date of seizure*	*Decision**	*Treatment of animal*	*Modus operandi*	*Gender*	*CITES listing*
109	Fish	30 tablets containing seahorse parts (*Hippocampus* spp.)	19.03.15	Dismissed		Sent from Latvia	M	CITES II
110	Fish	48 tablets containing seahorse parts (*Hippocampus* spp.)	28.04.15	Unknown		Sent from UK	M	CITES II
111	Fish	300 grams sturgeon caviar	25.04.16	Reported to the police Also fined 472 for bringing in alcohol above limits		Trafficked from Russia[4]	M	CITES II

*All fine amounts are in NOK.

Table A1.3 Details of cases: category 3 – non-CITES/unknown species

		Species/parts/products	*Date of seizure*	*Decision**	*Treatment of animals*	*Modus operandi*	*Gender*
112	Reptiles Arthropods	1 leopard gecko 15 crickets	28.08.08	5,000 fine	Confiscation	Bought in and trafficked from Sweden	M
113	Birds Mammals	3 canaries 1 Staffordshire terrier	10.11.08	5,000 fine		Trafficked from Sweden	M
114	Reptiles Mammals	1 bearded agama (*Pogona vitticeps*) 1 dog	27.02.09	Unknown		Bought in and trafficked from Sweden	M
115	Arthropods Reptiles	1 bottle with scorpion and snake	18.01.10	No reaction from enforcement authorities		For collection	M
116	Birds Mammals	2 budgerigars 2 desert rats, gerbil	15.08.12	Unknown		Trafficked from Sweden by car	M
117	Mammals	5 Pomeranian puppies	23.01.12	15,000 fine	Confiscated	Trafficked by car from Poland	M
118	Mammals	1 dog (species unknown)	06.02.12	10,000 fine		Trafficked from Tallinn, Estonia by plane	M
119	Mammals	Ratlerek puppies	11.05.12	12,000 fine		Trafficked from Poland together with steroids	M
120	Mammals	2 Irish wolfhounds	02.09.12	Unknown		Bought in Sweden	
121	Mammals	2 chipmunks	25.09.14	10,000 fine		Bought in Norway	M
122	Birds	3 dead hoopoes	19.11.10	15,000 fine and suspended prison sentence		Sent by post	M
123	Birds	90 partridges	02.09.12	Unknown		Bought in Sweden	M
124	Birds	67 birds: canaries, pigeons, quails	14.10.15	9,000 fine Charged under Customs Law		Trafficked by car from Germany	M
125	Reptiles	2 Greek tortoises (*Testudo hermanni*)	16.07.10	4,000 fine		Found in trash bin at women's toilet, arrival hall, Stavanger Airport	F?

*All fine amounts are in NOK.

Notes

1 Customs Directorate statistics list that he arrived with a belt made of elephant skin. This, however, is not mentioned in the seizure report.
2 These are used to make fishing flies.
3 Precise numbers of snake skins unknown as there are various numbers presented in the report. The offender had also previously imported python skins.
4 It should be noted that it is legal to bring up to 175 grams of caviar into Norway.

Appendix 2

Colombian legislation concerning wildlife trafficking

1 **Decreto 1608 de 1978**. Reglamenta el código nacional de los recursos naturales renovables y de protección al medio ambiente y la ley 23 de 1973 en materia de fauna silvestre.[1] (National Code of Renewable Natural Resources and Environmental Protection and Law 23 of 1973 on regulating wildlife.) In this law, Articles 30–34 are of particular interest. They state that: to take/use wildlife requires a permit; that authorizations and permits for the use of wildlife are personal, meaning they cannot be transferred to others; that the managing entity shall determine the species of wildlife for which a permit is to be granted, as well as the number, size and other characteristics of the wild animals that can be hunted, and the areas and seasons when hunting can take place and which species can be hunted. Hunting must never threaten the 'resource' (meaning the survival of the species). Those who intend to sell specimens or wildlife products must conduct a preliminary study to develop inventories, a business plan and an environmental impact statement. This ecological study is required to obtain the permit. Individuals, national or regional management entities seeking to conduct research on wildlife will have permission granted according to the next chapter III of the law, which concerns permissions to do research and investigations.

2 **Ley 1453 de 2011[2] (Law 1453 from 2011 [Codigo Penal])**. This law is a revision of the Colombian Penal Law (Ley 599 de 2000 The Colombian Penal Law, Articles 328, 329). Relevant is Article 29 (This was added to the revised Penal Law, Article 328).

- **Article 29** (whose content is currently Article 328 under the Penal Law) concerns the illicit use of renewable natural resources. It states[3] that a foreigner guilty of non-compliance with existing regulations to appropriate, enter, explore, transport, hold, traffic, trade and benefit from the specimens, products or parts of fauna and flora from Colombian biodiversity may receive imprisonment of 48–108 months and a fine of 35,000 minimum monthly minimum salaries. The penalty is increased by a third to half when species are categorized as threatened, endangered or migratory, rare or endemic to Colombia.
- **Article 30** concerns the illegal crossing of Colombian borders in order to exploit, explore or extract natural resources, violators of which shall

be sentenced to 64–144 months in prison and a fine of 133.33 to 45,000 monthly minimum salaries. This was added to Article 329 of the Penal Law.

- **Article 32** (330A) establishes that the treatment of, dispersal of, experimentation on, manipulation of exotic species that entails endangering humans or biodiversity is illegal and can be punished with 48–198 months in prison and fines of 133 to 15,000 minimum monthly salaries. This was added to Article 330A of the Penal Law.
- **Article 33**. Those who destroy, cause the disappearance of or otherwise harm natural resources will be punished with 48–198 months in prison and fines of 133 to 15,000 minimum monthly salaries (see Article 32). Article 33 was added to Article 331 of the Penal Law.

3 **Ley 99 de 1993**.[4] This is the act through which the Ministry of the Environment was established. This law is in response to the UN Rio Declaration on Environment and Development from 1992[5] and provides the framework for other Colombian environmental laws.[6]

4 **Decreto 84 de 1989 Estatuto Nacional de Protección de los Animales**.[7] (Animal welfare legislation.) This law's intention is, as it states in the second article, to promote the health and welfare of animals; ensure hygiene, sanitation and appropriate conditions of existence; eradicate and punish abuse and cruelty to animals; develop educational programs through the state, media and local officials; encourage private education to promote respect and care for the animals; and to develop effective measures for the preservation of wildlife.

5 **Decreto 2811 de 1974. Código nacional de los recursos naturales renovables y de protección del medio ambiente**. (Decree 2811 of 1974. National code of renewable natural resources and environmental protection.)[8] In this code, Articles 247–265 (Section IX, Wildlife) are of particular relevance. Article 247 sets standards to ensure the conservation, development and sensible use of wildlife as an indispensable basis for its continued use. In Article 248, all wildlife located in national territory belongs to the nation, except farm species and animals hunted on private property. It is, like CITES, a law that perceives wildlife as an exploitable resource. Article 2655 (I) forbids exporting individual animals, other than for scientific research or as expressly authorized by the government.

6 **Ley 165 de 1994**. (Law 165 of 1994.) By which the Convention of Biological Diversity[9] was adopted.

7 **Decisión Andina 391 de 1996**. Régimen común sobre acceso a los recursos genéticos.[10] (Andean Decision 391 from 1996. Common Regime on Access to Genetic Resources.) This agreement between the five Andean countries requires members to have in place regulations regarding the conservation and sustainable use of biodiversity according to the International Convention on Biodiversity.

8 **Decreto 1401 de 1997.**[11] Decree 1401 de 1997 designates the Ministry of Environmental Affairs as the authority responsible for CITES implementation and which will issue export and import certificates. CITES was signed and entered into force in Colombia in 1981. Decreto 1401 establishes further that personnel enforcing CITES in Colombia will receive the necessary training to manage the international commerce in live flora and fauna as it pertains to Colombia, and that IATA[12] and CITES regulations for transport of live animals will be applied.

9 **Ley 611 de 2000.**[13] (Law 611 of 2000.) This law establishes norms for sustainable use of land and aquatic wildlife who have not been domesticated, not been genetically bred, or who have returned to the wild. Sustainable use is understood to mean that animals will be used in a way and at a rate that does not lead to their decrease in the long term and safeguards the populations to meet the needs and aspirations of present and future generations. The aim is to regulate sustainable management of wild fauna and aquatic species, the use of them and their products, and their breeding. Most of the decree is dedicated to regulate breeding facilities. Registration, inspection and supervision of the farms will be provided by the authorities.

10 **Resolución 438 de 2001.**[14] (Resolution 438 of 2001.) This resolution describes the proceedings concerning permissions to transport or engage in commerce of natural resources.

11 **Ley 1333 de 2009.**[15] (Law 1333 of 2009.) This law establishes procedures and punishment for environmental crimes that breach Decree 2811 from 1974, Law 99 of 1993, Law 165 of 1996.

12 **Resolución 383 de 2010.**[16] This resolution lists the species which are endangered in Colombia.

13 **Resolución 2064 de 2010.**[17] This resolution determines how confiscated wildlife should be kept and treated. In accordance with Article 8, paragraph 5 of CITES, rescue centres are to be established by a management authority to look after the welfare of animals that are confiscated and that specific centres are to be established for this purpose, according to Law 1333 of and Decree 1401 of May 27, 1997, which determines Colombia's obligations towards CITES. Article 60 of the 1333 Act establishes an information system concerning wildlife seizures (PIFS [Portal de Información sobre Fauna Silvestre)], under the Ministerio de Ambiente, Vivienda y Desarrollo Territorial – MAVDT [Ministry of Environment, Housing and Territorial Development], which must contain the following information regarding seizures for each species: the number of individuals in a seizure; the location where they were seized, where they are kept and their condition; and the dates of seizures and planned destinations. The Ministry shall regulate the restitution or forfeiture of wild fauna and flora that correspond to alternative provisional or final disposal, according to Law 1333 of 2009. According to the law, there are to be centres for reception and rehabilitation of wildlife that are responsible for determining what will happen to the seized animals.

14 **Decreto 1376 de 2013.**[18] (Decree 1376 of 2013.) This decree contains the details of issuing permissions to collecting wildlife for scientific purposes.

Notes

1 www.alcaldiabogota.gov.co/sisjur/normas/Norma1.jsp?i=8241
2 www.alcaldiabogota.gov.co/sisjur/normas/Norma1.jsp?i=43202
3 El que con incumplimiento de la normatividad existente se apropie, introduzca, explote, transporte, mantenga, trafique, comercie, explore, aproveche o se beneficie de los especímenes, productos o partes de los recursos fáunicos, forestales, florísticos, hidrobiológicos, biológicos o genéticas de la biodiversidad colombiana, incurrirá en prisión de cuarenta y ocho (48) a ciento ocho (108) meses y multe hasta de treinta y cinco mil (35.000) salarios mínimos legales mensuales vigentes. La pena se aumentará de una tercera parte a la mitad, cuando las especies estén categorizadas como amenazadas, en riesgo de extinción o de carácter migratorio, raras o endémicas del territorio colombiano. http://leyes.co/codigo_penal/328.htm
4 www.alcaldiabogota.gov.co/sisjur/normas/Norma1.jsp?i=297
5 www.un.org/documents/ga/conf151/aconf15126-1appendix1.htm
6 This was mentioned several times in interviews as central.
7 www.alcaldiabogota.gov.co/sisjur/normas/Norma1.jsp?i=8242
8 www.alcaldiabogota.gov.co/sisjur/normas/Norma1.jsp?i=1551
9 www.cbd.int/doc/legal/cbd-en.pdf
10 www.wipo.int/wipolex/es/text.jsp?file_id=223520
11 www.minambiente.gov.co/documentos/dec_1401_270597.pdf
12 The International Air Transport Association. www.iata.org/about/pages/index.aspx
13 www.minambiente.gov.co/documentos/ley_0611_170800.pdf
14 www.icbf.gov.co/cargues/avance/docs/resolucion_minambiente_rma43801.htm
15 www.alcaldiabogota.gov.co/sisjur/normas/Norma1.jsp?i=36879
16 http://190.85.6.171/Sistematizacion_Normatividad/Fauna%20y%20Flora/Resol._383_de_2010_especies_amenzadas.pdf
17 www.icbf.gov.co/cargues/avance/docs/resolucion_minambientevdt_2064_2010.htm
18 www.datafauna.veterinariosvs.org/wp-content/uploads/Dec_1376_2013_ColectaCientifica.pdf

Index

Note: Page numbers in italics indicate a figure and page numbers in bold indicate a table on the corresponding page.

Made in the USA
Monee, IL
13 September 2026

62978974R10168